The History of Disruption

Mehmet Döşemeci is an anarchist, activist, and associate professor of history at Bucknell University. The author of two books and numerous academic articles, his writings on the meaning and significance of radical democracy and the uprisings, occupations, and riots of the twenty-first century have been published by Al Jazeera, *ROAR Magazine, openDemocracy*, and *Common Dreams*. In his spare time, he runs a website on the past and present of social disruption: disruptnow.org.

The History of Disruption

Social Struggle in the Atlantic World

Mehmet Döşemeci

VERSO

London • New York

First published by Verso 2024
© Mehmet Döşemeci 2024
Author and publisher express their gratitude to Haymarket Books
for permission to reproduce an image from Philip S. Foner,
Th e Black Panthers Speak, Haymarket Books 2014.

1 3 5 7 9 10 8 6 4 2

Verso
UK: 6 Meard Street, London W1F 0EG
US: 388 Atlantic Avenue, Brooklyn, NY 11217
versobooks.com

Verso is the imprint of New Left Books

ISBN-13: 978-1-80429-390-4
ISBN-13: 978-1-80429-391-1 (UK EBK)
ISBN-13: 978-1-80429-394-2 (US EBK)

British Library Cataloguing in Publication Data
A catalogue record for this book is available from the British Library

Library of Congress Cataloging-in-Publication Data

Names: Döşemeci, Mehmet, author.
Title: Thehist ory of disruption : social struggle in the Atlantic world /
    Mehmet Döşemeci.
Description: London ; New York : Verso, 2024. | Includes bibliographical
    references.
Identifier s: LCCN 2024002389 (print) | LCCN 2024002390 (ebook) | ISBN
    9781804293904 (paperback) | ISBN 9781804293942 (ebk)
Subjects: LCSH: Social movements. | World politics—21st century.
Classifi cation: LCC HM881 .D674 2024 (print) | LCC HM881 (ebook) | DDC
    303.48/4—dc23/eng/20240430
LC record available at https://lccn.loc.gov/2024002389
LC ebook record available at https://lccn.loc.gov/2024002390

Typeset in Minion Pro by Hewer Text UK Ltd, Edinburgh

To my daughter Willow,
May you also find yourself, and others, through refusal.

Contents

Acknowledgments

A very large thank you to all those who have read or thought through the various arguments of the manuscript over these past years. There are too many to name, but Mohammed Elnaeim, Yetkin Nural, Emma Downey, Ulus Atayurt, and, above all, Aylin Kuryel deserve special mention. Their suggestions and critical comments have been invaluable in bringing the book to its present form.

Special thanks to the American Council of Learned Societies, whose Burkhardt Residential Fellowship provided generous funds and crucial time away from teaching, ensuring the timely completion of the manuscript. To the Institute for Comparative Literature and Society at Columbia University and, in particular, Stathis Gourgouris, my old mentor and young friend, in whose nostalgic and noisy office on the top floor of Hamilton much of this text was written.

My mother Ayşe, while giving plenty of it, understood that criticism need not always be constructive. Thank you for both lending a scientist's eye to humanistic writing and never tiring of reminding me how long such writing was taking. *Oğlum, senin şu kitabın hâlâ bitmedi mi?*

My thirteen-year-old daughter cares more about the plight of animals than human liberation. A young willow who speaks for the trees. Thank you for teaching me that the circle of the social needs widening, needs to include the dogs, and rivers, and bees.

And, most importantly, Brittany Edmoundson, who, fortunately for me, though perhaps less so for her, has been there from the very start of this project, reading drafts for as long as we have been together. Because of you, both it and we have grown tighter with each passing year. Thank you for all the conversations, the edits, high fives, hugs, and vetoes you have given, the objections you have raised, for the patience you have always shown. Seeing my writing through your eyes makes me smile. I hope you feel the same way. This book simply would not have been possible without you.

Introduction: The Kinetics of Our Discontent

The impasse of the present, everywhere in evidence, is everywhere denied.
                                                    The Invisible Committee

Wherever one looks, the institutions of the post–World War II order are failing us. Concentration camps once again litter the globe, eight people hoard more wealth than half of humanity, and toxic combinations of xenophobia and austerity paralyze us with hate and fear. Long-standing legal and political safeguards have, seemingly overnight, been shattered, giving way to an atmosphere of violence, lawlessness, and dehumanization. Tomorrow, from every forecasted angle, looks dismally worse. We are hurtling toward a future of biometric surveillance, mass species extinction, and the impending collapse of a wage system that can no longer provide jobs nor the means for humans to exist without them. In the meantime, we gaze, year after year, at the funeral processions of failed climate summits as our only planet floods and burns. The global pandemic has only exacerbated these trends. In a little over four years, inequality between genders, races, classes, and geographies has exponentially accelerated, matched only by the disregard of the world's elite toward the fate of its surplus population.

Yet, despite the rapid and alarming deterioration of our planet, human agency, and the rule of law, cosmologies of progress and movement remain legion. Drawing profit from desperation, our political, corporate, and social justice leaders continue to peddle tonics of dynamism, determination, movement, and growth as solutions to our present catastrophe.

Faced with this impasse, a great many humans have turned to a markedly different politics—one that confronts the global catastrophe through interruption. From the 2011 uprisings through Black Lives Matter, Standing Rock, Abolish ICE, and Antifa in the United States; Nuit Debout and the Yellow Vests of France; Extinction Rebellion in England; and the recent revolts in Chile, Haiti, Palestine, Puerto Rico, Peru, Sudan, Ecuador, and Iran, social struggles across the globe are engaging in disruptive politics. A language of occupation, confrontation, sabotage, insurrection, revolt, and blockade now permeates the thoughts and practices of global discontent. Following Donald Trump's inauguration, even Hillary Clinton—to the delight of some and the chagrin of others—declared herself part of "the resistance." A politics of interruption, for forty years dismissed as the purview of fringe groups, has once again become mainstream.

But don't just take it from me. In 2020, Verisk Maplecroft, a global risk assessment firm that helps businesses map and manage the exposure of their operations, supply chains, and investments, began warning its clients of worldwide civil unrest and political instability in the years ahead. That same year, a research analyst for Deutsche Bank predicted the end of the "age of globalization" and the dawn of a new "age of disorder," supposedly the sixth distinct era of the modern world.[1] A few weeks before the global pandemic, the right-wing think tank Center for Strategic and International Studies released a lengthy report, "The Age of Mass Protests: Understanding an Escalating Global Trend," that warned of a coming "decade of rage, unrest, and shifting geopolitical sands."[2]

Commentators and scholars have likewise scrambled to make sense of this "new" politics. Outside of momentary instances during the Arab Spring, none of these struggles have led to what we would call revolutions. Neither do they conform to our accustomed understandings of social movements. Terms such as *civil strife, unrest, riot,* and *disorder* either flatten to illegibility what is decidedly not or, more often, reflect the racist and elitist views of the speaker. What then are we to make of this resurgence of disruptive politics? How should we read them? As the spasmodic reactions of a cornered humanity? Perhaps. As the inchoate and incipient tendencies of something yet to come? If so, what? These psychosocial or speculative queries do not interest me. What interests me is history. What turning an eye to past struggles can tell us about those of the present and future.

Thinking through these cosmologies of movement and interruption is, I argue, a way to overcome our conceptual impasse. Instead of trying to decipher what these various struggles want, how to categorize their tactics, organization, and intentions, I want to examine how they understand and manifest themselves in relation to the categories of movement and disruption. Is there a politics to this? Does this politics have a history?

The History of Disruption explores these questions by approaching modern social struggle *kinetically*—in relation to the flows and blockages within space and time. It is an investigation of how humans have thought of and practiced politics in terms of motion and its interruption. As a method, kinetic analysis examines social struggle across three registers. First, the physical movement or disruption of matter: of bodies, goods, and machines and the procedures, technologies, and laws created to move and stop them. Second, of mentalities: how humans have imagined their social struggles as moving or arresting the existing social order. And third, within time: how struggles have situated themselves within the flow or rupture of history. These three registers of thinking about movement and disruption, I argue, are intertwined. One of the central aims of the book is to show how the interruption or progression of matter, social order, and time are historically linked. Reading the history of struggle through this kinetic lens offers a new way to examine the tactics, motivations, and temporalities of those who sought to change the world they live in. Applied over a broad geographic area and long timespan, it uncovers how a politics of movement and its disruption, in both space and time, formed the terrain on which modern social struggle takes place.

If we are to approach struggle kinetically, we first have to interrogate the kinetic concepts we have used and still use to think about and practice social struggle. James Baldwin once wrote, "We must drive to the heart of every answer and expose the question the answer hides."[3] Kinetic analysis likewise begins by questioning the axiomatic association of modern social struggles with the category of movement. How, when, and why did this association emerge? What exactly are social movements putting into motion and where is this motion going? Conversely, has struggle been thought of and practiced otherwise? Not as movement, but as interruption, arrest, stasis? If so, what are struggles trying to stop?

While having a much longer history in the sciences and philosophy, the political use of the term *movement* is actually quite recent, of mid-nineteenth-century mint.[4] In its original entrance into the political realm, movement was used to distinguish the dynamic primacy of society over what its proponents called the "forces of order." In July 1830, the French revolutionaries pitted their *Parti du Mouvement* against this *Parti de l'Ordre*. Two decades later, *movement* received its first political analysis, briefly mentioned in the 1848 *Communist Manifesto* as the "proletarian movement" and, in 1850, given more systematic treatment by Lorenz von Stein's *The History of the Social Movement in France: 1789–1848*. By 1867, across the Atlantic, Emerson could state that "there are always two parties, the party of the Past and the party of the Future: the Establishment and the Movement."[5] As Giorgio Agamben has noted, in such instances, the use of the term movement was always social and in an antagonistic relationship with established and stagnant state and parliamentary institutions.[6]

In a less acknowledged history (at least by the left), the interwar period saw the term movement appropriated by the radical right, not as the dynamic element standing against state and party, but rather in service of them. Both German National Socialism and Italian Fascism incorporated movement as a central category in the constitutional apparatus of their one-party dictatorships.[7] This inversion of the political category of movement, from an antagonistic to a legitimizing relation to the forces of order, remains a continuing feature of many fascist, neo-Nazi, and radical nationalist parties around the globe.[8]

However, the present prevalence of the term movement as a political and analytical category has its roots in postwar progressive history, specifically in the first-world social struggles of the 1960s and '70s. It was the relative success of the civil rights, antiwar, student, women's, and gay liberation struggles that established the hegemony of the term among activists and academics alike. The victories of "The Movement" (as the New Left struggles called themselves) prompted the subsequent adoption of the term by future activists to describe a whole host of social struggles over nuclear power and weapons, fast-food culture, growth, evictions, human rights abuses, and environmental destruction, a trend culminating in the Zapatista-inspired alter-globalization struggles of the 1990s, often labelled as the Movement of Movements.[9]

In the 1960s, the term *movement* also became a category of academic analysis. As a subfield of political sociology, the empirical study and theorization of social movements originated at the intersection of political science and postwar sociology, since becoming a prolific interdisciplinary and global field in its own right.[10] These two trends, the adoption of the term by activists since the 1960s and the academic analysis of social struggle through the lens of movement, have been mutually reinforcing. The hermeneutic circle formed through the evolving interplay between the interpretation and practice of social movements (aided, in no small measure, by the 1980s migration of New Left activists into academia) accounts for much of the present ubiquity of the term *movement* to describe contemporary social struggle and, conversely, our difficulty in imagining modern struggle outside this category.

This is not just a semantic issue. Movement, as a political concept, is laden with a whole host of historical assumptions concerning both the aims and tactics of modern social struggle as well as the social order they are struggling against. If we are to make sense of the struggles of the twenty-first century, we need to fundamentally interrogate our kinetic understanding of their predecessors. In questioning movement, it does little good to begin within a literature—the study of social movements—that has, for the most part, taken this concept for granted.[11] Political theory, on the other hand, has had a long history of relating movement to the political. In fact, it has produced two distinct lineages that have, in very different ways, conceptualized the relationship between motion and the social order. The first, which I call States of Arrest, is key to understanding the historical assumptions buried within the term *social movement*. The second, States of Motion, allows us to conceptualize a politics of social disruption.

Political Kinetics

> *Freedom of movement is historically the oldest and the most elementary liberty. Being able to depart for where we will is the prototypical gesture of being free, as limitation of movement has since time immemorial been the precondition of enslavement.*
> Hannah Arendt, *Men in Dark Times*[12]

> *What [refugees] have lost are not specific rights but the right to* take place, *to reside, which conditions the possibility of political existence.*
> Hannah Arendt, *Origins of Totalitarianism*[13]

These two quotes, written seventeen years apart by the same author, offer contrasting takes on the relationship between movement, freedom, and the political. The first, which associates individual human freedom with the ability to move, is informed by classical strains of liberal thought. The second sees forced movement as antithetical to the formation of political community and hence, for Arendt, to public freedom. Drawing on Heidegger's notion of *clearing*, and prefiguring her work on revolution a decade later, Arendt argued that *stasis*, the ability to dwell, to come together in a fixed place, is the precondition for collective human emancipation.

Together, these quotes go to the heart of a kinetic tension between social order, freedom, and movement. As in physics, political movement is a relative phenomenon. Movement, or the arrest of it, is discernible only in relation to the field against which it operates. Many contemporary strands of leftist politics identify this field as a conservative and inertial social order that their progressive movements struggle against. For disruption, the answer is less clear. If we are to make disruption a legible category of social struggle—one not animated by conservatism or frustration—we need to trace the history of the kinetic interpretations of this social field.

States of Arrest

From Plato's *Republic* to postmodernist explorations of hybridity and nomadism, the category of movement has figured prominently in the history of political thought.[14] Yet it is to early strains of seventeenth- and eighteenth-century liberal theory that movement owes much of its prominence as a political category. In the first of the modern ideologies to challenge the order of things, key political concepts such as freedom, political community, subjectivity, and the state were all thought through a kinetic register.

From the earliest incarnations of liberal theory in the seventeenth century through to the present, movement has been central to liberal conceptions of freedom. Deriving from the Latin *liber* (free), the English word *liberal* came to mean "freely permitted" or "free from restraint" in the sixteenth and the seventeenth centuries. In its classical political formulations, liberalism stood as an oppositional ideology to all static or immovable structures within feudal regimes, including hereditary privilege, state religion, absolute monarchy, and the divine right of kings. In the late eighteenth century, as an economic doctrine, liberalism took aim at restrictive trade preferences, state grants of monopolies, serfdom, and slavery, calling instead for the unrestrained movement of goods, market forces, and human beings. As Arendt remarked, "liberty meant freedom from restraint, and as such was identical with freedom of movement. Freedom of movement was the materialization of the liberal conception of liberty."[15]

That is, for the white, male, and propertied members of liberal society. As Hagar Kotef has brilliantly argued, the twin historical contexts of capitalism and colonialism informed liberalism's demarcation of whose (and what kind of) movement was to be freely permitted and whose was to be regulated and constrained. Some subjects, based on their race, gender, class, or ethnicity, appeared free when moving (and as oppressed when hindered), and their good, purposive, rational, and often progressive mobility, liberalism sought to maximize. The movement of other(ed) groups was, by contrast, often marked as disorder, disturbance, danger, or delinquency. Colonized subjects declared to be nomads, dispossessed poor deemed to be vagrants, and women whose "fragility" necessitated "sedentary employments" became "unruly" and "excessive" subjects whose movement needed to be managed. This management of undesirable movement both made liberal regimes perfectly compatible with the proliferation of "nonliberal" state technologies (the prison, the asylum, the camp) and conditioned how some of its more managed subjects would later conceptualize their own liberation as the abolition of the carceral state.[16]

Its differentiated mobility notwithstanding, liberalism depicted itself as operating within a confining social field filled with barriers that inhibited both the motion of society and the individuals constituting it. In doing so, liberal thought coupled movement to the key political categories of liberty and progress. It was in this coupling that the movement of society as teleological progression and the motion of goods and people within it became inextricably linked. Early in the twentieth century, in one of the first reflections on the history of liberal theory, L. T. Hobhouse defined liberalism as a political critique whose main "business" had been "to remove obstacles which block human progress."[17] Liberal society, as he conceived it, was an organism literally moving forward. The free subject, in turn, was defined as an individual both capable of movement and understood as free by that mobility.[18] For the English jurist William Blackstone, whose *Commentaries* informed strains of American revolutionary thought, "liberty is the power of locomotion, of changing situation . . . to whatsoever place one's inclination may direct, without imprisonment or restraint."[19]

The coupling of the freedom to move with liberty and progress served as the guiding principle and theoretical foundation for social movements when they first emerged as a political practice in the early nineteenth century. The midcentury struggle for women's dress reform provides a case in point. The "bloomer campaign," an effort to replace the confining fashions of Victorian dress with loose trousers and a corsetless top, equated freedom with a woman's ability to move. Adopted by Elizabeth Cady Stanton, Lucy Stone, and Susan B. Anthony, the bloomer granted (middle- and upper-class) women, previously restrained both in bodily movement and to the domestic sphere, a new mobility. Stanton likened the change in dress to liberation itself: "Like a captive set free from his ball and chain . . . what a sense of liberty I felt with no skirt to hold or brush."[20]

As a response to perceived social and state intransigence, early social movements described both the goal and the means of a political project to put society in motion. Yet, for social movements to become intelligible as a political category, they required a conceptualization of a static and restraining social field to project themselves against. This conceptualization, first furnished by liberalism, provided the backdrop against which many social movements have been thought of to this day. In the quite different context of (a masculinized) anticolonial struggle, Frantz Fanon remarked on the affective register of confinement that had similarly animated early white middle-class feminism a century before:

The colonial subject is a man penned in . . . The first thing the colonial subject learns is to remain in his place and not overstep its limits. Hence the dreams of the colonial subject are muscular dreams, dreams of action, dreams of aggressive vitality. I dream I am jumping, swimming, running, and climbing.[21]

Fanon portrayed movement as a dialectical reaction to colonial regimes of restraint. The anticolonial struggle was animated psychically, but, above all, physically, by the spasmodic desire to free itself, violently, from confinement.

This "antisedentary metaphysics" has enjoyed a surprisingly long afterlife, informing the politics of an eclectic body of post-Marxist, postcolonial, and poststructuralist thought. Concepts as diverse as *slippage, flight, rhizome, exodus, flux, translation, nomadism, hybridity,* and *trace* all entail elements of movement that unsettle or disrupt modernist structures—from totalitarian politics to identarian patterns of thought— that fix, enclose, bind things into place. The mobile subjectivities present in carnival (Bakhtin), exile (Said), the vagrant (Bauman), the nomad (Deleuze and Guattari), as well as tactics "that overflow or drift over an imposed terrain" (Michel de Certeau) all employ this same kinetic register.[22] This connection between liberation and mobility is equally evident in the mature works of Michael Hardt and Antonio Negri, where the mobility of the multitude constantly threatens to destabilize sedimented global hierarchies, "a multitude that slides across barriers and burrows connecting tunnels that undermine the walls" of Empire.[23]

Within these political imaginaries, the state serves as the quintessential arresting apparatus, one that interrupts and confines movement in its pursuit of order. There is of course a long history in support of these claims. From institutionalized serfdom and slavery to the vagrancy and Black codes following their abolition, from internal passports to mass incarceration, metropolitan policing to colonial governance, the disciplinary power of the state brought a vast array of "antinomadic techniques" to the management of human bodies. As James C. Scott powerfully demonstrated, "the state has always seemed to be the enemy of people who move around."[24]

Yet this conception of the state restraining movement to maintain social order (and better tax its population) tells a one-dimensional and increasingly anachronistic story. Parallel to these readings, there exists a long tradition of thought that conceived of the modern social field as one of permanent flux and motion. To arrive at a liberatory politics of disruption, we must first trace these alternate historical interpretations. This means, above all, to take the claims of modernism seriously.

States of Motion

Constant, unceasing change has been the constitutive feature of modernist thought and its own historical self-interpretation. The self-erected boundary line of the modern period is, in the social, political, and economic domains, the transition from a largely static to an ever-dynamic social order. The first modernist historian attributed this transition to the rise of the bourgeoisie. For Karl Marx, the revolutionary potential of bourgeois society arose from its ability to put everything into motion: "Constant revolutionizing of production, uninterrupted disturbance of all social relations, everlasting uncertainty and agitation, distinguish the bourgeois epoch from all earlier times. All new forms become obsolete before they can ossify. All that is solid melts into air."[25]

Marxist scholars have since traced how, from the seventeenth century onward, the increasing penetration of market forces brought with it an ever-intensifying *regime of movement*. Rapid shifts in the means and social relations of production necessitated the massive mobilization of human bodies, where "whole populations [are] conjured out of the ground."[26] "The immense movements of peoples—to cities, to frontiers, to new lands—which the bourgeoisie has sometimes inspired, sometimes brutally enforced, sometimes subsidized, and always exploited for profit"[27] became the hallmark of the new social order. Beginning with the enclosure of the commons, peasants were pushed off their land and channeled into their new positions within the market economy.[28] If expropriation marked one mechanism of this conjuring of populations, the capture and movement of Black bodies marked another. As Marcus Rediker, Ian Baucom, Greg Grandin, and others have more recently demonstrated, forced unending movement became central to the establishment of the transatlantic maritime economy in the early modern world.[29]

In this regard, the colonies of the New World that received this human cargo were of particular importance. Creations of the regime of movement, they were not simply fixed territories to house and work those coerced there, but themselves terrains of flux and unending motion. As Ann Stoler has remarked,

> A colony as a common noun is a place where people are moved in and out, a place of livid, hopeful, desperate, and violent—willed and unwilled—circulation. It is marked by unsettledness, and regulated, policed migration. A colony as a political concept is not a place but a principle of managed mobilities, mobilizing . . . populations, dislocating and relocating peoples according to a set of changing rules and hierarchies that orders social kinds.[30]

Significantly, the forced movement of human bodies, so characteristic of primitive accumulation, was by no means confined to the initial establishment of the regime of movement, but remains a systemic feature that has haunted its entire history (a point clearly made by Marx in *Capital* and often unmade by his interpreters).[31] In the 1990 issue of their journal, the Midnight Notes Collective underscored this continuity in a special edition on the "new enclosures."

> The New Enclosures . . . name the large-scale reorganization of the accumulation process which has been underway since the mid-1970s. The main objective of this process has been to uproot workers from the terrain on which their organizational power has been built . . . The New Enclosures make mobile and migrant labor the dominant form of labor. We are now the most geographically mobile labor force since the advent of capitalism.[32]

Or, as Sandro Mezzadra succinctly put it, "there is no capitalism without migration."[33]

The violence needed to ensure a steady supply of docile mobile labor forced the market economy to enlist the services of the state. And it is in the history of this enlistment that the political theories of the "states of motion" departs most dramatically from liberal projections. Beginning with Hobbes, this trajectory conceptualized the state itself as both active (that is, itself in motion) and actively conscripted by the economy of movement. Informed by William Harvey's discovery of the human circulatory system, Hobbes's Leviathan is likewise a body in constant motion. As Gil Anidjar notes, it is marked by both an internal movement, where Hobbes speaks of the "sanguification of the commonwealth," the money and wealth that is the blood moving within and nourishing the state, and the external movement of its limbs of war, the expansion of the state's reach through conquest.[34] In contrast to liberal theory's depiction of a static, inertial, and intransigent state, Hobbes's Leviathan is one of perpetual internal and external motion; a conception that has since informed the practitioners (and historians) of mercantilism, colonialism, and imperialism, as well as the politics of modernist state development in the twentieth century.

More often, the state was deployed to construct, and when needed enforce, the continued expansion and smooth operation of the market economy. As Karl Polanyi remarked long ago, "for as long as that system is not established, economic liberals must and will unhesitatingly call for the intervention of the state in order to establish it, and, once established in order to maintain it."[35] Within this capacity, the principal role of the state was not to arrest, but rather to ensure (the right kind of) motion. In this light, early laws against vagrancy and vagabondage served not to prohibit mobility, but rather to direct human movement toward forms of labor desired by the regime of movement.[36] Paul Virilio, in his kinetic analysis of the French Revolution, stated as much:

> The events of 1789 claim to be a revolt against subjection, that is, against the constraints to immobility symbolized by the ancient feudal serfdom—a revolt against arbitrary confinement and the obligation to reside in one place. But no one yet suspected that the "conquest of freedom to come and go" so dear to Montaigne could, by a sleight of hand, become an obligation to mobility ... the institution of the dictatorship of movement.[37]

In his kinetic history of the modern state, John Torpey argues that this process was largely completed (in Europe) during the ninetheenth century, by which time states had consolidated the "monopoly of the legitimate means of movement" from rival claimants such as churches and private enterprises. The establishment of this monopoly, manifest through the invention of the passport as well as legal differentiations between the citizen and its others (the alien, the migrant, the colonial subject), became, Torpey argued, a central feature of the modern state.[38]

Seeing the state as active and complicit in the regime of movement has necessitated a similar reformulation of modern policing. In a clever kinetic inversion of Althusser's famous police injunction "Hey you, there! Stop!", Jacques Rancière underscores this new function: one encapsulated in the simple act of a police officer urging bystanders of an incident to "Move along! There is nothing to see here."[39] For Rancière, the purpose of the state apparatus is to ensure the constant circulation of people, goods, and services: "The police say there is nothing to see, nothing happening, nothing to be done but to keep moving, circulating; they say that the space of circulation is nothing but the space of circulation."[40] In their everyday operation, states are less concerned with the arrest and constraint of movement than they are with making sure that nothing appears that may itself arrest the functioning of society, cause society to pause. During the 2014 Black Lives Matter protests, this point was driven home by a Ferguson police department directive ordering "peaceful, law-abiding protesters to keep moving [barring them from] standing still for longer than five seconds."[41] Or, as an exasperated Paul Boden, an advocate for homeless people in the United States, lamented, "it's illegal to stand still, it's illegal to sit down, it's illegal to lay down, it's illegal to eat. You're breaking the law as soon as you stop walking."[42] Across the Atlantic, Liverpool police have similarly tested out a "dispersal zone" covering much of the city center to preemptively deter any human gathering.[43] The absurdity of such kinetic laws was underscored in 2013 when Erdem Gündüz, following the brutal crackdown of Istanbul's Gezi uprising, planned a performative protest of standing in place at the center of Taksim Square. Within hours, #standingman had gone viral, and Gündüz was joined by hundreds of other standers, all of whom were dispersed or detained. Describing East Asian communism but in ways now eerily familiar to twenty-first-century regimes of movement in liberal democratic states, Virilio remarked, "Ostensibly, there are hardly any more crimes of opinion, only crimes of gesture. The confession is superseded: bodies are guilty of being out of sync, they have to be put back in line, at the speed of an entire population in maneuvers."[44]

The increased deployment of "big data policing," where algorithms are used to track (and predict) the movement of humans in society, takes these "crimes of gesture" to new heights. It has created, according to Davide Panagia, "a new political corporeality—the perpetually mobile body." This body can be "datafied," traced, and correlated, automatically registering deviations from—or disruptions to—normalized patterns of motion. With big data, populations are policed, not through the carceral and disciplinary institutions that compartmentalize, measure, identify, and differentiate its subjects, but rather through the constant surveillance of their movements. If the efficacy of one requires and creates sedentary subjects, the other requires and creates bodies in perpetual motion.[45]

This new form of policing gives new meaning to Virilio's claim that "the political power of the State is *polis*, police, that is, the management of the public ways." Its function, as Deleuze and Guattari have argued, is "to ensure that all freely moving bodies . . . become the relative characteristic of a 'moved body' going from one point to another in a striated space."[46]

I have so far briefly sketched two historical-conceptual trajectories through which the state has been interpreted in the modern period: the first as an inertial entity arresting and confining motion toward the management of order; the second an active entity that oversees a regime of incessant movement. To be sure, the history and present reality of every modern state displays both sets of characteristics. Stop and Frisk and the Ferguson directive to keep moving coexist as twin technologies to manage the Black population in the United States. The brutal evictions of the 2011 occupations (in order to restore a disrupted regime of movement) went hand in hand with the physical arrest of many of their participants. Sites of mass incarceration and ordinances against loitering dot the same American landscape. Why then go to such pains to differentiate the two?

The answer lies in how the protagonists of historical social struggles have encountered the social field within which they struggled. For those who perceived a static state built on order and confinement, freedom meant putting things into motion. The right to mobility and, if restrained, the flight from servitude have for these groups been the paradigmatic form of liberty. Others, conversely, have conceived the modern state as aiding and abetting a regime of movement. It was within this imaginary of the compulsion to move, surrounded by social fields of violent flux, that a politics of disruption became theorizable for the first time.

Perhaps as importantly, these brief kinetic sketches of the state's theorization underscore how the practice and study of social struggle as movement is historically bound to early strains of European liberalism; one that forged a still-present connection between the ideas of freedom, progress, and mobility. Against these associations, I argue, stands a long but untold history of social struggle that sought freedom not in movement but through its disruption. The aim of this book is to tell this story.

Histories of Disruption

One thread of this story takes us to the Rio Nunez, a river that by the early eighteenth century had become a main artery for transporting kidnapped Africans to be sold on the Upper Guinea Coast. It was here, in the 1720s, that Chief Tamba and his people began a campaign of continuous warfare against African and European slave traders, "obstructing their trade and executing the middlemen they captured." After years of struggle, Tamba was eventually caught, sold, and transported to a slaver, where he organized a revolt among captives on the ship. It was brutally put down; Tamba was killed, his liver fed to his supporters, who were subsequently executed.[47]

Records of such active and organized resistance to the slave trade in Africa are rare. But as the regime of movement made greater and greater inroads into the continent, countless communities devised strategies to insulate themselves against forces seeking to uproot them. They settled into steep mountains, constructed fortified encampments, and developed intricate alarm systems to ward off slave raids. The names of these safe havens, "the village of free people" or "here where no one can reach us," were evocative of both their function and the surrounding regime of movement that sought to spirit them away. In such circumstances, the ability to dwell, to reside in place, became the goal of freedom.

Another could tell the story of Joe Hill, the Swedish immigrant and IWW worker, who in 1914 wrote the song "Workers of the World, Awaken," which imagined a general strike that would paralyze the economy of movement:

If the workers take a notion
They can stop all speeding trains;
Every ship upon the ocean
They can tie with mighty chains;
Every wheel in the creation
Every mine and every mill,
Fleets and armies of the nation
Will at their command stand still.[48]

Following this cataclysmic disruption, the working class would usher in a new world, one where, Hill continued: "No one will for bread be crying / We'll have freedom, love and health / When the grand red flag is flying / In the Workers' Commonwealth." Unfortunately, Hill did not live long enough to see the worker's paradise. Like Chief Tamba, Joe Hill was executed soon after, this time by the state of Utah, in the hands of copper bosses whose enormous profits depended on the metal's uninterrupted flow.

Yet, just a few years later, workers across the Atlantic nearly turned Hill's song into reality. In Italy, the *Biennio Rosso* "Two Red Years" of 1919 and 1920 saw a massive series of countrywide strikes and land seizures that culminated in a revolutionary moment of factory occupations in Milan and Turin. An estimated 1 million workers established factory councils, instituted worker control over production, and began to run their factories themselves. In Germany, a general strike on January 7, 1919, brought a half-million mostly armed workers to the center of Berlin. Over the following days, mass work stoppages in other major cities led to a countrywide insurrection. In April 1919, the entire state of Bavaria declared independence from the Weimar Republic, created a "Red Army," and expropriated factories placing them under workers' control. That same year, mass strikes crippled Spain and Ireland and, jumping the Atlantic, halted production and circulation in Seattle and Winnipeg, bringing instances of "dual power" to North America.

Yet a third tale could shift forward to the 1970s, describing the peculiar position of US radical feminists that led many to advocate for separatism, extracting themselves from the world of men. Such a story might begin with Almania Barbour, a Black militant woman from Philadelphia, who claimed that "the women's movement is the first in history with a war on but no enemy."[49] An observation repeated by many radical feminists in countless consciousness-raising groups. If individual men, however well intentioned, were the physical human beings who upheld the structures of patriarchy, then most women, Barbour argued, were living alongside their adversaries. As The Furies, a Washington D.C. based lesbian-feminist collective stated in plain terms: "You can't build a strong movement if your sisters are out there fucking the oppressor."[50]

For some radical feminists, the problem was marriage. Isolated from one another, each day the bodies and minds of married women were being contaminated with male definitions, male gazes, male expectations, and male norms. If women really were at war, this clearly was not a very suitable battle position. Others took a more hardline stance. The Boston-based feminist collective Cell 16 called for separation and celibacy as the only means for breaking out of the self-conditioning impressed upon women by patriarchal society. They advocated forming female-only communes and spoke only to female reporters, eschewing all interaction with men. The Feminists, led by Atkinson, institutionalized this principle of separation, stipulating that only one-third (and by 1971, none) of its membership could be comprised of women living with men—in legal or informal partnerships.[51] They described heterosexual love as a sort of Stockholm syndrome, "the response of the victim to her rapist," and married women as at best "hostages" and at worst "collaborators."

Resistance to the slave trade in Africa, general strikes in Europe, feminist separatism in America. How should we think about these stories? Contextualized within the abolitionist, labor, or feminist movements, they appear as localized, extreme, spontaneous, momentary, even spasmodic responses to the systems they struggle against. At the same time, such stories are often imbued with a certain aura, attributed a naïve heroic or tragic idealism whose romanticization has only served to marginalize them further. Both these tendencies are a result of a long history of understanding social struggle through the category of movement. This book is an attempt to switch kinetic lenses. To see what we find when we look at social struggle not as movement but as disruption.

The History of Disruption begins by tracing the establishment of a regime of movement whose profits derived from the forced motion of various goods and social kinds. It then details a 300-year history of transatlantic struggle predicated on disrupting this regime, examining struggles that aimed not to move society but rather to interrupt its incessant need to produce, circulate, and uproot. Doing so, it hopes to outline a different narrative connecting such stories, a narrative where Chief Tamba, Joe Hill, and Cell 16 take center stage.

The regime of movement, by its own logic, has shifted form over the past three centuries, constantly devising new channels of motion to profit from. To a large extent, these shifts have conditioned the strategies of the politics of disruption that has struggled against it. During the time of Chief Tamba, the regime of movement was in relative infancy, expanding geographically by forcing its way into and connecting distant markets. Disruptive politics, whether as resistance to kidnapping, mutinies, food, foreclosure, or impressment riots, sought to *obstruct* the intrusion of the regime of movement onto the terrain of various Atlantic communities. By the late nineteenth century, having secured and connected international markets for its goods, the main source of the regime's profit shifted to producing them faster and more efficiently. The concentration of labor this required—in cities, in enterprises—provided new possibilities for the politics of disruption, a time when workers like Joe Hill sought, through interruption, a way to *control* the regime of movement for their own ends. In the 1960s, diminishing returns from industrial production—itself the result of worker disruption—forced the regime of movement to seek profits outside the factory: in rents, immaterial labor, consumption, health care, and the marketization of leisure. In order to extract surplus-value from these domains, human existence was increasingly channeled toward commodified activity, while social relations outside the logic of exchange were invalidated or proscribed. This colonization of daily life recomposed the terrain of disruptive politics to universities, grocery stores, hospitals, and homes, and occasioned new disruptive subjects, including students, minorities, and women who, like Cell 16, sought to *extract* themselves from the regime of movement altogether.

These strategies—*obstruction, control, extraction*—signal significant shifts in the politics of disruption and loosely form the long arc of this book.

Chapter 1, "Movement," details how movement, as a practice and idea, was central to the establishment and legitimation of the capitalist economy in the eighteenth century. It demonstrates how this economy made its profits by moving goods, credit, and human beings across the Atlantic world. It examines the violence and coercion that accompanied this movement; of the force necessary to create regional, national, and international markets for goods; and the mobile, docile labor force required to supply, connect, and protect them. It argues that since this economy's inception, social struggle in the Atlantic world took place on a kinetic register, as the struggle over the power of movement and its disruption.

Chapter 2, "Obstruction," examines the initial resistance to the establishment of the regime of movement, detailing disruptions that aimed to block or arrest the reterritorialization of their life-worlds. In doing so, it connects the histories of slave ship mutinies, Caribbean piracy, maroons, and the food, enclosure, and impressment riots of the eighteenth century as attempts to disrupt the forced movement of the world's first globalization.

Chapter 3, "Control," traces the disruptive strategies of the nineteenth- and early twentieth-century workers' struggle, examining the theories and practices of sabotage, the barricade, the general strike, and propaganda of the deed as they were developed by transatlantic networks of anarchist, Marxist, and syndicalist laborers. It tells the story of a working class created by and already inscribed into the regime of movement. It underscores how working-class disruption in this period aimed not to obstruct but rather to control economic motion, the period when resistance to the regime of movement became increasingly equated to assuming power over it.

Chapter 4, "Extraction," turns to the post-1968 struggles in Italy and the United States, examining the Black Power, workerist (*operaismo*), and Italian and American radical feminist struggles during a moment of global economic restructuring. It describes another shift in the dominant mode of disruption, one where struggles largely discarded attempts to control the regime of movement in favor of extracting themselves from it. Heavily influenced by anticolonialism and the New Left, these struggles theorized and deployed disruption to create decolonized subjectivities and spaces from within territories already configured by capital. The chapter explores how Blacks, workers, and women rejected the roles ascribed to them by the existing social order in order to define themselves on their own terms. It details the new spaces, histories, languages, and frameworks these groups created and the unruly or unexpected subjects engendered through these disruptive struggles.

The book's Coda, "The Southern Wind," focuses on the Zapatista Army of National Liberation (*EZLN*) that emerged from the Lacandón Jungle in 1994 to overthrow the Mexican government and disrupt global neoliberalism. It frames the Zapatistas as both the product of the disruptive politics of the 1970s and the source for new frameworks of disruption that animated numerous global struggles of the twenty-first century.

Finally, the Conclusion, "Disrupt or Be Disrupted," brings the history of disruption up to the present day, exploring the recent co-option of disruption by capital itself and its implications for social struggles of the future. It traces the rise of *disruptive innovation* as a business model and its spread from the fringes of the tech sector to the education, health care, logistics, and gig economies. Coupling these developments with an examination of the post-2011 global crackdown on disruptive struggles, the conclusion argues that we are entering a moment when social struggle will take place not over movement, but rather the category of disruption. The book ends by tracing the emergent battles of this new terrain between a disruptive capital and those seeking to free themselves from it.

These chapters are themselves interrupted by two short excursus, which consider key moments that altered the signification of disruption, detailing shifts in how disruption was inscribed, practiced, and understood. The first examines the effects of the French and Haitian Revolutions, describing how they marked disruption as an act of sovereign will and inscribed disruptive struggle into (a newly universal) history. The second explores the changes in the meaning and temporality of disruption that accompanied the revolutionary uprisings of 1968.

Situating the History of Disruption

Disruption, modernity, and reaction

The politics and practice of disruption have historically gotten a bad rap. With some notable exceptions, disruption has been, and continues to be, disparaged or dismissed by activists, politicians, and scholars alike. The book details many historical instances of disruption's excision from the social body and its memory, including those carried out by the oppressed themselves. Here, I will comment only on its academic reception.

A major line of scholarly criticism is that the politics of disruption, ideationally and in praxis, is at best conservative and at worst reactionary. Fredric Jameson, commenting on the contemporary resurgence of disruptive politics, perhaps most vividly expressed a view held by many:

> We may pause to observe the way in which so much of left politics today—unlike Marx's own passionate commitment to a streamlined technological future—seems to have adopted as its slogan Benjamin's odd idea that revolution means pulling the emergency brake on the runaway train of History, as though an admittedly runaway capitalism itself had the monopoly on change and futurity.[52]

The suggestion being that, by giving capitalism a monopoly on the future, we concede, in advance, any alternative to remaking it on our own. Implied in this and many similar critiques is that disruptive politics can only slow or stall the future. That it is animated not by the society it wishes to bring about, but rather by an embrace of the past as shelter—if not in a lost feudal socialism (Marx's charge against the utopians), then perhaps a receding feudal Keynesianism.[53] Though I find this line of critique to be quite baseless, it does bring up a reception problem often faced by disruptive struggles: how to practice a nonrestorative politics of disruption? One that neither falls prey to right-wing conservative localism nor a romantic primitivism of the left. How can futurity be incorporated into a politics that itself disrupts the idea of progression? In the 235 years since the French Revolution which first made such questions askable, the practitioners of disruption have faced them head-on. Their answers have been creative, numerous, and form a central theme of this book.

A second vector of criticism against disruptive politics originates from social movement studies. Kinetically speaking, the historiography of social struggle has been, and, to a large extent, remains, dominated by the category of movement. The origin story of social movements, most notably put forth by the late Charles Tilly, recounts the story of a qualitative shift in the aim and tactics of social struggle that occurred in the eighteenth-century Atlantic world. "In the late 18th century, people in Western Europe and North America began the fateful creation of a new political phenomena. They began to create social movements." By the mid-nineteenth century, Tilly continues, "the people of most western countries shed the collective-action repertoire that they had used for two centuries and adopted the repertoire that they still use today."[54]

Tilly describes an evolutionary narrative of social struggle: from premodern (re)actions classified as localized, unmediated, spontaneous, spasmodic, and conservative to the organized, premeditated, (inter)national, and forward-looking character of modern social movements. The differentiation is by repertoire. Whereas premodern struggles involved riots, looting, veiled or explicit threats, and violence, modern social movements invented and utilized a new set of strategies: campaigns, associations, coalitions, public meetings, solemn processions, vigils, rallies, demonstrations, petition drives, public media statements, and pamphleteering. Tilly referred to these new strategies—somewhat clumsily—as *WUNC* displays: participants' concerted public representation of Worthiness, Unity, Numbers, and Commitments.[55]

Two important moves occur in this narrative. The first is the identification of disruption with premodern—and movement with modern—forms of struggle. This identification consigns disruption to an antiquated—and, when employed in the modern era—anachronistic tactic, vis-à-vis the modern practices of social movements. Second, Tilly places normative value on the evolution of social struggle repertoires, which, to a large extent, boils down to increasing their efficacy. In his reading, modern social movements can make legible claims to the existing system, seeking inclusion within, and recognition by, the regime of movement itself. Legibility allows their tactical and organizational forms to be assessed, evaluated, and further developed. The selection bias here is obvious, highlighting certain struggles while ignoring others. It is easy to see what Gandhi wanted. The 1965 Watts uprising, less so.

Tilly's principal narrative has, to a large extent, been adopted by many social movement scholars. It is one of the main reasons that the history of disruption has been so often written out of, tangentially referenced by, or seen as a primitive precursor to, the history of social movements. There is much to take issue with this narrative. Rather than do so explicitly, however, this book underscores that the practices and mentalities of disruption, so often treated as spontaneous, archaic, and disorderly outliers to the organization and structure of social movements, possess a long, continuous, and *modern* history of their own.

Periodizing disruption

Whatever the faults or merits of Tilly's account, it does reproduce a much older and broader tendency of social struggle scholarship: periodization. The periodization of social struggle, particularly the divide between *premodern* and *modern* forms of struggle, predates the academic study of it (the distinction is conceptually coeval with modernity itself and, at the very latest, was demarked by workers following the early nineteenth-century Luddite revolts). Within academia, periodization debates have either focused on tactics—where scholars have tended to replicate Tilly's main argument—or on the *temporal* or *religious/secular* imaginaries of historical social struggles. The former divide draws the line between premodern and modern forms of struggle along their orientations toward the past or future: whether struggles aimed to restore or create, were driven by the nostalgia for a lost age or the hope of a new and better world to come. The latter, following modernity's self-conception, marks the premodern/modern line as the shift from a religious to secular cosmology (and correspondingly, a switch from an irrational to a rational basis) animating social struggle.[56]

On the other side of modernity, the academic study of social struggle has also added a second boundary line, one distinguishing the *modern* from the *postmodern* eras (usually situated—for Atlantic struggles—in the decade surrounding 1968). Though what exactly this boundary marks has been the subject of much debate. Scholars have attributed the shifts in social struggle to: the demotion of the revolutionary role of the working class and the entrance of other political subjects (students, the colonized, women, Blacks); the transition from economic struggle to the identity-, issue-, or lifestyle-based politics of the New Social Movements; the transition from material to symbolic/performative struggle; from struggle for the future to a focus on the now; or from hierarchical to horizontal and leaderless forms of internal organization.

The History of Disruption does not intervene in these periodization debates. Instead, it postulates a single adversary, the regime of movement, whose effect on humans (though differential by geography, race, and gender) was continuous—if continually changing. These effects, and the 300-year history of human attempts to disrupt it, traverse the prevalent periodization of social struggle into premodern, modern, and postmodern forms. As such, *The History of Disruption* follows both older historians like Eric Hobsbawm (whose still quite remarkable little book, *Primitive Rebels*, described the presence of one era's imaginary in the other) and more recent scholars, including Michael T. Davis, Ilaria Favretto, Xabier Itçaina, and Joshua Clover, who have demonstrated the continuation and refinement of disruptive practices over the past three centuries.

This is not to say that this book lacks periodization. As Jameson and others have argued, the interpretation of history is impossible without it.[57] *The History of Disruption* also periodizes, but according to a different register. The book's fairly loose boundaries are not based on the tactics of social struggles, nor on their forward- or backward-looking nature, but, rather, on the relationship of disruption to history, of how and when disruption became inscribed into history, was made legible to it, seen as something that could change it, and when—at a different historical conjuncture—disruption ceased to be this way. These codings of disruption are detailed in the two short excursus of the book, which trace the significant transformations (or, more properly, interruptions) in the signification of disruption: changes in how disruption was inscribed, practiced, and understood.

Movement, disruption, and revolution

I decided to research and write this book as a way to understand the global resurgence of disruptive struggle since 2011. These struggles fit into neither our accustomed understandings of *revolution* nor a progressive politics practiced and studied as *social movements*. *The History of Disruption* is, conceptually, centered around this dual incommensurability. It details both the historical lineages of the disruptive struggles we are witnessing today and the challenges such a history poses to the two predominant categories by which scholars have approached and accounted for popular sociopolitical change.

Both revolution and social movements (as we understand these terms today) have their origins in the late eighteenth-century Atlantic world, coeval with the modern understanding that humans can collectively alter and refashion their own societies. They were differentiated and practiced in tandem by the nineteenth-century workers' struggle and reimagined once again by the anti-imperial impulses of decolonization and the New Left. It is all the more surprising, given their conjoined history, that the academic study of social movements and revolution have not only developed in isolation, but bear the mark of a near-total segregation.[58]

Revolutionary history and theory have had a long and varied historiography. Over the past century, the search for the "objective" causes and historical significance of revolution has largely given way to an analysis of the revolutionary moment itself: revolution as spontaneous creation; of new forms, spaces, meanings, temporalities, subjectivities; revolution as the analysis of both historical contingency and the emergence and repetition of historical scripts. Throughout, the study of revolution has interpreted social change as an outcome of exceptional politics, the self-recognized situation when the extant laws and forms of an established system break down, are transcended, discarded, and replaced. In other words, the popular counterpolitics to, and obverse of, the state of exception as developed by Hobbes, Arendt, Schmidt, and Agamben.

The academic inquiry into social movements, by contrast, has been concerned with the unexceptional. A child of political science and postwar sociology, social movement studies was born to explain how groups of people effect change within (not of) a system. Both its empirical studies and its theoretical framework have undergone significant shifts over the past half century. But it was not until the mid-1990s that it turned its eye to the past, inquiring into the historical origins, refinement, and resonance of social movement tactics, strategies, and organizational structures.

These independent academic trajectories have, over time, developed their own internal dynamics, vocabularies, and cosmologies to examine and interpret the history of popular social change. Though rarely appearing in each other's histories, the study of social movements and revolution are nevertheless conceptually codependent. A set of binary oppositions over legibility/illegibility, legality/transgression, flow/rupture, accretion/abruptness, recognition/liberation, and intentionality/contingency pervade and delineate the boundaries of what is and is not considered a social movement or revolution. As binary concepts, it is not possible to think through revolutionary change without implicit reference to the change brought about by social movements (and vice versa). The understanding of one, in this sense, is predicated on the ignored presence of the other.[59] Together they form a conceptual universe of historical analysis that has, to a large extent, circumscribed how we approach and examine collective social change.

The binary oppositions between revolution and social movement have only been solidified by their academic isolation from one another. This "arbitrary, ahistorical, and damaging move," to quote Sidney Tarrow, is, I argue, largely a result of the existing association of social struggle with the category of movement. In this sense, *The History of Disruption* is an attempt at desegregation. It underscores how revolution, both tactically and temporally, shares much in common with everyday practices of disruption. In doing so, it allows for the history of revolution, one that occupies a very tangential place within (if not altogether excluded from) the history of social movements, to be written back into a now much broader conceptualization of collective social change. Within this new field, disruptive practices and mentalities become the soil for, precursors to, or the aborted children of a now more expansive revolutionary history. This book is an attempt to outline the contours of this history in the Atlantic world.

In connecting the exceptional state of revolution to the unexceptional politics of interruption, *The History of Disruption* also challenges contemporary theories that position revolution as an abstracted moment of epistemic rupture, which speak of revolution's "unpredictable contingency," valorize the "event" and its "unnamable" causes and outcomes, or theorize its "inarticulable and impossible" political subjects. Against this philosophy of rupture that awaits the "yet unthought," *The History of Disruption* resituates rupture as a mentality that is harbored, fostered, and transmitted through human beings within history. In this sense, it sends a clear retort to contemporary purists of revolution that revolution's future, far from necessitating abstraction, is to be found in the disruptive subjects, spaces, and potentials of the now.

Kinetic History, Capitalism, and the Scope of this Book

The method underlying *The History of Disruption* is kinetic analysis: the critical use of the categories of movement and interruption to examine the tactics, mentalities, and temporalities of those who sought to change the world they live in. Unlike, say, the analysis of gender or class, kinetic analysis is not a universal framework for examining all social struggle across human history.[60] It is, in a foundational sense, suited to the analysis of social struggle under capitalism. This is because the object of kinetic analysis is made possible by capitalism itself.

For Marx, the internal logic of capitalism, its "sole driving force, [is] the drive to valorise itself, to create surplus-value."[61] This vampiric self-accretion of capital—whereby dead labor expands by feeding on the labor of the living—is governed by laws that Marx called, following Newton, *the laws of motion*.[62] The ultimate aim of *Capital* was in fact "to lay bare the economic laws of motion of modern society."[63] These were, as Ellen Meiksins Wood succinctly summarized, "the *imperatives* of competition and profit maximization; a *compulsion* to re-invest surpluses; and the systematic *need* to improve labor-productivity."[64] For Marx, the laws of motion constantly propelled the expansion of capitalism into new terrains. And wherever market economies and commodity production established themselves, these laws came with them, gradually restructuring economic and social life according to their principles.[65] As the laws of motion penetrated into new human communities—the feuds and grievances, births and marriages, hierarchies and religions that had pulled people apart and brought them together—entire human ecosystems with their histories and entanglements, ways of being, and the institutions that propped them up were all stripped of their ordering force.

This process, by which existing social relations lose their binding power, Deleuze and Guattari referred to as deterritorialization.[66] Deterritorialization involved a decoding of physical and symbolic space that had previously regulated the roles, conflicts, and bonds within a community. Once "decoded," the terrain is then reterritorialized with new codes that order what a human body can or must do, how it can or must move, in order to exist. For the regime of movement, this reordering has historically consisted of reconfiguring place into property, natural entities into commodities, and human beings into labor. Taken together, this dual process of de- and reterritorialization erases existing fields of conflict and reconfigures the terrain kinetically, according to the capitalist laws of motion.[67] Much like a magnet brought near metal filings, it establishes, conditions, and coerces new patterns of movement, channeling bodies and things along the newly striated spaces of capital. The introduction of the slave trade, the enclosures and marketization of rents, and the forced consignment of women to reproduction are all early examples of this kinetic reterritorialization. As we shall see, in the nineteenth and especially twentieth centuries, kinetic reterritorialization would expand beyond a recoding of physical terrain into the symbolic architectures of society and the psychic architectures of our minds. As various currents of Western Marxism have pointed out, by the mid-twentieth century, the regime of movement began conditioning, on a mass scale, what we desire, what we resign ourselves to, and even our fantasies of escape.

Capitalism creates kinetic terrains. Its internal logic, its laws of motion, compel constant movement along its ever-shifting lines. That the forced evictions of European peasantry, the brutal kidnapping of Africans, and the violent mechanization of the female body gave way to internalized fantasies of social mobility, national development, and individual self-improvement is nothing other than the sublimations produced by this kinetic compulsion—its penetration into, and reconfiguration of, our psychic and symbolic terrains.

On this level, then, *The History of Disruption* is the story of both the kinetic reordering of terrain according to the laws of motion and the various histories of those resisting it. Its central argument is that once configured by capital, these physical, symbolic, and psychic terrains can only be contested kinetically, through a struggle against movement, as disruption. Kinetic analysis, as the examination into the establishment and contestation of these terrains, is therefore *immanent* to the history of capital. This is the strong claim of the book. If true, this immanence to its object makes kinetic analysis a privileged method for interpreting the history of modern social struggles. Namely, that the organization of movement and the attempts to disrupt this organization form the "terrain" on which modern social struggles take place.

The immanence of kinetic analysis to the history of capitalism has guided many of the decisions over the book's temporal, geographic, and thematic scope. Kinetic analysis must follow its object. Accordingly, *The History of Disruption* begins in the eighteenth century with the widespread establishment of the regime of movement.[68] It ends (or, more appropriately, stops) in the present, at a moment when this regime is simultaneously omnipresent and radically unstable.

Similarly, the geographic scope of the book (at least initially) maps onto the kinetic reach of this regime. *The History of Disruption* is thus an Atlantic story, as this is where the regime of movement first emerged. Or, more accurately, since the Atlantic itself was a creation of the regime of movement, the book follows the terrain established by this regime. By the mid nineteenth century, this correspondence breaks down, as the regime of movement and the resistance to it become truly global, animating struggles from India to the Congo. For practical reasons, I do not expand my geography to keep pace.

Capital, itself compelled to move, ceaselessly etches new vectors of possible profitable movement. Kinetic analysis follows these shifting terrains. For this reason, the historical geography of disruption within the Atlantic world is also in constant flux. What begins as a largely maritime and rural history morphs into an examination of factories and urban centers and, by the end, extends to universities, the home, and the natural environment. These geographies are not objective but, rather, formed by the "maps" imagined by the people within the struggles I trace. Each of their worlds interacted with, envisioned, or were informed by a certain subjective geography of struggle. It is difficult to understand the German and American SDS without Vietnam. But quite easy without Iceland. These imagined geographies constitute the Atlantic worlds of the book as well.

Having said this, the selection of the particular struggles examined in the book was difficult. Rosa Luxemburg once remarked that "those who do not move, do not notice their chains." Kinetic analysis suggests the opposite. The chains of capital reveal themselves the moment people resist its forced movement. As a general rule, I have tried to follow the moments when practices of disruption revealed these chains. Thus, I have included struggles that either introduced new forms and meanings of disruption or transposed extant disruptive strategies to new terrains.

To be sure, any criterion involves the exclusion of many important social struggles. The obvious criticism of the above criterion is that it self-selects struggles that are particularly suited to kinetic analysis. This is unavoidable. All interpretations highlight certain elements and obscure others. It would be a sad reflection on the diversity of humanity's endeavors if they did not. Nonetheless, *The History of Disruption* does systematically privilege some forms of struggle over others. Because the book is concerned with the resistance to the regime of movement, it focuses on struggles that disrupt the motion of the things, bodies, and minds channeled by it. Yet, this same regime has, at different points and in different places, deemed certain people as surplus, unusable, or unnecessary to its functioning: The insane and disabled, the Indigenous, deindustrialized workers, refugees, urban minorities, and other discards of the "bulimic empire."[69] Instead of forcing them into profitable movement, it has excluded these excess populations from the terrain altogether. The technologies of this exclusion—the asylum, the reservation, mass incarceration, sterilization, narcotics, and camps— are ones of immobility. At their limit, they constitute a necropolitics. *The History of Disruption* does not deal with these technologies of social excision. They figure only as the carceral nightmare shrouding the edges of capital's kinetic terrain: a necessary and fantastic reminder of the consequences of not moving (or not being allowed to move) along its prescribed lines. This nightmare's temporal equivalent is, in Trotsky's infamous words, "the dustbin of history."

Finally, outside of the first chapter detailing the establishment of the regime of movement, the book is concerned with the history of attempts to resist it. Put another way, *The History of Disruption* is not a kinetic history of social struggle, but rather the history of one side of this conflict. This is intentional. My interest lies in the history of human attempts at liberation, not in detailing the technologies of our oppression.

How to read this book

This book can be read in a number of different ways depending on one's purpose. First, it is a tactical guide to disruptive action. Its chapters outline a multitude of strategies, mentalities, and practices that have sought to arrest or subvert the regime of movement. Here, the aim is to allow readers to reach outside their own contemporary struggles and histories to survey the phenomenal array of tactics and frameworks that humans have used to disrupt the various faces of capital. While the content and specific frameworks of both historical and contemporary struggles may seem unrelated, even at times unbridgeable, a certain unity of form, of strategic purpose, can illuminate pathways of solidarity. This resonance of form was particularly evident, for example, in the global occupations of the squares from 2011 to 2013 (themselves adapted from the sit-ins and occupations of workers and students of the twentieth century). The same can also be said of the reappropriation of and mutations to, say, the rough music and charivari of the eighteenth-century French peasant by Italian auto workers in the 1970s, or the adaptation of turn-of-the-century industrial sabotage by radical environmentalists in the 1980s. It is my hope that a grand survey of disruption will bring these and other connections to light.

Second, this book is a rebuke of the category of movement as a way to think about the social struggles against capital. This is admittedly a tall order, since the category is near ubiquitous across languages and subjects, activists and academia. My aim is not to change the terms we use—substituting movement for disruption—but, rather, to question the historical baggage and associations that have accrued into it. Ultimately, there is a depoliticizing element associated with movement that the practitioners of disruption noted time and time again. The main reason for this depoliticization, I argue, lies in the tactical and theoretical complicity of social movements with the order they oppose. As this book underscores, for capital, mobilization was always a military campaign, one that often recruited social movements as its shock troops. At a time when contemporary social struggles are explicitly targeting the many faces of neoliberal capital, *The History of Disruption* questions this complicity and claims that within a regime of movement, disruption stands as the precondition of the political as such.

Finally, for me at least, histories of disruption hold normative value. Scholars do not write in a political vacuum. They are both influenced by and address themselves to the assumptions and concerns of their own society.

We are currently living within a globalized regime of movement that employs the history of progress to understand its own past. For the purposes of its own self-reproduction, there is a tendency for this regime to inscribe past social struggles within a teleology of the present: a considerable interest in underscoring historical practices and imaginaries that conform to and explain its self-image—ones that are simultaneously legible for the present regime of movement and serve to make this regime itself legible. The contemporary popular narrative of New Left struggles as a period when various "movements" sought to incorporate the concerns and bodies of Blacks, students, and women more equally into the existing social order is a case in point.[70]

Normatively, then, kinetic analysis differentiates between accounts that read history with or against the grain. Yes, the worker's struggle was responsible for ensuring workplace safety, reduced working hours, and living wages, but it also sought an end to wage slavery and the alienation of humankind. Yes, the feminist struggle was responsible for ensuring women's franchise, de jure social equality, and control over women's bodies, yet it also sought to dismantle the hierarchical institutions of state and family that still structure contemporary society. These distinctions are not just a matter of emphasis but have serious political implications for the present. While feminism understood as movement can position the recent struggle for women to serve combat roles in the US military as the continuation of earlier battles for social equality, feminism as disruption would recover the significant currents within the feminist struggle that advocated not for the equal right of women to kill, but for the abolition of war. As Raymond Williams wisely suggested, "we cement our dissenting tradition by selecting the ancestors we need."[71]

Perhaps the worst form of this presentism occurs when social struggles are themselves seen as the products of the shifting values, categories, and operation of the regime of movement itself. Kristin Ross devastatingly argued this point in her discussion of the memory of 1968:

> The official story does not limit itself to merely claiming that some of May's more radical ideas and practices came to be recuperated or recycled in the service of Capital. Rather, it asserts that today's capitalist society, far from representing the derailment or failure of the May movement's aspirations, instead represents the accomplishment of its deepest desires.[72]

Inscribed into the regime of movement, May 1968 is stripped of its political subjectivity, becoming a necessary moment of cultural transformation itself produced by the modernization of France from an authoritarian industrial to a liberal financier state.[73]

Walter Benjamin once wrote, "thinking involves not only the flow of thoughts, but their arrest as well," a call for a politics of history that would interrupt the present's incessant tendency to remake the past in its desired self-image. Histories of disruption are one form of this politics. They fill the past with dead ends, alternative visions, and subjectivities of refusal that sought outcomes other than the ones that came to pass. In the coming years, we will need these more than ever.

1

Movement

The creation of a large and expanding market for goods and a large and available labor force go together, two aspects of the same process.
Eric Hobsbawm

Beginning in the sixteenth century, a series of developments in north-western Europe profoundly changed life on both sides of the North Atlantic. Technological advances in navigation that improved the speed and accuracy of oceanic travel, the formation of joint-stock companies and national banking that allowed for the pooling of capital, the establishment of the African slave trade, and the European agricultural revolution made large-scale commerce and colonization both possible and extremely profitable, creating the conditions for the formation of a transatlantic economy.[1] As David Armitage once noted, "The Atlantic was a European invention ... because Europeans were the first to connect its four sides into a single entity."[2]

This economy was made possible by, and derived its wealth from, movement. By the dawn of the nineteenth century, it had put into motion goods and bodies in a manner unprecedented in human history. This chapter traces the emergence of the regime of movement in the seventeenth and eighteenth centuries. It is not concerned with the abstract development of political economy or in highlighting techno-logical innovations. Rather, it examines the effects of this regime on the lives and experiences of human beings.

The stories that it describes have been told before. It is the story of commodification: of how both human beings and the things they made came to be bought and sold by others, in markets, for profit. It is also the story of primitive accumulation, of the violence by which a commercial and landowning class accumulated wealth through a system of expropriation and kidnapping that they themselves legalized. This chapter tells these old stories in a new way. It underscores how movement, as a practice and idea, was central to the establishment and legitimation of the capitalist economy. It examines the violence and coercion that accompanied this movement, of the force necessary to create regional, national, and international markets for goods and a mobile, docile labor source required to supply them. In this way, it links the liberalization of trade, European migration, African enslavement, and the disciplining of bodily motion, tying through a logic of forced movement histories of land and sea, bodies and goods, schedules and idleness across the Atlantic world.

I. The Movement of Goods

On the most elemental level, the transatlantic regime of movement involved taking things that people made in one place and moving them somewhere else. The spread of this regime, and its penetration into the lives of human beings around the Atlantic, was dictated by the profits to be made from this movement. In order to move goods "freely" from one place to another, it was necessary to link producers and consumers in far-flung places and to tear down the barriers that lay between them, that is, to establish regional, national, and international markets through which goods could easily flow.

The regime of movement's own narrative describes the process by which this occurred: subsistence-based communities, isolated by distance, law, and custom, were gradually brought together by a commercial class that overcame oceans and state monopolies and linked town to country, increasing the commonwealth through division of labor and comparative advantage. First formulated by Adam Smith and the French Physiocrats in the late eighteenth century, this narrative, with little variation, continues to inform the ideational basis of contemporary trade regimes, including GATT, the Common Market, NAFTA, and the TTIP.

Often left out of this story is the process by which these markets were created. The free movement of goods, both as practice and idea, did not emerge ex nihilo, but rather fought a real and ideological war with economic practices and cosmologies that existed alongside it. The establishment of free markets brought with it wholly new ways of thinking about nature, right, and order; new occupations, classes, and social kinds; and new ways of accumulating wealth, all based on movement. The establishment of the "free movement" of goods provoked popular resistance at almost every turn and was forced to enlist an increasingly centralized state to implement, by force, its design.

What did the free movement of goods replace? Before the onset of liberalism, there existed a reciprocal bond between the rural populace of western Europe and the early modern state. In this paternalistic political economy, the state "purchased" domestic obedience by guaranteeing people the right to fairly priced basic provisions. The authorities in this economy had the responsibility to ensure subsistence and, if abridged, the people were justified to rise up and secure this right for themselves. E. P. Thompson, the pioneer of this historical process in England, called it the moral economy. The French simply referred to it as *taxation populaire*. Both involved a complex relationship between rulers and ruled that fed the people of early modern Europe.[3]

Ensuring fairly priced basic provisions meant, in day-to-day life, maintaining a set of customs and practices over the functioning of local markets. Regulations governed when, where, in what form, to whom, and how much goods—especially wheat—could be sold (or left unsold).[4] Though varying by region, these rules were everywhere precise. In Preston, Lancashire: "None but the townspeople are permitted to buy during the first hour, at nine others may purchase: but nothing unsold must be withdrawn from the market till one o'clock, fish excepted."[5] In other areas, farmers or middlemen could not sell by sample, could not sell standing crops, could not sell outside of the prescribed market hours, in bulk quantities, or to anyone outside of the prescribed people (usually limited to the consumer). Buying to later sell in the same market, or in neighboring markets, was strictly prohibited. Throughout France, similar subsistence regulations and practices, referred to as *la police de subsistance*, prohibited millers and bakers from buying excess grain, forced all purchases to take place at market, and allowed families purchasing for consumption the first dibs.[6] The aim of these measures was to prevent excessive profits from forestalling or regrating by farmers and middlemen and to ensure the local and direct sale of provisions to consumers at a reasonable price. Within the cosmology of the moral economy, the freedom of the farmer to move his corn as he pleased was branded a "natural" as opposed to a "civic" liberty (the liberty to buy fairly priced goods), one fit for "savages" and thus not deserving of the protection of the community.[7]

In both countries where the paternalistic model held sway, these customs had the sanction of local authorities. Whether at village, municipal, or royal level, authorities were either outright sympathetic to the claims of ordinary people or felt compelled to assist them as part of an older compact. This meant not only upholding established practices that regulated the food market, but also "turning a blind eye to crowds that stopped merchants from moving supplies, protecting commoners accused of violent actions, or joining and sometimes leading rioting crowds."[8]

A similar, though nonpaternalistic, cosmology of exchange was also taking shape across the ocean, in Britain's thirteen colonies. Colonial settlement, made possible by the economy of movement, included two distinct, though interrelated, economies: those tied up within large-scale long-distance trade (concentrated around merchants in larger cities along the coast) and those based on small, relatively independent farmers and craftsmen, producing and consuming locally (concentrated, though not exclusively, in rural communities). These two coexisting economies animated two different societies and societal visions, what Charles Sellers has called the cultures of market and of land. The first fostered individual competitive pursuit and accumulation of wealth through the commodification of goods. The second, a subsistence culture, nurtured family obligation, communal cooperation, reciprocity, and concern for the public over the private interest.[9] Many scholars have since traced the self-formation of this local culture, the rather complex rules governing the exchange of labor, tools, manufacture, produce, and debt, and the social and ethical frames they developed to guide them.[10] Exchange in these communities was conducted according to widely shared local ideas about what was customary and fair. These included expectations that trade should be "mutually advantageous" and not conducted at another's expense. For most inhabitants of a locality, maintaining a reputation for probity and fairness conditioned how neighbors related to one another. Scholars would later term such exchange relations between families "civic humanism." For a Delaware farmer writing in his notebook, the concept was far less abstract: the households simply "neighbored." Similarly, credit and debt were extended and incurred in these more insular communities, but were practiced differently—and for other motives—than those that guided international trade. A local debt might persist for years without interest and would more than likely be paid off in kind or labor than cash. As Bruce Mann has argued, there were different rules by which these communities dealt with "neighbors" and "strangers."[11] Within the community, mutuality and reciprocity were paramount.[12] Much like the moral economies of Europe, the culture of land ordered a social and cultural universe of human relations and exchange that was inimical to (if in this case made possible by) the economy of movement.[13]

In the eighteenth century, the economy of movement challenged these alternate practices on both sides of the Atlantic. In Great Britain and France, demographic shifts and changes to traditional landholding arrangements (particularly in England) increased pressure to both abandon the moral economy and the state's support of it. The introduction of rack rent and the growth of population centers removed from the main growing districts meant large profits for those who could move foodstuffs from one area to another. The result was a push for deregulation. As urban and export demand for grains increased, less of it was locally consumed, and local markets were increasingly drawn into and incorporated within larger regional, national, and international economies. Toward the end of the eighteenth century, marketing procedures became less transparent as the grain passed through the hands of a more complex network of intermediaries. Farmers, instead of selling directly to local markets, turned more and more to dealers, who were in a better position to hold stocks and keep prices high.[14] In many places, farmers (and millers) increasingly refused to sell (or grind) grain in small quantities, preferring larger contracts with merchants. As a consequence, the local markets either disappeared or became wholesale, leaving the poor to turn to higher priced merchants or bakers for subsistence.[15]

On the heels of the increased profits to be made through the movement of goods came the economic cosmology to legitimize it. In France, the physiocrats, or *économistes*, as they called themselves, directly challenged the paternalistic regulationism of the markets and urged the government to "*laissez faire, laissez passer*," arguing that deregulation would increase productivity and thus revenue for the Crown. Similar ideas were also afoot in England. Beginning with Charles Smith's *Tracts on the Corn Trade* in 1758 , a whole host of ideologues came out for the economy of movement. "Let corn flow like water and it will find its level," wrote agriculturalist John Arbuthnot in 1773. Three years later, Adam Smith demanded the "unlimited, unrestrained freedom of the corn trade."[16] In a complete reversal of their standing within the moral economy, the movers of corn, the middlemen and merchants, were not only seen as necessary but depicted as laudable members of society, transporting corn from areas of surplus to scarcity. Rather than harboring interests opposed to common folk, these political economists felt the commercial class was in fact teaching commoners the principles of a totally different—though equally moral—economy. "By raising the price to that fetched in the market," Adam Smith wrote, the merchant "encourages thrift and good management, especially among the inferior ranks of the people."[17]

The issue for Smith and other classical political economists was the state's ongoing role in upholding outmoded customs. The civic liberty of market regulation, which Smith characterized as the meddlesome interference of "popular prejudice" akin to "beliefs in witchcraft," was being sanctioned by the state itself. Rather than condone this violence, what liberalism, "the self-adjusting economy," demanded of the state was the "protection of the law."[18] In both France and England, the ideologues of movement pitched their case that deregulation would further increase the division of labor, comparative advantage, the productivity and cultivation of land, and thus the Crown's taxable revenue.

These arguments began to have their effect, shifting the relationship between state, merchants, and commoners over the second half of the eighteenth century. In France, the monarchy, struggling to extract more and more taxes from its subjects, came to recognize that economic growth held the key to treasury replenishment. Beginning in 1763, it encouraged everyone to participate in the grain trade, permitted transactions outside the local market, and allowed previously outlawed business practices, such as regrating. Though reversing policy several times, the monarchy's preference toward expanding regional, national, and international markets, urbanization, the commercialization of agriculture, and a greater division of social labor marked the beginning of a long-term trend.[19] As the state gradually abandoned its paternalistic role to favor profits made from the marketization of basic foodstuffs, the moral economy that ensured the security of its subjects gave way to Physiocratic, laissez-faire, and liberal economic thinking.[20] Accompanying this shift was a state-sustained effort to depoliticize subsistence issues and delegitimize popular claims that "need" took precedence over the rights of property.[21]

The state's transition—from siding with commoners to protecting the interests of merchants and large producers—signals a fundamental shift in the history of kinetic struggle. It marks the emergence, within the marketplace of eighteenth-century Europe, of the regime of movement: the moment when the state, which had previously sanctioned the disruption of the grain trade, committed itself to ensuring the right of movement for goods. The transition of the state from paternalism to being harnessed by the economy of movement was a gradual process that, despite hiccups based on local idiosyncrasies or international wars, neared completion in the North Atlantic world by the mid-nineteenth century.[22]

Siding with the economy of movement put the state at odds with the commoners of France and England, creating an antagonism that was increasingly resolved through violence. Simply put, most people were unwilling to watch their food supply be carted away so that others could make a profit, especially when this movement put their families at the risk of starvation. As resistance to the movement of goods rose, the state was initially unprepared to defend it. In 1700, police as we recognize them did not exist; the occasional bailiff or beadle summed up its presence in most marketplaces.[23] The provincial magistracies were often in extreme isolation. Troops, if they were sent for, would take days to arrive and many showed sufficient ambiguity and a marked lack of enthusiasm for this "Odious Service," making those that called upon them more than a little nervous.[24] To ensure the free movement of goods, the state retained larger and more reliable domestic armies, regularized policing, and increasingly used them against their own population. It took 25,000 royal troops to re-establish order in the Paris Basin during the 1775 Flour War. As John Bohstedt has noted, "in England, the free market was delivered by armed guards," while Robespierre claimed that if the government wanted free trade in commerce, it would need "bayonets to calm fears and pacify hunger."[25] As we shall see in the next chapter, the "food riots" that peaked in the eighteenth century were the response of a rural population bent on disrupting the flow of foodstuffs: a kinetic struggle between "natural" and "civic" liberties waged on the highways, rivers, granaries, mills, and bakeries of early modern Europe.

II. Making Movable Bodies

If movement was central to the commodification of goods, the same held true for human beings. The political and technological ability to move goods from place to place, and to make profit from this movement, similarly coerced people into motion. As Eric Hobsbawm remarked in 1954, "The creation of a large and expanding market for goods and a large and available labor force go together, two aspects of the same process."[26] The establishment of New World plantation systems and the need to produce, transport, and secure its products unleashed a monstrous hunger for labor power.

In this regard, the decimation of the New World populations through conquest coupled with the population crisis in Europe proved to be a damning combination for the fate of women across the Atlantic. For labor power was itself produced by one source, and the transatlantic economy had a seemingly insatiable need for it. To meet this need, the regime of movement, with unparalleled violence, set about the great task of turning a woman's body into an unceasing procreative machine. As Silvia Federici has devastatingly shown, through the criminalization of contraception and abortion, the (male) supervision of birthing, the exclusion of women from wage labor, and a public campaign of sexocide and terror to quash all dissent, the wombs of women were made public territory, controlled by men and the state, and directly placed into service of producing the human labor supply.[27] In fact, Federici argues that the rationalization, disciplining, and control of women's bodily movement in order to maximize their "output" predated (and was the condition for) the similar disciplining of male bodily movement during the Industrial Revolution. What she also underscores is that the expropriation of the female womb and its transformation into the first factory did not go uncontested, requiring the demonization and burning of hundreds of thousands of European and African witches.

As with their procurement, the physical movement of human beings was likewise brought about by force. By the eighteenth century, the eviction and displacement of small landowners in England, the capture and displacement of Blacks in Africa, and the dispossession and displacement of the Native populations of the Americas had torn tens of millions of people from their ancestral lands, "freed" land for "productive" cultivation, and forced millions of laborers to the far-flung edges of empire to take their part in the "largest planned accumulation of wealth the world had yet seen."[28]

For two centuries following the initial voyages of discovery, ship after ship disgorged its human cargo from the Old World to the New. The majority of people who moved to the New World came bound. African captives composed 69 percent of the total migrants between 1600 and 1800. If one adds to that the 80 percent of European migrants who were brought as indentured servants, redemptioners, and convicts, a staggering 94 percent of migrants to the Americas initially consisted of unfree labor.[29]

In examining the involuntary displacement and coerced motion of labor power across the Atlantic, I corral the movement of European bodies into the generally established histories of the slave trade and Native removal within the early modern Atlantic world. This is not to suggest an equivalence, in either moral or historical terms, between the coerced movement of whites and the Africans subjected to the slave trade or the wholesale displacement of Native populations in the Americas. It fully acknowledges that many of these Europeans were complicit in, and themselves became perpetrators of, genocide and slavery. The transatlantic regime of movement, while forcing people of all colors to move, was, in its epistemology and operation, a highly racialized regime. Moreover, the differential privileges and discourses regarding movement, oftentimes erected to prevent interracial solidarity among the New World's laboring classes, were a primary factor in the emergence of institutionalized racism in the Americas. Still, the regime of movement, while racialized, was animated above all by the need to create movable human labor. White or Black, it produced people who were bound to move.

The long-standing popular narrative of early European migration to the New World, as opposed to the history of the slave trade, has been a narrative of opportunity or escape from (political or religious) persecution. The voluntary nature of this migration, though still persistent in many national and ethnic histories, has been revised by historians who have examined why so many European (especially English) men left their ancestral homes and undertook the voyage to the Americas. The story that they have uncovered tells a harrowing tale, one based far more often on compulsion than the willful pursuit of a better life.

The story, in short, is this: how a large segment of the rural population lost the ability to sustain life in a sedentary fashion and were compelled into motion in order to survive. The creation of a landless mass of white laborers took two principal forms: outright expropriation through enclosure and dispossession through the establishment of market economies for the lease of land. Both processes fundamentally changed how land was owned and worked as well as the understanding of property that lay claim to it. Both were enforced by state violence. Neither, as was often claimed, was the product of "natural" market forces. The transformation of land tenure in western Europe spanned several centuries, occurring in several waves from the sixteenth through the nineteenth century. Though it was not unique to the British Isles, it occurred there earlier and more completely, and was more integral to the success of British overseas empire than in any other European country.

Though medieval systems of land use varied throughout England, as a general rule, much of the arable land was organized by an open-field system, where rights were shared between landowners and villagers (commoners). Commoners had the "common right" to graze their animals on fallow or common pasture, as well as the right to forage food and firewood from common forests. In this way, "crab apples to cob nuts, wild herbs and flowers ... almost every living thing in the parish could be turned to some good use by the peasant laborer or his wife."[30]

Enclosure, broadly speaking, referred to the process of consolidating scattered holdings of the open-field system as well as the "fencing in" of common lands and forests. First carried out through brute force by landowners, enclosure was later enforced by parliamentary laws, known as Enclosure Acts, in the eighteenth and nineteenth centuries. Enclosure entailed legal changes in the definition of property, not simply replacing "common" with "private," but marking this private property as something exclusive. It was in this new understanding of exclusivity that the common and customary use rights on which many had depended for their livelihood were extinguished.[31]

Or as a popular protest rhyme from the 1700s put it:

> The law locks up the man or woman
> Who steals the goose from off the common,
> But lets the greater felon loose
> Who steals the common from off the goose.[32]

Alongside and complementary to the outright theft of land through enclosure was the gradual introduction of rents determined by short-term market forces. From the 1600s onwards, landlords began to "auction off" leases to the highest bidders. With the emergence of a market in leases—a market for access to land—rents themselves, which had previously been fixed by customary arrangement, began to move. By 1700, two-thirds of England's customary tenants had been subject to increased rents that outstripped the rise in food prices.[33] Known as rack rent (the word "rack" evoking the medieval torture device), the marketization of rents led to a transformation of social property relations. Whereas the English peasant of the open field system had paid set dues to the lord while supplementing his farm through foraging and husbandry on common land, the situation facing the new English tenant farmer was altogether different. Marketization of rent brought competition and, with it, the imperative to improve labor productivity—naturally favoring those in a position to make capital investments, namely larger landowners. In these changing conditions, subsistence farmers, or those who had lived from harvest to harvest, increasingly faced eviction.

The combination of enclosure and the marketization of rents, processes that worked in tandem, displaced hundreds of thousands of people from their homes, creating a large class of landless poor.[34] Smallholders in open-field villages were the hardest hit by enclosure and the commercialization of agrarian relations; in Chippenham, a small town east of Bristol, the proportion of landless householders rose from 3.5 percent in 1279 to 32 percent in 1544 and finally to 63 percent in 1712. Throughout England, farm laborers without land (including family plots) rose from 11 percent in 1550 to 40 percent in 1650. By the end of the seventeenth century, there were twelve times as many propertyless people as there had been at the beginning.[35]

The loss of land increased long-distance subsistence migration dramatically, as desperate migrants trekked long distances from town to town, "overshadowed by the tramping curse of necessity."[36] Many traveled to towns and port cities in search of means to stay alive. London's growth was the most significant: the city grew from 40,000 people in 1500 to 900,000 in 1801.[37]

As Marx wrote in *Grundrisse*, humans expelled from the countryside were

> thrown into the labor market . . . dependent on the sale of their labor capacity or on begging, vagabondage, and robbery as their only source of income. It is a matter of historic record that they tried the latter first, but were driven off this road by gallows, stocks, and whippings, onto the narrow path of the labor market.[38]

The forced movement of human bodies was, and remains, a central feature of the regime of movement.[39] Many economists and quite a few historians have seen these as natural and even favorable developments within the history of capitalism. They argue that enclosure and the marketization of rents increased agricultural efficiency, population growth, division of labor, and urbanization, laying the groundwork for the transformation of England from a subsistence agrarian economy into a commercial and later industrial power. What is almost always absent from this narrative is the coercion that was required to put these human beings into motion.

Most people did not want to leave their homes to eke out an existence within the transatlantic regime of movement. Enclosure and marketization deprived people of their ability to provide for themselves and forced them into motion. Further force was required to channel this now propertyless mass toward the maritime "deployment of hands" and New World colonization. New and brutal laws against the "masterless men" were enacted nearly simultaneously throughout northwestern Europe in an effort to keep them from finding alternate survival strategies outside the system of wage labor.

The vast sea of propertyless laborers thrust upon the roads with no means of feeding themselves gave rise to a "vagrancy epidemic" throughout premodern Europe. In response, governments legislated that every able-bodied person lacking independent means must have a master; otherwise, they were to be legally classified as vagabonds.[40] Vagrancy became a "social crime," one based on the status of a person rather than their actions. People recently forced into mobility became subject to the merciless cruelty of a labor and criminal code "as severe and terrifying as any that had yet appeared in human history."[41] Vagabonds were subject to whipping, branding, ear severing, and (for repeat offenders) death by hanging unless taken up by "masters." For many, this equated to forced labor in galley service, corrections houses, or indentured servitude. Imprisonment—and with it—penal transportation to England's new colonial empire became the fate of others.[42] As Marx noted, workers were "tortured by grotesquely terroristic laws into accepting the discipline necessary for the system of wage-labor."[43] In a cruel twist of fate for English peasants, laws against vagabondage criminalized an existence forced onto them by the same state.

Misery for many became an opportunity for the few. The swelling numbers of "masterless men" were a boon to overseas ventures that required personnel, especially young, able-bodied laborers. The mechanisms that dislodged so many young men from their home parishes and launched them on the road to port towns were not coincidental but causal in the success of English colonial expansion. Government concerns about vagrants in England coincided with investor's hopes for men to populate their holdings. As one plantation agent reminded his employer in Barbados, "a plantation in this place is worth nothing unless they be good store of hands upon it. Without able hands, there is no way to live."[44] The Virginia Company was quick to capitalize on the state's increasing concern with vagrants. Alongside arguments beckoning national glory and the duty to convert savages, it portrayed itself as an answer to the emergent "social question": the movement of people to the colonies would serve to remove the swarms of idle people recently forced off their land.[45]

In the seventeenth century alone, around 300,000 English migrated to the Americas (primarily to the West Indies and the Chesapeake colonies), joined by another 100,000 German-speaking migrants from the Rhineland. English migration also had cascading effects throughout its emerging empire. The infusion of British colonial settlers into Ireland, accompanied as it was by repeated wars and the steady encroachment on native lands, prompted emigration from Ireland. Approximately 350,000 Irish left their homes between 1600 and 1775 for Atlantic destinations.[46] This new mobile humanity was conducted, by force, subterfuge, and law, into the transatlantic regime of movement. Their bodies were appropriated through three main channels into service of the new economy: indentured servitude, penal transport, and impressment.

The vast majority of landless migrants came to the New World as indentured servants, often viewing indenture as a means to escape the stiff penalties for vagrancy and idleness in Europe.[47] By 1840, over half a million Europeans were brought as indentured servants to the Caribbean and an almost equal number to Britain's thirteen colonies.[48] Arriving at Bristol or London to seek bondage in return for passage was merely the last point on a long process of internal mobility; by the time emigrants arrived at these port towns, they had exhausted their possibilities for survival within the domestic economy. At port, they were met by shadowy recruiting agents known as spirits, who kidnapped or enticed unsuspecting migrants aboard ship. Stories abound of parents pitifully following ships carrying their children to the West Indies downriver to Gravesend, "cryinge and mourninge for Redemption from their Slavery."[49] Indentured servants were individuals who bargained away their labor for a period of four to seven years in exchange for passage to the New World. Their entrance into the economy of movement, that is, their ability to move, was purchased at the price of their freedom. Arriving in the New World, ships from English ports carrying servants "plied the Chesapeake's major rivers, stopping to sell their cargoes wherever there was demand."[50] Once sold, indentured servants could not marry without the permission of their master, were subject to physical punishment, and could be bought and sold in secondary markets.

Those not lucky enough to escape the criminal codes fell upon a worse fate. Between 1620 and 1775, upward of 100,000 convicts were transported to Britain's American colonies.[51] The majority of convicts were picked up for crimes of economic necessity (theft, prostitution), but also included the Irish (especially during the time of Cromwell) and political prisoners of the numerous rebellions against the British Crown in the late seventeenth and eighteenth centuries. Like African slaves, convicts were laced into irons and shackles and stowed beneath deck. Forced into cramped quarters, receiving insufficient rations, and plagued by typhus (gaol fever), they suffered an unusually high mortality rate for whites making the Atlantic crossing (about 14 percent in 1720).[52] Upon arrival, they became commodities, "sold in the manner of horses or cows in our market or fair," chained in pairs, driven in lots, their "teeth and limbs inspected to see if they were sound and fit for their labor."[53]

Many felons ended up in the "penal colony" of Barbados, where severe laws such as the 1686 Act prohibited manumission through self-purchase or intermarriage, created a registry to track convicts, established penalties for those assisting escape, regulated the use of small vessels, and prescribed punishment (lashes, pillory, and the "branding of F.T.—Fugitive Traitor—so as the letters may plainly appear on the forehead" for those who tried to run away).[54] Others were transported to British North America. Between 1718 and 1775, around 50,000 convicts were shipped to the American colonies from the British Isles, some 17 percent of the total white emigration to America in the eighteenth century.[55] The British Transportation Act of 1718 gave courts the statutory authority to banish felons from the realm for the first time, greatly increasing (and regularizing) the flow of convict labor within the transatlantic economy. Convicts were then sold on seven-year contracts, much like indentured servants. Though unlike indentured servants (but similar to slaves), they were barred from giving evidence in court. In some colonies, such as Virginia, they were also denied freedom dues.[56]

Besides the obvious profits derived from their expropriated labor power, the trade in indentured and convicted bodies itself presented a lucrative opportunity for transatlantic captains and merchants. The headright system enacted to encourage the colonization of Virginia awarded 50 acres for every person brought into the colony. The colony of Maryland initially offered 2,000 acres for every five servants brought in. So, in addition to the money made from the sale of bonded labor, merchants claimed large tracts of land for each shipment of their human cargo.[57] If the movement of indentured bodies was backed by the colonies, the opposite held true for the forced transport of penal labor. Merchants were subsidized by the British Treasury between three and five pounds for each convict transported, and received additional local contracts from towns and counties for dispatching their felons. Upon reaching the New World, they were at liberty to sell these people to the highest bidder, pocketing the entirety of the sale.

Impressment formed a third channel through which "masterless men" were conducted into the economy of movement. The transatlantic trade would not have been possible without the armed support of the state. Sea power provided the means for the near-continuous flow of goods and bodies across the Atlantic world. As John Evelyn, a British commissioner during the Second Anglo-Dutch War put it, "Whoever commands the ocean, commands the trade of the world, and whoever commands that, commands the world itself."[58] Command of the ocean required men. The issue was finding them. Pay in the navy was usually half that a sailor could earn on merchant vessels, and the discipline, not to mention mortality rates, much higher.

Of the 450,000 men who served in the British navy between 1740 and 1815, 40 percent were impressed. This amounted to 180,000 men (a figure that omits those sentenced to maritime labor) in a seventy-five-year period.[59] In many instances, impressment differed little from kidnapping. Press gangs would scour the port towns of Britain and her colonies, seeking able-bodied men, preferably those with some previous experience at sea. They burst into taverns with press warrants, abducting sailors from their homes. Others were turned over to press officers by merchant captains, who used the threat of impressment to maintain harsh discipline on their own vessels. The British Empire also obtained naval recruits as punishment for resistance to its own colonial endeavors, especially among Irish Catholics, who generated thousands of sailors for the British fleets.[60] A 1757 Act of Parliament erased the distinction between evading impressment and desertion. This, coupled with King George II's Royal Proclamation marking desertion a capital crime, made death the punishment for dodging or resisting impressment.

Destitute and landless whites were not the only people forced into motion. While the European poor formed the early laborers of (especially the British) colonies and continued to work the ships that supplied them with labor, this supply was increasingly met by the kidnapping and forced movement of humans from the African continent.[61] The transatlantic slave trade began in 1444 with the Portuguese and ended in the 1880s with the collapse of the Brazilian and Cuban slave economies. In the intervening 440 years, over 27,000 voyages transported 13 million slaves to the New World. Ten million slaves were captured and transported in the 150-year period between 1700 and 1850 alone.[62]

The creation of a mobile mass of Africans, the mechanisms by which they were integrated into the regime of movement, were much cruder than those used to force whites into its service. The latter required the deprivation of self-sustenance, the forceful removal of people off their lands, and the criminalization of itinerant life outside those prescribed by the economy of movement. Africans were kidnapped and transported against their will to the New World. The self-evidence of this coercion is the primary reason this chapter has spent so much time on how Europeans were compelled to move. There are two other reasons as well.

First, compared to narratives of the slave trade, descriptions of how most Europeans came to take part in the transatlantic economy of movement are less common and, in their filtration to popular understandings, oftentimes quite wrong. Much of the above history stands against the still-common narrative that attributes early transatlantic European migration to opportunity or persecution. Every step of the process, initial dispossession, the alienating and dehumanizing effects of being torn from traditional kinship networks, the corralling of itinerant whites into New World colonization, and the early experiences of indenture upon arrival, were carried out by force. In this, they bear striking resemblance, not least kinetically, to the capture and movement of Black people that constituted the transatlantic slave trade. Similarly, it was through the organization of the transatlantic regime of movement, of the sailing ships and their human or nonhuman cargo, that the elites of Europe learned to think about people, free or unfree, as a commodity— as something to buy and sell on the international market, for money. As Marcus Rediker has noted, "The fundamental class relationships of modern capitalism, involving both slave and free labor, were mediated by the ship."[63] These similarities are in fact the reason it is possible to talk about *a* regime versus multiple regimes of movement in the first place.

That being said, there are key differences between the regimes of slavery and coerced wage labor that provided the mobile bodies for this economy. The first concerns violence, which by any qualitative and quantitative account, was far more pervasive and systemic to the slave trade. Complementing the harrowing narratives of torture, torment, and death that began with capture and transfer to the African coast, storage conditions awaiting transatlantic shipment, the Middle Passage, and the agony of separation in the New World are the hard statistics. The transatlantic slave trade murdered 5 million Africans in Africa, during passage, and in the first year of labor in the New World. In the eighteenth century alone, some 500,000 perished en route to the ships, another 400,000 on board, and yet another 250,000 shortly after their arrival at port.[64] While similar experiences are recounted for Europeans (especially convict transportation), they were the exception to which the slave trade was the rule. African slaves were not just physically but also culturally ripped from their homes. Torn from their families, packed into the dark holds of ships, they were often unable to decipher the languages spoken around them or their destination. As we shall see in the following chapter, instances of uprisings, mutinies, and suicide among enslaved people far outweighed those of white laborers, offering further proof of the difference in brutality. In this light, recent scholarship tracing the plight of "white cargo" across the Atlantic needs to be put into proper context, without which it risks becoming an apologia for Black enslavement itself.

A second key difference was the fate of those transported to the New World. While many indentured servants had their terms of bonded labor extended (often under dubious pretexts) or were worked to death before these terms expired, many did not. Those who managed to free themselves through work—and, equally as significantly, their offspring— enjoyed privileges that were categorically denied to African slaves and their children. This included earning an independent living not just from economies dependent on slavery but also through direct participation in the slave trade. While similarly dislodged and forced into the regime of movement, some whites (and more so their children) were given, and readily took, the opportunity to profit from it.

Alongside humans of European and African descent, there was another group of people compelled into motion by the establishment of the economy of movement. The removal of Native populations in the Americas began with the arrival of Europeans in 1492 and continued through the nineteenth century. Indigenous people were displaced, died of disease, and were killed by Europeans through slavery, rape, and war. In 1491, about 145 million people lived in the western hemisphere. By 1691, the population of Indigenous Americans had declined by 90 to 95 percent, or 130 million people.[65] Though equally coerced, Native removal (particularly in North America) was carried out not to procure a source of mobile labor, but rather to clear land for the expansion of the transatlantic economy. Europeans and Africans were forcefully brought to work in the New World; Native Americans were driven from their homes in order to provide space for them to do so. Despite these differences, the effects were equally, if not more, devastating. While it is difficult to ascertain with certainty (especially in the sixteenth and seventeenth centuries) the numbers of Natives who succumbed to disease or were murdered from those displaced, it is not difficult to attribute historical motivation to Europeans who wanted the land cleared of its population. Though by a different logic, they too became causalities of the regime of movement.

III. Discipline and Bodily Motion

The geographic displacement of millions of people was the most visible consequence of the regime of movement and one that indelibly altered the social makeup and future histories of the four continents surrounding the Atlantic. Less noticed, though equally as impactful on human lives, were the mechanisms by which this economy regulated the motion of people in their given environment. From the early eighteenth century onward, in an effort to increase the productivity of labor, a series of technologies, practices, and moral exhortations began to condition *how* humans could move, *when* they could move, and *why* they should move (and not remain idle).

The disciplining of the bodily motions of labor, which became a hallmark of the industrial factory, had maritime roots. Trapped onboard, under the constant supervision of their employers, sailors had less control of their bodies, schedule, hours, and what was to be done with them. In such self-contained environments, captains of the royal navies, merchant ships, and privateers could and did impose a violent disciplinary regime upon their crews.[66] Sailors were paid not for the outcome of their labor, but for the time they spent engaged in it. This arrangement made the bodies of sailors the property of their employer, giving them (at least in their eyes) the right to regulate these bodies as they saw fit.

As nonagricultural production gradually shifted away from piecework and putting-out to timed and supervised wage labor, many of the maritime mechanisms of bodily control were brought ashore. The movements of workers who were paid for their time were increasingly scrutinized, corrected, and punished. The introduction of regular working hours, time sheets that kept records of the "Come" and "Run" of workers, the observation of work by foremen, bells and clocks, and, hovering over them all, an intricate system of fines and punishments regulated, down to the minutest detail, the motions of people during their hours of work.[67] Early sciences of management calculated the maximum exertion per day capable by man (and horse) and sought to refine motion to get the most out of it. The famous French physicist Charles Augustin Coulomb "search[ed] for a way to combine the different degrees of force, of speed, and of time, so that a man, with equal fatigue may furnish the greatest quantity of action." This would enable one to find, he claimed, "the quantity that expressed the maximum of action relative to the level of fatigue."[68] The English mathematician and inventor Charles Babbage applied these studies of human labor to the bodily movements of shoveling. He set out to demonstrate that the most productive use of the spade was in teaching the laborer to "ascertain that a given weight of earth raised at each shovelful, together with a certain number of shovelfuls per hour, would be more advantageous for his strength than any other such combination." His calculations led to devising the optimum shape of the shovel, the precise ways the worker should bend and dig, the height he should raise the shovel above the wheelbarrow, and how many repetitions of this motion were to be done in one hour.[69]

Across the Atlantic, eighteenth-century plantation overseers were conducting similar experiments on cotton picking, using immense data sets to calibrate and fine-tune the motions of slaves.[70] A recent study of records from just 114 US plantations between 1801 and 1862 tabulated a total of 602,000 individual observations of cotton-picking times and methods recorded by overseers in efforts to improve the rate of productivity of slaves under their charge.[71]

The sciences of human labor required the participation of workers in conditioning their bodily movements to specification, something that they proved less than willing to do. *The Law Book of the Crowley Iron Works*, a 100,000-word volume of civil and penal code designed to govern Crowley's refractory labor force, is both a testament to this indisposition and the attempt to overcome it. On the section on pay, all human activity at the ironworks not engaged in production was to be deducted from wages. This included, "deductions for breakfast, dinner, playing, sleeping, smoaking, singing, reading of news history, quarelling, contention, disputes or anything forreign to my business, any way loitering."[72]

To deter these inefficient "preoccupations" from entering the workplace, the disciplining of bodily motion for work began to increasingly regulate social life outside of it. A chorus of eighteenth-century moralists launched a crusade against the perceived idleness of the lower classes. As they turned their attention to the "problem" of leisure (a category incidentally created by the division between the employer's time and what remained for the worker), they discovered that a considerable proportion of manual workers would, after concluding their work, "for hours together sit on a bench, or lie down on a bank or hillock . . . yielded up to utter vacancy and torpor . . . or collect in groups idle by the road side."[73] The Reverend J. Clayton's *Friendly Advice to the Poor*, "written and published at the Request of the late and present Officers of the Town of Manchester" in 1755, preached that "if the sluggard hides his hands in his bosom, rather than applies them to work; if he . . . Saunters, impairs his Constitution by Laziness, and dulls his Spirit by Indolence . . . then he can expect only poverty as his reward."[74] John Wesley, in his 1786 tract *The Duty and Advantage of Early Rising*, inveighed against "the slothful spending of Morning in Bed" where "By soaking . . . so long between warm sheets, the flesh is, as it were, parboiled, and becomes soft and flabby."[75] For early Puritan moralists, the body was to be engaged in purposeful movement at all times, utilized not just by the employer but internalized by the individual as well, toward some end. Staying idle, in place, oversleeping, passing the time, or doing nothing even while not at work was both morally unacceptable and used to justify the worker's position within the regime of movement.

These exhortations soon found their way into practice. Over the course of the eighteenth century, a vast institutional framework was erected to condition human bodies to move properly. Prisons, hospitals, churches, military barracks, schools, and families became sites for the creation of docile bodies that, as Michel Foucault argued, would be "pliable," capable of being "manipulated, shaped, trained" for the motions required of them by industrial capitalism.[76] Within these institutions, bodies were molded to move to tightly organized signals that maintained order. This "political anatomy," as Foucault described it, "defined how one may have a hold over others' bodies, not only so that they may do what one wishes, but so that they may operate as one wishes, with the techniques, the speed, and the efficiency, that one determines." Controlling how bodies moved required "an uninterrupted, constant coercion, supervising the *processes of the activity* rather than its result, and [was] exercised according to a codification that partitions as closely as possible time, space, movement."[77]

The Rules for the Government, Superintendence, and Teaching of a Methodist school in York speaks volumes to this disciplining of bodily motion at an early age. At the start of the school day,

> The Superintendent shall ring—when, on a motion of his hand, the whole School rise at once from their seats—on a second motion, the Scholars turn—on a third, slowly and silently move to the place appointed to repeat their lessons—he then pronounces the word "Begin."[78]

The introduction of the machine into manufacture in the late eighteenth and early nineteenth centuries was both a product of and solved the problem of correct bodily movement. A mechanized labor process would require workers to move at the same speed as the machine, to follow its arithmetically precise rhythms, and to reshape their bodies to the demands of the machine's movements. From about the 1770s onward, the machine was marketed on the basis that it would discipline labor and "act as a safeguard on dishonesty, mistakes, and laziness," thereby fueling economic growth.[79] The machine was to serve a trifold function: it enabled the use of less labor, thus reducing cost; it trained the human body to move in precise rhythms; and it stamped out idleness by putting the body into constant forced motion.

Perhaps the best example of this multifunctionality was crafted not for factory use, but within one of the many institutions designed to condition bodies to move properly for it. The prison treadwheel, a machine that literally converted man and metal into a single mechanical contraption, was introduced in 1818 by the British engineer Sir William Cubitt as a means of usefully occupying convicts in the prisons of Brixton. Cubitt observed prisoners lying around in idleness and opined that it was better "reforming offenders by teaching them the habits of industry."[80] Known by contemporaries as the "discipline mill," the device consisted of two wheels some twenty feet in length and five feet in height, with each wheel having twenty-four stepping boards. Within this giant gerbil cage, prisoners were forced to climb forty-eight to fifty steps per minute for ten hours in the summer and eight hours in the winter. "Every now and then as the wheel revolved, a whitened step appeared, and then one of the workers would drop down, and one of the walkers would get up, and so the wheel and the punishment was kept moving."[81] Significantly, the original aim of the treadmill was not economical, but disciplinary. As a professor of the Woolwich Royal Military Academy put it, "a tool for the correction and improvement of the morals of the idle, vicious, and disorderly part of the community."[82] By 1850, now attached to pumps and mills, the treadmill was in operation in over half of British prisons.[83]

Though a particularly odious example, the prison mill underscores, both in its design and use, the aim of bodily discipline: to induce the human body to conform to the laws of efficient motion. The machine was not simply a technological innovation to make things quicker and cheaper, it was also, if not primarily, designed to condition the bodily movement of those who used it. In this sense, the machine was not the start (as both its proponents and critics claimed) but rather the culmination of a long process of moral and institutional training to create bodies that could be moved in very particular ways.

Conclusion

The establishment of the regime of movement put into motion goods and bodies in a manner unprecedented in human history. This movement, associated with freedom by ideologues of liberalism both then and now, required a sustained and terrific amount of force, applied at multiple points throughout the Atlantic social body. The seizure of land, eviction, the criminalization of itinerancy, kidnapping, the Middle Passage, and the disciplining of free and unfree labor through intricate and draconian punishment were, in this sense, not an unfortunate by-product, but rather constitutive of movement itself.

By the end of the eighteenth century, the Atlantic economy had reached a stage of maturity, stability, and profitability.[84] The threats arising to it, from piracy to revolt, had been largely contained. More significantly, the regime of movement proved resilient enough to withstand significant changes in its political and social makeup, including the independence of the New World colonies, the abolition of the slave trade, and the French and Haitian revolutions.

Once established, the regime of movement became self-perpetuating. The subsequent changes brought about through the global expansion of the market; nineteenth-century industrialization and the transportation revolution; Taylorism, motion studies, scientific management, the transition from coal to oil; post–WWII trade regimes; containerization, intermodal transport, logistics, and just-in-time global supply chains; bodily fitness and the corporatized mantra of self-improvement can all be seen as intensifications and expansions of an economy, first established in the seventeenth and eighteenth centuries, whose profits derived from the more efficient movement of goods and the bodies used to make them.

2

Obstruction

We shall not, we shall not be moved
We shall not, we shall not be moved
Just like a tree that's planted by the waters
We shall not be moved[1]
                    Anonymous African-American spiritual

From its very inception, the regime of movement has had its detractors: those who resisted both the forced movement of their bodies and the penetration of market forces into their lives. Resistance took many forms and came from all quarters of the Atlantic world: food rioters, pirates, maroons, impressed sailors, indentured servants and the enslaved. However different their aims and tactics, each in the their own way sought to stave off the compulsive motion of this regime through a politics of disruption.

Through this politics, there emerged a practice and idea of liberty totally at odds with liberal conceptions: one that equated movement not with freedom but coercion. For the vast majority of people caught up in the emerging transatlantic economy, the freedom to subsist and, in the last instance, exist was systematically taken away by the force of movement. Within this world of constant coerced flux, the disruption of movement became equated with freedom and security, a means to let food and humans stay, to remain in place, or to find and maintain lives outside of this economy.

The pioneering work of Marcus Rediker, his students, and fellow travelers notwithstanding, the scholarship on resistance in the early modern Atlantic world remains, to a large extent, racially and thematically compartmentalized. Subsistence struggles in northwestern Europe, slave revolts off the coast of Africa, impressment riots in British North America, and the maroon communities and pirates of the Caribbean have been analyzed as discrete cases, each with their own structural and contingent dynamics. The interconnection and resonance of these struggles, evident to many who took part in them, has largely been ignored by their commentators. The results of this compartmentalization are all too predictable. Instead of a single image of transatlantic resistance, we are left with fractured portraits of localized discontent. This chapter seeks to connect these struggles through a shared history of disruption. Its central argument is that, taken together, the disparate efforts to prevent the intrusion of the regime of movement into Atlantic communities, constituted the world's first antiglobalization struggle.

The condition they struggled against is today termed *precarity*: the marked decrease in the predictability, security, and stability of both physical and psychological existence due to the marketization of land, goods and human labor. Today, precarity is usually attributed to a set of global neoliberal reforms that has strengthened management and weakened the bargaining power of workers since the 1970s. The main cause of precarity in the eighteenth century was the establishment of the regime of movement. As the following pages detail, disrupting this regime was a near-ubiquitous practice and mentality. In the long run, it failed. Its history has something to tell us today.

I. Disrupting the Market

The liberalization of the Atlantic market led to intensifying subsistence struggles throughout the eighteenth century. These struggles were fueled by the movement of more and more basic provisions from producer to consumer areas and—especially in years of war or bad harvest—supply shortages and price hikes. In England, there were major outbreaks of food riots in 1709, 1740, 1756, 1766, 1773, and 1782; in

France, major riots over food occurred in the years 1764 to 1768, 1770 to 1775, 1784, and from the eve of the revolution through the Republic of Virtue (1788–1793).[2] Riots over foodstuffs, albeit to a lesser extent, were also a feature of social life in British North America, with major waves occurring between 1709 and 1713, the 1720s, and much more frequently in the lead-up to and during the American War of Independence. As the British and French governments lent their support to liberal trade policies, the frequency of food riots markedly increased. While the period of 1690 to 1720 saw 182 such disturbances in France, food riots in the thirty years preceding the French Revolution totaled 652, nearly four times as many.

The predominant mode of land-based social struggle in the eighteenth century, history has not been kind to the riot. Bourgeois commentators, tending to prefer moral over social understandings of social antagonism, have convicted the riot as violence. This trend was as prevalent in contemporary bourgeois accounts of eighteenth-century riots as it is today; the language and tone condemning rioting in Ferguson, Tottenham, or the banlieues of Paris are almost identical to those used 300 years ago. Bourgeois scholars have largely expanded on this connection. David Halle and Kevin Rafter have described the riot as "one group publicly, and with little to no attempt at concealment, illegally assaulting . . . or illegally attacking or invading property . . . in ways which suggest the authorities have lost control." Paul Gilje, the author of *Rioting in America*, defined it as "any group of twelve or more people attempting to assert their will immediately through the use of force outside the normal bounds of the law." A scintillating number, as Joshua Clover sarcastically notes, whereby the riot becomes the obverse of the orderly distribution of justice, the jury.[3]

More surprising has been the denigration of the riot by the practitioners of its successor: the strike. Leaders of the nineteenth- and twentieth-century workers' movement often depicted the riot as a disorderly irruption of momentary discontent, the foil against which organized labor appeared as disciplined and methodical resistance. Speaking to this distinction, Joshua Clover writes,

The strike becomes the strike via being *formalized* against the riot. It is order itself, the unbroken window. The riot's form is disordered, and this disorder becomes its content. [From the point of view of the strike], it wants nothing but its own disorder, its bright opacity. Glints and shards of broken glass.[4]

From the mid-nineteenth century onwards, both trade union and Marxist (especially Leninist) groups have pushed forward this opposition, either as earnest political strategy or to exert control over their more anarchically minded rank-and-file members or opponents. Both have adopted a militaristic, regimental vocabulary, invoking the virtues of discipline, order, and hierarchy, to do so.

Worse still have been the intellectuals of the working class, who have embedded the distinction between premodern riot and working-class organization within history itself, where the riot, when compared to the orderly progression of the proletariat through world history, appears as ahistorical, thus apolitical and without teleology. In both bourgeois and leftist readings, "the riot is understood to have no politics at all, a spasmodic irruption to be read symptomatically and perhaps granted a paternalistic dollop of sympathy,"[5] having little in common with either the more organized campaigns of middle-class liberal social movements or the discipline of class warfare. E. P. Thompson summarized this "spasmodic view" of popular history, stating:

> The common people can scarcely be taken as historical agents before the French Revolution. Before this period, they intrude occasionally in moments of sudden social disturbance. These irruptions are compulsive, rather than self-conscious or self-activating; they are simple responses to economic stimuli.[6]

Since its publication in 1971, Thompson's critique of the prevalent understanding of early modern riots has created a large cottage industry of historians who have painstakingly shown how "subsistence struggles," as they prefer to call them, were methodical actions rooted in long-standing moral or civic claims.

But these debates are old. I want to position the riot as the first mode of resistance to an emerging regime of movement, one that began a politics of disruption that carries through to the present day. But what did food riots consist of? At the most general level, food riots were direct interventions into the market forces governing the sale and transport of food. They involved blockages of food shipments from rural communities to urban or export centers, as well as the forced sale of goods that merchants were hoarding to fetch a higher price. The aim of the food riot was to disrupt the transport of a particular agricultural province's food supply to other provinces with higher purchasing power.[7] Principally, it took two forms. Either it involved the direct and physical obstruction of food through seizure, sabotage, and blockade or "price setting": the practice of forcing grain holders to sell their goods locally (rather than transport them to distant markets) at a "fair price." Food riots were about disrupting the movement of food made possible by liberalization. In fact, the French term, *entraves*, meaning "obstruction" or "hindrance," perfectly conveys the kinetic politics behind this practice that is somewhat lost in the English.

As demand rose with the growing urban population, big city merchants went further afield to secure large contracts from farmers, particularly around the London and Paris basins. Faced with the disappearance of their local markets, increasingly forced into buying grain or flour from intermediaries, if not baked bread itself at marked-up prices, commoners repeatedly disrupted the new distribution practices of the regime of movement.

As Tilly notes, these disruptions were the means by which commoners themselves took over the state's previous duty to provide basic subsistence.

> During the period from 1650 to 1850, people kept grain from leaving town by seizing the shipment . . . The authorities called those actions food riots, but in fact they consisted of ordinary people doing almost exactly the same thing as authorities did in times of shortage—forbid grain from leaving town, commandeer local supplies, regulate the price.[8]

Exported grain was often a first target of food riots, especially when subsidized or thought to be subsidized by taxpayers themselves. As early as 1631, a Suffolk magistrate noted, "To see their bread thus taken from them and sent to strangers has turned the impatience of the poor into licentious fury and desperation." In British North

America, a wave of riots between 1709 and 1713 attacked ships and snapped rudders in order to prevent the shipment of wheat out of the colonies.[9] Export riots increased in number and organization in the second half of the eighteenth century. In 1783, a notice affixed to the market cross in Carlisle targeting local exporters stated the issue quite directly:

> Peter Qemeseson & Moses Luthart this is to give you Warning that you must Quit your unlawfull Dealing or Die and be Darned your buying the Corn to starve the Poor Inhabitants of the City and Soborbs of Carlisle to send to France and get the Bounty Given by the Law for taking the Corn out of the Country but by the Lord God Amighty we will give you Bounty at the Expence of your Lives you Darned Roagues.[10]

Though no one was immune. Merchants who transported food away, the farmers who sold to them, and the miller who refused to grind grain in small quantities all became legitimate targets. Rioters would often pay visits to those forestalling or engrossing goods, sacking granaries and seizing grain intended for transport. In 1795, a Tiverton farmer complained to the War Office of riotous assemblies "threatening to pull down or fire his house because he takes in Butter of the neighboring Farmers and Dairymen to forward it by the common road wagon to . . . London."[11] Adam Smith told the tale of a dealer's lament:

> In years of scarcity the inferior ranks of the people impute their distress to the avarice of the corn merchant who becomes the object of their hatred and indignation. Instead of profit, he is faced with ruin, in danger of having his magazines plundered and destroyed by their violence.[12]

Profound feeling arose in times of dearth, particularly in areas peripheral to urban centers where dealers could up their profits, aggravating already stressed local markets. In these instances, rioters resorted to the direct disruption of trade by erecting obstacles to channels of transport and communication, obstructing the rivers and roads that took grain from their communities. During the

French Flour War, when over 300 food riots erupted in the spring of 1775, inhabitants from over seventeen neighboring villages descended on a grain barge moored at Stors and walked off with 19,400 livres worth of wheat. The uprising at Pontoise of that same year, after emptying out the market, turned to "intercept several grain carts, raided two barges, and sacked the homes and granaries of six flour merchants" who sought to transport grain to Paris.[13] In 1795 and again in 1800, rioters around Carlisle, England, blockaded roads to prevent export from the parish. Wagons were intercepted and unloaded in the towns from which they passed. To the lament of merchants, "the movement of grain by night-convoy assumed the proportions of a military operation."[14] Ships were stormed at ports and threats were made to destroy the canals. Near Haverfordwest in Wales, rioters nearly closed the estuary at a narrow point, all in an effort to "stay the transport of food."[15]

The regime of movement polarized communities into those that suffered or profited from it, changing the composition of rioters over the course of the eighteenth century. In France, what had once been a fairly heterogeneous mix of the social population, with bourgeois and property owners at times partaking in riots, increasingly took on a class character. By the 1760s and 1770s, workers, unskilled and semi-skilled, urban and rural, constituted the backbone of most food riots—particularly during the Flour War.[16] In eighteenth-century England, these "risings of the people" were led by the "lower orders," agricultural laborers often joined by colliers, tinners, weavers, and hosiery workers. For wage earners lacking the opportunity to grow food for themselves, fluctuations in the market price meant starvation in times of dearth. The marketplace became the point at which "working people most often felt their exposure to exploitation" and therefore "as much the arena of class war as the factory and mine became in the industrial revolution."[17]

Some of these acts were violent. Others simply demanded that the goods be brought to market at a fair price, often set on the spot by rioters themselves. As E. P. Thompson, at pains to record the orderly and peaceful nature of many food riots, points out:

> During the extensive disorders in the West in 1766 the sheriff of Gloucestershire, could not disguise his respect for the rioters who

went . . . "to a farmhouse and civilly desired that they wou'd thresh out and bring to market their wheat and sell it for five shillings per bushel, which being promised, and some provisions given them unasked for, they departed without the least violence or offence."[18]

On other occasions, rioters visited farmers, millers, bakers, and hucksters' shops, selling their corn, flour, bread, cheese, butter, and bacon at fair prices.

They returned in general the produce [i.e., the money] to the proprietors or in their absence left the money for them; and behaved with great regularity and decency where they were not opposed, with outrage and violence where they was: but pilfered very little.[19]

The same "orderly conduct" was, despite the popular image of the Boston Tea Party, an even more common feature of food riots across the Atlantic. In July of 1776, commoners broke into Samuel Colton's locked store in Longmeadow, Massachusetts, and carried away his rum, sugar, molasses, and salt. Though Colton later complained that they "ransacked [the house] from top to bottom," causing "great Fear and Terr'r," the local minister Stephen Williams reported no destruction or indiscriminate looting.

The crowd delivered the goods to the town clerk, who sold them at "reasonable" prices. Eventually, crowd leaders offered the proceeds of the sales to Colton and, when he refused them, took along witnesses and left the money on a table in his house.[20]

French rioters—following earlier custom—would very often first appeal to the local lieutenant general of police, summoning him to fix fair prices. In 1775, when commoners of Beaumont-sur-Oise dragged the exporting merchant Descroix in front of the local authorities, demanding that they "come police the market and force down the price of grain," the head of police replied that "the sale of grain was free at all times and that they should let the market continue without trouble."[21] Denied justice by the local police, they resorted to their own form of regulation.

The repeated insistence of local communities, on both sides of the Atlantic, on "orderly conduct" in ensuring fairly priced provisions is a testament to the regulatory rather than unruly character of subsistence struggles, their interventions into free trade rooted in ideas of fair and just practice that had become unraveled by the regime of movement. Though rarer, such momentary disruptions of the food trade could lead to more extended regulations of the market, with rioters themselves taking over the operation of the movement of goods. "Sometimes the mob would control the marketplace for days, the women regulating its practices as parties of men intercepted grain on the roads, at the docks, and on the rivers."[22] This latter aspect blurred the distinctions between riot as intervention and the outright regulation of the economy, between momentary action in defiance of the law and the crowd itself becoming political authority. These distinctions, as well as their dissolution, were to become key features of the American food riots, especially during (and following) its independence from Britain.

Much like the moral economies of England and France, food riots in the thirteen colonies drew upon an alternate set of societal norms and practices in disrupting the free movement of goods. Here, the "culture of land," or "civic humanism," furnished the cosmology to resist the regime of movement as well as the vocabulary to define this regime as oppressive. While sharing ideas of "just" and "fair" exchange, of reciprocity and civic duties, a significant difference existed between the cosmologies of the Old and New World settlers.

Many commoners in England and France retained faith in the moral compact between commoner and king and viewed breaches to this compact as occurring outside the bounds of the Crown. "If only the king knew what was happening under his realm," they reasoned, he would put a stop to these practices. Many went further, often rioting in his name, calling themselves "King Mob," seizing shipments "By Order of the King," or setting "The King's Price." The civic humanism of the colonial settlers by contrast, eschewed royal authority in favor of political and economic senses of community self-control. This distinction was to prove incendiary during the 1770s.

In the 1710s and 1720s, commoners in Boston, the city most vulnerable to grain shortages, carried out a series of food riots, successfully securing legislation that limited exports and a public granary that would buy and sell at cost. As British policies became harsher after midcentury, American colonists began to associate the regime of movement with the British Crown. There was a widespread conviction that indebtedness, even engagement in British trade itself, was eroding a precious independence. To regain that independence, many withdrew from the Atlantic market. Faced with the Sugar Act, Stamp Act, Townshend Acts, and Coercive Acts, colonists joined together in nonimportation and nonconsumption pacts, eschewing imports and banning occasions that required or promoted their use.[23] It was at this moment that the disruption to the regime of movement became linked to "patriotism," lending explicit political significance to economic and cultural activity. The trade boycotts that began in 1764 and continued through the eve of independence, those "solemn leagues and covenants," the mushrooming "associations," were ways of relating to neighbors and formulating community outside both the Crown and the Atlantic market.

When war broke out in 1776, the ensuing embargo and rising demand by armies increased incentives for withholding goods or selling them for more money elsewhere. Higher prices and forestalling by colonial merchants ignited a series of food riots across the thirteen states. In 1776, crowds in Kingston, New York, broke into stores and warehouses. In rural Dutchess County, exiles from occupied New York City forcibly stopped outgoing wagons in search of foodstuffs. On several occasions, farmers from various Maryland counties seized quantities of salt. The following four years saw a further thirty food riots. What differentiated these riots from their counterparts in Europe was the degree to which rioters assumed political authority over the marketplace, with rioters not just intervening, but negotiating with, and at times superseding, the power of local committees. Their political character combined the disruptive tactics of older direct actions against the regime of movement with a deliberative democratic model that mimicked the revolutionary bodies of patriot elites.

In March 1777, with food prices rising and supplies of grain and produce growing scarce, a Boston town meeting appointed a body composed of thirty-six men "not in trade" to supplement their ineffectual town committee and began calling out town merchants to publicly declare their holdings of flour. In December of 1777, crowds aggressively confronted engrossing merchants. About 900 gathered in Boston's North End, forming their own town meeting, where they resolved to offer paper money for engrossed goods and to take the goods "in some other way" if refused. On the next day, some 500 inhabitants met at the store of Jonathan Amory, a merchant long known for hoarding, carted Amory's sugar to a nearby store, weighed it, and left it for storage under the supervision of the three committeemen. To Amory's supply the crowd soon added the sugar held by other merchants (including patriot Isaac Sears). The three men supervised the sale of West Indian sugar and other goods well into the summer of 1778, "[keeping] down the Price of Wood and Grain for above a Year."[24] In Beverly, Massachusetts, a crowd of women took similar measures, breaking into a distill house, seizing sugar, forcing other merchants to hand over their supplies, and setting up one of their number, a storekeeper, to supervise retail. In May 1779, when the price of foodstuffs in Philadelphia soared, men armed with clubs visited shopkeepers to force them to lower prices. The mass meeting that followed resolved that, in the face of monopolizing, hoarding, and price gouging, "the public have a right to enquire into the causes of such extraordinary abuses, and prevent them." The meeting established committees to investigate flour engrossing and to set price ceilings in the upcoming months. After the meeting, crowds escorted a merchant, a butcher, and a speculator accused of raising prices to the city jail.[25]

In all these instances, lower-class rioters either forced patriot leaders to abide by their rules or established their own political authority within the marketplace. Disruption of the free movement of goods not only served the immediate need of provisioning at affordable prices but also involved the construction of institutional frameworks to continue doing so. These fledgling institutions, based on the "culture of land," backed by the power of the crowd, combined political with economic practices of liberty.

Unsurprisingly, the new revolutionary potential of disruption caused considerable alarm among the patriot elite, especially those whose fortunes were tied to the regime of movement. Ostensibly fighting the same enemy, the growing tension between the cultures of land and market turned into outright conflict following the War of Independence. As early as 1776, the colonial elite had become wary of riotous crowds that sought to introduce price controls and force their will onto the marketplace. Boston merchants argued that such actions were "directly opposite to the Idea of Liberty," which they explicitly equated with free trade.[26] Following the war, the merchants, financiers, and land speculators of the East Coast went on the offensive to ensure that the culture of the market became the law of the land. In an effort to both re-establish ties with European investors, who had become wary of the "excess of popular democracy in the newly independent states," and to guarantee themselves full payment of the war debt (which they had amassed at vastly discounted rates), they passed a series of deeply unpopular taxes and anti-inflationary measures while crafting a constitution to occlude popular participation. The result was a credit crunch through the new states that led to a loss of property and land rivaling that of the Great Depression. Lacking hard specie, barred from paying their debts or the new taxes with paper currency, independent landowners and craftsmen faced the forced auction of their assets, which included everything from their land, animals, and tools of trade, down to personal items such as pots and pans.[27]

With their vision of the revolution slipping away, ordinary whites, particularly in rural communities, mounted one last disruptive effort against the regime of movement. Between 1783 and 1795, small communities in backcountry areas devised intricate methods of resistance to interrupt the forced movement of goods out of their communities. Locally appointed tax officers and elected Justices of the Peace refused to collect "unjust" taxes or hear bankruptcy cases, facing fines or even imprisonment for their actions. Local constables, often drawn from the poorest ranks of the community, refused to foreclose property, at risk of dismissal. Where auctions were held, residents would conspire no-bid pacts so that goods and property remained unsold and in the hands of the original owner. As the elite-dominated state and federal governments began to crack down on such practices, many rural communities took to closing roads to prohibit their goods from being carted away. Between 1787 and 1795, sixty-five major roads leading to rural communities in Pennsylvania were shut down to prevent the seizure of goods by the sheriff's wagon. Banding together, they constructed six-foot-high fences reaching fifty feet wide, felled trees, and moved large boulders onto the road. Others dug deep trenches, flooded roads by diverting canals onto highways, or simply built small mountains out of manure to block incoming coaches. When local supervisors were sent out to clear them, it was often the case that state authorities found the roads narrowed even further.[28] Though these disruptions served to momentarily insulate rural populations from the culture of the market, they also isolated rural regions from each other. Left to fend for themselves, these backcountry communities became increasingly distrustful of all government, fueling a conservative strain of libertarianism that has impacted American politics to this day.

Much like in Europe, riots in North America were, in the long run, unsuccessful in disrupting the regime of movement. Though subsistence struggles continued into the nineteenth century, with large food riots erupting in France in 1801, 1811, 1816, and 1829; in German lands prior to and during the 1848 revolution; and in Italy following unification, their moment had passed.[29] Gradually, the kinetic struggle over the movement of goods would take place not at the sites of their circulation or distribution, but of their production. Despite their ultimate shortcomings, it is all too simple to view food riots as the localized, apolitical, reactionary, and spontaneous response of besieged communities. On both sides of the Atlantic, food riots were animated by a compelling cosmology of exchange, replete with notions of a right and just social polity.

There has been a longstanding debate among scholars over the political significance of the food riot, whether it manifested reactionary or (proto)revolutionary tendencies.[30] Rather than impute the motivations for riots through anachronistic categories, it is better to see them on their own terms: as local disruptions of the "free" movement of goods guided by the idea that provision, not profit, was the ultimate purpose of the marketplace.

II. No Masters

Peter Linebaugh and Marcus Rediker open their history of the radical early modern Atlantic with the story of the *Sea Venture*, a ship chartered by the Virginia Company of London in 1609 to bring 150 new settlers to reinforce the ailing plantation colony in Jamestown. Caught in a tempest, the ship capsized, marooning the survivors on the island of Bermuda. On board the *Sea Venture* were representatives of the three main agents that organized the transatlantic regime of movement: the captain (police), shareholders (capital), and the governor (political authority). These leaders immediately set the crew to building new ships. The remaining Bermuda castaways, finding abundant fruit, hog, fowl, fish, and having got wind of the wretchedness awaiting them in Virginia, had other ideas. For ten months, there raged a fierce battle between "those who wanted to go ahead with the money-making venture in Virginia and those whose hands were supposed to get them there."[31] The mutinous crew "promised each onto the other not to set their hands to any travail or endeavor" that would take them off the island, and with this vow, withdrew into the woods to form their own settlement. In the span of forty-two weeks, the Virginia Company encountered four further insurgencies and meted out the first capital punishments in English America to quell them. When the authorities finally restored order and set sail, three men jumped ship to remain on the island, where they "began to erect their little common wealth . . . with brotherly regency."[32]

For Linebaugh and Rediker, the ten-month struggle following the shipwreck of the *Sea Venture* was a vivid snapshot of the origins of capitalism and colonization, about world trade and the building of empires. While the authors focused on alternate ways of living and the official use of violence, terror, and class discipline to deter or destroy them, the *Sea Venture* also encapsulates another story: a story of kinetic struggle, a struggle over the movement of bodies in the early modern transatlantic world.

Aside from providing the basis for Shakespeare's *Tempest*, the voyage of the *Sea Venture* was not remarkable. Though an early adventure of British colonialism, it was just one of the hundreds of thousands of voyages that served as the arteries of the transatlantic economy. Some 232 years later, an American slaving brig the *Creole* left Virginia carrying 135 African slaves en route to the port of New Orleans. The United States had officially abolished the importation of slaves in 1808, and a rapidly commercializing domestic trade in human property had boomed to supply much-needed labor throughout the southern states. A week into the voyage, nineteen of the enslaved orchestrated a mutiny, killed the slave agent, severely wounded the captain, and gained control of the ship. They then set sail for the Bahamas, which being a British colony, had abolished slavery three years earlier. The *Creole* mutineers arrived in Nassau on November 7, 1841, to find "embrace in the wider tradition of black Atlantic resistance and cooperation."[33] The ship was warmly greeted by African troops (themselves kidnapped Africans who had been "rescued" and were now "apprenticed" by the British navy for a period of fourteen years following their emancipation). Within days, news of the mutinous ship had spread throughout the town, and a crowd of nearly 2,000 free Blacks had assembled to ensure that the ship's Black population was released to the island. Meanwhile, the American Consul, Bacon, and the surviving first mate of the *Creole* were hatching other plans. They aimed to reclaim the ship by force and resume sail with its human cargo back to New Orleans.

Just as with the *Sea Venture*, a kinetic struggle took place over the fate of the human beings on board the ship. The Americans quickly went about town trying to acquire guns to retake the sequestered vessel. The African troops, and the crowd gathered in the harbor front, clearly sided with the rebels. So too, it turned out, had the island's weapons dealers. They refused to sell to the Americans, who were forced to scrape together guns from two other American ships. As the first mate later wrote, the two were subjected to jeers and insults by both the Black and white residents of the island. As tensions rose, the crowd at the harbor, armed with clubs, boarded small boats and headed toward the *Creole*, planning to forcibly bring the captives on board to shore. Bacon and the first mate acted quickly, loading the guns onto a boat of their own and setting off to arm the white crew aboard the ship. Yet "with a line of twenty-four West India muskets trained down on them and surrounded by masses of armed fishermen, stevedores, and droughers, they had no option but to withdraw." The spectacle of the crowd's numbers, their noise, and the threat of violence had prevented the Americans from recapturing the ship. The captives boarded the smaller boats, greeted by "enormous cheers as they disembarked onto the harbor."[34]

The shipwreck of the *Sea Venture* and the mutiny aboard the *Creole* stand as relatively early and late instances of resistance to the transatlantic regime of movement. Each became the scene of a struggle between forces that sought to (re)assert the movement of human bodies and those who attempted to disrupt it. The intervening years saw a great deal of changes: the removal of Native peoples from large swaths of North America, the transition from white servitude to Black slavery as the main source of New World labor, the rise and fall of Atlantic piracy, and a large expansion in imperial navies to decide who got all the profits. Remaining unchanged throughout was the unremitting demand of the regime of movement for mobile labor.

Resistance to this coerced movement of human bodies was constant and ubiquitous. Whether in direct actions against land expropriation, impressment riots, uprisings aboard slave, merchant and naval vessels, *marronage* and piracy, as well as sailor work stoppages, desertion, strikes, and port blockades, a politics of disruption pervaded the Atlantic labor force. Some disrupted the forced removal of or from their homes, some sought through disruption a return to them, while still others revolted from the regime of movement to found homes elsewhere on their own terms.

Disrupting impressment

In the fall of 1747, Commodore Charles Knowles was anchored in Boston Harbor, refitting and replenishing his ships en route to the West Indies when fifty sailors of the HMS *Lark* deserted to escape the harshness and danger of the British navy. Desperately in need of men, Knowles ordered his press-gangs into Boston's waterfront, where they rounded up forty-six sailors, carpenters, and laborers and chained them below the tender deck, awaiting transport to his British warship. The following morning, the riots began. Working-class Bostonians rampaged through town, seizing British officers and seamen as hostages. For three days, the rioters (numbering in the thousands) controlled Boston and paralyzed the provincial government. They surrounded the governor's house, beat his deputy, and put him in the stocks. They confiscated and burned a barge and, after an intense standoff with Knowles, who had trained his guns on the harbor, ensured the release of the impressed men in exchange for the hostages, cheering gleefully as Knowles sailed out of Boston. Samuel Adams, writing for *The Independent Advertiser*, praised the rioters as an assembly of people defending their natural rights to life and liberty when these were breached by the government.[35]

Twenty-four years later, in 1771, the Royal Navy was mobilizing for another presumed war with France. As in the past, it sent its press-gangs to the port and shipping towns of England to round up sailors to man its warships. The Newcastle gang had captured 160 men and loaded them onto the transport tender that was to ferry them to the HMS *Conquestador* waiting at the Nore, a sandbank in the mouth of the Thames. The captain of the navy warship reported that he received only eighty-five men. The remaining seventy-five pressed sailors, along with two volunteers, had "risen against the crew," seized control of the vessel, destroyed the lists that recorded the names and residencies of those to be pressed, and made their escape back home.[36]

These anti-impressment riots, on opposite sides of the Atlantic, were just two of thousands of disruptions of forced naval recruitment in the eighteenth-century Atlantic world. When, after a quarter century's peace, England declared war on Spain in 1739, sailors in every port of the British empire, from the British Isles to Antigua, Saint Kitts, Barbados, Jamaica, and the thirteen mainland colonies, fought tooth and nail against press-gangs who sought to carry them away.[37] They had good reason to, since the kidnapping of men into service was one of the principle ways of manning the navies of empire. Of the 450,000 men who served in the British navy between 1740 and 1815, a staggering 40 percent were forcefully coerced into military service.[38]

The ideas animating much anti-impressment disruption had popular roots in seventeenth-century English radicalism. Throughout the 1640s, Levellers had argued against the government's use of impressment as a violation of their liberties. "There was nothing more opposite of freedom, no greater form of slavery," they argued, "than impressment."[39] Impressment was, for many Levellers, one of the most egregious violations brought on by the regime of movement. Thomas Rainborough, speaking during the New Model Army's Putney Debates in 1647, grouped impressment, alongside the forcible appropriation and distribution of poorer English laborers to overseas colonies, with African slavery, calling for an end to both.

Anti-impressment resistance was pure collective direct action. When news of a press-gang's presence spread, a core group of principals would form a collective, usually ranging from a few dozen to several hundred maritime laborers, that would badger, hound, fight, and, if need be, kill those attempting to force them into service. Much like the *Creole* off the coast of Newport, collective intimidation helped disrupt the regime of forced movement. In 1775, when Vice Admiral Samuel Graves, commander of the British fleet of North America, directed the captain of the HMS *Lively* to press thirty seamen outside Marblehead, Massachusetts, collective resistance was quickly set in motion. An armed tender carrying ten pressed sailors was quickly surrounded by whale boats filled with locals from the port's commercial fishing industry. As an observer noted, "with harpoons pointed they demanded the release of men, who took the opportunity to secure freedom by jumping overboard where they were quickly taken up by the awaiting boats."[40]

Often conducted in ritualistic fashion, the literal burning of the transport tender became a large-scale feature of anti-impressment riots. Mobs burned tenders on a number of occasions, in New York City in 1764 and 1765 and three separate times in Boston during 1768. The final instance was precipitated by a mob of 2,000 angry sailors, who dragged the navy vessel from the waterfront to Boston's liberty tree. "The mob conducted a mock Vice Admiralty Court, condemned the navy's property, then carried the boat to the commons to set it ablaze."[41] In Saint Kitts, when Captain Abel Smith of the *Pembroke Prize* pressed wandering sailors, a crowd of seamen "seized the King's boat, hawled her up . . . and threatened to burn her if the Captain would not return the Prest Men, which he was obliged to do to save the Boat & Lives, to the great Dishonour of the King's Authority."[42]

At their extreme, anti-impressment disruptions arrested or killed press-gangs. In September of 1767, the armed sloop *Hornet* landed in Norfolk, Virginia, with a press-gang of thirty men. Having strong-armed several laborers from the seamen quarter, they were met by an impressment collective of around 100 sailors, who overpowered the gang and placed them under arrest in the port's jail for the weekend. In the case of the 1769 *Pitt Packet* affair, a smaller group of four sailors attacked their captors, killing the naval officer with a harpoon.[43] In describing the fight aboard the ship, a New York newspaper reported that "this Outrage of the Press Gang, far from intimidating, increased the Resolution of the Men to die, rather than surrender themselves to such lawless Banditti."[44] Significantly, at their trial, the sailors were defended by John Adams (the future second president of the United States), who got them acquitted on the basis of justifiable homicide in self-defense (an argument that mutinous enslaved Africans would not have recourse to).

Whether in colonial ports or in England, sailors mutinied, intimidated, arrested, and killed to obstruct the normal workings of press-gangs. They burned the boats that were to spirit them away. These disruptions proved effective in the short run. In 1746, the captain of the HMS *Shirley* "dared not set foot on shore for four months for fear of being . . . murdered by the mob for pressing."[45] Yet, resisting recruitment into imperial navies did not deter colonial expansion or the battles fought over it. Nevertheless, within the thirteen colonies, anti-impressment actions, alongside food riots, fueled a form of popular disruption that would become a key feature of patriotic resistance during the American Revolution. On a longer timescale, they instantiated a long line of direct actions, from mutinous soldiers in World War I to the draft dodgers of Vietnam, by "free men" against their forced participation in imperial war.

Disrupting slavery

Far more prevalent were the attempts to disrupt the movement of enslaved bodies. Yet, unlike impressment—where resisting forced movement ensured one's liberty—the kinetic struggle over slavery was more complex. Within the New World plantation systems that were the final destination (or birthplace) of many Africans, slavery was a system of confinement. Confinement existed on both a material level—in that slaves were not allowed to leave and found freedom by running away—and an ideological one, in so far as the abolition movement, heavily influenced by liberal thought, equated freedom with the ability to move.

Though undeniable, this kinetic struggle describes the last decades of slavery much better than its first 300 years. It is a narrative that became firmly entrenched only in the nineteenth century, produced by economic and political shifts, including the abolition of the transatlantic slave trade, the social reproduction of slavery within the New World, the maturing of the abolitionist movement, industrial capitalism's own self-serving distinction between unfree (slave) and free (wage) labor, the end of slavery in the northern United States and Canada, and the formation of the Underground Railroad. These nineteenth-century developments all focused attention on slavery as a static system of confinement and equated movement with liberty. Within this imaginary, the literal movement of slaves to achieve liberty, the progressive movement of society toward freedom, and the economic idea that—just as in trade—the ability to move made labor markets more freely, all combined to position slavery as the antithesis of movement.

This relation of slavery to movement obscures as much as it reveals. Its focus on the plantation system as opposed to how slaves got there, on the end of slavery rather than its establishment, and on the New World versus the Atlantic and African context offers a very partial account of both the historical and geographical scope of the Atlantic slave system, as well as the practice and ideas of resistance to it. The more we zoom out—in both time and space—the more slavery becomes an essential component of, rather than the exception to, the regime of movement. Through this wider lens, a different kinetic struggle emerges: one where freedom was both practiced and understood, not as movement, but rather as the disruption of it.

Disruption of the slave trade began from the resistance to kidnapping and continued over the forced voyage to the coast, in the barracoons of port cities, during the loading onto the slaver ships, and throughout the Middle Passage. As the regime of movement made greater and greater inroads into the African continent, whole communities, especially those who found themselves on the frontiers of more powerful slaving empires, came under increasing risk of raids that spirited off men, women, and children to be sold into Atlantic slavery. In such circumstances, the ability to stay, to reside in place, became the goal of freedom.

The first line of disruption against this economy was to resist being kidnapped. To ward off slave raids, frontier communities became more densely clustered, abandoned scattered holdings in unprotected areas, constructed fortified encampments, and altered their interior architecture, all to disrupt attempts to corral them into the regime of movement.[46] Paleonigritic populations surrounding Lake Chad warded off organized raids by the Bornu, Bagirmi, and Adamawa states by settling into steep mountains, forming shelters under rocks and in caverns, and erecting high fences made from live hedges or the thorny branches of trees.[47] Muslim refugee enclaves within the Cayor and Baol kingdoms in present-day Senegal cultivated venomous plants to halt the advance of slavers and developed intricate alarm systems to alert themselves of raiding parties.[48] The names of these *sauvetés*, or safe havens, such as "the village of free people" and "here where no one can reach us," were evocative of both their function and the regime of movement that surrounded them.

Alongside the defensive strategies to disrupt the slave trade were Africans who actively resisted it. In the 1720s, Chief Tamba of the Rio Nunez and his people waged continuous warfare against the African and European slave traders of the Upper Guinea Coast, "obstructing their trade and executing the middlemen they captured." Tamba was caught, sold, and transported to a slaver, where he organized a revolt among captives on the ship. It was brutally put down; Tamba was killed, his liver fed to his supporters, who were subsequently executed.[49]

The moment of boarding the giant transatlantic ships signaled a transition from African to European control, where slaves passed what they would later refer to as "the door of no return." After this moment, defensive strategies of remaining in place gave way to more active disruptions, as slaves rebelled in increasing numbers to make their way back home or, in desperation, removed themselves from the regime of movement altogether.

In 1770, the slaver *Unity* on a two-year triangular route from Liverpool to Whydah (a large slave port in what is present-day Benin), to Jamaica, and back again, had just picked up its human cargo off the African coast. Within a week into its transatlantic voyage, the first of four insurrections aboard the ship was "quelled with ye Loss [of] two Women."[50] Two weeks later, the slaves rose up again and were put down again, the lead women "receiving 24 lashes each." Three days later, it happened again when the women "got off their Handcuffs, forced ye Grating in the Night, with a design to murder ye whites." The women confessed upon their fourth attempt the next morning that they "had resolved to burn the ship." According to the captain, Robert Norris, "their obstinacy, put me under ye necessity of shooting the ringleader." This still did not end matters, as two others continued to resist and died in fits of madness.[51]

Norris's log entry from the *Unity* details just one of more than 550 slave mutinies during the 27,000 voyages of the Middle Passage as recorded in the Transatlantic Slave Trade Database.[52] Other accounts, using estimates for nonrecorded uprisings, put this number even higher at 2,700, suggesting that one in ten slave ships experienced some sort of insurrection.[53]

Shipboard insurrections sought to interrupt the movement of enslaved bodies across the Atlantic. As Eric Robert Taylor's detailed study of slave-ship mutinies put it quite succinctly, "Before true freedom could be hoped for, the Africans on board had to stop the progress of the ship."[54]

Some were successful. In 1750, around 100 captives led by a Fula named Old Mano rebelled on board the Danish slave ship *Claire B. Williams*, managed to flee to shore, and established a free settlement in the mountains off the Sierra Leone coast.[55] Most were not. In 1765, forty slaves broke free from their iron manacles and successfully took over a Boston slaver. They killed the captain and most of the crew, sparing a few needed to steer them back home. When the ship ran (or was run) aground, they were met by an armed party of slavers, who shot most of the rebels and set the others back on their way across the Atlantic.[56] The odds against a successful uprising were daunting. The slaving ships themselves were intentionally designed to prevent mutiny. Besides the chaining up of slaves below deck, slavers were outfitted with barricades separating the hold from other parts and equipped with extra crew (typically 50 percent higher than on produce ships of similar size). When an uprising overcame these obstacles, what to do afterward posed further dilemmas. If the mutiny occurred off the African coast, there was at least the chance to make one's way back home, though again under constant threat of recapture. With little knowledge of where they were or navigational skills, slaves who took over a ship during the Middle Passage or off the American Coast found getting home nearly impossible.

Instances of outright rebellion were the most explicit, and most often recorded, disruption of the slave trade. Yet, they were not the only weapon available to the enslaved. Because the captain's main charge was to deliver as many live, healthy African bodies as possible to a New World port, anyone who refused sustenance, for any reason whatsoever, endangered profits and subverted authority.[57] Slaves were well aware of this fact. Hunger strikes could spread quickly aboard ships, as when in 1730, the entire human cargo of the *City of London* rejected their daily rations. This was, as the captain explained, but one instance of a widespread problem: "The nature and disposition of Negroes on Merchant ships where the whole Company of them on board grow Sullen and refuse to eat and many of them pine away and die."[58]

At its extreme, this disruption took the form of suicide. The willful ending of life and, with it, the African's role in the regime of movement, occurred frequently on board the ships of the Middle Passage. In 1737, 100 men jumped off the *Prince of Orange* as soon as they had been released from their chains at Saint Kitts. In 1803, seventy-five Igbo slaves, having been recently auctioned in the markets of Savannah, took control of the ship, killed its crew, then drowned themselves in the Georgia marshes.[59] Enslaved women, having more freedom of movement, also had more occasion to choose this form of resistance. In 1714, four women, one "big with child," jumped overboard the slaver *Florida*. In 1732, Captain James Hogg reported that six women had gone overboard and that only "brisk effort from the crew prevented the rest from following." The practice was so prevalent and feared by the organizers of the slave trade that they warned their captains about it in their instructions. Many captains in turn retrofitted their ships with nettings all around.[60] When jumping overboard was not feasible, slaves resorted to hard-edged tools, sharp objects, or even their own fingernails. An account by the son of Naimbanna, king of the Temne, described the desperation of some enslaved on their voyages: "Unless secured, it is common for them to cut their own throats or otherwise destroy themselves."[61] Tracking the reports of eighty-six slave ship physicians between 1788 and 1797, Marcus Rediker calculated that one-third of the vessels they served on witnessed some sort of suicide.[62]

Combining insurrection and suicide, the least common but most spectacular disruption of the regime of movement was the destruction of the slaving ship. In 1777, after an insurrection on board the *New Britannia*, the rebellious slaves, sensing defeat, "set fire to the magazine, and blowed up the vessel," killing 300 on board. In 1785, after a similar failed insurrection, slaves blew up their vessel "with a dreadful explosion, and every soul on board perished."[63] This combination of failed rebellion ending in suicide carried over to slave communities in the New World, where many slaves chose death over recapture. Mass suicides took place in Palmares in 1695 and on the Virgin Islands and Jamaica in the 1730s, when insurgent slaves, facing defeat, preferred throwing themselves off cliffs over forced reintegration into the slave economy.[64]

Not all suicides were out of desperation. Many slaves believed that committing suicide would facilitate the return to Africa, a way to disrupt their forced movement through a death that would bring them back home. Faith in the transmigration of the soul and body, prevalent throughout much of West Africa, is thought to have been behind many ship suicides.[65] A woman of Old Calabar who starved herself to death aboard a slaver in the 1760s told her fellow captives that "she was going to her friends." Enslavers, well aware of the hold that transmigration had on their cargo, often severed the body parts of those who died by their own hand to impress upon the living that if the dead made it back home, it would be in mutilated form.[66] The abolitionist Thomas Clarkson wrote,

It is an opinion, which the Africans universally entertain, that as soon as death shall release them from their oppressors, they shall immediately be wafted back to their native country, there to exist again, to enjoy the sight of their beloved countrymen, and to spend the whole of their new existence in scenes of tranquility and delight. And so powerfully does this notion operate upon them, as to drive them frequently to the horrid extremity of putting a period to their lives.[67]

In such instances, returning home, when not possible by rebellion, was achieved through the disruption of life itself.

~

By the end of the months-long Middle Passage, enslaved Africans had very little realistic hope of finding their ways back. Once in the New World, the disruption of slavery took on a different form: *marronage*. The historian Kevin Mulroy remarked, "As the history of slavery unfolded, true freedom would acquire connotations of living in exile and establishing communities on hostile frontiers."[68] Marronage was the process of extricating oneself from the slave economy through the establishment of new societies in which formerly enslaved people took control of their own lives.

The history of Atlantic maroon communities is as long as the history of African slavery in the Americas. The first recorded act of marronage dates to 1503 in Hispaniola, a decade after Columbus made landfall on the island. They lasted until the end of slavery in the New World. (Semi) permanent maroon communities numbered in the thousands, many surviving for decades, some for over a century. By numbers, albeit hard to come by, marronage represented a significant disruption of the transatlantic slave economy. Suriname in the late eighteenth century is thought to have had a maroon population of 7,000, or 10 percent of a total enslaved population of 70,000. The available figures for Venezuela, if even close, are even more striking; somewhere between 20,000 and 30,000 maroons, equal to nearly half of the total slave population. Maroon communities typically had between 20 and 200 members, though there were exceptions, such as Palmares in Brazil, which, at its height, was home to anywhere from 15,000 to 30,000 ex-slaves. An expedition returning from Palmares in 1675 recounted a well-garrisoned city of more than 2,000 houses, with many two-story dwellings in its center.[69] Though predominantly initiated and populated by ex-slaves, maroon communities formed a refuge for all manner of fugitives and exiles of the regime of movement: Native Americans, Europeans, and Creoles; the formerly enslaved as well as free people; and adherents to African religions, Christianity, and Islam.

To be viable, maroon communities had to be inaccessible, and villages were typically located in remote, inhospitable areas. In the southern United States, isolated swamps were a favorite setting. In Jamaica, some of the most famous maroon groups lived in "cockpit country," where deep canyons and limestone sinkholes abound, but water and good soil were scarce. And, in the Guianas, seemingly impenetrable jungles provided maroons a safe haven.[70] In such areas, maroons engaged in many of the same defensive strategies to avoid (re)capture as frontier communities in West and Central Africa, including intricate fortifications, alarm systems, and ingenious uses of their local environment.

Maroons throughout the hemisphere also developed extraordinary skills in guerrilla warfare. They struck and withdrew with great rapidity, making extensive use of ambushes that bewildered their colonial enemies. Many maroon communities used these tactics to continually disrupt the plantation system, organizing regular raids that wreaked havoc on the white settlements. In some instances, maroon raids led to the complete abandonment of plantations, and discouraged planters and investors from establishing new ones close to known maroon settlements. Agents of the slave economy, from plantation managers to colonial administrators, referred to maroons as "the enemy in our bowels," "African malignancies," or the "intestinal enemies," "chronic plague," and "gangrene" of many plantation societies, right up to final emancipation.[71] As the American historian William Freehling noted of maroon communities, "the job of an underclass, when it seeks to overturn a crushing dominion, is to find the spaces where successful resistance can be mounted."[72]

The systemic disruption of slavery, from resistance to enslavement within Africa to maroon communities in the New World, took a material toll on the slave trade. Defensive strategies of frontier communities forced slave traders farther into the continent. Middle Passage suicides and insurrections deprived the slave trade of around 100,000 valuable commodities and forced slaving ships to take expensive precautions to prevent them (increased crew size, retrofitting of ships, and so on).

Raiding maroon communities required greater colonial forces to protect plantation societies. All of this raised the cost of the slave trade considerably. David Richardson argues that these increased costs "significantly reduced the shipments of slaves to the Americas, by a million over the full course of the slave trade, 600,000 in the 18th century alone."[73]

The disruption of slavery also made its way into the white reading public, where tales of bloody insurrections and suicide were increasingly chronicled on both sides of the Atlantic. Especially after 1787, when public debates over the slave trade erupted in the Anglo-American world, white abolitionists used slave disruptions to counter the arguments about the decency and fair treatment of slaves aboard ships and as evidence of the "humanity of Africans" rising up to recapture their "lost liberty and natural right," in "Splendorous actions [that] eclipse those celebrated Characters of Greece and Rome."[74] Most significantly, the systemic disruption to slavery by the enslaved created a culture of rebellion, a breeding ground for the self-emancipation of Afro-Americans that would later be carried out on a grand scale, beginning with the Haitian Revolution.

Disrupting Atlantic trade

At age twenty-seven, William Fly, a sailor "of very obscure parents," signed on to the Bristol-based merchant ship *The Elizabeth* on a voyage to West Africa. Receiving ill rations and harsh discipline, Fly and a few other of the crew orchestrated a mutiny, killing the captain and first mate. Having taken possession of the vessel, the mutineers prepared a bowl of punch. They then installed a new egalitarian shipboard social order, stitched the skull and crossbones onto a black flag, and, renaming their ship the *Fames' Revenge*, sailed away in search of prizes. So began the life of one of the more than 200 pirate ships that sailed the Atlantic during the golden age of piracy between 1716 and 1726. Over the next four years, Fly and his mates captured five merchant vessels, lashed their captains, recruited their crew, and, plundering the ships' cargo, sent them to the bottom of the ocean.[75]

Pirates epitomized the politics of disruption of the eighteenth century. Like resistance to impressment, mutiny, or marronage, piracy offered a way to escape the clutches of the transatlantic regime of movement. But, unlike these other disruptions of forced movement, piracy—like a parasite to its host—was also uniquely dependent on this same regime. Disrupting it brought pirates money, food, goods, wine, and fresh recruits. However much they waged war on the regime of movement, without it, there would be no pirates at all.

Not that there were many of them. Probably no more than 5,000 at any given time. A small number, perhaps, but they wreaked havoc on the Atlantic economy, capturing thousands of merchant vessels, many of which they burned or sank, all of which they plundered for valuable cargo. The previous occupations and life stories of pirates were as diverse as they are telling. Running through the past histories of the navy deserters, debtors, political prisoners, vagabonds, demoralized soldiers, indentured servants, slaves, convicts, dispossessed small-holders and all those who took up the "pyratical way" was a common thread: the refusal of the life thrust on them by the regime of move-ment. Most pirates had previously worked as maritime hands within the transatlantic economy, either on merchant, naval, or privateering vessels. Yet not all pirates were disgruntled sailors. Escaped slaves, if given the chance to join an attacking pirate vessel, opted for piracy in great numbers. During its golden age, it was not uncommon for runa-way slaves to make up a quarter or more of the pirate ship's crew.[76] Marcus Rediker, a leading historian of Atlantic piracy, claims, "Piracy was a way of life voluntarily chosen, for the most part, by large numbers of men who directly challenged the ways of the society from which they had excepted themselves."[77] In an age when forms of life outside the regime of movement were being systematically extinguished or criminalized, piracy—which fed off the arteries of this regime—stood as the ultimate crime.

How did one become a pirate? A few, like William Fly, were muti-nous crew members of merchant vessels who had collectively seized control of their ship. Yet this way of turning pirate was rare. The most common path to piracy was through the (mis)fortune of coming under attack by a pirate ship. In fact, the social reproduction of piracy and the disruption of maritime shipping went hand in hand. Pirates found their greatest recruits from among the surviving crew of their targets, especially in the early eighteenth century, when "seamen turned to the black flag by the thousands." Edward England's pirate crew took nine vessels off the coast of Africa and found 55 of the 143 seamen ready to sign their articles of agreement. "I fear they will soon multiply," Colonel

Benjamin Bennet wrote to the Council of Trade and Plantation in 1718, "for so many are willing to joyn when taken."[78]

That so many sailors voluntarily chose to sail under the Jolly Roger is telling, both of the allure that piratical life offered and of the misery, poor wages, and exacting discipline of the life they left behind. Sailors-become-pirates often complained of the "thin commons" and "ill-treatment" they had received in their previous line of work. Many decided that "a merry if short life" was better than no life at all.

The "merry life" of Atlantic piracy was vouchsafed and "codified" in the articles of agreement that each new pirate signed when joining a crew. The articles laid out the rules and customs of the pirates' social order and make for fascinating reading. The very first item of the pirate Bartholomew Roberts's articles, for example, guaranteed every man not money, but rather "A Vote in Affairs of Moment" and "equal Title" to "fresh provisions and strong liquors."[79] In its twin affirmation of egalitarian democracy and indulgence, the article was a clear and conscious rejection of the hierarchical order that governed the lives of sailors on the high seas.

Pirates elected their officers, distributed their own justice, divided loot equally, established their own disciplinary codes, and set up social insurance funds to provide for those injured or old. Such practices were made possible by taking common ownership over their ship. In this act, pirates dissolved the distinction between those who owned and worked for private property, ending the system of wage labor and the hierarchy, discipline, and moral preaching that had maintained it.

The promise of this "world turned upside down" was a threat to the Atlantic social order. What pirates did to sustain this world went even further, putting in danger the enormous profits to be made from it. At their height in the early eighteenth century, the pirates who haunted the sea-lanes of the Atlantic did serious material damage to the regime of movement, disrupting trade in strategic zones of capital accumulation in the West Indies, North America, and West Africa.[80] They seized thousands of vessels, plundering their holds and coffers. What pirates could not use or sell (large shipments of tobacco or sugar were tough to fence), they destroyed. As sea captains never got tired of telling, they "descended into the ships hold like a 'Parcel of Furies,' slashing boxes and bales of goods, throwing them overboard, and laughing uproariously as they did so." When they were done, partly to prevent news spreading from ship to shore, partly to practice "indirect terror against owners of mercantile property," pirates often targeted the ship, the key technology of the regime of movement.[81] They cut masts, set ships afire, or sunk them, destroying around 250 merchant vessels between 1716 and 1726 alone.

Ships were not the only targets of Atlantic piracy. In 1717, the infamous pirate Blackbeard and his crew blockaded the city of Charleston, South Carolina, prompting one merchant to write that "the Trade of this Place is totally interrupted" and the whole province is in "a great Terror." Five years later, Bartholomew Roberts, a Welsh pirate who had 400 captured vessels to his name, blockaded the port of Philadelphia, halting all maritime commerce to and from the city for an entire week. Cries of lament made their way back to London. "Unless effectual measures are taken, the whole trade of the Americas will cease." If these disruptions, others argued, remained unchecked, "All the English Plantations in America will be totally ruin'd in a short time." One colonial observer claimed that piracy was damaging not only transatlantic and intercolonial trade, but also industry in England. "The outbound voyages of the American and African trades which carried manufactures were being especially hard hit."[82] To be sure, such comments must be taken with a grain of salt, as fearmongering statements by a colonial elite trying to move governments to protect their economic self-interest. Nonetheless, the strategic targeting of difficult-to-protect sea-lanes and colonial ports allowed a relatively small number of pirates to cause significant disruption to the transatlantic economy.

To rest, recruit, regroup, provision, and share news, Atlantic pirates needed land: a Madagascar of their own. Isla de Providencia in the southwest Caribbean and the rocky coastal shores of war-torn Maine had served such functions in the past. In the golden age of piracy, Blackbeard and many other pirate captains gravitated to the largely uninhabited island of New Providence in the Bahamas. New Providence was well suited for piracy. It was within easy reach of the Florida Strait and its busy shipping lanes as well as accessible by fugitives from both the Caribbean Islands and the North American mainland. Equally important was its harbor, which could easily accommodate hundreds of ships but proved too shallow for the Royal Navy's larger vessels.

It was here that the outcasts and runaways from the regime of movement set up an informal pirate republic, one that stood for eleven years between 1706 and 1718. Amid the palm trees, palmettoes, and tropical shrubs, hundreds of huts—made from driftwood and the hulls of captured ships all thatched with bits of old sail— mushroomed around the island. As word of the pirate republic spread throughout the Western Hemisphere, people from all walks of life flocked to New Providence. And not all of them were sailors. Ex-indentured servants, unable to find land amid the large plantations of Barbados, South Carolina, or Virginia, came to farm small plots. They were joined by logwood cutters from Campeche and criminals on the run from everywhere. With money pouring in from pirate raids, women too began to settle on the island; wives, wenches, and workers tending alehouses, mending clothes, and keeping the men company at night. Some, like Anne Bonny, who came to New Providence as the young Irish wife of a sailor, ditched their husbands to become pirates themselves. The pirate republic also became a magnet for ex-slaves, drawing large numbers of Black or Indigenous people on the run from their masters on the nearby islands of Cuba, Hispaniola, and Jamaica. Intermarrying extensively with whites, they took up as pirates or joined the hundreds of merchants, tradesmen, and farmers who supported them. Though short-lived, the presence of the rogue state became destabilizing to the slave societies surrounding it. "The negro men [have] grown so impudent and insulting of late that we have reason to suspect their rising [against us]," the Governor of Bermuda reported. "We can have no dependence on their assistance and . . . fear their joining with the pirates."[83] With plenty of wine, food, and money well-protected by stolen guns, and boasting a nonauthoritarian social order, New Providence was a place a pirate could think of retiring to.[84] As long as the agents of empire could be kept away.

Unsurprisingly, these agents were not long in coming. Faced with ongoing and increasing losses, the colonial landowners and merchants went on the offensive. They petitioned kings and parliament, who obliged them with the resources of their royal navies and new laws that hung pirates by the hundreds.[85] One of their first targets was New Providence. In 1718, Woodes Rogers, appointed by King George I as the new royal governor of the Bahamas, arrived in Nassau with a large fleet.

He offered the king's pardon to those who would take it and ruthlessly hunted down the rest. Within the year, Rogers had re-established British control and ended the pirates' republic in the Bahamas. In the early 1720s, the Atlantic empires, led by Britain, carried out a successful international campaign of terror to eradicate piracy throughout the Atlantic, bringing an end to its golden age by 1726.

Conclusion

As the mutinous slaves aboard the *Creole* happily discovered, those who carried out disruptions were not alone. Across the Atlantic, and in increasing numbers as the eighteenth century advanced, they were surrounded by communities who provided them both active aid and passive support. Port workers and sailors offered pirates valuable intelligence on shipping routes and the movements of navies. Local townsman joined anti-impressment collectives, took part in riots, and hid those sought by the press-gangs. Plantation slaves traded with and gave information to nearby maroon communities while keeping maroon hideouts a secret from their masters. Authorities found the loyalty of troops wanting in the suppression of food riots, while local officers in rural American communities outwardly refused to do the bidding of East Coast merchants and state governments. These networks were crucial to the success of those directly disrupting the regime of movement. They also attest to the widespread support that the politics of disruption had throughout the larger Atlantic: among sailors and slaves but also itinerant small traders (higglers), bandits, witches, renegades, and musicians, the so-called dangerous populations of the Atlantic world. This support drew from shared experiences of dislocation and deprivation caused by the regime of movement, creating a "fictive kinship" among those who had suffered at its hands.

The same movement that caused such hardship also circulated the ideas and practices that resisted it. The politics of disruption drew inspiration from ideologies old and new that were, along with the bodies and goods, carried aboard the ships that traversed the Atlantic world. Older customary rights and a newer civic humanism anchored food riots on opposite sides of the Atlantic. Kidnapped slaves brought with them belief systems of African origin, while English radicalism crossed the seas by captured Levellers who were transported to work and die in the New World. The pirates of the Caribbean, a motley crew of maroons, indentured servants, impressed sailors, Native Americans, runaway slaves, political refugees, and Muslim Africans, combined elements brought by its members into intricate codes that informed both the piratical disruption of Atlantic trade and the lives they led while disrupting it.[86]

Most often, people used what worked. Some employed the language of liberalism against the liberal regime of movement itself, playing off the contradictions between its advocacy of natural rights and liberty and the coerced movement of the transatlantic economy. Others had recourse to alternate cosmologies, from the moral economy to the culture of land, as platforms from which to resist the liberalizing practices of the market. Pirates fashioned their own universe of a fair, merry, and equal order in the obverse image of the lives forced on them by the regime of movement. There were countless more who did not need, or never for posterity articulated, a reason to resist the movement that had ripped them from their homes. If one were to generalize, the disruptions of the regime of movement were motivated by visions of a more just, civic, and bountiful world, which was being denied by the movement of things and bodies. But such sweeping statements oversimplify.

While the mentalities were multiple, the practices of disruption were not. Resistance everywhere took the form of direct action to stop the motion of goods and bodies across the Atlantic world. "Premodern" disruptions targeted the *immediate* vehicles of the regime of the movement: the press-gang, the slaver, the grain cart, the ship. The often-laid criticism of such actions is that in doing so, they missed the forest for the tree, mistook the symptom for the cause. As Lenin would famously declare at the birth of the twentieth century, these early "revolts" were merely "the spontaneous resistance of the oppressed," yet to develop consciousness in even embryonic form.[87] There is some truth to these claims. Aside from the end of slavery (to which slave resistance contributed a great deal), premodern disruptions were not successful in deterring the dislocations of the regime of movement nor the wars that were fought for its sake. But such critique is also anachronistic. Talk of "underlying

causes," of "consciousness," its emergence and "historical development," as well as the role disruption was to play in it would only
come later, in the mid-nineteenth century. Before we get there, we
need to pause briefly and examine the two monumental events that
made it possible to think about disruption in such terms.

Excursus I

Disruption and Revolution

France

On January 25, 2011, around 50,000 Egyptians occupied Cairo's Tahrir Square. In the following days, their numbers swelled to over half a million, and a makeshift tent city with areas for sleeping, food, medicine, art, media, and childcare mushroomed at its center. The crowd gathered at the square were protesting deteriorating social conditions brought on by thirty years of dictatorship. It was not the first time people had come to Tahrir. In 1977, hundreds of thousands of lower-class Egyptians had rioted after the World Bank forced the government to end subsidies for basic foodstuffs in what became known as the Bread Intifada. But this time, events played out differently. The crowd had not assembled around a particular grievance but rather called for a wholesale change to the existing order. "The people demand the downfall of the regime" became the rallying cry of Tahrir. Over the course of the next eighteen days, foreign governments and the international press chimed in, characterizing the crowd as "expressing the sovereign will of the Egyptian people." When the president Hosni Mubarak finally stepped down on February 11, commentators within the square, in Egypt, and across the world declared the birth of the Egyptian Revolution, reflecting on its significance and future direction.

To a mid-eighteenth-century observer, the occupation of Tahrir would have been incomprehensible. How could a disruptive crowd demand the downfall of the regime? How could outside observers equate this crowd (500,000 out of 80 million) with the Egyptian people? When a young Egyptian man stated, "Starting today, the 25th of January, I take charge of the affairs of my country," what did this mean? How could the resignation of the leader of Egypt usher in the beginning (and not the end) of a revolution? These statements, observations, and outcomes were simply not imaginable for the disruptions examined in the previous chapter.

The fundamental changes in the perception and possibility of disruption that allowed a crowd camped out in a square to overthrow a regime have their origin in the opening month of the French Revolution. Over the course of July 1789, the politics of disruption became *sovereign*, *self-reflexive*, and *revolutionary*. These changes happened abruptly, simultaneously, and were conceptually linked. Taken together, they altered how disruption was thought about and practiced for the next 200 years.

Sovereign disruption

On June 17, 1789, the delegates of the Third Estate broke away from the Estates General, declared themselves the National Assembly, and claimed to be the sole representatives of the French nation. For the next two weeks, an uneasy tension existed in France between two distinct political apparatuses (King and Assembly), what Trotsky would later famously term the period of "dual power." By July 11, it seemed that Louis XVI had had enough. He ordered his royal troops to encircle Paris and Versailles, signaling his intent to move against the Assembly. In response, on the morning of July 14, 1789, a large Parisian crowd gathered at the Hôtel des Invalides in search of arms. Fearing a Saint Bartholomew–type massacre, the crowd had amassed to defend themselves. Finding 20,000 to 30,000 muskets but not ammunition, they headed across the city to the Bastille, an old military fortress that was rumored to store large quantities of powder. After a short battle, they made their way inside. They captured the commandant of the fortress as well as a municipal official, severed their bodies from their heads and, putting the latter on pikes, paraded triumphantly around the city.

In and of themselves, the actions of the Parisian crowd were nothing new. Though occurring under particularly charged circumstances, they were but another instance of popular resistance against authority that had

had many predecessors in the eighteenth-century Atlantic world. Previous terms to describe such disruptions included uprising, emotion, revolt, riot, mutiny, insurrection, rebellion, or sedition. And this was precisely how the elites of France first understood the events of July 14. The king, returning from a hunting trip, inquired if it was the beginning of a revolt, while the delegates of the Third Estate treated the popular violence as "disastrous news," fearing that the "bloody massacres" and "excess of fury" would strengthen the king's hand and undermine that of the Assembly.

Yet, in the week that followed, something remarkable happened. The actions of the crowd began to be understood in a new way, one that would have a profound impact on the politics of disruption—changing its meaning, prospects, and history for the next two centuries. The immediate effect of the taking of the Bastille was sensational. The king recalled his troops the following day and, on July 16, made a humiliating visit to Paris, essentially conceding the self-proclaimed authority of the National Assembly. Parisian orators and commentators jumped on the capitulation, characterizing the storming of the Bastille as "a rising of liberty against despotism." They began using the word "citizen" to describe participants of the crowd and referred to the armed militia who had seized weapons as the "soldiers of the nation." This new language soon seeped into the National Assembly, whose delegates, despite their inclination, were forced to acknowledge that their political fortunes had been reversed by the Parisian masses. By July 16, the same "bloody massacres" of July 14 were being referred to as "the courage and energy" of the people who had made Paris "worthy of liberty." By July 20, the Assembly had gone further, stating that not only had the "courage of the people taking up arms" preserved their liberty, but implied that such action, far from being condemned, might be required once again in the future. In a stirring speech, the delegate François Buzot remarked, "Who will tell that despotism will not be reborn among us? If one day it draws together its forces to strike us down, what citizens will arm themselves in time to save the fatherland?"[1]

What had hitherto been regarded as a spontaneous irruption of unrestrained violence had, in under a week, become acknowledged by both the king and National Assembly as the self-conscious act of the "people" imposing their sovereign will. This construal, as the sociologist William Sewell pointed out, required a dramatic and utterly unforeseen articulation between two modes of activity not previously understood to be linked: on the one hand, political and philosophical claims about the sovereignty of the people of the sort that the delegates of the Third Estate had used when declaring themselves the National Assembly; on the other, popular actions of the sort that the Parisian populace had used against the king's troops on July 14.[2] This interpretation of the storming of the Bastille, associating disruptive crowd action with an act of sovereign will, became the mainspring for the modern conception of revolution.

Nothing is more indicative of this new sanctioning of disruption as an act of sovereignty than the date chosen, a year later in 1790, to mark the beginning of the French Revolution. The elites of the Third Estate would have no doubt preferred to celebrate their own actions: June 17, when they broke away to form the National Assembly, or June 20, when they took the (tennis court) oath to provide France with a new constitution. But they were forced to acknowledge the popular action of the crowd that had saved them on July 14. To grasp the symbolic meaning of this date—celebrated around the world as Bastille Day—and its significance for the politics of disruption, one need only compare it with its American counterpart. The contrast is perhaps best illustrated by two paintings that have become the iconic images of the two revolutions, John Trumbull's *The Declaration of Independence* and Jean-Pierre Houël's *Prise de la Bastille*.

John Trumbull, *Declaration of Independence* (1818), National Portrait Gallery

Jean-Pierre Houël, *The Storming of the Bastille*
(1789), Bibliothèque nationale de France

Trumbull's painting, originally begun at the behest of Thomas Jefferson in 1786 and completed thirty-two years later in 1818, has, over the past two centuries, been reproduced in countless American schoolbooks and graces the back of the (albeit rarely used) two-dollar bill. It depicts a grouping of rich white men in an adorned hall fixated on a legal document that symbolized the will of the American people to become independent of Britain. It is, in many respects, the perfect encapsulation of Habermas's notion of the Bourgeois Public Sphere: rational men addressing "the opinions of mankind," making "self-evident arguments" as to "the causes which compel their separation."[3] The second painting, by Jean-Pierre Houël, one of the iconic images of the French Revolution, is a scene of mass disruption. Buildings are on fire. There is an air of fury and chaos. It is the scene of a struggle, yet unlike depictions of military operations, the main protagonists are dispersed, seeming to act spontaneously and independently from one another, almost reminiscent of a riot. If in the former, the will of the nation is expressed through the deliberation of men compelled toward the writing of a declaration, the latter depicts the disruptive actions of a crowd as the true face of liberty.

Revolutionary disruption

The new language of disruption, linked for the first time with the conception of sovereignty, was intimately bound to another fundamental innovation of July 1789: a new meaning and use of the word *revolution*. This shift would likewise have profound implications for the politics of disruption. Before 1789, the term *revolution* had two connotations. The first, and much older one, was astronomical, referring to the cyclical rotation of celestial bodies. In the late seventeenth and early eighteenth centuries, the word *revolution* took on its second meaning, no longer referring to cycles but to changes in fortune—to accidental mutations in human affairs, to innovations and disorders erupting within human time. In this way, it was possible to speak of the eighteenth century as a century of revolutions, that is, innovations and disruptions in political thought, in art, in music, and so on. The 1772 French *Encyclopédie* gave its political definition as "a considerable change in the government of a state," the fall of a minister, the death of a king, the loss of a battle. Other eighteenth-century French dictionaries referred to revolution as "a change which occurs in public affairs, in things of this world," citing examples such as "there are no states that have not been subject to revolutions" or "time makes strange revolutions in human affairs" for its contemporary usage. In all of these, as Keith Baker masterfully points out, revolution was usually used in the plural, or when singular, the indefinite article was preferred over the definite (*a* revolution, not *the* revolution). Significantly, revolution was also and always an ex post facto category of historical understanding, referring to something that had already occurred, usually abruptly and without the conscious choice of human actors.[4]

Yet, in the weeks following July 14, the usage of revolution underwent a profound change, taking on the meaning it has today. Nowhere was this shift more evident than in the pages of *Les Révolutions de Paris*, the most widely read account of the events taking place in the French capital. In his detailed study of the journal, Pierre Retat explains that the first issue of *Révolutions de Paris* (not counting the brief pamphlet rushed out on the evening of the 14th) was initially intended as a single publication, printed on July 18, whose aim was to describe the happenings of the past four days. Its enormous popularity made the editors promise (by its fifth edition) to continue giving a weekly account of events and to extend publication indefinitely. Similarly, the journal's usage of the term *revolution* transformed; a succession of revolutions became first "a revolution," then "the astonishing revolution now taking place" in this, "the first year of French liberty."[5] These changes signified a radical shift in the understanding of revolution, no longer describing events that had already occurred but now, for the first time, referring to something actively being made by humans. Revolution, in this sense, was opened up in time, indeed came to possess its own time, as something that could be altered and directed by the human beings living through it. In fact, the weeks following July 14 mark the birth of the active tenses of the word. It became possible, for the first time, "to revolutionize" or to be an agent of revolution itself ("a revolutionary"), terms that simply did not exist before 1789.[6]

These shifts in meaning and association, first articulated in July 1789, fashioned a new script for disruption that would be restaged multiple times over the coming years. Less than three months after the taking of the Bastille, a group of women from the poorer Faubourg Saint-Antoine district, complaining of food shortages and fearing famine, set out with makeshift arms on a six-hour march to Versailles. Once there, they occupied the benches of the National Assembly, and the following day stormed the Royal Palace. That evening, they forced both the institutional powers of France (King and Assembly) to relocate to Paris, where they could be dutifully watched over by the people. On June 21, 1791, crowds disrupted the planned escape of the king, arrested his entourage, and returned the royal couple, now essentially prisoners, back to the French capital. At key moments, popular disruption went beyond buttressing an alternate elite body to initiating active insurrection itself. On August 4, 1792, forty-seven of the forty-eight sections of Paris presented an ultimatum to the Assembly to deal with the treason of Lafayette and the king, announcing that they had "resumed their sovereignty." Less than a week later, on August 10, 1792, armed crowds forced their way into the Tuileries Palace, suspended the king and dissolved the Legislative Assembly. The resolution of the insurrectionary commune stated that "when the People puts itself into a state of insurrection, it withdraws all powers and takes it onto itself." Between 1792 and 1794, Parisian crowds disrupted the new National Convention on at least fifteen occasions, impressing their will upon their new republic. The most famous of these disruptions took place on September 5, 1793, when the poor of Paris invaded the Convention, demanding "food. And to have it, force for the law," leading to the General Maximum (price ceiling) on basic foodstuffs in September 29, 1793. Each of these *journées*, as they were called, mimicked, further legitimized, and carried into new realms the association between popular disruption and sovereignty first fashioned in July 1789. Each of them further proved that the future and direction of the revolution was something that could actively be shaped by those living in it. Through these continued disruptions, the "people" inserted themselves repeatedly into the revolution, consciously altered its course to their will, and ensured that the revolution would not "be closed" without their consent.

These repeated acts, their political efficacy, and the significance attached to them brought about fundamental changes to the politics of disruption. Popular disruption was no longer something that, usually abruptly and spontaneously, happened, but now something (often reluctantly) sanctioned by elites, as a conscious act of a common people seeking liberty. This sanctioning imparted a universal dimension to disruption, elevating particular and localized action into acts against tyranny and for the liberation of mankind. In this way, the French Revolution inaugurated disruption onto the historical stage, becoming the moment when the politics of disruption could determine the course of the future, the moment it became inscribed into history.

Self-reflexive disruption

Finally, the French Revolution imparted to the politics of disruption a dimension that it has not lost since: self-reflexivity. From its very beginning, the revolution produced a discourse on itself. Within a few weeks of the initial publication of *Les Révolutions de Paris* in July 1789, the detailed day-to-day accounting of events were supplemented and, after October, replaced by new rubrics that not only chronicled occurrences, but sought to structure and interpret them. By the end of the year, the journal had developed a new chronological organization, a schema by which the revolution existed and developed in its own time, now with a definite beginning that broke from the old and an indefinite and open-ended future.[7] While Prudhomme's *Les Révolutions de Paris* was the most popular, reaching a circulation of over 10,000, it was just one of over eighty contemporary journals and periodicals that commented on the momentous events taking place in the country. Alongside these were the thousands of political clubs (the Jacobins alone had 900 branches by 1793) as well as the neighborhood and village meetings that appeared spontaneously throughout France after 1789. In all of these venues, the revolution, its meaning, and, most importantly, its future direction, were endlessly discussed and debated.

This self-reflexivity of the revolution—present from its birth—both stemmed from and contributed to the recognition that ordinary human beings could sculpt their own future. Debating the meaning and direction of the revolution opened up a new relationship between human politics and time. It made the present that "we, Frenchmen are living in" pregnant with possibilities, where every moment could lead to liberty or the restoration of despotism. The revolution both created the modern political categories by which people approached time (conservative, moderate, radical) and cast a normative stamp on it, situating freedom in the self-created future and relegating the past to reaction.

The emergence of self-reflexive popular struggle had lasting effects on the politics of disruption. Disruption, after 1789, took place in time, as something that changed the course of history. That this alteration could be self-conscious and directed transformed disruption from a momentary and spontaneous irruption to something that could be prepared, developed, and cultivated. In doing so, the French Revolution laid the framework for the later theorization of disruption. Nineteenth- and twentieth-century ideas of (class) consciousness, of objective conditions, of quantitative to qualitative change, the relationship between party, people, and revolution (to name just a few Marxist concepts), *foco* theories of guerrilla warfare, as well as debates over the efficacy of disruptive tactics such as the general strike or sabotage, are all products of, and made possible by, the self-reflexivity of disruption that emerged in 1789. So too was the nineteenth-century split between those who carried out day-to-day disruptions and those who theorized about them: between rank-and-file workers on the one hand and the intelligentsia and professional revolutionaries on the other. Self-reflexivity allowed the new breed of socially engaged intellectuals to position the tactics and mentalities of workers into the history and development of disruption that they themselves wrote. As something theorized, disruption could have a teleology, a future destination independent of its immediate aims; it became possible for disruptions to wane or accrue, to work toward or against their "final" goal.

Haiti

Nowhere were these new inscriptions of disruption more evident than in Haiti. In 1791, two years into the revolution in France, a general slave uprising swept through the Caribbean colony of Saint-Domingue. Thirteen years later, the Black population of the island had emancipated themselves, altered the structure of landownership, and created a new nation.

Over the last thirty years, Haiti has attracted intense scholarly interest as historians have finally given it its due place among the eighteenth-century Atlantic revolutions, questioned why it has been overlooked for so long, and positioned the Haitian revolution as a central event, both within world history and the longer framework of Black self-emancipation. The debates on the issue have largely followed postcolonial lines: class versus race analysis, the import of European ideas versus African traditions, of a restorative versus radical politics, of the legibility and erasure of subaltern history.[8]

Marronage

Of concern to us is how this momentous event transformed the politics of disruption. Rather than delving into these admittedly fascinating debates, perhaps it would be better to start in a public square in present-day Port-au-Prince. On this square, at the very center of the capital across from the National Palace, stands a 3.5-meter bronze statue of a maroon. He holds a conch in one hand—the shell used to initiate the slave rebellion of 1791—and in the other, a machete. Since its completion in 1967 by Haitian architect Albert Mangonès, *Le Marron Inconnu* has become not only the most prominent symbol of the Haitian Revolution, but also a globally recognized symbol of Black liberation and human freedom, adopted in 1989 by the United Nations in its commemoration of Article 4 of the Universal Declaration of Human Rights. Much like Bastille Day, *Le Marron Inconnu* stands as a marker of

Albert Mangonès, *Le Marron Inconnu* [The Unknown
Maroon] (1967), Port-au-Prince, Haiti

how particular disruptive practices (in this case, marronage) became
elevated into sovereign, revolutionary, and universal acts that were
inscribed into history.[9]

Marronage on Saint-Domingue, though on a smaller scale than those
of other slave colonies like Jamaica or Suriname, was nevertheless a

widespread and persistent practice.[10] And, like these other colonies, both the intentions of maroons, as well as their relationship with the plantation system, were ambiguous and shifting. Most scholars have interpreted pre-1791 marronage as small-scale and immediate responses by the enslaved to their life conditions, as an escape from—or retribution against—their former plantations. The long history of accommodation that maroon communities forged with the regime of slavery certainly confirms this view. Though not as complicit as their counterparts in Jamaica, the maroons' communities of Saint-Domingue concluded informal cease-fires, trade, and longer-term peace treaties with the plantation system, leveraging disruption for security and survival. One rebel chief even requested that his son be sent to Europe to receive a proper education. During the Haitian Revolution itself, some maroons sided with the whites against its leader Toussaint Louverture, choosing the guarantee of their personal liberty over the promise of a universal one.

There were exceptions. Those who interpreted their disruptions within a more general context. In 1697, the maroon leader Padre Jean called for a "new state of black power" to replace the state of white power, while the maroon Medor in 1757 encouraged his followers to free those enslaved so as to "destroy the colony." The most famous of all of Saint-Domingue's maroon leaders was a West-African Muslim named Mackandal, who incited his band to poison whites and their property, be it slaves or livestock. The head of a group of fifty-plus maroons, Mackandal created a vast network of free and enslaved Blacks, in towns and on the plantations, that provided refuge, intelligence, and materials for his crew.

While exact figures are hard to come by, estimates range in the area of hundreds of whites and 7,000 to 8,000 slaves who, over the years, were poisoned to death through Mackandal's network.[11] Poison as a disruptive tactic had many benefits. It was very difficult to identify its source and could be applied in large or measured doses to individuals or to entire plantations. It could be targeted for specific purposes, such as the poisoning of heirs to ensure that slave families would not be broken up upon their master's death, or as indiscriminate economic sabotage of the plantation system. Equally as important, it sowed paranoia and fear into the slaveholding class. Through the threat of poison, slaves themselves placed the masters in a position of uncertainty and dependence, underscoring how their economic survival, not to mention their own lives, could in equal measure be determined by those they oppressed.[12]

This fear materialized in 1757, when, after six years of planning, Mackandal launched an organized attempt to poison the water supply of Le Cap and its military barracks, killing the whites and overthrowing the regime of slavery in order to make "blacks the final masters of the country."[13] The plan failed. Mackandal was captured and burned at the stake in the central square of Port-au-Prince. Historians have long debated Mackandal's intentions, some positioning him as a revolutionary, others as a premodern millenarian. Regardless, Mackandal stands as an exemplary instance of how marronage could become an organized and collective center of Black resistance targeting the institution of slavery in Saint-Domingue.

Irrespective of whether their maroon leaders chose a more accommodationist or confrontational stance, marronage, in both a real and a symbolic sense, was a disruption of the plantation system. Even before the 1791 uprising, the economic impact of marronage on the colony was undeniable. In both its short-term individual (*petit*) or long-term collective variants (*grand*), marronage was a disruption of plantation labor, "a stopping dead and point-blank refusal of work."[14] In addition to the refusal of their labor, maroon communities in Saint-Domingue also engaged in more active disruptions of the plantation system, including setting fire to sugarcane fields, destroying plantation installations, and killing stewards and overseers.

On a more abstract though equally real register, the very act of marronage, in its performance, turned a slave into a free person. It not only disrupted the status of the person, but called into question the very institution of slavery. For the masters, acceding that fugitive slaves had fled to become free people, that they had the ability to consciously negate the condition of perpetual bondage, would have undermined the ideological foundation of slavery and, with it, the economic basis of their wealth and power. An accession that no ruling class has ever granted voluntarily.

Rather, whites in France and the colonies continued to characterize marronage as "desertion" or "brigandage," often brought about by "laziness," "hunger," or "natural delinquency." Oftentimes, colonists recorded that their slaves had become maroons seemingly "without reason," "without subject," or "without any visible motive."[15] Such language was in keeping with how the elites of the Atlantic characterized other popular disruptions—from food and impressment riots to Atlantic piracy— adding, of course, a racial element.

These characterizations also go a long way to explaining why the white slave-holding class was so shocked when the mass insurrection finally materialized. From hindsight, the connections between the long history of marronage on Saint-Domingue and the Haitian Revolution are clear. It was a maroon, Dutty Boukman, who incited and led the 1791 general slave uprising that destroyed 1,800 plantations and murdered 1,000 slaveholders in under a week. From that moment onward, Black resistance in Haiti had all the markings of maroon disruption now applied on a colony-wide scale: the refusal to work, the burning of fields and installations, the use of guerrilla tactics, the formation of maroon bands, the killing of whites.

1791

In the fall of 1789, the enslaved of Saint-Domingue began to receive news of both a major slave uprising in Martinique and the extraordinary events that were taking place in France. On their own island, they heard accounts of whites torturing and lynching mulattoes and free Blacks in response to the latter's demands for the civil rights of free people of color. It did not take long for the enslaved to begin interpreting and acting upon the news of uprising, revolution, rights, and equality in their own way. For many, this meant marronage. In the two years between the storming of the Bastille and the colony-wide slave insurrection that began in August 1791, the practice of marronage greatly increased on the island. On some plantations, the entire workforce along with its *commandeur* were reported maroon. One plantation manager wrote the owner telling of the new mood among his slaves: "The sight of the cockade is giving them ideas." Another that "one must lend a deaf ear and pretend not to hear what they are saying to avoid a general uprising."[16]

In June and July 1791, the slaves of several plantations in the North Plains left their fields and began holding gatherings in the woods. Soon these gatherings were joined by delegated slaves from nearby plantations. By early August, these meetings encompassed slaves from over 100 estates, covering nearly the entire central region of the Northern province, and had turned into full-scale political assemblies, where issues, points of view, and differing strategies were presented and discussed. It was in one of these meetings, held on August 14, that a final agreement over the manner and timing of the uprising was reached, and where a call to arms was issued for the night of the 22nd.

The general insurrection began at 10 p.m., when the slaves of the Flaville-Turpin estate deserted en masse and joined forces with the maroon leader Boukman. The assembled rebels made their way to the neighboring plantation, whose slaves, through prior agreement, had already murdered the manager, owner, the sugar refiner, and his apprentice. By midnight, the entire plantation was aflame, the rising cloud of smoke sending signal to others in the Northern province that the insurrection had begun. The rebels then went plantation to plantation, at times instigating, at times joining in on an uprising already taking place. Within these first few hours, the finest sugar plantations of Saint-Domingue were devoured in flames. An account of that night from the Robillard estate details the pattern of revolt replicated across the north. The rebels set fire to the Robillard's sheds, the boiler house, the curing house, the mill house, and all the cane fields. They sledged the boilers, the mill, and sugar manufacturing equipment to pieces. Alongside Robillard's own house, they torched the lodgings of the cooper, the carpenter, and the refiner, whom they had just killed. "In a word," wrote Robillard, "all that was left of my property were two large tables which the Brigands spared to take their meals."[17] A passage from C. L. R. James's *Black Jacobins* put the mass disruption into context:

> The slaves destroyed tirelessly. Like the peasants in the Jacquerie or the Luddite wreckers, they were seeking their salvation in the most obvious way, the destruction of what they knew was the cause of their sufferings; and if they destroyed much it was because they had suffered much. They knew that as long as these plantations stood, their lot would be to labour on them until they dropped. The only thing was to destroy them. From their masters they had known rape, torture, degradation, and at the slightest provocation, death. They returned in kind.[18]

Within eight days, the slaves had devastated seven parishes and destroyed 184 sugar plantations throughout the Northern province. Within the month, the rebellion had spread to the coffee-growing areas, setting ablaze an additional 1,200 plantations with fires that burned for days. At each plantation, the rebels set up a military camp and augmented their numbers. By the end of the first day, they were close to 2,000, by week's end, 10,000, divided into three armies. In September, as many as 40,000 slaves were in revolt. By November, they numbered 80,000.

On the south side of the Island, the insurrection took a more traditional maroon form. Following the burning of the plantations, the slaves in the Southern provinces retreated to set up a new life in the mountains, building dozens of large camps along its cliffs, each encompassing 800 to 900 cabins with hospitals for the sick. The largest of them was *Les Platons*, an entrenched camp walled with woven liana, surrounded by ditches five meters deep, and lined at the bottom with sharpened stakes.[19] By the end of 1791, *Les Platons* had become a bustling socially and militarily organized marron community of 10,000 to 12,000 former slaves.[20] From here, they continued their disruptive raids, stealing mules or food, attacking army camps, and soliciting new recruits. Meanwhile, those who had remained on the plain "had simply stopped working altogether."

The disruption of the plantation system was made all the more complete by the simple fact that those disrupting it were humans who were also, and by definition, property. As the insurrection grew in size to eventually encompass the entire colony, the full implications of this revolt of property soon became clear. As one planter lamented,

> If we do not defeat and destroy these rebel slaves, the monsters will slaughter us, and by destroying them we destroy our fortunes. For it is in these slaves that our fortunes exist. Whichever way things turn out, our ruin is total.[21]

From marronage to emancipation

By 1792, the slaves in rebellion had disrupted nearly all the island's export production and formed a considerable fighting force of their own. The continued, spreading, and undeniable success of the slave uprising created an opening to reassess and reevaluate the aims of the insurrection. Initially, the rebel leaders had asked for a limited number of emancipations and basic reforms to the institution of slavery (three days of rest and a ban on whipping). These had been rejected by whites in both the Northern and Southern provinces. A year later, the leaders of the uprising, Jean-François and Georges Biassou, were drafting letters to the Colonial Assembly, casting their uprising in universal terms. Referencing the Declaration of the Rights of Man, they argued that because "men are born free and equal in rights," of which "resistance to oppression" was a stated one, their uprising against slavery was clearly within the rights given to them by the Declaration that the Colonial Assembly had "formally sworn" to follow. Accordingly, they argued, they would lay down their arms only upon "the general liberty for all men retained in slavery" and a "general amnesty for the past."[22] In less than a year, the rebel leaders had gone from asking for the freedom of a small number of slaves and a more tolerable servitude for others (each request reaffirming the institution itself) to demanding universal emancipation and the recognition that their insurrection had been and continued to be a sovereign act of a people against bondage and tyranny.

It was one thing for fugitive slaves to demand such things, another thing entirely for these demands to be acknowledged by whites. Here, developments on the other side of the Atlantic proved fortuitous. In France, the revolution was entering its more radical phase, having overthrown the monarchy, instituted a republic, and formed a new National Convention dominated by the Jacobins. By 1793, the new republic was at war with England and Spain and faced with a total revolt in its most prized colony. Nearly two-thirds of the white planters of Saint-Domingue had abandoned the Republic and were actively plotting against the new republican government. They were soon joined by the mulattoes, many of them slaveholders themselves, whose slightly privileged status was threatened by talk of a general emancipation. Most important for the Convention was the increasing and increasingly undeniable power of the maroon rebels, who had established full control of the north and reached a stalemate against the planter class in the south. Where, just a year before, the National Assembly had reaffirmed the importance of slavery for the functioning of the colony, it was becoming clear to the newly appointed civil commissioners sent from Paris that winning over these rebel slaves was the only hope of not losing the colony altogether.

So it was that, soon after arriving on the island, the new commissioners Sonthonax and Polverel were forced to acknowledge the freedom that the slaves had already attained for themselves. In much the same way that the National Assembly had recast the riotous mobs of Paris as the defenders of liberty, it was in this acknowledgment that the colony-wide marronage of the slaves became stamped as the sovereign act of a people claiming their universal rights.

Events proceeded fairly quickly. On June 21, 1793, Sonthonax issued a proclamation guaranteeing freedom and the full rights of French citizenship to all slaves who joined the republican army to defend France against her foreign and domestic enemies. Once-fugitive maroon slaves were now free republican soldiers fighting in the "Legion of Equality." On July 11, freedom was extended to their present or future wives and children. On August 29, Sonthonax proclaimed the total abolition of slavery in the north. Finally, on October 31, the civil commissioners declared that slavery was abolished and the Rights of Man now proclaimed universally throughout the colony. A few months later, these colonial proclamations were acknowledged by the metropole. On 16 Pluviôse of Year II (February 4, 1794), the Republican Government of France issued the following decree:

> The National Convention declares the abolition of Negro slavery in all the colonies; in consequence it decrees that all men, without distinction of color, residing in the colonies are French citizens and will enjoy all the rights assured by the constitution.

In less than three years, the understanding of marronage had transformed from the spontaneous irruption of discontent into a recognized, self-conscious, sovereign, and revolutionary act by Black slaves to achieve their own liberty. By the time Haitians declared their independence in 1804, marronage, as both idea and practice, formed a path to the universal liberation of mankind.

These transformations in the meaning and possibility of disruption, begun by the poor of France, extended and amplified by the enslaved of Saint-Domingue, were both unforeseeable and irreversible. Following the French and Haitian Revolutions, every disruption *could* become revolutionary, changing the course of, and thus inscribing itself into, history. This was not a theoretical possibility, but a lived one. After Haiti, every slave uprising had the potential of repeating its script, a prospect that roused the enslaved and terrified slaveholders until the end of the institution of Atlantic slavery.[23]

Of course, not every disruption after 1789 took on world historical significance. This was not even the case for disruptions in the midst of the French Revolution. The *Grandes Journées* described here directly impacted the political, and at times economic, trajectory of the revolution, consequently becoming the disruptions focused on by most historians. Yet taken as a whole, the *journées* made up but a small fraction of the crowd disturbances in the decade following 1789. Alongside these were thousands of acts of machine breaking, food riots, and naval mutinies. Most of these acts were not equated, at the time or afterward, as expressions of a grander national or universal will. The point is that, beginning in 1789, they could have.

The cumulative impact of these shifts opened up a new period in the history of disruption. The French and Haitian Revolutions propelled disruption into the modern era, to be arbitrated upon by the modernist concepts of development and project. It would remain there until the upheavals of 1968.

3

Control

If the workers take a notion,
They can stop all speeding trains;
Every ship upon the ocean
They can tie with mighty chains;
Every wheel in the creation,
Every mine and every mill,
Fleets and armies of the nation,
Will at their command stand still.

Joe Hill

Thinking involves not only the flow of thoughts, but their arrest as well.

Walter Benjamin

These two epigraphs offer snapshots of disruption as it was practiced and conceived by the workers' struggle. The first is from a song, "Workers of the World, Awaken," written by the IWW singer Joe Hill in 1914. Born to a working-class family of nine in Sweden, Hill immigrated to New York in his early twenties, moving from job to job across the United States. In 1910, he joined the International Workers of the World. In the preceding stanza, Hill sang of the general strike, a massive work stoppage that would paralyze the regime of movement. This cataclysmic disruption, the song continued, would "crush the greedy shirkers," ending their reign and, with them, the slavery of the old order. The freed workers would then usher in a new world, one where, as the song ends:

> No one will for bread be crying
> We'll have freedom, love and health
> When the grand red flag is flying
> In the Workers' Commonwealth.

The song stressed how the workers themselves, through their labor, were essential to the regime of movement. Workers enabled the regime to move, and if it could not serve their ends, they could make it stop moving. In its lyrics, we can see the legacy of the French Revolution at play. The workers are portrayed as a universal subject who would impose their will upon the world, changing the course of history. Through their general strike, the workers would understand themselves as a disruptive power, one that is sovereign, revolutionary, and self-aware.

If Joe Hill's song encouraged workers to disruptive action, the second quote, by the German-Jewish intellectual Walter Benjamin, spoke of the renewed necessity for disruptive thought. Written in 1940, Benjamin's words were a stinging criticism of German social democracy, which, captivated by the idea of orderly social progress, had abandoned revolutionary politics for a program of gradual parliamentary reform. "The *movement* is everything," social democracy's leading theoretician had written in 1900, "the end goal [of socialism] is nothing."[1] Such ideas, Benjamin felt, were based on a conception of time that saw the present as the steady transition from a less-perfect past into an ineluctably more-perfect future. The working class was marching onward in time, improving its life conditions and freedom with each forward step. For Benjamin, this was an extremely dangerous idea. "Nothing has so corrupted the German working class as the notion that it was moving with the current."[2] The twenty-five preceding years certainly seemed to confirm Benjamin's critique. The belief in the inevitability of human progress had led the largest worker movement in the world to endorse the slaughter of the First World War and remain toothless against the rise of fascism in Germany. In failing to avert the twentieth century's twin catastrophes, social democracy's promise of a redeemed future had, ironically, condemned the German workers' struggle to self-destruction.

What was needed, according to Benjamin, was a return to the disruptive tradition of the French Revolution that many workers had embraced in the nineteenth century. One in which the insurrectionary acts of the lower classes inserted them into human history, disrupting the flow of time itself. The worker required "a notion of a present which is not a transition, but in which time stands still and has come to a stop," Benjamin wrote. "In this structure he recognizes the sign of a Messianic cessation of happening, or, put differently, a revolutionary chance in the fight for the oppressed past."[3] Without this revolutionary rupture of time, workers would be dragged along from one catastrophe to the next, swept up in the disastrous storm called progress.

Both writers died within a year of penning these lines. Walter Benjamin committed suicide on the Franco–Spanish border attempting to escape Nazi persecution. Joe Hill was arrested, questionably tried, and executed by the state of Utah. In one sense, this chapter is a reclamation of their thought. It traces how workers developed and practiced a politics of disruption that had been made possible by the French and Haitian Revolutions. It details the disruptive strategies workers developed as they sought to debilitate and wrest control of the regime of movement. To do so, the chapter examines how working-class disruption was *theorized*, *organized*, and *practiced* from the 1840s to the 1920s. A part-intellectual, part-structural, and part-tactical analysis of labor struggle, it traces the centrality of disruption in the various projects workers undertook to emancipate themselves.[4]

I. Disruption Theorized

To understand how a politics of disruption became central to worker emancipation, we need to widen our scope to consider the changing political context within which workers struggled. So far, our examination of disruption has been spatial. We have largely been concerned with how people interrupted or arrested the motion of goods and bodies across the eighteenth-century Atlantic world. These disruptions were physical and geographic in nature, in that they aimed to disrupt a particular motion taking place in a particular space. This way of under-standing disruption, as the physical arrest of the regime of movement, made sense for us since this regime functioned by moving goods and bodies in space.

In the nineteenth century, the ways in which movement was understood, as a political category, began to change. Alongside its spatial connotation, it took on a temporal meaning, referring to the motion of societies through time. This, too, was a legacy of the French Revolution. That ordinary human beings could act collec-tively in deliberate ways and, in so doing, change the course of history opened up a new relationship between time and human poli-tics. Political ideas were articulated not just in relation to the present, but as something that belonged to a wider arc of human activity stretching from the past into the future. With this shift, it became possible to talk about collective politics as a *movement*, as a project that people engaged in to change (and, later on, preserve) their soci-ety over time. It was in this sense that, during the 1830 July Revolution, the agents of liberal change called themselves *Parti du Mouvement* (the earliest instance this author could find of the term's political usage).[5]

As it emerged in the early nineteenth century, the new language of movement naturalized change, cementing the view that political and social transformations were normal and not exceptional. It also gave these transformations a direction. Change, when understood correctly, was neither random nor cyclical, but guided by the devel-opment of society toward its own ultimate realization (though what this realization was differed immensely). Taken together, these two characteristics became the basis for the liberal idea of human progress.

In one (Marxist) sense, the idea of progress was the ideological corollary to the rising hegemony of the bourgeois mode of production. The regime of movement dramatically altered where people lived, how they produced, what they consumed, and the ways they related to one another. Moreover, and this was particularly true in areas where the industrial revolution had spread, this movement was itself constantly evolving, even accelerating. Liberalism, as the championing political ideology of the regime of movement, imagined society as an organism moving forward along a new temporal vector. Propelled by man's scientific and mechanical domination of nature and the gradual tearing down of the world's physical and political barriers, society was progressing toward an end where freedom—understood increasingly as the freedom to transact and produce everywhere and without hindrance—would be realized. This view of human progress, to the extent that it increased the productivity or the market reach of the regime of movement, became the ideological basis for a whole host of corollary projects, from urban planning and public health to the civilizational narratives that legitimized colonial expansion. The liberal category of movement and its attendant faith in progress soon spread to other emancipatory "movements," including middle-class calls for women's suffrage and the abolition of slavery. Toward the end of the nineteenth century, it had infiltrated the working-class struggle in the form of social democracy.

The liberal hegemony in imagining politics, what Immanuel Wallerstein called the "geo-culture of the modern world system," formed the ideological context for the politics of working-class disruption. Within its worldview, the category of disruption took on increasingly negative connotations. It no longer implied a disturbance of the present order, but one whose chaos upset the orderly progress of society toward freedom. It was on this basis that liberal and, later, social democratic champions of progress joined conservatives such as Edmund Burke in criticizing the greatest of all upheavals, the French Revolution. For these critics, the Revolution became an anomaly; the very French (read *violent*) way of enacting social change that could better be accomplished by more peaceful means, such as the British had done between 1688 and 1832. The latest manifestation of a moderating impulse that sought, as Robespierre had once remarked, "a revolution without a revolution."[6]

The new configuration of movement and disruption was something that the mid-nineteenth-century theorists of working-class disruption had to contend with. Their solution was to come from the most unlikely of sources, the theoretical patriarch of the modern state and order, Georg Wilhelm Friedrich Hegel.

Hegel's ideas of historical change shared many assumptions with the liberal model. He, too, felt that the social world, much like the natural, was in a state of perpetual movement, and that this movement was governed by fundamental laws of development. He, too, was confident that the application of reason (or, for Hegel, its unfolding through human history) would lead to greater freedom. What distinguished Hegel's theory of historical progress from others was the way in which this movement occurred. For Hegel, the world was in constant flux, but this motion was neither orderly nor linear, but rather brought about by antagonism, contradiction, and dialectical tension.

Hegel's theory of dialectics as the engine for the unfolding of world history was directly influenced by the upheavals of the French and Haitian Revolutions, the latter becoming the inspiration for his analysis of the master–slave relationship in the *Phenomenology of the Spirit*.[7] For Hegel, the dialectic began after an initial confrontation between two people, when the losing side chose slavery over death. In the ensuing relationship, the master was recognized by the slave as free, and the master recognized the slave as his property. While philosophers have generally taken this relationship as an allegory for the development of consciousness, political theorists have stressed its more material dimensions. According to the political philosopher Susan Buck-Morss, Hegel had understood "the position of the master in both political *and* economic terms":

> "The master is in possession of an overabundance of physical necessities, and the other [the slave] in the lack thereof." At first consideration, the master's situation is "independent, and its essential nature is to be for itself," whereas the slave "is dependent on and has an existence for another."[8]

Yet, as the slave works with nature and begins to shape it into products for the master, she begins to see herself reflected in the products she has created; she understands, in fact, that they are her products. The apparent dominance of the master is then reversed, with the mutual awareness that the master (and his overabundance) is totally dependent on the slave. At this point, the contradiction inherent in slavery is recognized and the relationship breaks out into an open "struggle to the death," whereby the slave risks her life for her freedom. The goal of this struggle cannot be, for Hegel, the subjugation of the master in turn, which would merely repeat the master's "existential impasse," but, rather, the elimination of the institution of slavery.[9] What was crucial for Hegel is that this freedom from slavery cannot be granted to the enslaved from above, but must be the result of their self-liberation from below. Social and political transformation, in Hegel's view, was therefore never orderly or self-evident, but always violent and destructive.

By stressing the necessity of violent confrontation in the resolution of the dialectic, Hegel inserted disruption into the very heart of the unfolding of world history. Disruption became the means of advancing society forward, of moving from a lower or less free stage to a higher and freer social order. For Hegel, the culmination of this dialectical development was, in the realm of politics, the enlightened despotism of the Prussian state, and in the realm of thought, himself. It would be left to a later generation to translate his ideas into a theory of working-class liberation.

Beginning in the 1840s, a group of philosophers, intellectuals, and militants, comprised mostly of communists and anarchists, took up Hegelian dialectics to argue for the necessity of disruption as a means of emancipating the working class. They argued that human society was filled with contradictions that, at moments, would irrupt into outright conflict, destroy the existing order, and rupture history. As with Hegel, their dialectical view of how human societies developed through time embedded disruption into the very logic of movement. Disruption, however it was to be conceptualized, precipitated, or deployed, was, in both Marxist and anarchist thought, the mechanism by which society would resolve its contradictions and advance to a freer stage of historical development. In doing so, this group transformed disruption from a reactionary force retarding historical movement into the engine of progress itself.

Marx, and Marxism more generally, advanced by far the most coherent and sophisticated theory of social development and, within it, the necessity of disruption. Though there have been innumerable elaborations of, and interventions into, this theory since its first articulation, the basic outlines of the "materialist conception of history" are as follows. For Marx, human history could be divided into different eras based on a society's dominant mode of organizing production. He argued that within each era, the development of the productive forces (how we make stuff) pushes against the confines of how society organizes that production (what he called social relations or the relations of property). This tension, between the productive capacities and organizational makeup of society, manifests as a conflict between two classes (that is, between those who hold economic and political power through the current organization of production and the new class created by the development of the productive forces). The mounting class conflict, a "more or less veiled civil war raging within existing society," increases "up to the point where that war breaks out into open revolution": the moment when the class created by the development of the productive forces violently overthrows the old social order and institutes its own property relations, accompanied by a corresponding social and political constitution. For Marx, this violent disruption of the social order was the engine by which society resolved its existing contradictions and advanced to create new ones.

The mounting tension between feudal property relations and the productive forces of the bourgeoisie had been, for Marx, the materialist context for the great French Revolution. This tension had broken out in the massive disruptions of 1789 that "burst asunder" the existing order. "Into its place stepped free competition, and the legal and political sway of the bourgeois class." In turn, Marx argued, the productive forces unleashed by industrial labor were pushing up against the limits of the new bourgeois property relations. The accumulation of capital by big business, the attendant pauperization of the working class unable to purchase the goods they made, would lead to periodic and ever-intensifying economic crises. For Marx, "the conditions of bourgeois society [had become] too narrow to comprise the wealth created by them." This tension would be resolved through a violent proletarian revolution, whereby the working class would seize political and economic power, replacing the relations of private property with an association of workers in which "the free development of each is the condition for the free development of all."[10]

Revolution was, for Marx, a necessary and inevitable disruption within humanity's historical development, one that dismantled the social organization of an older age and ushered in the sway of a new one. As Marx wrote in the *Manifesto*, "Communists . . . openly declare that their ends can be attained only by the forcible overthrow of all existing social conditions." In this way, disruption was built into the very logic of society's movement through history.

Anarchism, while never developing so coherent a theory as Marx's, was nevertheless equally influenced by revolutionary Hegelianism, and likewise positioned disruption at the heart of its own theories of social development. More geared toward action than contemplative philosophy, anarchist thought has been a notoriously difficult literature to theoretically pin down. Nevertheless, its principal adherents all shared the belief that conflict and struggle were essential components of human development and social progress. If the triple evils of religion, the state, and private property that enslaved mankind were to be overcome, anarchists held, it would be through a revolutionary interruption that would immobilize the social order, destroying its existing institutional framework. It was this shared belief that centered disruption in their praxis of liberation.

Contemporaries of Marx, the European anarchist intellectuals Pierre-Joseph Proudhon and Mikhail Bakunin, as well as later anarchist thinkers James Guillaume and Peter Kropotkin, were all influenced, to varying degrees, by the revolutionary strain of Hegelian thought popularized by the Left Hegelians of the 1830s. Proudhon argued that human history was animated by a "Serial Dialectic" that operates through the reconciliation of opposing forces. This "theory of antinomies" determined the development of human society and "was the basis for all movement."[11] "Every antagonism, whether in Nature or in ideas, is resolvable in a more complex formula, which harmonizes the opposing factors by absorbing them, so to speak, in each other."[12] For Proudhon, the political and economic concepts of the present age (whether property, god, or the state) are marked by contradictions that become exposed when examined through a future socialist lens. His more famous phrases, *Property Is Theft, Anarchy Is Order, God Is Evil* and *Government Is Civil War*, all bear the markings of this examination, highlighting the misery, exploitation, and servitude of life under existing institutions from the standpoint of a just society. The reconciliation of these contradictions was, for Proudhon, to be brought about by the disruption of extant institutions (church, property, state) through social and economic revolution. Despite a brief and disillusioning stint as deputy during the 1848 revolution in France, Proudhon declared "universal suffrage [to be] the counter-revolution," took to the streets, and argued that human liberation could only be achieved through the "social liquidation" of existing relations. This disruption would simultaneously destroy the coercive and unjust elements of the present while creating space for humans to reforge social and economic bonds based on moral, mutual, and federal principles.

The writings of Mikhail Bakunin, the Russian émigré anarchist who first translated Hegel into his native tongue, are similarly marked by a Hegelian cosmology. For Bakunin, human societies moved through time toward a teleological end where "liberty [stood] as the goal of humanity's historical progress." As with Marx and Proudhon, the engine of this movement was disruptive conflict. For Bakunin, historical change occurred through the clash of opposite forces. "Continual struggle is the real condition of life and of movement," he wrote. "In nature, as in society, order in the absence of struggle is death."[13] Among all the intellectuals of the working class influenced by revolutionary Hegelianism, Bakunin was the one to most fervently embrace its politics of negation. "Let us therefore trust the eternal Spirit which destroys and annihilates only because it is the unfathomable and eternal source of all life," he wrote. "The passion for destruction is a creative passion, too!"[14] For Bakunin, revolutionary disruption was the only means of advancing the cause of liberty. "I await my fiancée, revolution. We will become ourselves only when the whole world is engulfed in fire."[15]

Destruction for Bakunin meant disruption in almost all forms, including secret conspiratorial societies, selective assassination, and the barricades of social revolution. In two 1869 texts, *Principles of Revolution* and *Catechism of a Revolutionary*, he preached "emancipation through practical action," advocated the drawing up of kill lists, and "recogniz[ed] no other activity but the work of extermination [whose means nevertheless] will be extremely varied—poison, the knife, the rope, etc."[16] On the other extreme, Bakunin favored a spontaneous uprising of the masses in social revolution, arguing that the opportune time was to turn a war between two states (in this case, Prussia and France) into a civil guerrilla war of the armed people against both foreign invader and domestic enemy—one that would awaken the ferocious energy of the workers, "let[ting] loose this mass anarchy . . . until it swells like an avalanche destroying everything in its path."[17] In other writings, while never officially renouncing targeted assassinations, Bakunin turned his attention to the destruction of the institutional order.

> The revolution may well be bloody and vengeful in its early days but waged more on positions than on men. It will open with the universal destruction of all institutions and all establishments, churches, parliaments, courts, administrations, armies, banks, universities, etc. which constitute the very existence of the State. The state must be demolished and declared bankrupt in terms political, bureaucratic, military, judicial, and policing . . . All legal papers (trial, property, and debt) will be consigned to flames.[18]

All institutions of the old order were suspect. "Not a stone upon stone should be left standing in the whole of Europe."[19]

James Guillaume took many of Bakunin's ideas into the Anarchist International and, with the watchmakers at Jura, Switzerland, laid down the theoretical outlines of what would later be termed *revolutionary syndicalism*. Guillaume's ideas of social disruption were also directly influenced by Hegel, especially those of quantitative tension irrupting in qualitative change. "The waters rise slowly and by degrees; but once they have reached the desired level, the collapse is sudden, and the dam crumbles in the blinking of an eye." It was the same with society, he wrote. "First the slow conversion of ideas, needs, and methods of action and when far enough to be translated into deeds, comes the abrupt and decisive crisis, the revolution."[20] Much like other anarchist militants, Guillaume held that this qualitative change needed to be, by nature, disruptive.

> The character [of revolution] has to be above all negative and destructive. It is not a matter of improving certain institutions from the past so as to adapt them to a new society, but rather of suppressing them. Thus, radical suppression of government, the army, courts, the Church, the school, banking, and everything connected with them.[21]

The Russian geographer and revolutionary Peter Kropotkin agreed with Proudhon, Bakunin, and Guillaume that destruction was necessary for creation. "In demolishing, we shall build," he wrote, arguing that all social progress in the past had come about "by the force of popular revolution" and not "an evolution created by the elite."[22] Like Bakunin, he advocated any and all means of insurrection that could aid in bringing about the social revolution, from economic terrorism to mass uprising. The social revolution would, for Kropotkin, involve the total disruption of the apparatuses of society:

> Once the machinery of State has been derailed, the hierarchy of officers thrown into disarray and no longer knowing in what direction to go ... then there looms before us the mammoth undertaking of demolishing the institutions which serve to perpetuate economic and political slavery.[23]

He equated revolution with "disorder, the toppling and overthrow of age-old institutions within the space of a few days, with violent demolition of established forms of property, with the destruction of caste." As such, Kropotkin argued, "it is the precise negation of government, the latter being synonymous with established order, conservatism, and the maintenance of existing institutions."[24]

In tracing the disruptive elements in anarchist thought, the above account has admittedly ignored the vast amount of anarchist literature that has outlined future visions of nonhierarchical government. In doing so, it has omitted not only the major rift between anarchists and Marx over the postrevolutionary role of the state, but also significant divisions among anarchists concerning the organizational structure of an emancipated society. In fact, by underscoring its violent and destructive tendencies over its generative ones, the above account stands closer to bourgeois critiques of anarchism as chaos, nihilism, and terror—a view that continues to haunt common perceptions of anarchism to this day.

The debates among anarchists and with Marxism are important and have been extensively discussed elsewhere.[25] Our interest lies in the theorization of worker disruption. This was made possible by the adoption of a particular strain of revolutionary Hegelianism, one that advanced a theory of human progress through conflict and historical rupture as the cosmology of both Marxist and anarchist thought. This cosmology animated both anarchist and radical Marxist militants in their relentless attacks on parliamentary and gradualist solutions toward freedom as well as their calls for the total disruption of the existing order.

Most workers, to be sure, could not read, nor cared for the finer points of Hegelian philosophy. Anarchist and Marxist theories, for all their advocacy of worker emancipation, were thoroughly middle-class products. The biographical backgrounds of its creators, their philosophical and scientific training, had little in common with the experiences of an industrial labor force of recent peasant origin. Despite this, two factors helped translate their ideas to the emergent working class: a tradition of Atlantic disruption in the eighteenth century and popular ideas of emancipatory rupture commonly referred to as millenarianism.[26]

On a tactical level, nineteenth-century practices of disruption advocated by anarchist and Marxist theorists were either already used by, or resonated with, earlier disruptive practices common to the laboring classes (much more so than the newly developed repertoires of liberal social movements, such as petitions, demonstrations, electoral campaigns, and pamphleteering).

The new temporality of disruption also found elective affinity with popular strains of millenarianism. The belief in a coming apocalyptic transformation of society, after which all things would be changed, had a long history among religious, spiritual, and later secular underclasses across the Atlantic.[27] To the extent that these millenarian traditions combined a deep and total rejection of an existing evil world and a passionate aspiration to another better one, with the belief that only a complete and radical rupture would allow passage between the two, their understanding of social development and disruption shared a similar trajectory with much of radical Marxist and anarchist thought.[28]

II. Disruption Organized

Marx famously ended his *Theses on Feuerbach* with the dictum "philosophers have hitherto only *interpreted* the world; the point is to *change* it.[29] For Marxists, and even more so for anarchists, the theoretical framework of disruption was inseparable from the organizational forms needed to achieve it. The relationship between the theory and form of worker disruption was dynamic and reciprocal; experiments in one realm led to reformulations and deployments in the other.

Broadly speaking, the organizational structures of worker disruption from the mid-nineteenth to the early twentieth century took two principal forms: *popular insurrection* and *revolutionary syndicalism*. The first waged class warfare in the political sphere against the forces of the state; the second took disruption into industry, directly targeting the workings of capital. The split over organizational form led to bitter disputes within the labor struggle over which would best assure worker emancipation. In the years immediately following the First World War, when the high point of syndicalism coincided with the aftershocks of the Bolshevik Revolution, the two currents combined into a generalized worker revolt that nearly brought down the regime of movement.

Popular insurrection

As a way of organizing disruption, popular insurrection took inspiration from the spontaneous rebellions of the French Revolution and the subsequent worker uprisings of 1848 (across Europe), 1871 (Paris), and 1905 (Russia). In each of these, the working classes had confronted the state, subverted its operation, and created alternate institutional structures governing society. The ultimate failure of these revolutions and their all-too-seldom occurrence led the revolutionaries of the working class to formulate ideas of how they could be prompted and sustained. Between the 1840s and the Bolshevik Revolution (when the success of the Leninist model largely resolved the debate), insurrectionary organization took many paths. All agreed, however, that a group of dedicated militants would prompt, and later direct, popular insurgency toward its desired (usually more radical) end.

For Marx and other German expats in London during the late 1840s, the Communist Party was to form the backbone of militant organization. As laid out in the *Manifesto*:

The Communists, therefore, are, on the one hand, practically the most advanced and resolute section of the working-class parties of every country, that section which pushes forward all others; on the other hand, theoretically, they have over the great mass of the proletariat the advantage of clearly understanding the lines of march, the conditions, and the ultimate general results of the proletarian movement. The immediate aim of the Communists is . . . Formation of the proletariat into a class, overthrow of the bourgeois supremacy, conquest of political power by the proletariat.

History was producing a single force of deliverance known as "the proletariat," with a single head or "organ of consciousness," the Communist Party. This bifurcation of the working class into a body and head, the result of a self-reflexivity that had created the intellectuals of the working class, was a central feature of nearly all organizational forms of popular insurrection. The communist parties were to be composed of militants who had both an understanding of the historical development of society (including the centrality of class warfare and revolution in it) and the radicalism of tactics necessary to achieve its ends. They were to undertake the trifold task of educating the workers (class consciousness), leading them to revolution (overthrow of bourgeois order), and directing its aftermath (the dictatorship of the proletariat).

The original organization, known as the Communist League, drew inspiration from Gracchus Babeuf's 1795 Conspiracy of Equals, a failed coup d'état that sought to overthrow the Directory in order to set up an egalitarian republic on Jacobin ideals. The League nevertheless shunned secrecy in favor of open and undisguised confrontation with the bourgeois state. "The Communists disdain to conceal their views and aims. They openly declare that their ends can be attained only by the forcible overthrow of all existing social conditions."[30] Despite such lofty rhetoric, there was very little in the way of actual organization. The Communist League never rose beyond a small grouping of militant intellectuals, remained ineffectual during the 1848 revolutions, and disbanded a few years later, a casualty of the general Europe-wide repression that followed in their aftermath. As James Billington once noted, in the 1840s, "the word communism spread before there were any communists."[31]

Yet, Marx's own politics changed over the next decades. His years in British exile and experience with its trade union movement led him to abandon the Jacobin model of violent insurrection for an evolutionary one of slow, gradual change. Under Marx's leadership, the International Workingman's Association, a clearinghouse of socialist ideas with a worldwide membership of 8 million, began to conceptualize revolution as a long process rather than a single dramatic event and settled into spreading "a new and lasting language of social democracy."[32] Only after the 1871 Paris Commune did Marx's own politics revert back toward their initial insurrectionary roots.

Much more prevalent in the early years of insurrectionary organization were secret societies. These clandestine groups dedicated themselves to provoking a small uprising that would initiate a chain reaction among the workers, leading to massive social disruption and, ultimately, revolution. As early as 1848, Bakunin developed the outlines of what was to be the first of many such conspiratorial organizations. Composed of individual battalions of 400 to 500 men, each directed by a central committee of three or four militants, this organization would serve as the "invisible force" of the revolution, dismantling states across Europe.[33] In 1866, he founded the International Brotherhood, a secret international revolutionary society, that would first act as the "invisible pilots in the thick of popular tempest," therefore "assist[ing] the birth of the revolution by sowing seeds corresponding to the instincts of the masses."[34] Though Bakunin's societies existed more on paper than in reality, they did inspire real efforts in Russia (the Organization, Black Repartition, the People's Will) and among Italian anarchists in both Italy and the United States (the Committee for Social Revolution, the Right to Existence Group). These organizations, especially in Russia, were successful in attracting disgruntled workers and popularized the insurrectionary tactic known as the propaganda of the deed.

In France, the leading proponent of insurrection by secret society was Louis Auguste Blanqui, who argued that revolution should be carried out by a small group of professional dedicated militants who would overthrow the bourgeois order in an organized coup d'état and set up a temporary dictatorship before handing power over to the working classes. More concerned with fomenting revolution than the future society that would result from it, Blanqui was a pure agent of disruption. A tireless revolutionary, Blanqui attempted to instigate armed insurrection in 1832, 1836, 1839, 1848, 1865, and twice in 1870. Each of these ended in failure. His revolutionary theory, Blanquism, nevertheless exerted a large influence on French worker struggle, attracting many adherents during the short-lived 1871 Paris Commune and becoming the basis for the Central Revolutionary Committee (CRC) and the Socialist Revolutionary Party following his death in 1881.

By the 1880s, the limited success of conspiratorial groups acting independently of the workers prompted a change in insurrectionary strategy. Inspired by Kropotkin's ideas of spontaneity, the Italian anarchists Carlo Cafiero and Errico Malatesta sought to join the "spontaneous movement of the people [wherever it] erupts," turning their industrial grievances into a direct confrontation with the state. This insurrection would widen the arena from industrial conflict to the disruption of all existing social institutions "by barricades or otherwise," where the decisive battle would take place. As Malatesta claimed, "A river of blood separates us from the future."[35] Malatesta and Cafiero first attempted to put their activism into effect in 1877, when they seized the village of Lentino, issued arms to the population, and torched the public records. Malatesta went on to organize anarchists throughout Europe, the Middle East, Argentina, the United States, and Cuba, returning to Italy in 1913 to become a key instigator of Italy's "Red Week" in June 1914, a weeklong working-class disruption involving widespread rioting and large-scale strikes throughout the Italian provinces of Romagna and the Marche.

Alongside the anarchist tradition, the turn of the century witnessed a revived insurrectionary spirit among radical Marxists dissatisfied with the reformism of social democracy. Spearheaded by Vladimir Lenin in Russia and Rosa Luxemburg in Germany, this new current resurrected the vital role of disruption within Marxist worker organizations. In a direct retort to Eduard Bernstein's legislative revisionism, which had called on the German Social Democratic Party (SPD) to renounce its revolutionary rhetoric, Luxemburg wrote that

> Bernstein, thundering against the conquest of political power as a theory of Blanquist violence, has the misfortune of labeling as a Blanquist error that which has always been the pivot and the motive force of human history. From the first appearance of class societies . . . the conquest of political power has been the aim of all rising classes. Here is the starting point and end of every historic period.[36]

Stating that "the final goal is nothing, the movement is everything," Bernstein had renounced the need for a millenarian break in the social order.[37] For Luxemburg, this amounted to a denial of the proletariat's role in history. "Revisionism leads not to the suppression of the wage labor system but the diminution of its exploitation, that is, the suppression of the abuses of capitalism instead of suppression of capitalism itself." In contrast, Luxemburg reinserted the necessity of disruption into the logic of movement. "In order to advance society to socialism from the capitalist 'social form,'" she argued, "a social revolution will be necessary."[38]

Two years later, in his 1902 pamphlet *What Is to Be Done?*, Lenin attacked the reformist tendencies of both social democracy and simple trade unionism. "The worst sin we commit is that we degrade our political and *organizational* tasks to the level of the immediate, 'palpable,' 'concrete' interests of the everyday economic struggle."[39] Instead, Lenin proposed that a revolutionary vanguard party, mostly recruited from workers, should undertake a political insurrection that would see state power transferred from the bourgeoisie to the working class. This party would then establish a dictatorship of the proletariat that would democratically organize workers and peasants into soviets, while "suppressing by force, i.e. excluding from democracy, the exploiters and oppressors of the people."[40] Though the booklet became a guiding star for revolutionaries of the twentieth century, there was little new in Lenin's ideas of disruption. They were a distillation of over a half century of insurrectionary politics adapted to the "objective conditions" of Russia. Its later claim to fame was based on the simple, and at the time unique, fact of its triumph.

All told, however, the historical balance sheet of worker disruption via popular insurrection was bleak. Almost all attempts led to disappointment, prison, death, or exile for its organizers and resulted in waves of repression against the broader working-class struggle. The few occasions when insurrection prevailed, the Paris Commune and the two Russian Revolutions in 1905 and 1917, it followed on the heels of military defeats, where a discredited state and generalized worker/soldier discontent allowed both disruptive ideas and their proponents to circulate freely. In these instances, political insurrection acquired the mass worker following that proved elusive elsewhere. Of these three, two ended in defeat. The lone success of the

Bolshevik Revolution hides the colossal historical failures that came before (and after) it.

The other organizational form of worker disruption was revolutionary syndicalism. Taking as its motto that "the emancipation of the workers will come from the workers themselves," revolutionary syndicalism eschewed all politics (legislative or insurrectionary) in favor of direct industrial warfare by workers against the regime of movement. While organized into industrial unions, revolutionary syndicalists felt that there could be "no compromise, no lasting peace" between capitalists and workers and advocated for the "open revolt" by workers "against the sordid conditions of life which the capitalist system compels them to put up with."[41] As "Big Bill" Haywood told the 1905 founding convention of the Industrial Workers of the World (IWW):

> We are here to confederate the workers of this country . . . for the purpose of the emancipation of the working class from the slave bondage of capitalism. This organization shall be formed, based, and founded on class struggle, having in view no compromise and no surrender, and but one object and one purpose and that is to bring the workers of this country into possession of the full value of the product of their toil.[42]

Tom Mann, founder of the British Industrial Syndicalist Education League, concurred. "Syndicalism is revolutionary in aim, because it will be out for the abolition of the wage system, thereby seeking to change the system of society from Capitalist to Socialist."[43]

Revolutionary syndicalists across the Atlantic believed that this shift would be precipitated by continuous worker disruption of capitalist production. Nonstop industrial war, from sabotage to ever-intensifying strike waves, would eventually culminate in a massive and generalized work stoppage. This "revolutionary general strike" would bring the entire regime of movement to a grinding halt, allowing workers to take democratic control of their factories "without regard to capitalist masters."

Revolutionary syndicalism had its heyday in the first two decades of the twentieth century. It was strongest in Latin Europe (France, Italy, Spain) and the United States and, to a lesser extent, influenced worker struggles in the British Isles. Its broad-based support and theoretical attractiveness in this period were the direct result of two largely independent trajectories taken by previous Marxist and anarchist traditions. On the one hand, revolutionary syndicalism came of age during a lull in radical Marxist practice between the pioneering revolutionary ideas of Marx in the mid-nineteenth century and the Leninist conception of the revolutionary vanguard party that culminated in the 1917 Russian Revolution. At a time when many socialist parties had given themselves over to a deterministic conception of history that combined a theory of the economic inevitability of socialism with increasingly reformist and bureaucratic tendencies, the practice of direct worker action became alluring. On the other hand, anarchist militants, having largely abandoned insurrectionary politics after the failures of both the propaganda of the deed and the Paris Commune, gravitated in increasing numbers toward radical worker unionism by the turn of the century. Their new message, that the workers' struggle needed to develop outside of the state and create the institutions that would replace it, found a receptive audience. Faced with limited franchise and governments that rarely failed to intervene on behalf of capital, workers who had soured from "political solutions" flocked to radical syndicalism in droves.[44]

By numbers, the growth of revolutionary unions was stunning. In France, the *Confédération Générale du Travail* (CGT) rose from an initial membership of 120,000 in 1902 to 600,000 by the end of the First World War, and then to a peak of 2.4 million in 1920, where it represented over half of the organized workers of France.[45] Its influence, as F. F. Ridley argues, was even greater than this. "In a real sense, [the CGT] spoke for the labor movement as a whole."[46] In much less populous Ireland, the *Irish Transport and General Workers' Union* (ITGWU) grew from some 5,000 members in 1911 to over 100,000 in the early 1920s. Its official papers, *The Irish Worker* and *People's Advocate*, averaged between 20,000 and 100,000 copies per issue.[47] In Italy, the anarchosyndicalist *Unione Sindacale Italiana* (USI), founded in 1912 with a membership of 80,000, had enrolled about 300,000 by 1919, while in Spain, the *Confederación Nacional del Trabajo* (CNT) formed in 1911 with 50,000 members (almost exclusively in Catalonia), grew spectacularly to nearly 800,000 by 1920. Viciously pursued by the Rivera dictatorship in 1923, it was driven underground only to resurface undeterred, with membership surpassing 1.7 million by the outbreak of the Spanish Civil War.[48] Across the Atlantic, the Wobblies' own brand of industrial unionism reached its membership height of 150,000 in the summer of 1917 before being brutally suppressed that same year. Though, given the very large turnover rate of the IWW, it has been estimated that as many as 2 or 3 million probably passed through its ranks, with millions more subject to its influence.[49]

Though striking, these statistics should be taken with a grain of salt. With few exceptions, many of these unions tempered their revolutionary zeal as more and more workers joined their ranks. Or, more precisely, the delicate balance struck between the millenarian goal of abolishing capitalism and short-term gains in working wages and hours began to tilt in the latter's favor. It was a paradox that plagued revolutionary syndicalism across the Atlantic. Radical unions experienced an explosion of membership following successful strikes. While this introduced new members to the revolutionary goals of the union, it also increased pressure to secure more concessions from capital at the expense of overthrowing it.[50]

In 1872, hearing of the anarchist/Marxist split in the First International, the German chancellor Otto von Bismarck had remarked, "Crowned heads, wealth, and privilege may well tremble should ever again the Black and Red unite!"[51] Though each had its drawbacks and often engaged in rhetorical war with the other, the two organizational forms of worker disruption—political insurrection and radical syndicalism—converged in the years following the First World War to create a revolutionary moment throughout Europe. Their simultaneous irruption between 1917 and 1921 delivered the largest disruptive shock the regime of movement had seen (or would ever see), nearly leading to its collapse.

Several factors, including: the social and economic chaos brought on by the demobilization of World War I armies; the discrediting of both European monarchies and reformist socialist parties who had supported the war; and the astonishing success of the Russian Revolution—all contributed to elevating worker grievances into a full-scale indictment of the capitalist system and the need for its overthrow.

In Italy, August 1917 saw a general strike and spontaneous insurrection

in Turin, where anarchist and syndicalist defenses of barricaded workers' districts were crushed with machine guns and tanks. This was a
mere prelude to the *Biennio Rosso* ("Two Red Years"), where a massive
series of countrywide strikes and land seizures culminated in a revolutionary moment of factory occupations in Milan and Turin. An estimated 1 million workers established factory councils and worker control
over production and began to run their factories themselves. In Spain,
1918 to 1920, dubbed the "three Bolshevik years," saw syndicalist workers in Valencia renaming streets *Lenin, Soviet, and October*, while the
worker occupation of Barcelona's main power plant paralyzed public
transport and plunged the city into darkness.[52] In 1919 Ireland, the
30,000-strong engineering and dock builders union strike was termed,
if a little hastily, the "Belfast Soviet," though the following year brought
the first workplace seizures and the occupation of thirteen factories in
Limerick.[53]

In Germany, a general strike on January 7, 1919, brought a half
million mostly armed workers to the center of Berlin. Spearheaded by
Rosa Luxemburg of the Spartacus League, their manifesto called for the
use of "all instruments of political power to achieve socialism, to expropriate the capitalist class in accordance with the will of the revolutionary
majority of the proletariat."[54] What began in Berlin soon spread to a
countrywide insurrection, in which workers in Bremen, the Ruhr,
Rhineland, Saxony, Hamburg, Thuringia, and Bavaria led uprisings to
overthrow the SPD-led government. Failing to win over key regiments
of the armed forces and facing right-wing paramilitary units called up
by their own socialist party, the workers fought bloody street battles
until the uprising was finally put down on January 19. A few months
later, in April 1919, the entire state of Bavaria declared independence
from the Weimar Republic, created a "Red Army," and expropriated
factories and placed them under workers' control. By May, 30,000
Freikorps units had entered Munich and, after a fierce battle featuring
summary executions, brought an end to the Munich Council. A few
weeks earlier, in Hungary, a successful insurrection formed the world's
second Soviet Republic, which nationalized industrial and commercial
enterprises and socialized housing, transport, banking, medicine,
cultural institutions, and all landholdings of more than 40 hectares,
until it, too, was overtaken by Romanian forces in August 1919.

In the United States, between 1919 and 1921, 4 million workers, totaling 20 percent of the labor force, halted production in the largest US strike wave to date, while general strikes in Seattle (lasting six days) and Winnipeg (lasting six weeks) brought instances of "dual power" to North America. The wave included the armed uprising of 10,000 coal miners at West Virginia's Blair Mountain who waged a fierce battle against the state and mine owners. After five days, which saw over 1 million rounds fired and hired planes that dropped gas and explosive bombs on the strikers, President Harding sent in federal troops to finally suppress the rebellion.

The pace and force of these worker disruptions were staggering. Not all were undertaken by radical Marxist or syndicalist sympathizers. Yet, the generalized suspicion of parliaments and collective bargaining as well as the speed with which workers escalated to political or industrial direct action clearly demonstrated how widespread such ideas had become.[55] In a memorandum to the Versailles Conference of 1919, British prime minister Lloyd George wrote:

> Europe is filled with revolutionary ideas. A feeling not of depression, but of passion and revolt reigns in the breasts of the working class against the conditions of life that prevailed before the war. The whole of the existing system, political, social, and economic, is regarded with distrust by the whole population of Europe. All signs go to show that the striving is as much for social and political changes as for increases in wages.[56]

III. Disruptive Practices

Workers have, over the past two centuries, developed, discussed, and carried out an astonishing array of strategies to achieve their aims: the strike, unionization, petition, barricades, collective bargaining, marches, occupations, revolutionary communes, arbitration, political parties, soviets, armed struggle, cooperatives, blockades, mutual aid societies, insurrection, slow-downs, sit-ins, and sabotage, to name just a few. Some of these tactics have been employed for the recognition or betterment of workers' lives within the existing social order; others have been deployed to overthrow it. Many have, depending on historical circumstance and the groups using them, been a tool for both.

Among these, the barricade, propaganda of the deed, the general strike, and sabotage were most directly associated with worker disruption. Taken together, they are a testament to the inventiveness and originality of workers' attempts to liberate themselves. The four practices are presented in roughly chronological order as they appeared and were popularized among Atlantic workers in the nineteenth and early twentieth centuries. The first two of these practices were most often used during, or to instigate, moments of political insurrection. The latter two were tactics of industrial warfare. Though, as we shall see, combinations of these practices often blurred the lines between the two. This section in no way aims to describe the full history of these practices. Its intent is to show how the workers who thought through and deployed them conceptualized what they were doing through the category of disruption.

The barricade

The barricade as a disruptive practice has been central to both the tactical and symbolic tradition of insurrection as it emerged in modern Europe. Its use stretches half a millennium, from the early sixteenth century to the 2013 uprising in Istanbul's Gezi Park, making the barricade one of the few tactics of popular struggle to have bridged the premodern, modern, and postmodern eras.[57]

The first recorded instance of barricading dates to 1588 Paris, when the popular comte Cossé de Brissac led Parisians to rebellion in response to the posting of soldiers in the streets of the city. In the first "day of the barricades," chains were strung across streets to disrupt traffic, and these points of closure were reinforced with barrels (*barrique*) filled with stones to restrict military movement.[58] During the Fronde (*Fronde Parlementaire*) of August 1648, an uprising by the Parisian population in response to the arrest of feudal parliament leaders led to the first city-wide use of barricades, with some estimates putting the number constructed as high as 1,260. "For three days running, all normal business was halted and freedom of movement within the city curtailed. A state of near paralysis overtook the capital of France," thus "immobilizing the greatest metropolis on the continent."[59]

Yet these early instances of the barricade served mainly to resolve conflicts between elite claims to state power. It was only during the final sansculottes uprising of the French Revolution (May 1795) against the Thermidorian Convention that the barricade picked up its insurrectionary use as a tactic intended to facilitate the overthrow of the existing regime in the name of the people. The insurrection marked the beginning of the barricade's seventy-five-year golden age, between 1795 and 1871, when it was used on twenty-one separate occasions in France alone.[60] July 1830 saw over 4,000 barricades constructed throughout Paris, depicted most famously by Delacroix's *Liberty on the Barricades*. A generation later, in 1848, the barricade conquered Europe. The Parisian uprising began on the 23rd of February. By the next morning, some 1,500 barricades had been built. Three days later, on the day of King Louis-Philippe's abdication, the number had reached 6,000.[61] Within days, barricades had spread to the Belgian provinces, the German states, Ireland, and the Austrian Empire, becoming the symbol of generalized insurrection in 1848.

The barricade, in its construction, as a structure, and in the ways human beings behaved on and around it, created a near-total disruption of the urban life world. The most obvious aim of the barricades, at least for those who built them, was to disrupt the movement of troops into the city. The combination of narrow urban streets and military tactics requiring wide lines of soldiers made bottlenecks fairly common. As the historian Mark Traugott noted, from 1648 onwards, barricades served the function of neighborhood defense. "Their first concern was naturally to inhibit the free circulation of royal troops through the inner-city."[62] If the barricade arrested or retarded the motion of soldiers, it was also designed to allow free passage to insurgents. Sometimes, barricades stretching partway across the street were staggered, permitting revolutionaries to pass without climbing over. On other occasions, a network of supporting passages was established through adjoining gardens and houses, disused land and alleyways, so barricaders could move up and down the street rapidly under cover.[63] As an early instance of urban guerrilla warfare, their power was kinetic, revolving around the control or disruption of movement. Yet, by the time it was adopted as a tactic of class war, the barricade's role in restricting the movement of troops had largely become obsolete. The evolution of military tactics after the mid-nineteenth century, especially the development of modern artillery, made short work of hastily assembled fortifications, a reality that the 1871 Parisian Communards were to realize all too late.

For the workers' struggle, the real disruptive value lay in another possibility opened up by the barricade: fraternization. Friedrich Engels, in his introduction to Marx's *The Class Struggles in France, 1848-1850*, remarked, "Even in the classic time of street fighting, the barricade produced more of a moral than a material effect." It was a means of shaking the steadfastness of the military. The barricade forced troops to momentarily stop moving, creating a standoff between them and the insurgent workers. Arresting the physical motion of soldiers presented workers with the opportunity to disrupt their allegiance—the crucial moment where the soldiers would either confront "the manifestation of the people" or, if the spell of the barricades was broken, "rebels, agitators, plunderers, levelers, the scum of society."[64] Echoing Engels ten years later, Leon Trotsky commented on this "moral role":

> The barricade is insurrectionary because, by creating a barrier to the movement of troops; it brings them into contact with the people. Here, at the barricades, the soldier hears—perhaps for the first time in his life—the workers' conscience, his fraternal appeal.[65]

This disruptive function of the barricade was not just limited to troops. It forced everyone—soldiers, supporters, and, above all, neutral bystanders—to take a stand, to define their relation to the barricade and, through it, the insurrectionary situation. Passersby were each invited to contribute a paver. By its very presence, the barricade became a means of engaging the disengaged, of converting observers into participants.[66] In this sense, its function was akin to the original meaning of *resistance*, whose etymology, from the Latin *stare* and Greek *stasis*, meant "to come to a stand" or "to cause to stand."

In many instances, the construction of the barricade itself became a source of disruption. Victor Hugo's famous account of the Saint-Antoine barricade during the 1832 June Days offers a vivid portrait. The barricade was three stories high and seven hundred feet long:

> It ran from one end to the other of the vast mouth of the Faubourg—that is to say, across three streets. It was jagged, makeshift and irregular . . . Everything had gone onto it, doors, grilles, screens, bedroom

furniture, wrecked cooking stoves and pots and pans, piled up haphazard, the whole a composite of paving-stones and rubble, timbers, iron bars, broken window-panes, seatless chairs, rags, odds and ends of every kind . . . The Saint-Antoine barricade used everything as a weapon, everything that civil war can hurl at the head of society . . . a mad thing, flinging an inexpressible clamor into the sky . . . It was a pile of garbage, and it was Sinai.[67]

Hugo's eye-witnessed if fictional account account is supported by an military reconnaissance report describing the basic material of the barricade: "street paving, which was torn up, stacked or mounded. Mounding was typically supplemented by piling up whatever material was to hand: construction materials, furniture, rubbish, carriages, etc."[68]

Amassing available materials as well as the means to transport them disrupted and redefined existing property relations and norms of social use. The commandeering of carts, carriages, wheelbarrows, and wagons, the uplifting of paving stones, and door-to-door requests for arms and goods, made barricades collective construction projects that tore down existing relations of property and instituted their own unique economy. As Carl Douglas has noted, "Under the regime of the barricades, divisions into tenancies and properties were no longer respected. Space and materials were appropriated, shared, and stolen as the barricaders converted the city into a continuous field of urban matter."[69] This disruption and redefinition was particularly significant for the workers' struggle, since the construction of barricades mimicked and prefigured, in microcosm, the very transition from private to communal property relations the insurrection sought to bring about.

Once erected, barricades similarly disrupted the normal functioning of urban life and the social roles within it. Describing the February 1848 insurrection in Paris, Mikhail Bakunin wrote,

In every street, virtually everywhere, barricades towered like mountains stretching to the level of roof-tops: atop these barricades, amid the rubble and broken furniture were workmen . . . blackened with dust and armed to the teeth. There was not a single vehicle on the streets or in the boulevards."[70]

Their existence severely "dislocated habitual patterns of sociability," creating a "break with the everyday experiences of one's private occupations."[71] In its place, barricades instituted social spaces in which insurgents, most of whom had never previously met, came together with a powerful sense of common purpose. The Countess Éléonore de Boigne, whose apartment directly overlooked a barricade during the July 1830 uprising, remarked, "This place had become a center. Neighbors gathered around the 25 or 30 men on guard ... bringing them food or drink." The barricades developed into regular "places of assembly and chat," a scene, she added, that was "being repeated ... in every road throughout the city."[72]

The erection of these new social spaces further disrupted the traditional division of labor within urban life, creating new roles and ways of interacting. This was especially true for women, children, and the elderly, who not only aided in constructing and supplying, but "manned" the barricades as well. The disruption to customary norms caused by the barricade allowed for the expression of new ones. What it was possible to do and to be became open to redefinition. Barricades facilitated this openness to change "even to the point of modifying one's self conception."[73] Much like the disruption of previous property relations, this shift in urban subjectivity—from private individuals to communal subjects— became prefigurative; the barricade turned into a tiny stage on which workers acted out the new social relations that would follow the coming revolution.

Aside from the disruptions created by it, the barricade's very familiarity (especially in France) also imparted to it a certain ritualistic function. Each new instance of barricading became at the same time a re-enactment of previous ones. By 1871, Communards were eager to have themselves photographed alongside the barricades as a testament to their insurrection. With its repeated use, the barricade became a symbol of disruption itself, a marker for the transition between "the state of everyday political existence, with its presumption of stasis or continuity ... and the insurrectionary situation, which remained exceptional, and was perceived to hold both the potential for sudden violence and the promise of meaningful change."[74] After 1848, when the call, "To the barricades!" was sounded, almost everyone knew what to do. The barricade, in this sense, furnished its own script. This symbolic dimension of the barricade, whose erection signified the disruption of everyday politics in favor of an insurrectionary one, "invited people to question the presumption of normality, including the legitimacy usually employed by duly constituted government."[75] When used effectively, the barricade helped create instances of dual sovereignty, in which competing visions of how society should be governed openly struggled for supremacy. These disruptions to existing property, social, and political relations, which long outlasted the barricades' usefulness as a site of military confrontation or fraternization, explain why barricades have continued to be erected into the twentieth and twenty-first centuries.

As a disruptive practice, barricades required the existence of a popular uprising, which could then be turned into an insurrectionary situation. Outside of France, such uprisings, at least for the more radical segments of the workers' struggle, did not occur as often as hoped. Faced with this reality, militants stretching from Russia to the United States focused on instigating them.

Propaganda of the deed

In 1862, a short pamphlet titled "Young Russia" circulated around student and worker circles of Saint Petersburg and Moscow. The leaflet came on the heels of a spate of arson attacks in the Russian capital. Its tone was millenarian, militant, and apocalyptic.

> The day will soon come when we will unfurl the great banner of the future, the red banner. And with the violent cry of "Long live the Russian Social and Democratic Republic" we will move against the Winter Palace and exterminate all who dwell there.[76]

The leaflet argued that, in a time when a small number of capitalists controlled the fate of the rest, "only a violent and pitiless revolution . . . forged in rivers of blood" would "change everything down to the very roots" and set the stage for the redistribution of land to peasant communes and the establishment of "social factories" run by elected worker-managers. Its author, Peter Zaichnevsky, who was caught a year later carrying his unfinished Russian translation of Proudhon's *What Is Property?*, ended the text with a dire warning for those who would come to the Romanov's aid, stating, we will kill them in the squares . . . kill them in the houses, kill them in the narrow alleys of towns, in the broad avenues of capitals, kill them in the villages and the hamlets.[77]

In the following years, secret revolutionary committees emerged across Russia and Europe to make these words a reality. Dmitry Karakozov, a member of the conspiratorial group the Organization and leader of its even more secretive subsection Hell, attempted the first assassination of Czar Alexander in 1866. The manifesto from the European Revolutionary Committee he left behind, his secret trial, public execution, and subsequent martyrdom were the opening salvos of a new means of instigating revolution: the propaganda of the deed.

Propaganda of the deed, in its original practice, referred to violent acts of political action against the state. These included, but were not limited to, targeted assassinations of leading government figures, capitalists, regicides, and tyrannicides. The intent was to sow disruption in two distinct ways. First, and most immediately, targeted assassinations lay bare, in quite literal form, the vulnerability of the state. They showed that those most privileged by the existing order were not unassailable and that their lives could be disrupted by the workers' struggle. Second, its practitioners believed that propaganda of the deed would usher in a wave of state repression (white terror) against the working class, crystallize antagonisms, and display to the workers the brutal nature of the bourgeois state. This would in turn bolster the revolutionary spirit of the people, leading to an effective state of insurrection.

State repression invariably followed. Insurrectionary situations usually did not. Nevertheless, propaganda of the deed was adopted by the Bakuninist wing of the International at their 1876 Berne Congress and again by the International Congress of Anarchists in 1881 as a legitimate means of carrying out the class struggle.

Its sensational popularity was also greatly enhanced by a technological innovation of the 1860s. From Alfred Nobel's first underwater detonation of dynamite in 1862 through the perfecting of nitroglycerine compounds in the early 1870s, the Atlantic world was presented with a powerful new explosive. The use of dynamite in coal mining, railroad tunnels, and the construction of the Panama Canal proved a great boon to the regime of movement. It was also to provide a most spectacular weapon for those trying to disrupt it: the bomb.

In the most concrete sense, the bomb served as the perfect agent of disruption. The explosion brought the normal functioning of the area to a complete and sensational halt. The more public the space, the better. The Russian revolutionary group, People's Will, attached special importance to the bomb even while recognizing that shooting was far simpler and cheaper. "It would not have created such an impression," they wrote after their 1879 assassination attempt on the czar. "It would have been seen as an ordinary murder and thus would not have expressed a new stage in revolutionary movement."[78] The French, after the famed improvised "bomb" created by Giuseppe Fieschi in his 1835 assassination attempt of King Louis-Phillipe, called them *les machines infernales*, or hellish machines, while a 1908 Spanish anarchist periodical extolled the poetic power of dynamite:

> Its irresistible force, its formidable power. It seems that the spirit of Shiva, the god of destruction, eternal destroyer of life, resides in the depths of this strange composition . . . It creates and it destroys, illuminates and darkens, it annihilates and it gives life; it is at once chained Prometheus and angry Jupiter.[79]

Back in Russia, Karakozov's failed attempt soon inspired the formation of other conspiratorial groups, which sought to instigate a generalized revolt through targeted acts of terror. Black Repartition, operating under the slogan "Worker, take the factory; peasant, take the land!" organized among Ukrainian and South Russian workers and had a membership of about 800 in Kiev alone. They advocated terrorism against economic exploiters as "the first step toward a complete reconstruction of society on socialist foundations."[80] The group Land and Liberty created secret cadres of "urban terrorists" pledged solely to "disorganization," including prison breaks, assassinations of police, and "systematic destruction of the most harmful or prominent members of government." Between 1878 and 1880, they carried out several unsuccessful assassination attempts against the czar and killed the Kiev chief of police. The execution of its members and the resulting state of military siege within Russia led to the formation of the largest insurrectional Russian group, The People's Will, which boasted some 2,000 to 3,000 members drawn from the student and industrial proletariat. They waged nonstop war against the Russian government via an underground apparatus of local, semi-independent cells coordinated by a self-selecting Executive Committee, a war that culminated in the assassination of Czar Alexander II in March 1881.[81]

Interest in the new disruptive tactic was not confined to Russia. Three months before the czar's assassination, in a famous article published in *La Révolté*, the Geneva-based newspaper founded in 1879 by Peter Kropotkin, the anarchist Carlo Cafiero called for "action and yet more action. Our action must be permanent revolt . . . by the dagger, the rifle, dynamite."[82] The czar's death seemed to confirm the validity of Cafiero's advice and sparked a wave of interest across the Atlantic in the propaganda of the deed.

The German-American Johann Most, whose drift toward anarchism resulted in his expulsion from the SPD in 1880, extolled the Russian regicide and advocated its emulation in acts of targeted violence that would inspire the masses and sweep them up in revolutionary fervor. "The existing system will be quickest and most radically overthrown by the annihilation of its exponents. Therefore," he argued, "massacres of the enemies of the people must be set in motion."[83] In 1885, he published *The Science of Revolutionary Warfare*, a technical manual on bomb making based on knowledge he had acquired working in a New Jersey explosives factory, a text that earned him the moniker *Dynomost*. In 1892, influenced by Most, Alexander Berkman, the anarchist and lifetime lover and friend of Emma Goldman, attempted to kill American industrialist Henry Clay Frick in retaliation for Frick's hiring of Pinkerton detectives to break up the Homestead Strike. In 1901, the president of the United States, William McKinley, was assassinated by the Polish-American anarchist Leon Frank Czolgosz.

But it was the Italians who did the most to popularize the tactic outside of Russia. In fact, from 1894 to 1902, Italian anarchists alone were responsible for the assassinations of a president of France, a prime minister of Spain, the Empress of Austria, and King Umberto I of Italy, and made unsuccessful attempts on the lives of an Italian prime minister and King Leopold II of Belgium. At the turn of the century, facing an increasingly repressive atmosphere in Europe, many migrated to North America, bringing the propaganda of the deed with them. Perhaps none was as outspoken or instrumental in extolling its virtues as Luigi Galleani, a fiery anarchist orator who escaped from an Italian prison in 1900 and, via Egypt and London, made his way to

New Jersey. There, as editor of *La Questione Sociale*, the leading anarchist periodical in the United States, and the newsletter *Cronaca
Sovversiva* (Subversive Chronicle), he advocated relentlessly for the
violent overthrow of established government and institutions through
the use of bombings and assassinations. *Cronaca Sovversiva* regularly
published a list of addresses and personal details of the "enemies of the
people": capitalists, industrialists, politicians, judges, and chiefs of
police. As Carlo Buda, the brother of Italian bomb maker Mario Buda,
once put it, "You heard Galleani speak, and you were ready to shoot
the first policeman you saw."[84] In 1905, Galleani published the bomb-
making manual *La Salute è in voi!* (Health Is in You!), which supplied
to his readers the chemical formula for nitroglycerine. It sold for 25
cents and was billed as a must-have for any proletarian family. Between
1914 and 1932, Galleani's followers in the United States (known as
Galleanisti) carried out a series of bombings and assassination attempts
against institutions and persons they viewed as class enemies, chief
among them the 1920 Wall Street bombing that killed thirty-eight
people.

From an ethical standpoint, propaganda of the deed was seen as a
counter to the state's monopolization of the legitimate use of violence.
Among anarchism's founding premises was the idea that social peace
could not exist within capitalism. Violence permeated all aspects of
capitalist society, where every murdered worker, every law, every
church, every paycheck was based on force.[85] What propaganda of the
deed did was to disrupt this monopoly, showing that workers need not
suffer idly. In terms of achieving its intended result, fomenting mass
insurrection, it was a spectacular failure. More often than not, it led to
repression. States across the Atlantic passed a series of laws, known in
France as *les lois scélérates* (the villainous laws), that restricted freedom of press and enacted states of exception, leading to brutal clamp-
downs on the labor struggle. Far from fearing the tactic, many states
welcomed it, even utilizing agent provocateurs and false flag operations in order to justify further repression and to discredit the labor
struggle as a whole.

Propaganda of the deed was attractive to radicals in southern Europe
and the United States at a time when labor unions were either systematically suppressed or drifting toward conservatism. Its demonstrated
inability to instigate insurrection, coupled with recriminations by

workers for the repressions that followed, led to a sharp drop in its popularity by the end of the century. In the first two decades of the twentieth century, militant workers turned their attentions to more collective forms of disruption.

The general strike

In broad terms, the general strike was the theorization and practice of a generalized work stoppage in which significant numbers of workers, across multiple industries and dispersed geographically, brought production and distribution in an area to an effective standstill. Unlike the barricade and propaganda of the deed, whose conceptualization and use were exclusively revolutionary in intent, the disruptions envisioned by the general strike (and as we shall later see, sabotage), operated on multiple registers.

Over its long history, the general strike has been viewed both as a tactic to advance the agenda of the working class within the capitalist system as well as the strategy to radically subvert it. On the one hand, the general strike stands as a tactic of temporary disruption within a broader integrationist movement. In these cases, it has had a political use, to obtain franchise and trade union rights, or been employed for economic gain—solidarity strikes as manifestation of union power or for the eight-hour work day. On the other hand, the second "profoundest conception of the General Strike," historically adopted by anarchist, syndicalist, and radical socialist groups, saw its disruption as an eschatological event, one, as the German Stephen Naft put it, "pointing to a thorough change of the present system: a social revolution of the world; an entire new reorganization; a demolition of the entire old system of all governments."[86] Our concern is primarily with the disruptive strategy that was often referred to as the revolutionary general strike.[87] Despite the, at times, acrimonious rhetoric between the various advocates of the general strike and the even starker typological divides of post–World War II sociologists, the lines between these two intents often blurred into one another. This was especially the case when general strikes begun over economic grievances took on revolutionary character (as in 1916–1917 Russia), or when workers *experienced* the paralyzing power of purely political or sympathy strikes in revolutionary terms.

Though the revolutionary general strike as a disruptive strategy had its golden age in the decades preceding and immediately following World War I, its history goes back to the eighteenth century, where it was introduced as a way of manifesting the power of the "productive over the idle classes" through a general work stoppage. Well before Abbé Sieyès's championing of the Third Estate, Jean Meslier (1729), Sylvain Maréchal (1775), and Constantin Volney (1788) all advocated for a generalized arrest of work as a means to overthrow the deadweight of the First and Second Estates.[88] In the first year of the revolution, the moderate Comte Honoré Gabriel de Mirabeau, in a call for practical action over lofty rhetoric, urged his fellow revolutionaries to "take care. Do not irritate this people that produces everything, and that, to make itself formidable, has only to become motionless."[89] Though no general strike materialized during the course of the revolution (in fact, the revolution produced its kinetic opposite, the first *levée en masse*), these eighteenth-century conceptualizations of the Third Estate are highly significant. Alongside natural rights, numerical majority, or its productive capacity vis-à-vis the first two estates, they highlight how the Third Estate's power and legitimacy within society was understood through the people's ability to disrupt production on a mass scale. Quickly overshadowed by the insurrectionary Jacobin script and hampered by the limited means of communication and organization to carry it through (a problem that plagued the Glasgow strike of 1820), the general strike went out of favor as a revolutionary tactic of social struggle.[90]

It resurfaced briefly in the early 1870s as part of the larger theoretical feud between the anarchist and Marxist wings of the International, but its revival as concerted praxis came only in late nineteenth century, both in Latin Europe and the United States, coinciding with the emergence of syndicalism.[91]

Georges Sorel, an ex-civil servant in the elite corps of engineers turned armchair philosopher, became the unlikely theorist for the syndicalist general strike. Eschewing the materialism of both the anarchist and socialist traditions, Sorel argued that society was made sense of, or grasped, through myths. Myths were, for Sorel, a collection of images that could only be experienced intuitively through action. The general strike was not some future goal to be attained, but rather a myth that "acted upon the present." Its power lay in how the general strike framed class conflict for the worker, crystallizing both the present-day antagonism between capital and labor and the concrete, even imminent possibility of its overcoming. "The general strike, allows the individual worker an instantaneous perception of the world as a whole," a moment when "all oppositions become extraordinarily clear" and "society is plainly divided into two camps, and only into two, on a field of battle."[92] In its light, he argued, "the slightest incidents of daily life become the symptoms of the state of war between the classes, every conflict is an incident in the social war, every strike begets the perspective of total catastrophe."[93] In Sorel's formulation, the disruption caused by the general strike served as a way of orienting, giving form to, and directing the worker's day-to-day struggle.

For syndicalist leaders, and even more so for the rank and file, the starting point for the general strike was more practical. Coming predominantly from union backgrounds and generally proud of their anti-intellectualism, syndicalists imagined the great rupture as the magnification of what workers already did, but on a massive scale. The general strike was just a bigger and better strike that signaled their ultimate victory. The task, as they saw it, was to transform individual strikes against a particular employer into a generalized confrontation with the capitalist class as a whole. As William E. Trautmann, founding general secretary of the Wobblies stated,

> [Workers] will first stop production on a small scale . . . in any one industry, then in all industries of a locality, then an entire nation. And when they are powerful enough, they will shut the factories against the present employers the world over.[94]

For syndicalists, the general strike was nothing other than the intensification of industrial struggle taken to its logical conclusion, one that would abolish the wage system, overthrow capitalism, and replace it with workers' control over industry and society. Or, in the more poetic prose of French CGT leader Victor Griffuelhes, the general strike would be "the curtain drop on a tired old scene of several centuries, and the curtain rising on another, more fertile field of human activity."[95] The Amiens Charter, containing the founding principles of the CGT, stated the confederation's goal as "the complete emancipation of the proletariat through the expropriation of capitalists," and recommended the general strike as its core strategy. Its working group laid out a four-stage plan of disruption. "1. Strikes of federations. 2. Withdrawal of labor throughout the country on a given date. 3. Complete and general standstill, placing the proletariat in a state of open war with capitalist society. 4. General strike—revolution."[96]

Repeated experience with strikes had taught workers to look at class conflict and power kinetically. From the workers' standpoint, every attempt they made to stop production was met by an equal attempt on the side of capital to get it up and running again. Work stoppages were countered by bringing in scabs from other areas, soldiers were sent in to break pickets or even put to work themselves. The strength of the general strike lay in the possibility for total immobilization. According to Stephen Naft, it would "completely interrupt production in the whole country, stop communication and consumption for the ruling classes long enough to totally disorganize the capitalistic society; allowing for the complete annihilation of the old system."[97]

As the idea of the general strike gained popularity among syndicalist, anarchist, and Marxist circles in the first decade of the twentieth century, disagreements arose over how such a strike would actually play out. Some took the stance that, if all workers simply stopped working (the *bras croisés* mass strike laid out by Pelloutier and Briand), the existing order would simply crumple through nonviolent and legal disruption. "If the workers of the world want to win," an Italian IWW organizer of the 1912 Lawrence, Massachusetts, strike echoed,

> they have nothing to do but fold their arms and the world would stop . . . With the workers absolutely refusing to move, lying absolutely still, they are more powerful than all the weapons the other side has for attack.[98]

The sheer size of the strike would itself be enough to immobilize the state's response. For the advocates of this nonviolent approach, the bloody lesson to be drawn from the Paris Commune was that a "war of position" (to use the later Gramscian term) was disastrous. Instead, Fernand Pelloutier, leader of the French *Bourses du Travail*, saw the general strike as a way to circumvent a direct confrontation with the state. A general strike would provide either no precise targets or, conversely, too many of them. It would be "everywhere and nowhere," so diffuse that the army, unable to attack every factory or railway line, would have nowhere to turn.[99] Eugène Guérard backed up these claims with some calculations he presented to the 1896 CGT Congress. "At the moment [in France] there are 300,000 soldiers to guard 39,000,000 meters of railway track, one man for every 130 meters with none left for the stations, arsenals, and public buildings, not to mention the factory gates themselves."[100] In such circumstances, the general strike would be the revolution itself.

Others were more realistic about the state's military intervention on the side of capital. Faced with what Georges Yvetot referred to as the inevitable "establishment of terror," the proletariat would need to respond in kind.[101] Malatesta believed that the general strike would inevitably lead to "soldiers, policemen, forcing the question to be resolved by bullets and bombs. It will be insurrection, and victory will go to the strongest."[102] This insurrection would widen the conflict from the industrial sphere to the disruption of all existing social institutions "by barricades or otherwise" where the decisive battle would take place. The radical Marxist Rosa Luxemburg agreed. Her famous pamphlet, *The Mass Strike*, written soon after the insurrectionary general strike in 1905 Russia, argued that the spontaneous rising of the masses in the form of a general strike would precipitate an inevitable armed confrontation with the state.

These formulations both helped shape and were shaped by the increasing frequency of general strikes, which enjoyed a global if brief historic moment in the two decades before and immediately following the First World War. The ephemeral instances of general strikes, whether revolutionary or not, gave workers direct experience of the power of disruption. When a general strike was successfully implemented, disruption went beyond a generalized work stoppage and overflowed into the total paralysis of the social order. Throughout the series of turn-of-the-century general strikes in Belgium and Spain, it was often the "first thought of the workers to cut off all means of communication and transportation to prevent police and military coordination as well as the movement of troops and their supplies."[103] Whether in a city, a region, or at times a whole nation, disruption of the old order was coupled with the establishment of a new regime of movement now in worker control. During the 1905 Russian general strike, worker control of the railroad, postal, and telegraph services disrupted communications and troop movements while simultaneously allowing the newly formed soviets to carry out day-to-day operations. General strike committees and trade councils, from Seattle and Winnipeg in 1919 to the UK in 1926, put in place new regimes of movement to contend with the logistics of providing basic supplies and keeping emergency services in operation. The kinetic shifts brought about by the general strike were a frequently remarked facet that signaled the (hoped-for) transition of power. As R. E. Scouller, a Glasgow member of the National Union of Clerks, explained during the 1926 UK general strike:

> I handled most of the requests for permits to move. Some were granted immediately, supplies for hospitals, etc. But those trying to move commercial stuff never got beyond Glasgow. It was quite an experience to have contractors ask permission to move stuff and be refused. Some young people thought the revolution had arrived.[104]

Formal and informal systems managing movement were central features of the temporary bodies of "dual power" that emerged through the general strike. By taking effective control over the power of movement, workers realized that power lay in the hands of those who decided who and what could and could not move.

The sheer number of general strikes in the first two decades of the twentieth century and the experiences of workers in them had many believing that the revolutionary general strike was not only possible, but immanent. A 1918 report by the Rockefeller Foundation in New York relayed in quite fearful terms the danger to the economy of movement of this, the most disruptive of all worker strategies:

> If the recent past revealed the frightful consequences of industrial strife, do not present developments all over the world afford possibilities infinitely worse? Syndicalism aims at the destruction by force of existing organization, and the transfer of industrial capital from present possessors to syndicats or revolutionary trades unions. This it seeks to accomplish by the "general strike." What might not happen if the coal mines were suddenly to shut down and the railways to stop running? Here is power which once exercised, would

paralyze the . . . nation more effectively than any blockade in time of war.[105]

Sabotage

If the revolutionary general strike stood as the rarely attained holy grail of workers' struggle, sabotage was a routinely employed strategy of industrial warfare. Unlike the general strike, which required daunting degrees of coordination and participation, workers could sabotage individually and at any time. Etymologically, the word "sabotage" derives from two meanings of the French *sabot*: the first referring to a wooden shoe, thrown as early as the fifteenth century by Dutch workers to break the cogs of textile looms, the second to the brake applied to the wheel to bring a horse wagon to a stop.[106]

Within the labor struggle, sabotage as a tactic of disruption referred to a great number of historical practices, including soldiering on the job, playing dumb, working to rule, slowdowns, machine tampering, diversion, all the way to direct actions that crippled the means of production. Elizabeth Gurley Flynn, the IWW activist and founding member of the ACLU, claimed that even contraception, as the purposeful arrest of the labor supply, was a form of working-class sabotage.[107] Sabotage was understood as a practical tactic to disrupt local production (and prevent blacklegs from resuming it), oppose the rationalization of work time, as well as a revolutionary tactic to debilitate the entire social order. As with the general strike, one can distinguish between the uses of sabotage as a strategy to enforce "a fair day's work for a fair day's pay," a claim made to, and legible within, the system of wage labor, and sabotage understood in its eschatological sense, what the Italian-American Arturo Giovannitti claimed was "nothing more or less than the chloroforming of the organism of production, the knockout drops to put to sleep the ogres of . . . King Capital."[108] In this latter conceptualization, sabotage was conceived not as a way to better the conditions of the working class, but rather as a series of debilitating disruptions that would bring about the destruction of the existing social order.

In its application, sabotage has been playful: "a bar of soap tossed into a boiler," "a thousand trees planted root-side up in a field in Washington," or the mischievous misdirection of railway wagons to random destinations.[109] Sabotage has also been organized, "hundreds of plant workers split[ing] the week into 20-minute periods, each shutting the line down when it was his turn," or the systematic snipping of telegraph and signal wires to disrupt the communication and transportation networks of the regime of movement.[110] Sabotage could also be a violent means of disruption used to terrorize capitalists into surrender. In 1902 Marseilles, dockers smashed cranes, set fire to warehouses, and destroyed goods to force the hand of their employer. At Brest, a few years later, workers threw cargo overboard and rolled barrels of wine from the warehouses into the sea.[111] This "revolutionary vandalism," as workers called it, was a use of disruption that went beyond the withdrawal of labor to an attack on its expropriated products. As Emile Pouget made clear, "It is necessary that the capitalist recognize that the worker will respect the machine only on the day when it has become for him a friend, and not, as it is today, an enemy."[112]

Sabotage as a collective practice was most often employed in the context of the strike. The Wobblies urged "the tampering of machinery in order to make impossible the work of scabs and thus to secure the complete and real stoppage of work during a strike."[113] Similarly, Bousquet, in a 1905 article published in the *Voix de Peuple*, declared that the first duty of strikers before leaving their place of work was to immobilize their machines. "The smell of a few gallons of petrol, poured into ovens, will make the baking of bread impossible for months to come; a handful of sand into the oil cups can shut down an entire steel plant."[114]

Sabotage also reached beyond the factory setting to disrupt the state's response. In Parma, Italy, during a farmworkers strike, engineers removed vital parts of the locomotives, forcing government troops to take a long walk to the city. On route, bridges disappeared in advance of their march.[115] During a strike in Holland, saboteurs sunk a ship crosswise under a bridge, preventing all traffic by water.[116] This hope in the collective application of sabotage led many of its proponents to see it as a revolutionary tactic of mass disruption. Emile Pouget's classic 1908 work, *Sabotage*, likened it to "a pestiferous epidemic, becoming to the body social of capitalism more dangerous and incurable than cancer and syphilis are to the human body."[117]

Predictably, its labor opponents saw sabotage as an archaic weapon "not fitted for the *movement* of our day." One that "must be rejected to give place to the weapons of civilization—the ballot and orderly industrial organization."[118]

Though each had distinct histories and proponents, the disruption wrought by the barricade, propaganda of the deed, the general strike, and sabotage displayed a certain symmetry that contemporaries were aware of. Rudolph Rocker, a leading figure of the Syndicalist International, argued that "the general strike is to industrial warfare what the barricades are to the political uprising."[119] The Spanish anarchosyndicalist CNT, which, from 1920 to 1923, funded professional *pistoleros* to carry out targeted assassinations of employers, viewed such action as a form of sabotage.[120] Tactically, the barricade/general strike and propaganda of the deed/sabotage lay at opposite ends of the spectrum; the first pair required the coordination and consciousness of a sizable percentage of the working population, the second, only the will of an individual worker. Yet, what all their practitioners shared in common was the belief that worker power both lay in and could be realized through the disruption of the existing regime of movement, be it of production or the state apparatuses in its service.[121]

At the root of this power was the simple fact that disruption could not be ignored. Disruption revealed and crystalized the fundamental antagonisms between those who sided with and against the regime of movement. It forced workers, bystanders, communities, liberals, the state, and its soldiers to take a stand, to declare "which side of barricade" they were on. In this way, the politics of disruption disclosed a very particular and agonistic social field to the worker: an unceasing regime of movement set up by capital, ensured by the state, hostile to, yet utterly dependent on, the working class. Within this social field, workers understood themselves and were understood as an arresting power.[122]

In terms of both efficacy and deployment, disruptive organizations and tactics were not the most common weapons of the labor struggle. Historically, collective bargaining or the push for, and use of, political franchise has been utilized more often and yielded far more tangible fruit. Advocated by vocal, though numerically smaller, groupings of anarchists, syndicalists, and radical Marxists, the politics of disruption has also had a much rockier history within more mainstream currents of North Atlantic trade unionism and social democracy. Nonetheless, it remained an important and cohesive political subculture of worker struggle: an undercurrent of thought and practice inherited from the eighteenth century that would soon be picked up and amplified by their successors in the New Left.

Excursus II
The New Left

In 1964, students at the University of California at Berkeley staged a sit-in of Sproul Hall to protest campus restrictions on political activism. Shouting through his bullhorn, the leader of the Free Speech Movement, Mario Savio, likened modern society to an unhearing, unfeeling oiled machine that needed to be immobilized:

> There is a time when the operation of the machine becomes so odious, makes you so sick at heart, that you can't take part. You can't even passively take part! And you've got to put your bodies upon the gears and upon the wheels, upon the levers, upon all the apparatus and you've got to make it stop! And you've got to indicate to the people who run it, to the people who own it, that unless you're free, the machine will be prevented from working at all![1]

A handful of years later, students the world over had seemingly made good on Savio's words. In Italy, the occupation of the University of Turin in 1967 ignited a wholesale student takeover of campuses in Florence, Pisa, Venice, Milan, Naples, Padua, and Bologna. By March 1968, the spreading disruptions had paralyzed the entire system of higher education in Italy. Tens of thousands of students had gone on strike; the universities were blocked up, besieged, or occupied; and professors faced locked rooms or empty lecture halls.[2] In 1968 France, student protests begun at Nanterre soon spread to occupations throughout the French university system. The same year, German students occupied the Free University in Berlin and barricaded the entrances to campuses in Frankfurt, Hamburg, Göttingen, and Aachen, while high school and university students in Mexico occupied their school buildings under the slogan, "We don't want the Olympic Games, we want a revolution!"[3] In the United States, the 1968 occupation of Columbia University by the Students for a Democratic Society (SDS) was, within two years, replicated across the country as over 4 million students (joined by 350,000 faculty in over 800 universities) went on strike, taking over university buildings and burning down army recruitment offices.[4] Between May 1 and June 30, 1970, nearly a third of all US universities witnessed "incidents which resulted in the disruption of the normal functioning of the school."[5]

Initially centered on campuses, students soon took these tactics beyond the university to disrupt "business as usual" within society at large. In the United States, students blocked railroad tracks, city streets, and held sit-ins on America's highways, engaging stalled drivers in debates about the state of the nation (though how well this last tactic worked is open to some debate).[6] Antiwar demonstrators chanting "Hell no, we won't go!" occupied the Pentagon steps, blockaded draft-induction centers, and obstructed draftees in attempts to disrupt the movement of American bodies to Vietnam. In May 1971, 35,000 antiwar protestors occupied West Potomac Park in Washington and announced that "because the government had not stopped the Vietnam War, they would stop the government."[7] In 1966, West Berlin student groups kicked off the "promenade demonstrations," blocking traffic by engaging passersby in long discussions. Two years later, the German New Left were building street barricades and overturning the Springer publications delivery trucks in order to physically arrest the distribution of false reports of their activities.[8] In 1968 France, the government crackdown of the universities led to the construction of barricades in the streets of Paris and the spread of the occupations to factories that paralyzed the country for the better part of May and June.[9] All told, between 1968 and 1970 alone, tens of millions of students and workers across the Atlantic, spontaneously and en masse, shut down thousands of universities and factories and, however briefly, took effective control of their places of study and work.

The occupation of space was not a new tactic in the politics of disruption. It had roots in the revolutionary takeover of factories in post–World

War I Spain and Italy and the "sit-in strikes" that swept across France and the United States in 1936.[10] In the postwar period, civil rights activists had occupied the segregated lunch counters of the American South, refusing to move when they were denied service.[11]

Despite such continuities, and almost immediately, the nonviolent disruptions of the New Left became the subject of intense criticism. The leftist militant Pierre Goldman claimed that New Left students were "satisfying their desire for history using ludic and masturbatory forms."[12] Senior left-wing critics excoriated the student uprisings: "For a number of weeks, [the rebels] were the masters, not of French society, nor even its university systems, but of its walls." To many of an older generation, the imagination may have seized power, but it was only an imaginary power. "Because they no longer wished society to be a spectacle," critics damningly continued, "they mistook a spectacle for society."[13] Even the sympathetic Jean-Paul Sartre remarked that "a regime is not brought down by 100,000 unarmed students, no matter how courageous."[14] This understanding of the New Left, as engaged in a war between an all-powerful military state and powerless students adrift in a purely symbolic realm, has been a near-constant refrain over the past half century. Twenty years after the '68 events, David Caute dismissed the tactics of the American SDS and the white New Left as the "playground stuff" of middle-class kids "enacting their nursery rebellions."[15]

The ghost of Lenin drools over these, and countless similar, comments, judging disruption by its ability to appropriate political or economic power. Like Lenin, they see disruption through the eyes of the state, as something that does or does not pose a threat to its existence. From this vantage point, as Kristin Ross has pointed out, "people in the streets are people always already failing to seize state power."[16] Such views cannot help but see the New Left disruptions as the failed, symbolic, and self-indulgent reenactment of what workers had attempted before. Yet, in doing so, they fundamentally misconstrue what the New Left was attempting to disrupt. To understand what was new about the disruptions of the New Left, we have to stop judging them from the lens of the old. As the Italian student activist and later cultural historian Luisa Passerini remarked, "We realized that, notwithstanding its fascination, the idea of an assault on the Winter Palace was archaic."[17]

The Administered Society

In the half century between the tumultuous postwar worker disruptions and 1968, the regime of movement underwent a serious restructuring across the Atlantic world. The combination of the Great Depression and the Second World War altered its economic operation, means of accumulation, and its impact on and attitude toward the working class. These changes necessitated new forms and practices of disruption.

From its inception in the seventeenth century through World War II, the economy of movement had itself had a disruptive effect on the lives of the lower classes, *the* cause of both mental and physical dislocation, deracination, and alienation throughout the Atlantic world. The massive mobilization of weaponry and bodies conjured by the Second World War was the devastating culmination of these experiences, resulting in the deaths of 80 million human beings (3 percent of the world's population) and displacing 15 million in Europe alone. In its aftermath, a great chunk of the old continent lay in rubble, its families and societies torn apart.

In the immediate postwar period, people wanted to get on with their lives. Across the Atlantic world, there was a generalized retreat into the personal sphere, a distaste for the great transformations and disruptions of the past three decades. It was a time when politics written with a capital *P*, history with a capital *H*, became anathema.

The architects of the postwar Atlantic economy, with the mistakes of their predecessors fresh on their minds, were more than ready to oblige, putting in place broad initiatives aimed at social and economic integration. On the international level, the Bretton Woods monetary order, GATT, the Marshall Plan, and the formation of the European Economic Community created an institutional framework that sought to avoid the twin disruptions of economic depression and war that had plagued the Atlantic world since 1914. On the domestic level, the creation of national welfare states, full-employment economic policies, codetermination between labor and management (especially in the UK and the Federal Republic), and coordinated efforts to discredit communist parties and unions all aimed to end the disruptive politics of class warfare by assimilating the working class into postwar society.

These institutional frameworks were accompanied by ideological war against the Soviet Union and, at the national level, "postideological" discourses that depoliticized social transformation under the rubric of rational social growth. Modernization and development became the catchwords of the age, society's train ride into the future, but one now powered by rational technocratic administration rather than the engine of disruption. Postwar theories of social transformation eschewed critical concepts (exploitation, contradiction, alienation, class) that had provided a systematic critique of the regime of movement. In its place, the new "value-neutral" social sciences focused on the family, bureaucracy, Keynesian economics, and pluralist democracy, categories that could be rationally modernized, but not transcended.[18] Finally, in an effort to close the circle, they promoted theories of "mass politics" and "charisma" that dismissed all attempts to overcome the status quo as irrational.

What the regime of movement offered in return, at least to white members of this society, was commodities. Consumer culture, which gave the promise of fulfilling one's desires and needs through the consumption of goods, became both pacifier and safety valve for millions of individuals throughout the Atlantic world.

Strikingly, the Old Left put up little resistance to, and at times actively embraced, this new social order. With the failure of the worldwide communist uprising that was to follow the Russian Revolution, the Soviet experiment had turned inward, intent on developing "socialism in one country." By the time of Stalin's ascension, Carl Schmitt was depicting Marxism as generically similar to capitalism, a form of "economic thinking" hostile to all genuine politics. "Bolsheviks and American financiers shared the ideal of an electrified earth," Schmitt asserted, "differing only on the correct method of electrification."[19] From the Second World War onward, Communism would be spread (and maintained) by Soviet tanks rather than Leninist calls for global insurrection. For the rest of the world, Moscow's brand of Communism became either a third-world pathway to industrialization or an opposition party with a long history of social democratic capitulations within first-world parliamentary democracies. In either case, it had given up on a politics of disruption.

Anti-Imperial Disruption

The crack in the armor came from international politics. In this regard, the year 1956 proved seminal to the emergence of New Left disruption. Within the span of a few months the British and French invaded Egypt to reassert Western control over the Suez Canal, the French social democratic government pursued a brutal crackdown of Algerian freedom fighters in the Battle of Algiers, and the Red Army's tanks rolled into Hungary. These interventions were a wake-up call for many on the left, exposing the imperial violence with which both the USSR and the West enforced their respective social systems.[20] A decade earlier, in their sweeping analysis of the dialectic of enlightenment, the leading theoreticians of the Frankfurt School had claimed that "the fully administered world radiates disaster triumphant."[21] The scientific and managerial administration of society, rather than guaranteeing human liberation, had led to the gas chambers of Auschwitz. For a younger generation of the left, the postwar world seemed to confirm this trajectory. Wherever they looked, the myths of technocratic and rational progress promoted by their own societies shattered against the harsh reality of Soviet tanks, napalm, and the very real threat of global thermonuclear Armageddon. The 1960s would bring these horrors into sharper relief. America's war in Vietnam, its failed intervention into Cuba, the normalization of French torture in Algeria, the Soviet invasion of Czechoslovakia, and the West's military and political support for repressive regimes in Latin America, Africa, and the Middle East all underscored imperial oppression along a newly imagined global north/south axis.

What was more, unlike the complacency of the European and American left, the third world was fighting back. In Cuba, Algeria, and Vietnam, ordinary men and women had taken up arms to disrupt and remove imperial regimes from their countries. These third-world liberation struggles, in particular, the resistance of the Vietnamese people to foreign domination, served as the catalyst for the birth of a New Left, one that would resurrect the politics of disruption throughout the Atlantic world. From the very beginning, the New Left was internationalist to its core, drawing inspiration, tactics, and their subjectivities from their analyses of (and connections with) third-world struggle.

The guiding principle of this New Left subjectivity was anti-imperial. For its members, the world was governed by an imperial authority, a global, unfeeling, unhearing machine that mobilized bodies and desires to buy its products and carry out its genocidal policies. New Left activist Tom Hayden, writing about the occupations of Columbia University, stated as much: "The Columbia Students were taking an internationalist and revolutionary view of themselves in opposition to imperialism." They aimed "to stop the machine if it cannot be made to serve human ends."[22] Though expressed in many different forms, the New Left shared the feeling that the existing organization of human beings, how they related to one another, the ways they spoke, what they saw and desired, the evaluation of their circumstances, were mechanisms of social control. For New Left activists, these more subtle mechanisms worked alongside the explicit forces of state and economic repression to colonize the lives and even minds of people in late industrial society. The New Left conception of imperialism widened the understanding of oppression, previously thought of in economic terms, to one that extended from foreign policy to domestic social relations, down to individual consciousness itself. As Eldridge Cleaver, an early leader of the Black Panther Party in the United States, put it, "People are colonized, oppressed, and exploited on all levels. Intellectually, Politically, Economically, Emotionally, Sexually, and Spiritually, we are oppressed, exploited, colonized."[23]

This broader critique of imperialism is crucial to understanding the politics of New Left disruption. For the New Left, the social order was not simply in the wrong hands—something that could either be reformed or wrested—but itself suspect. Anti-imperialism, in this sense, meant neither the modification nor the seizure of power but rather, and more profoundly, the devolution or destruction of it. Herbert Marcuse, the leading theoretician of the New Left, called this politics the "Great Refusal."[24] Whether they were attacking a racist or patriarchal system, Vietnam or the university's complicity in it, the New Left conceived of their political action as the desire to either withdraw from or completely irrupt the oppressive movement of the world around them. The Great Refusal was a saying no, an elemental opposition to a system of oppression, a noncompliance with the rules of a rigged game, a form of radical resistance and struggle.[25] As a Berkeley leaflet on student self-management stated, "Protest becomes an outmoded concept ... we are not intent on petitioning leaders to take action on our behalf. We are no longer interested in protesting someone else's politics. Reconstitution is about making our own politics."[26] A sentiment echoed by the popular slogan of the French student revolt first written on the Sorbonne amphitheater: "We won't ask, We won't demand, We will take and occupy."[27] For New Left activists, from the naïve student to militant groups on both sides of the Atlantic, politics became less and less about making claims for inclusion or reform and increasingly marked by a total repudiation of the sociopolitical system. As the Yippies provocatively claimed, "We are not protesting 'issues'; we are protesting Western civilization. We are not hassling over shit so that we can go back to 'normal' lives: *our 'normal' lives are fucked up!*"[28] Or, in the words of Stokely Carmichael, "When you talk of black power you talk about bringing the country to its knees . . . of smashing everything Western civilization has created."[29]

Anti-imperial disruption was a stand against the encroachment of social control into the national, institutional, communal, and individual domains of human existence. Or, put positively, a politics of disruption that asserted the autonomy of these spheres in the face of their colonization. It took place at multiple sites and across multiple registers, informing the politics of efforts to stop the global war machine, arrest police intrusion into Black neighborhoods, or to redefine the social roles, perceptions, and language of everyday life. Though the New Left applied various epithets to denote the imperial mechanisms of social control, "the machine," "the establishment," "the regime," "the man," the most common name used was the *police*. The term referred to both its literal meaning and the wider sense of how modern society policed the desires, horizons, occupational roles, boundaries, and experiential universe of its members. The concept of the police and policing became central to the way the New Left understood subjugation, a multilayered target for the disruptions they undertook to liberate their lives.

The Decolonization of Everyday Life

Whether material or symbolic, the police derived its power from authority. To dismantle (or abolish) the police meant in effect to locate and root out all of the authoritarian structures that governed over human lives. It led the New Left to a profound questioning of the hierarchical and authoritarian tendencies within liberal societies and a politics of disruption against the mechanisms or institutions through which they operated.

As students formed a major part of the New Left, education—its form, content, and purpose—was an early target. The student occupations sought to disrupt both the educational system within the universities and the university's role within society. For many New Left students, these two disruptions were fundamentally linked. University and high-school students disrupted examinations, the "control centers" of education that conditioned students to accept (even seek out) arbitrary authority and hierarchy within the classroom and acquiesce to it within society at large.[30] Students targeted not just how, but also what they were being taught. They asserted that higher education had lost its critical function, becoming a site where future leaders were inculcated in the principles and rules of the social order. "University education," Robin Blackburn, member of the editorial collective of the British *New Left Review*, claimed, "has been reduced to the acquisition of technocratic skills ... vocational training for the market researchers, personnel managers, and investment planners of the future."[31] Students sought to disrupt this integrative function of education, to blockade the reproduction of society in its existing form. "We refuse the role assigned to us: we will not be trained as your police dogs," wrote one student on the walls of Nanterre. Alain Touraine, the French sociologist who witnessed first-hand the Nanterre insurrection, claimed that the 1968 student uprisings were about "transforming the relationship between the young person and society. He was being taught to enter society; he wished to learn how to change it."[32]

The student occupations and strikes that resulted in blockaded or empty classrooms were accompanied by efforts to revamp the higher educational system across the Atlantic world. Initiatives in countercurricula, alternative education courses, and "critical" or "free universities" were often launched during or shortly following student strikes and occupations. First proposed and put into practice by the Free Speech Movement at UC Berkeley, by 1969, the Free University of Berkeley (FUB) was offering 119 courses, with such titles as the "Dialectics of Alienation" and "Revolutionary Thought and Action."[33] By 1970, there were between 300 and 500 Free or Critical universities in the United States alone, with an estimated 100,000 students having taken one or more of their courses. During the occupation of the University of Trento in northern Italy, insurgent students invited leftist guest lecturers, performance artists, and published a countercurriculum in a direct challenge to both the form and content of education administered by the university. A year later, the same groups circulated the "Manifesto for a Negative University," a blueprint for radically reshaping the university from an instrument of class domination to one of liberation.[34] In 1968, Free Universities had been established in England, West Germany, France, Canada, and the Netherlands. Throughout these counterinstitutions, sociological and political vocabulary was stripped of its "false neutrality" and radically moralized in terms of the Great Refusal. Or, as one French student graffitied on the walls of the Sorbonne, "When examined, answer with questions."[35]

To their credit, students quickly realized that the hierarchical and authoritarian nature of education was simply a reflection of the society that had created it. The much bigger problem, as other New Left groups had pointed out, was the material and psychological colonization of everyday life. First and foremost, there was the literal presence of the police, encountered by the white New Left in the form of the National Guard or riot squads, and by Blacks, daily, as the street patrols in their communities. In this context, decolonization meant confronting the authority the police wielded over human lives. "Liberate the Sorbonne from police occupation!" became a key demand of the French student uprising in 1968, one soon to be replicated across universities in Europe. In the United States, decolonization was the explicit intent for the 1966 formation of the Black Panther Party of Self-Defense, whose armed patrols shadowed law-enforcement officers, disrupting their attempts to racially police the "Black colony." Significantly, their projects of neighborhood decolonization embraced the full gamut of anti-imperial politics, from confronting the reign of predatory slum lords (a project also taken up by the Latino Young Lords of Chicago and New York) to burning draft cards, refusing to "fight and kill other people of color who . . . are being victimized by the White racist government of America."[36]

For other, mostly white and educated, members of the New Left, the police became a synecdoche for the social order in its entirety, a generalized epithet by which to implicate and dismiss all authoritarian tendencies within society and the individual. Through this equation, the New Left marked authority itself as fundamentally antisocial. For the most part, the white New Left preferred (and had the luxury of) insolence over violent confrontation as a way of disrobing vested authority. The first principle of the *Antiauthoritarian Manifesto of the Artistic Avant-Garde*, issued by the German collective *Gruppe Spur* in 1961, stated that "whoever does not see politics, government, church, industry, military, the political parties, and social organizations as a joke has nothing to do with us."[37] Jerry Rubin, in his three appearances before the House Un-American Activities Committee (HUAC), dressed as an American Revolutionary War soldier, a bare-chested armed guerrilla, and Santa Claus. Even Eldridge Cleaver, who took up a more militant approach, saw the merits of insolence. "A laughed at pig is a dead pig," he claimed, "barbequed Yippie style."[38]

These provocations toward vested authority were part of a larger project to disrupt the habituated behaviors and norms of modern society, a policing of the self that enabled the smooth operation of the regime of movement. "The consumer economy has introjected into the very nature of man aspirations and patterns of behavior that ties him libidinally and aggressively to the commodity form," Herbert Marcuse wrote. "It instills the need for possessing, consuming, handling, and constantly renewing the gadgets, devices, instruments, and engines offered to and imposed upon the people."[39] For Marcuse, this "voluntary" servitude, so internalized as to have become second nature, militated against any change that would disrupt it. Within late industrial capitalism, the individual—her roles, experiences, language, and desires—had become wholly determined by society, to the point where humans were not even aware of their subjugation. The things we wanted, saw, spoke, and felt imprisoned us to a society not of our making. In short, we had become our own police. A sentiment perhaps more pithily encapsulated by another of the French May's famous slogans, "A cop sleeps inside each one of us. We must kill him."[40]

Killing the cop inside us meant driving a wedge between the individual and the administered society, a disruption into the mechanisms by which human beings internalized its worldview as their own. At the forefront of such initiatives were the small group of artists and activists that formed the Situationist International (SI). Deeply influenced by Marx, the Situationists adopted and expanded the concepts of alienation, reification, and commodity fetishism to make sense of the administered society. For the Situationists, these concepts no longer or not only described economic relations (the nature of work or commodities) but characterized life under late industrial capitalism in its totality.

Objectification and estrangement typified all of our social relations, the situationists argued, occluding the possibility of authentic encounters and relationships. To counter what they termed the "society of the spectacle," the SI constructed public disruptions intended to jolt or shock people out of their uncritical submission to the regime of movement. Called "situations," these brief moments in space and time would underscore the colonization of life by interrupting its mechanisms and flows. For the Belgian SI theorist Raoul Vaneigem, this was an essential step toward liberation. "People who talk about revolution and class struggle without explicitly referring to everyday life, without understanding what is subversive about the refusal of constraints—such people have a corpse in their mouths."[41]

The Situationists' often-playful theatrical disruptions of everyday life were soon adapted by many New Left groups on both sides of the Atlantic. In Amsterdam, the Dutch *Provos* wreaked havoc on rush-hour traffic by releasing thousands of chickens onto the streets, while students at the University of Santa Barbara treated the main road leading into campus with lard, bringing traffic to a standstill.[42] In 1970, over 1,000 students at the University of Connecticut walked into an ROTC building armed with brushes and painted the walls with flowers, cartoons, and peace symbols.[43] The Yippies brought panic to the New York Stock Exchange by throwing money onto the trading floor and staged a "yip-in" that shut down Grand Central Station before being brutally dispersed by the police.[44] In both these events, Yippies took aim at the city's most famous sites of circulation, momentarily disrupting the flow of financial capital and human beings within the regime of movement. The point of such disruptions, as the West German Situationist group *Subversive Aktion* proclaimed, was to "interrupt the influences on the individual posed by society, allowing them to pause and reflect so that they could define themselves independently from authority."[45]

The self-policing of modern society, many in the New Left claimed, ran through language. "We live within language as within polluted air," Guy Debord wrote. "The problem of language is at the heart of all struggles between the forces striving to abolish present alienation and those striving to maintain it."[46] The colonization of human beings by the language they used, how speech had itself become a way of policing the population, became a staple critique across the New Left spectrum. Linguistic colonization took two principal forms: the individual's uncritical reproduction of words (and thereby concepts) necessary for the war and consumer machines and the sterilization of once subversive speech now reincorporated into mainstream society—a "recuperation" that took place increasingly through product advertising (*A Revolution in Motor Oil!*).[47]

The effort to free words from the distortion of their meanings by the administered society required "a transfer of moral standards (and of their validation) from the Establishment to the revolt against it."[48] Word play, irony, and reversal, by disrupting ordinary speech, challenged the individual's uncritical internalization of the language of the social order. These reversals of meaning were evinced across the New Left, from the hippies' "flower power," with their attendant act of placing flowers in the gun barrels of soldiers and police, to the Black Power slogan "Black is Beautiful," which disrupted centuries of the Western concept's association with the color white. Disruptive language was employed to delegitimize authority—as when the Black Panthers took to calling government leaders President X or Governor Y, Pig X or Pig Y, and translated their speech as "oink oink"—or to discredit establishment phrases of submission, such as "Be realistic," to which the French 1968 uprising famously appended, "Demand the impossible." As Stokely Carmichael put it, "We shall have to struggle for the right to create our own terms through which to define ourselves and our relationship to the society, and to have these terms recognized."[49] A sentiment shared by the left anthropologist Michel de Certeau, who, reflecting on the power of speech in '68 Paris, remarked, "We began to speak, as if for the first time. The previously self-assured discourses faded away and the 'authorities' were reduced to silence."[50]

The New Left's Politics of Disruption

By the mid-1970s, the anti-imperial consensus that had animated New Left disruptions had dissolved. An internal dynamic of radicalization, the end of the major third-world liberation struggles, and the state-targeted repression of militant groups all contributed to the fragmentation of the New Left alliance. In its brief life span, the politics of anti-imperial disruption straddled two worlds: the last manifestation of an older politics and the first of a new one.

Whether arresting the war machine or decolonizing universities, minority neighborhoods, and minds, the New Left framed their anti-imperial disruptions as part of a wider global politics of human liberation. This linking of the particular and the universal, a marriage first formed in the initial weeks of the French Revolution, allowed New Left activists to identify and struggle against a single enemy. The hierarchical and authoritarian structures of higher education and the workplace, the compartmentalization of life into discrete spheres of activity and competence, the internal policing of minorities, and the waging of foreign war were understood by the New Left as the multiple faces of a singular underlying oppression, though experienced differentially according to one's geography, class, race, and gender.

Moreover, the identification of a single enemy enabled the New Left to understand the interconnectedness of their struggles, allowing them to draw connections and solidarities across national and identarian grammars of discontent. They linked student and worker struggles, associated anticapitalist disruption in Europe with anti-imperialism abroad, and took a few awkward steps on the path intersecting racial, gender, and class liberation.

Beyond this universalism, the New Left also borrowed tactically from past disruptors. The sit-in strikes and industrial sabotage that arrested production in the factories found their counterparts in the occupations and theatrical disruptions of public space. In fact, New Left politics was very self-consciously articulated and fashioned in relation to the old. It was an attempt to recenter a politics of disruption that had, the New Left felt, been largely abandoned by the official wings of the workers' struggle. As Marcuse noted,

> The disruptive politics of the Parisian students momentarily broke through the memory repression of organized labor and recalled, for a very short moment, the historical power of the general strike and the factory occupation, of the red flag and the International.[51]

It is possible to trace this undercurrent of disruption in the periodicals and magazines of the early New Left on both sides of the Atlantic. Publications such as *Dissent*, *Liberation*, *Monthly Review*, and later *Radical America* in the United States, *New Left Review* in the UK, and their continental counterparts, such as *Funken*, *Pro und Contra*,

Sozialistische Politik, and *Die Andere Zeitung* in Germany; *Arguments* and *Socialisme ou Barbarie* in France; and *Passato and Presente*, *Quaderni Rossi*, and *Classe Operaia* in Italy all examined worker tactics and strategy while eschewing the orthodoxies of old labor.[52]

What had changed was the sites on which these disruptive strategies were carried out. Where workers had targeted capitalist production, the New Left sought to interrupt the circulation of the entire social body, itself oftentimes likened to a giant machine. In this sense, the disruptions of universities, of public throughways, of newspapers, police patrols, courthouses, draft induction centers, and even language were all part of a larger shift that gave primacy to social relations over the forces of production.

The New Left disruptions also inaugurated two others shifts in the politics of disruption. First, though by no means ubiquitous, there was a general trend away from strategies of seizing power to those that sought its dissolution. The aim of many New Left disruptions became less and less about the control of authority centers and more and more an effort to extract humans from their subjugating influences. Second, these same anti-authoritarian impulses led to a reformulation of the role of disruption within history. Certain vanguardist groups notwithstanding, there was a general reluctance to inscribe disruption within a longer predetermined progressive project, a turn away from the Hegelian idea—central to the radical praxis of the workers' struggle—that disruption was the engine that pushed society from a less free to a freer state of existence. For a good majority of the New Left, disruption was not a stepping stone to future utopia, but a way to change the social relations of the present. As Jerry Rubin averred, "Revolution did not mean the end of the war or the end of racism. Revolution meant the creation of new men and women. Revolution meant a new life. On earth. Today."[53]

4

Extraction

Europe now lives at such a mad, reckless pace that ... she is running headlong into the abyss. Let us flee from this motionless movement where the dialectic has given way to the logic of equilibrium. This pathological tearing apart of humanity's functions and the crumbling away of its unity ... the differentiations, the stratification, slavery, and exploitation.

Humanity is waiting for something other from us. Comrades, we must invent and we must make discoveries ... we must work out new concepts, and try to set afoot, a new human being.

Frantz Fanon

On May 24, 1968, a 100,000-strong crowd of students and workers, chanting "Your struggle is ours," began their march on the Bastille. This conjoining of the university and factory uprisings, no less through a symbolic reenactment of the events of July 14, 1789, sent chills down the spine of De Gaulle's government. The French state, faced with the terrifying prospect of workers and students uniting to form a new revolutionary subject, sprang to action, creating a wall of police to drive the demonstrators back to the Latin Quarter. In the days that followed, the careful and tactical policing of the streets was matched by an even more calculated media operation to segregate the masses of revolting French into their constituent parts. As Prime Minister Georges Pompidou later remarked, "I wanted to treat the problem of the youth separately." To divide the two back into their sociological identities, where the strike would become a wage, or "bread and butter issue," and student demands treated as an "educational" problem.[1] As long as the workers remained sequestered inside their occupied factories while the students relived the "myth of the barricades" in the confines of the Latin Quarter, the French state would remain intact. A few months later, Alain Touraine underscored this tactic of compartmentalization. "In the hands of its managers," he argued, society was "dismantled like a machine, each piece dealt with in a special shop or milieu."[2]

In the 1960s, the compartmentalization of the social terrain, the differentiation of human beings into exclusive spheres and functions, became a focal point of analysis and action for both the regime of movement and its detractors—profoundly altering the politics of disruption. For its upholders, the compartmentalization of subjects and spaces was a divide-and-conquer strategy wrapped in new clothes. It gave rise to different experiences, vocabularies, and hierarchies among the oppressed, creating distinctions (as with the workers and students of France) that segregated opposition to the regime. At the same time, the compartmentalization of daily life, the delineation of what kinds of people, under which conditions, could do what and where became a means for marketizing activities such as leisure, education, housework, and health care, creating new pathways of predation for the regime of movement.

As early as 1961, Frantz Fanon had appraised the differentiated spaces and subjects of colonialism in similar fashion. To understand capital accumulation in the colonies, Fanon argued, one had to move beyond the factory gates: to see the extraction of surplus value not only in the sites of commodity production, but as a process that was embedded into—and made possible by—colonial social relations in their entirety. For Fanon, exploitation was built into the very terrain of the colony, into the racial organization of colonial space and subjectivity. It was enforced and operated through multiple nodes: the mines, to be sure, but also the schools, living quarters, churches, transport, infrastructure, and the army. The colonial spatial order was composed of manifold zones of exclusivity that both created and kept separate the social kinds of the colony. The organization of these zones and the subjectivities within them, the policing of their gates, what it was possible to do or think inside each, were as fundamental to the functioning of the colonial economy as the industries and plantations set up by the colonizer. The central aim of anticolonial struggle, Fanon argued, was nothing other than the total destruction of these zones.

Fanon's analysis of space and subjectivity, while manifest most starkly in the colonies, resonated with struggles throughout the Atlantic. It was first and most directly adapted by advocates of Black Power, who argued that Blacks constituted an internal colony of the United States whose segregated ghettos had become new sites of predation. Around the same time, and in a quite different context, the Italian theorists of *operaismo* (workerism) were developing a similar spatial and subjective framework for analyzing capitalism. Much like Fanon's description of the colony, the workerists contended that the advanced economies of the capitalist world had reached a stage where every social relation had come under the sway of capital, collapsing any distinction between society and its sites of commodity production. In such a stage, the workerists argued, society itself became a factory and social relations *directly became relations of production*. A few years later, radical feminists turned this same lens onto the home, directing attention toward the social differentiation of subjects and spaces by gender.

And they were not alone. Influenced by the ideas of the global anticolonial and American civil rights struggles, New Left groups across the Atlantic were elaborating a more intricate understanding of the regime of movement. Rather than seeing the regime as a homogeneous force compelling the motion of goods and bodies, they underscored its production of, and reliance upon the segregation of human beings by social kind. On the broadest level, various currents of the New Left began to explore the mechanisms of this differentiating power, the grooves etched into the social terrain that demarcated the possible motions of specific subjects. They began to understand the regime as an ordering power: as the power to name, sort, distribute, and partition people into discrete subjects with separate functions, capacities, and geographies.

And, just as quickly, they took to disrupting this power. Across the Atlantic, New Leftists created new institutional and situational forms, some ephemeral and others more enduring, that tore down the rigid pathways of the regime of movement by bringing together people of different ages, races, occupations, and social milieu. Opposition to the Vietnam War occasioned thousands of such groupings in the United

States, creating unforeseen alliances across different social sectors. In 1968 France, *comités d'action* sprang up in factories, neighborhoods, high schools, and university campuses, crisscrossing the boundaries that divided French society. By the end of May, there were over 420 such committees in the Paris region alone. These often-leaderless groups explicitly rejected the idea of expertise, of segregated and exclusive spheres of human activity, and naturalized domains of competence. As the radical art collective *Atelier Populaire* that occupied the *École des Beaux-Arts* in May 1968 affirmed, "Bourgeois culture separates and isolates artists from other workers. It encloses artists in an invisible prison. We have decided to transform what we are in society."[3] Within these new collectives, the New Left questioned what it meant to be a student, an artist, a worker, and a woman, as well as why these roles took place at specific and segregated sites (the school, the factory, the studio, the home). Outwardly, their very existence disrupted the demarcation and regulation of who should be doing what, why, and where.

If the regime's power derived from its authority to differentiate subjects and demarcate spaces, liberation from this power rested in the refusal and appropriation of this authority. This chapter examines the politics of disruption from the mid-1960s through the 1970s via three instances of this refusal/appropriation: Black Power, *operaismo*, and radical feminism in Italy and the United States.

The bulk of the chapter focuses on subjectivity, tracing the history of the self-creation of Blacks, workers, and women as political subjects. It underscores how this becoming-subject was carried out through disruption. This disruption involved, crucially, two simultaneous actions. The first was a negative one, the withdrawal of consent—a refusal to be categorized, ordered, dispensed, and understood on the terms assigned by the regime of movement. Disruption, in this negative sense, meant the extraction of oneself from one's ascribed place and role, a deactivation, a "radical subtraction," a becoming "inoperable" to the regime of movement. Second, simultaneous to, and made possible by, this negative act was the positive assertion of subjectivity—"the entering into history," the deployment, self-valorization, and self-determination of a political subject by itself on new terms that had been previously unrepresentable, if not uninhabitable, within the regime of movement.

Antagonism was key to this disruptive politics. The new subjects not only rejected their present ascription within the regime but made clear that their subjectivity was incompatible with its future continuation. They did not seek to recalibrate the existing distributions of the regime or to be incorporated on equal footing with other social kinds. They were "unruly" or "unexpected" subjects precisely because (and only in so far as) they disrupted the ordering power of the regime itself.

But what were workers, or women, or Blacks if they refused both the categories that had oppressed them *and* integration into the universal order of their oppressors? This chapter examines the radical solutions to this question as they were articulated by Black Power, workerism, and radical feminism in Italy and the United States. It details how, in less than a decade, these disruptive subjects created new forms of politics, new ways of being with each other, new definitions of justice and humanity, as well as new institutions of care, belonging, provisioning, and policing.

Yet, to bring these to birth, they needed space. For these disruptive subjects, the question of who they were became intimately bound to where they were, the structure and purpose of the spaces they inhabited. They pointed out the overt or hidden rules and procedures that governed these spaces, the institutions and norms that established a connection between "activity" and "location" that defined the behaviors "suitable" to a given place. The more they examined the often-naturalized environments in which they (were) raised, worked, exchanged, tidied, created, and lived, the more they became aware that these spaces were designed for segregation, predation, and domination.

Three short vignettes, interspersed throughout the chapter, tell the stories of these spaces. They describe how these spaces were transformed by disruptive struggle. How the subjects who inhabited them challenged not only what was done there and those doing it, but also what could be seen, heard, named, and understood in a given place. The disruption of the established spatial order and the simultaneous creation of new patterns of movement, behavior, and norms was a very visceral experience, the material complement to the discourses of self-valorization, autonomy, and self-determination deployed by the emergent disruptive subjects.

Rather than analyzing the history of these spaces from above, I have sketched the vignettes horizontally, imagining how it felt to inhabit such spaces as they were transformed through disruptive struggle. The three vignettes are narrated in the first or second person from the point of view of three characters: a Black feminist in New York; a young male autoworker in Turin; and a three-story building in Oakland, California.

These characters, while drawn from a variety of historical documents, including worker questionnaires, autobiography, pamphlets, oral histories, newspapers, memoirs, plays, and secondary literature, are fictional. They are composite narratives created by me in the hope of providing a topographic sense of the politics of disruption.

Black Power

The American Negro can no longer, nor ever again, be controlled by white America's image of him.

James Baldwin

We blacks must respond in our own way, on our own terms ... The definition of ourselves, the roles we pursue, the goals we seek, are our own responsibility.

Stokely Carmichael

In August 1965, the people of Watts, Los Angeles, rebelled against their life conditions. For five days, they burned and looted white-owned businesses and engaged in continuous warfare with city police and federal troops. Over 30,000 Blacks actively took part in the rebellion, confronting an occupying force of 14,000 guardsmen and 16,000 officers.[4] Chief Parker of the LAPD called the uprising an "insurgency," compared it to fighting the Vietcong, and decreed a "paramilitary" response to the disorder. By the time the smoke had settled, thirty-four people had died, 3,000 people had been arrested, and 977 buildings had been damaged or destroyed. Within three years, similar Black uprisings tore through the urban United States. The long summer of 1967, led by Newark and Detroit, saw 159 rebellions; the assassination of Dr. King the following year sparked over 100 more. All told, the official reports tallied nearly 300 deaths, 13,000 injuries, 60,000 arrests, and hundreds of millions of dollars in property damage.[5]

Of all the disavowals of the regime of movement, the Black rebellions that scorched the United States in the second half of the 1960s were, both in form and voice, the most democratic. Spontaneous in origin and largely leaderless, Black Americans burned the withdrawal of their consent on cities across the country. From their ashes rose the organizations of Black Power: the Black Panther Party in Oakland, the US Organization in Los Angeles, the Congress of African People in Newark, and the Shrine of the Black Madonna, the Republic of New Africa, and the League of Revolutionary Black Workers in Detroit all joined newly radicalized civil rights organizations, including the Student Nonviolent Coordinating Committee (SNCC) and the Congress of Racial Equality (CORE).[6]

That the Watts Rebellion occurred less than a week after the passage of the landmark 1965 Voting Rights Act did not go unremarked by contemporary observers. For its supporters, the VRA was the outcome of years of civil rights organizing, a testament to the inclusion of Blacks within the democratic social order. Hands that once picked cotton, it was noted at the time, could now pick presidents. Those same hands, it turned out, could also throw Molotov cocktails. Watts sent a clear signal that, for many Blacks, the legal victories of the civil rights movement had done little to address, much less resolve, the systematic racism that pervaded the social and economic fabric of the United States.

Led by a younger, more militant generation, the dominant strands of Black Power rejected both the institutional structures of the United States and the recent attempts of the civil rights movement to integrate Black people into them.[7] The Black nationalist and poet LeRoi Jones, among the thousands arrested in the long, hot summer of 1967, aptly conveyed this new orientation.

> Again and again, we have sought to plead with reference to a progressive humanism. Again and again our complaints have been denied by an unfeeling, racist government. Now, we will govern ourselves, or no one will govern Newark, New Jersey at all.[8]

The "Negro's" place in the regime of movement

The transatlantic economy had, from its very beginning, been a racialized regime of movement. The inexhaustible need for labor to exploit the newly established colonies of Americas, initially provided by the Indigenous, then white indentured servitude, had over the course of the seventeenth century been addressed by the kidnapping and forced movement of Black humans from Africa to the thirteen colonies. The end of the transatlantic slave trade in 1808 led to a large and dynamic internal market of human property within the United States that continued to uproot slaves, rip apart families, and reproduce a supply of labor through institutionalized rape.

This initial racialization, differentiating discrete pathways by which Black and non-Black populations were moved, their relation to the means of production, the uses of their labor, and the techniques by which this labor was disciplined, all became fundamental to the operation of the regime of movement. The end of slavery in the United States did little to change this racialized ordering. Following abolition, new Black Codes were put in place proscribing a range of actions—including vagrancy, absence from work, breach of job contracts, possession of firearms, petty theft, even insulting gestures or acts—that were crimes only when the person committing them was Black. The "criminalization of Blackness" reversed the racial composition of prison populations and led to a fundamental shift of the Southern criminal justice system: from disciplining poor whites to a regime for managing Black labor. Convict leasing, or the practice of paying the state a monthly sum in exchange for a prisoner's labor, became both a means to extend slavery after its formal abolition and the primary engine of Southern industrialization.[9]

In the late nineteenth and early twentieth century, Jim Crow laws in the South and de facto segregation in the north and west—excluding Blacks from white schools, white unions, white churches, and white neighborhoods—formalized the economic, educational, and social inferiority of Blacks throughout the country. The racialized application of the GI Bill, federal housing programs, and the redlining practices of the postwar period—effectively foreclosing Black home and business ownership—became the new hallmarks of a state-sanctioned racial capitalism begun over 300 years ago.

Meanwhile, in the century following the Civil War, African Americans had watched as successive waves of European immigrants—the Irish, then Italian, then Slavs—became white. While the racial assimilation of the new European arrivals allowed them access to the stolen land and productivity gains of American capitalism, the "negro was always and forever a negro." This racial consensus, as Nikhil Singh has brilliantly traced, depended upon the fundamental exclusion of blackness from American cultural and social life.[10] Within white America, Black people were the part of no part, lying outside; yet for precisely this reason, foundational to America's representational order.

As more and more European immigrant workers traded in their prewar radicalism for the promises of the American Dream, few Blacks could internalize the aspiration to personal advancement, progress, and constant upward motion offered by the regime of movement.[11] By the mid-1960s, the racial capitalism of the United States had excluded Blacks from the modest capital accumulation of the emerging white middle class and removed Blacks from its social imaginary. The massive urban uprisings that began with Watts were plain recognition that the de jure end of segregation and the legal integration of "the Negro" through the Civil Rights Acts did not and could not alter the material, cultural, or psychic registers of this structural exclusion.[12]

If the urban rebellions were the disruptive withdrawal of consent to being Black in America, Black Power was the positive assertion of Black subjectivity on its own terms. In this very general sense, Black Power meant self-determination. The opening point of the 1967 Black Panther Program was clear, "We want Freedom. We want the power to determine the destiny of the Black community." Or as Stokely Carmichael averred, Black Power meant "exercising control over our lives, politically, economically, psychically."[13] Such ideas caught on like wildfire. In less than a year, Black Power had effectively replaced civil rights as the dominant ideological concept among a majority of Black youths and significant portions of the Black working and middle classes.[14] But what did self-determination mean? How was it to be put into practice? By 1970, dozens of Black Power organizations attracting tens of thousands of members attempted to answer these two questions. The astounding breadth of ideas and institutions they generated speaks volumes to both the richness of the Black radical tradition and the radical indeterminacy of a political subject at its birth.

Self-definition: from "Negro" to Black

In 1903, W. E. B. Du Bois argued that whites had the power to define and determine not only how a Black person was perceived by others but also how Blacks saw themselves. "It is a peculiar sensation, this double-consciousness; this sense of always looking at one's self through the eyes of others."[15] Through the eyes of white society, the Negro is filled with doubt, Du Bois claimed, and begins to question his "worth as a human being." Black Power, in this sense, was the explicit rejection of this gaze, a refusal to understand oneself through the present eyes and past scripts of white America. As James Baldwin remarked as early as 1960, "The American Negro can no longer, nor ever again, be controlled by white America's image of him."[16]

The fulcrum of this disavowal swung through the politics of naming: discarding of a name within a white lexicon in favor of a name that the new subject could imbue with its own meaning. The passage from Negro to Black. "Negro was invented by our oppressor," Stokely Carmichael asserted. "We must redefine ourselves. This is the first necessity of a free people, and the first right that any oppressor must suspend."[17] "The *Negro* is not a man," Lewis Michaux, the owner of the renowned African National Memorial Bookstore in Harlem, claimed. "*It's* a thing to be used, abused, accused, and confused."[18] If, as S. E. Anderson stated, "the aim of black power was to change Negroes into Blacks,"[19] this required a transition from objectification to subjectification, the process by which Blacks would begin to define who they were themselves.

Culturally, Black Power was an affirmation of the Black body and speech. The kinky hair, the thick lips, ethnic English, an entire "heritage of demeaning definitions imposed on us, over centuries of colonial conditioning" were reappropriated as markers of dignity and pride.[20] Black was Beautiful. As the conk hairstyles of the 1950s—and with them the self-degradation of applying burning chemicals to one's hair—gave way to the Afro, Black Power "mark[ed] the end of an era in which Black men devoted themselves to pathetic attempts to be white men and inaugurated an era in which black people will set their own standards of beauty, conduct and accomplishment."[21]

For others, becoming Black was about economic and political self-determination. At the Black Political Convention in Newark, amid the tumultuous unrest following the assassinations of Martin Luther King Jr. and Robert Kennedy, LeRoi Jones called for "The Political Emergence of the Black Man." Herman Ferguson of the Revolutionary Action Movement (RAM) distinguished between a Negro politics that did not "minister to our struggle for survival and liberation" and a Black politics that would find "radical solutions" to ghetto economics and life in the racist workplace. For the Black radical Marxist and auto worker James Boggs, blackness as it existed within the racist capitalism of America "exposed the failure of a system that had put economics in command of politics." He urged Blacks to take up a subjectivity that "put politics in command of economics." In other words, the creation of Black revolutionary subjects able to determine their own motions rather than resign themselves to the predatory pathways provided by the regime of movement.[22]

Becoming Black also prompted a deep dive into history.[23] The passage from Negro to Black wasn't just a new label for one's skin color, but was about understanding what had been inscribed and invested into that skin ever since the first Africans were kidnapped from the shores of Africa. It meant to *think* Black. This intense and far-reaching historical project involved a brutal examination of that inscription, an understanding of blackness as a unique form of historical oppression. The Maoist activists of RAM called for a "cultural revolution" that would purge the slave mentality from Black people in the United States by rooting out the habits, traditions, customs, and philosophies taught to them by white oppressors.[24] Others saw in this history a potential power. Earlier socialists like C. L. R. James had argued that the "special degradation" of the Black proletariat made them "the more revolutionary section of the population." Ironically, it was their exclusion from American capitalism that provided Black workers with autonomous impetus to challenge it.[25] In the 1970s, James Boggs furthered this line of thinking. For Boggs, Black people's status as the most wretched of the earth was also the source of their strength, a ward against the allures of an American Dream that had consumed so many others, the guarantor of the Black worker's privileged place in igniting and leading the revolution against capital.[26]

Alongside the inquiries into Black enslavement and resistance was the recuperation of the history of Blacks outside of it. As the sociologist Orlando Patterson remarked in 1971, "The present Black Movement in the US is perhaps singular in the intensity of its involvement with the past and in the demands made upon history for the affirmation of racial pride and dignity."[27] For cultural variants of Black nationalism in particular, the historical investigation into blackness meant eschewing the period of slavery altogether. The wide-reaching search for self in African culture, involving earnest if often dislocating pilgrimages, the importation of African clothing, and inquiry into precolonial African sociological formations were among the pathways of this exploration. As was the renaming of the self: the shedding of slave names and the reclamation of African ancestry. So it was that LeRoi Jones became Imamu Baraka, Stokely Carmichael became Kwame Ture, Stanley McClinton became Kimathi Mohammed, Edward Cooper became Modibo Kadalie. Malcolm Little was the name that "the white slavemaster . . . had imposed upon [his] paternal forebears," one he replaced with an *X*, representing the unknown name of his African ancestors and the culture he had been uprooted from.[28]

Autonomy, not integration

For Harold Cruse—among the foremost theorists of 1960s Black nationalism—the Negro was the product of colonization, a type of subjectivity corresponding to the Black colony. "The man that inhabits these countries is a dependent being, a sub-man," Cruse argued. "Such a man depends not on himself but on other men and other outside worlds that order him around, counsel and guide him like a newly born infant." A sentiment echoed by Stokely Carmichael, who likened the well-meaning white liberal NGOs to modern-day colonial missionaries that "come into our ghettos to Head Start, Upward Lift, Bootstrap, and Upward Bound us into white society."[29] As the political scientist James Wilson in his 1960 tract *Negro Politics* put it, "Things are often done for, or about, or to, or because of Negroes."[30] The history of slavery, its literal objectification of the Black human being as property, had left deep marks. For advocates of Black Power, disavowal of white America's gaze could never simply be a reflexive act of self-definition. It was not enough to think Black; one had to *do* Black as well.

The need for Black autonomous organizations, separate from whites, was a near-unanimous principle of the Black Power struggle. Self-determination, in this sense, meant not only the democratic ability to govern one's life, but an act of negation, the disruption of a half millennia of blackness as object. One pathway of this self-organization, the only one less actively resisted by the regime of movement, was Black capitalism: the development of Black free enterprise and a Black bourgeoisie. The economic power gained from organizing Black capital would, its advocates argued, translate into political power: the integration of Blacks into American civic life and representation in the councils of government. In fact, the first Black Power conference organized by Nathan Wright, a Black Republican, in a plush white-owned hotel, drew together middle-class Black professionals for whom Black Power meant getting a "fair share" of American capitalism. A message quickly picked up by Richard Nixon, whose re-election campaign likened Black Power and its slogans of Black "pride," "ownership," "capital," "self-assurance," and "self-respect" to the credos of private enterprise itself.[31]

Employing the sociological critique of the Black bourgeoisie theorized by Franklin Frazier and Frantz Fanon, the dominant strands of Black Power subjected the advocates of Black capitalism to heavy critique. Leading the charge was Harold Cruse, who lambasted integrationism as the philosophy of the Black middle class, serving their economic self-interest and pursuit of establishment credentials. Instead, Cruse argued that "the Negro is not really a part of the American nation ... not related to the 'we'—the Negro is the 'they,' a colonial being."[32] The Black nationalist minister, Albert B. Cleage Jr., founder of the Shrine of the Black Madonna Church and author of The Black Messiah, likewise excoriated integrationism as an individual escape from the psychological and physical condition of the Negro. The Negro was the product of a collective oppression. One that could only be overcome through collective struggle. Salvation for Blacks, Cleage preached, lay not in the individual redemption taught by white Christianity but as and through the Black population as a whole.[33]

For most Black Power struggles, self-determination did not mean gaining access to markets, equal citizenship, or integrating Black people into a common national subjectivity. Rather, these struggles explicitly pointed out the false universalism of American civic discourse, which was to them, fundamentally structured by Black exclusion. Autonomy meant a rejection not only of "the Negro's" place within the social order, but of the very principles on which that order was founded. Robert S. Browne, founder of the Black Economic Research Center in Harlem in 1969, saw in the "disproportionately large number of Negro law violators, of unwed mothers, of non-working adults" the Black's rejection of the core values of "the Anglo-Saxon system of organizing human relationships" in the United States.[34] For Stokely Carmichael, the values of this white middle class, ones that favored "material aggrandizement" over the "expansion of humanity," the "sanctity of property" over the "dignity of man," "free enterprise" over "free people," formed the backbone of institutional racism in America. In its place, Carmichael argued, "We blacks must respond in our own way, on our own terms . . . The definition of ourselves, the roles we pursue, the goals we seek, are our own responsibility."[35]

In etching this new terrain, Black Power organizations drew inspiration from intellectual sources outside the sanctioned boundaries of US political culture, including Islam, international socialism, Caribbean and African nationalism, and Third Worldism. In this sense, Black Power was polyvalent in both its roots and expression. The political subjects formed through these framings allowed Blacks to not only disassociate themselves from the subjectivities offered within the US regime of movement but to deploy new subjectivities that widened the circle of a common humanity.[36]

Yet, if the Black struggle in the United States had shifted from integration to disruption, how was this disruption to be organized? Would it be through directing spontaneous rebellion? Industrial action? Vanguard insurrection? Who would lead it? The Black worker? The lumpenproletariat? The students that Du Bois had called the Talented Tenth? Where was this struggle to take place? At the point of production? Within the Black ghetto? The mosque? The university? In international forums? These questions and the answers to them would animate the organizations of Black Power from the mid-1960s through the 1970s.

Despite the, at times, very incompatible visions and practices of Black autonomy, one thing was clear to all strains of Black Power: the liberation of Blacks in the United States was fundamentally linked to global liberation. As Stokely Carmichael put it, "There is nothing unilateral about the movement to free black people."[37] Internationalism enabled Black Power struggles to reject the integrationist ideologies now reluctantly on offer to Blacks by the regime of movement (equal opportunity, upward mobility, racial advancement) in order to discover autonomous political subjectivities that sought the disruption of this regime itself. This internationalism drew from a long twentieth-century tradition of Black radicalism, was theorized from the very beginnings of Black Power, and remained a constant throughout.[38] W. E. B. Du Bois, in his 1928 novel *Dark Princess*, had argued that the Black nation in America was just one faction of what he referred to as the "Land of the Blacks," a conglomeration of all racially subjugated groups around the world.[39] In the 1930s, the founder and prophet of the Nation of Islam, Fard Muhammad, claimed that Blacks were the original people who ruled from Asia and rejected the term "Africa" as a colonial invention for dividing the "East Asian" Blacks from other Asiatic people of color.[40] In his 1961 masterpiece, *The Wretched of the Earth* (whose French title derived from the opening lyrics of "The Internationale"), Frantz Fanon argued that only global solidarity could create an international consciousness necessary to discover values for a new liberated human being. Echoing Fanon, the author and essayist John O. Killens argued that Black Americans were tied to other people of color of the world through the heel of white supremacy. "We have all been 'niggerized,'" Killen stated. "And all of us are determined to 'deniggerize' the earth. To rid the world of 'niggers' is the Black Man's Burden, human reconstruction is the grand objective."[41]

The story of autonomy, internationalism, and the Black Power struggle is fascinating and tendrilous: its vines extend from a meeting between Castro and Malcolm in Harlem, weave through the Palestinian Liberation Organization and the Vietcong, and reach Algeria, North Korea, and West Germany. As good a place as any to enter into this story, however, is with RAM. One of the earliest Black Power organizations in the United States, the Revolutionary Action Movement was founded in Ohio in 1962, with subsequent major chapters operating in Philadelphia and Oakland, California. In its theoretical journal, *Black America*, RAM insisted that Blacks in the United States must "internationalize our struggle" and join what Malcolm X, who became a RAM officer in 1964, referred to as the "worldwide struggle of the oppressed against the oppressor."[42] Its stated aims were as follows:

To present a revolutionary program of national liberation and self-determination for the African captives enslaved in the racist United States of America. To forge a revolutionary unity among peoples of African descent and to give a new international spirit to Pan-Africanism. To unite Black America with the Bandung world (Asia, Africa and Latin America). To fight for the liberation of oppressed peoples everywhere.[43]

For RAM activists, these objectives were interlinked; their disruptive actions were part of a broader strategy of encircling capitalist countries to challenge a global imperialism. "The Afroamerican revolutionary, being inside the citadel of world imperialism [has] a position so strategic that victory means the downfall of the arch enemy of the oppressed (the US) and the beginning of the birth of a new world."[44] Solidarity, for RAM, meant fighting at home alongside other anticolonial struggles in China, Japan, Zanzibar, Cuba, Vietnam, Panama, Indonesia, and Algeria.[45]

In its fall 1964 issue, RAM painted a portrait of this fight, envisioning a scenario of mass disruption. A Black mutiny from the Armed Forces, joining the Black Liberation Forces who would "strike by night, sparing none," "sabotaging the cities," and take down "the electrical power, then transportation grids," engage in nonstop guerrilla warfare, leading to total chaos, a Wall Street crash, and the incapacitation of Washington, DC, through Black riots.[46] To organize such a force, RAM advocated a three-pronged approach that entailed: (1) the formation of an armed revolutionary Black Guard, (2) the creation of Black worker "liberation union" cells inside US factories, and (3) a national liberation struggle that would establish a sovereign Black state in the American South. Heavy on ideology but lighter on praxis, RAM's ambitious aims never got off the ground.[47] However, their ideas, and the internationalism on which they were based, became the three main organizational models of Black Power liberation.[48]

The last of these projects for Black autonomy, Black separatism, had a long history in both Black leftist and nationalist thought. RAM's addition was to imbue this separatist impulse with the decolonial internationalism that crested in the mid-1960s. RAM activists averred that the colonized peoples around the world, including the "internal Black colony" of the United States, had a right to self-determination that would materialize through a global uprising against the "universal slavemaster." To do so, Black Americans would join their anticolonial brothers and sisters in a war of national liberation that would establish revolutionary socialism on sovereign liberated lands. This entailed the creation of a Black nation in all or part of the states of Mississippi, Louisiana, Alabama, Georgia, Florida, Texas, Virginia, and the Carolinas that, in their eyes, rightfully belonged to Black people. The least worked-out (not to mention plausible) of RAM's approaches to Black liberation, RAM's Black separatism nevertheless informed the aims of a number of Black Power organizations, perhaps most prominently the New Republic of Africa, which advocated for the creation of an independent Black-majority country situated in the southeastern United States that would reject white property relations in favor of Black communalism.[49]

While advocating for a Black national liberation struggle, RAM also sought out more concrete ways of autonomous Black organizing. There was a strong belief among many RAM activists that the gang members of the urban north were the most revolutionary group in Black America. The lumpenproletariat that Fanon had described as the "pimps, hooligans, the unemployed and petty criminals" of the colonial slums, "these workless less-than-men" immune to false promises of uplift and social mobility became, in the eyes of RAM, the potential heroes and liberators of the new Black subject.[50] Modeled on the Congolese Youth Army and the Mau Mau guerrillas, RAM aimed to recruit these "hopeless dregs of humanity" into an armed militia of Black Guards who, with proper revolutionary guidance, would redirect Black-on-Black violence toward the dismantling of white power structures in the urban ghettos of America.

RAM's Northern California branch, operating under the name the "Soul Students Advisory Council," published a radical Black magazine, *Soulbook: The Revolutionary Journal of the Black World*, whose editorial board included Huey Newton and Bobby Seale. Through their interactions with RAM activists, Seale and Newton were exposed to the anti-imperial, socialist, and revolutionary nationalist currents of Black liberation. A few years later, the two would go on to found the Black Panther Party, with a self-defense wing recruited from the Black lumpenproletariat. Its ideology, intercommunalism, heavily influenced by the Black internationalism of RAM, understood Blacks as an "internal colony" of white America. For the Black Panther Party, imperialism—deterritorialized and operating everywhere—could only be disrupted if "pockets" among the global oppressed recognized their collective struggle against a common oppressor. What united the Black people of Oakland and the Vietnamese, Huey Newton argued, was their anti-imperial and autonomous "desire to run their own communities."[51] By 1970, the Black Panther Party had established sixty-eight such autonomous "pockets" of Black resistance and self-governance across the United States.

3106 Shattuck Avenue, Oakland: Panther Communalism

Com' on now Brother
shape a space
love your face
make a place.

A large three-story, multiroom residential house, I stand on 3106 Shattuck Avenue—about halfway between the largely white university town of Berkeley and the Black ghetto of Oakland on the east side of the San Francisco Bay. I'm a quiet house, in a quiet neighborhood, meant for quiet families. Until the summer of 1968, that is, when David Hilliard, Chief of Staff of the Black Panther Party moved in with his wife Patricia and three children. From that moment on, my life changed completely.

The first days seemed normal enough. The kids were set up on the top floor and Patricia and David settled into the master bedroom. But soon after, a steady stream of workers in leather jackets and black berets began to unload truckloads of material. They reinforced the front and back doors with steel sheets, put wire mesh on all the windows, and sandbags along the walls. They installed double bunk beds in the second-floor rooms and placed about ten desks, each with a telephone, in the main living space downstairs. Crews of men would disappear into the basement and re-emerge with bags of dirt they dumped in the backyard. Turned out they were digging a tunnel, not tall enough to stand in but enough to crawl through. 3106 Shattuck Ave is a half-block north of the city line dividing Berkeley from Oakland, on the Berkeley side. And even though the Berkeley Police Department was marginally more civilized than its Oakland counterpart, to the Hilliards, pigs were pigs and you could never be too careful.

By the end of the month, I was filled to the brim with people. My living room had become a command center, the kitchen a mess hall. During the day, section leaders manned the phones, handed out bundles of *The Black Panther* newspaper for distribution, and coordinated activities and the police patrols in the neighborhood. Evenings were taken up with political meetings, last-minute edits, and organizing work. My stoves and ovens were worn from use, glancing wearily at the sign-up sheets for cooking and cleaning shifts. It got a little quieter at night, but there was always a large group of mostly younger panthers who stayed over, tucked into sleeping bags placed on wood pallets when all the bunks were taken. It was hard to keep track of everybody. Outside of the Hilliards, who actually lived here and for how long was a constantly shifting mystery. Part home for the Hilliard family, part headquarters for the Party, part boardinghouse for the politically itinerant, part barricaded refuge from the police, I had become a jambalaya of intents and architectures.

But it wasn't just Panthers who came and went. As word went around about 3106 Shattuck, people from the community started pouring in. I became the place you turned to when you had a problem with the powers-that-be or one they wouldn't deal with. Old and young would walk up to my door, greeted by the on-duty security officer asking who they wanted to see or the nature of their business. They came with every gripe imaginable. People having issues with their boss, people struggling to pay rent or coming in with eviction notices, people with legal problems, moms whose kids had just been arrested, moms demanding a traffic signal at Alcatraz Ave., people complaining about racist store owners or school principals, about utility bills, about the police— and the Panthers tried to deal with them all. On top of everything else, I was becoming the city hall you went to when you realized the real one not only didn't give a shit, but was actually there to keep you down.

And the Hilliard Children? What were they doing in all this commotion? David and Patricia had been among the first to take their kids out of the Oakland school system, and were educating from home. Though, both of them were just so busy all the time, and maybe the kids suffered because of that, I'm not sure. Their relationship was different, a little distant perhaps, missing the that intimacy of a typical family. But maybe David and Patricia wanted it that way; maybe remaking the world into a better place for their kids through revolution was more important than sitting round the dinner table playing Monopoly. I guess things only got complicated when that revolution never came. In the meantime, the little cubs were surrounded by Panthers: making up in numbers, in communal embrace, what they lacked in parental affection. Being raised by Panthers was a little like that boy in *The Jungle Book*—nothing like most other kids in America. Instead of nursery rhymes, they sang liberation songs. While regular boys re-enacted Vietnam with their G.I. Joe figures, Darryl and Dorian wrote letters to incarcerated prisoners. For the entire time they lived here, the Hilliards never had a TV set, and not because they couldn't afford one.

Black Panther Party, "Defend the Ghetto" (1970).

Six months after they moved in, the Panthers decided to take a more proactive approach. They found a place about three miles down the road at the Episcopal church on 29th Street and started to serve breakfast to needy children. On its first day, eleven kids ate a hearty meal before school. Within a year, the

Panthers were serving breakfast in twenty-three cities: in churches, in the homes of parents, junkies, and prostitutes. At its height, the Free Breakfast Program fed about 100,000 kids a day across the country. This meant even more activity under my roof. Moms would come by to sign up their kids, and store owners would drop off boxes full of donated bread, eggs, bacon, milk, and paper napkins.

When the Breakfast Program caught like wildfire, the Panthers took up other pressing issues facing the Black community. They opened up a People's Free Medical Clinic in Oakland, offering general health screenings, vaccinations, door-to-door service, drug rehabilitation, and testing for lead poisoning and sickle cell anemia. This was more high-budget stuff than cooking up breakfast. But like the breakfast program, the Panthers relied on, and helped construct, a communal network in the neighborhood. Local pharmacists and Bay Area suppliers like Libby's Lab would bring by trucks full of free medical goods and equipment. Doctors, interns, nurses, lab techs, and medical students from Berkeley came by to volunteer their services, coordinate schedules, and to teach Party members health screening, first aid, and vaccination procedures so they could do these themselves. Oakland's "barefoot doctors" they called them, though I never got why.

As more and more people joined the Panthers, Hilliard began to expand operations. I was becoming a buzzing beehive of Black resistance. By 1970, my windows were covered with postersand sign-ups for the Free Clothing Program, the Free Shoe Program, the Free Pest Control Program, the Free Ambulance Program, the Free Plumbing and Maintenance Program, for free legal aid, renter's assistance, and senior escort programs. They even started a prison busing program that transported relatives to visit inmates incarcerated in rural penitentiaries far from Oakland. All this meant an incredible amount of organization: collecting donations; lining up plumbers, exterminators, drivers, and lawyers; figuring out schedules; making appointments. When there wasn't space to put all this stuff, it stayed here with me. Boxes filled with shoes, with food, clothes, and toys, stuffed in every corner of every room. I was a warehouse full of goods to distribute to the community.

For David and Patricia, it wasn't just about giving the poor people of Oakland things and services they sorely needed. It was about people helping out. People trusting each other. About coming together to take charge of their community. Some people called it socialist care. For the Hilliards, this was the meaning of Black self-determination. And I was its hub, the nodal point of all these connections. Well, at least for my little nook of North Oakland.

If the Panthers focused their energies on communalizing the Black lumpenproletariat, RAM's third model for autonomous Black organization looked to the Black working class as the subject of Black liberation. This model was inspired by the Johnson–Forest Tendency, a humanist Marxist group founded by C. L. R. James and Raya Dunayevskaya and later joined by Grace Lee Boggs. The Black Marxist tradition had long argued that the double curse of the Black industrial worker made it simultaneously the most exploited and most revolutionary segment of the global proletariat. Rejecting both inclusion into, as well as the ideological reformism of, the white-run labor unions, RAM organized several autonomous Black Worker Units in factories across the Midwest. One of these units would eventually morph into the League of Revolutionary Black Workers (LRBW).

The need for autonomous Black worker organization in the Midwest stemmed from the experiences of 1967 and '68, where the brutal repression of the urban uprisings had underscored the expendability of Black life. General Baker of the LRBW, describing the Detroit curfew imposed by the state, recounted:

If you got sick, you couldn't go to the doctor. If you got hungry, you couldn't get no food. But if you had a badge from Chrysler, Ford, or General Motors, you could get to the police line, the National Guard line, the army line, all of them to take your butt to work. The conclusion we drew from that was that the only place in this society that Black people had any value was at the point of production.[52]

On May 2, 1968, Black laborers made use of this value. At the Dodge Main Plant, bypassing union leadership, 4,000 workers walked out against an announced speedup of the automaker assembly line. The following day, the Black strike organizers founded the Dodge Revolutionary Union Movement (DRUM). Within a few months, several sister RUMs had sprouted up across the auto factories of Detroit, staging a series of wildcat strikes throughout the city's auto sector. By the following year, these RUMs combined to form the League of Revolutionary Black Workers (LRBW).

In some auto factories, Blacks made up over 70 percent of the workforce, and their motion was critical to the functioning of the line.[53] Yet despite their overwhelming presence within the plant, the same structures of white supremacy outside the factory were replicated within it. For the autoworker James Boggs, who argued that the United States was "a fascist state with a master majority race," it was not surprising that Blacks worked the most grueling and dangerous positions and had little to no representation within the racist union bureaucracy. Therefore, Boggs claimed, "It is not possible for blacks to free themselves without turning over every institution of this society, all of which have been structured with blacks at the bottom."[54] This included the unions. For the members of the RUMs and the LRBW, only the Black proletariat, autonomously organized, had the disruptive power and revolutionary consciousness to liberate itself (and everyone else) from the regime of movement. Echoing an earlier RAM analysis that American racism had led the white working class to abandon its class allegiance, Boggs argued Black Power was the "scientific recognition" that "there is no historical basis for the promise, constantly made to Blacks by American radicals, that the white worker will join them against the capitalist enemy."[55]

Becoming Black as the celebration of Black bodies and speech, as economic and political self-determination, as the revaluation of values, as anti-imperial internationalism. Becoming Black as historical inquiry into the centrality of slavery, into Black resistance to slavery, into ancestral social forms pre-dating slavery. Becoming Black as revolutionary subject, whether this be the lumpenproletarians of the ghetto or the Black industrial workers caught in the brutal death throes of American manufacturing. These differences of content and organizational form, while determinative of the future of Black politics, obscure the disruptive subjectivity of Black Power that made them possible. The refusal of "the Negro's" assigned place within the symbolic and material order of America and the assertion of the ability to define, an ambition to practice, on their own terms, the meaning of blackness.

Operaismo and Self-Valorization

> *I would prefer not to.*
>> Bartleby from Melville's "Bartleby, the Scrivener"

In March 1973, 10,000 workers occupied Fiat's giant Mirafiori automotive plant in Turin, blockading all entrances to the factory. A terrified union leadership, whose credibility rested on its ability to control such wildcat actions, issued a call to "strike for two hours." The workers of Fiat were not in a mood to listen. Neither it turned out, were those in the rest of the city. The following day, the occupations spread to shops in Lingotto, Bertone, Pininfarina, Spa Stura, Ricambi, Lancia, Carello, Spa Centro, Ferriere, and Grandi Motori. By evening, most of Turin's factories were in the hands of their workers. The unions and bosses scrambled to get hold of the situation and, in three days, hammered out a new national contract with terms extremely favorable to the workers. The first back-to-work day, announced with the new contract, was ignored completely. In the second, 60 percent of Fiat workers didn't show up. The ones who did continued their assembly work behind barricaded factory gates.

Factory occupations as a form of disruptive politics were nothing new, especially in Italy. They had been used to both extract concessions from capital and, at moments, as a revolutionary tactic for worker control. So what was different about these takeovers? To one Fiat line worker, the historical context was clear:

> This occupation is different from the one the workers did in 1920. In 1920 they said let's occupy but let's work. Let's show everyone that we can run production ourselves. Things are different today. In our occupation, the factory is a starting point for the revolutionary organization of the workers—*not a place to work!*[56]

Another line worker added:

> If the police had come to the gates, we wouldn't have attacked them there. We would have drawn them inside the factory, onto our own ground . . . where we're always ready to answer violence in the terms we understand . . . If the police had come into Mirafiori, the place would have been out of action for three years.[57]

In their analysis of the occupations, the group *Potere Operaio* (Workers' Power) concluded that "the workers took over the factory, not to defend it, nor to run it, but to use it as an enormous resource of political strength."[58]

What were these Italian workers saying? What did it mean that the factory was "not a place to work"? That they would meet police violence with the destruction of the factory that employed them? For over a century, workers had regarded their labor as the source of their current and future political power. How could not working in the factory be "an enormous resource of political strength"?

Between 1969 and 1977, Italian workers went to war with the entirety of Italian society. They waged war against capital and the Italian state, against the unions and political parties that were supposed to represent them, and, perhaps most profoundly, against the order of work itself. The scale of industrial conflict was astounding. In terms of lost working time, the Hot Autumn of 1969 alone registered as the third largest strike wave in human history (after May 1968 in France and the 1926 British general strike). Yet, unlike these intense but short-lived disruptions, Italian workers maintained a near-constant state of industrial agitation, with ebbs and flows, for nearly a decade. This state of "perpetual conflict," confounding bosses, political parties, and unions alike, spilled outside the factories and at times became unassimilable.

Worker disruption both informed and found political expression through the simultaneous explosion of extraparliamentary groups operating outside Italy's postwar institutional structure, most notably the militant intellectuals who coalesced around the banner of *operaismo*. This imbrication of radical thought and direct action first questioned, and ultimately rejected, long-cultivated understandings of proletarian subjectivity and rearticulated, in radical terms, what it meant to be a worker.

Operaismo, or workerism, emerged from an attempt by dissident leftist intellectuals to reground analysis of workers' struggle in the actual experience of workers within the factories. It was heavily influenced by two Trotskyist splinter groups, the Johnson–Forest Tendency in the United States and *Socialisme ou Barbarie* in France, both of which had advocated for workers' self-organization and self-management outside (and in spite of) the institutions and doctrines of the labor movement.[59] Building on these efforts, the Italian workerists scrapped the "objective" analysis of capitalism and class undertaken by almost all of orthodox Marxism and set about investigating capital as it was experienced at the point of its production, by workers, on the shop floor.

These "workers inquiries"—involving rich descriptions of the "microsystems of struggle" inside the factory—illuminated the shifting class composition of Italy's industrial workforce. The postwar Fordist restructuring of Italian manufacturing and the mechanization of southern agriculture had led to a massive uprooting of Italians as 9 million workers—nearly a fifth of the total population—resettled into the "Industrial Triangle" between Milan, Turin, and Genoa.[60] Bound to repetitive machines, socially degraded by and economically segregated from their northern counterparts, the newly arrived migrants from the rural south found themselves at the bottom of a hierarchical world enforced through abusive foremen and divisive pay scales.

Whereas the Italian Communist Party (PCI) perceived their high rates of absenteeism and turnover, their lack of integration into the established unions, and their low participation in official strikes as a sign of the new migrants' primitive or prepolitical consciousness, the workerists drew different conclusions. For the militant intellectuals of the group *Potere Operaio*, the passivity of the "new forces" signaled not the absence of politics, but the sign of a profound disavowal of the organization of industrial work. Workers' inquiry revealed that these new mass workers had no stake in the established unions, did not take part in strikes because they thought they were useless, and, more radically, rejected the union's emphasis on skill and worker pride, as well as its representational and bureaucratic form of organization. In their refusal of, and insubordination toward, the totality of industrial organization, the workerists saw the germ of a new revolutionary subject. A worker, animated not by the dignity of labor that creates all wealth but by a desire to not work, by the hatred of work.[61]

These interpretative differences were founded on radically divergent understandings of worker subjectivity. Within both bourgeois and orthodox Marxist analyses, class was a sociological and economic concept. It described a social aggregate to which one belonged, either through existing social stratification or one's relationship to the means of production. In both cases, class was something you were placed into; it existed as an external and objective category. For the workerists, such interpretations turned the working class into a very strange entity. Supposedly the subject of history, its entire definition had been given to it by others: by capital, by sociology, by economics, by the state, by unions, by communist parties, by intellectuals—by everyone, that is, but themselves.

In contrast, *operaismo* sought the basis of class in worker subjectivity—in how workers reacted politically to the world of capital. This subjectivity did not exist naturally, externally, or objectively, but was created by the workers themselves through struggle. Without struggle, the workerists argued, there could be proletarians but no proletariat, workers but not a working class. The first of these terms referred to the laborer's function within the regime of movement, their objective existence as humans forced to sell their labor power in order to survive. The second set of terms were subjective: the political self-understanding of workers that came about through the refusal of this existence. While capital produced workers, that is, restructured human beings as labor power, the workerists argued that struggle produced the working class. In these claims, *operaismo* went even further than E. P. Thomson's landmark shift in Anglophone new-left historiography. Workers were not just present at their own making, they became the proletariat, understood themselves as a class, by disrupting what capital had forced them to be. For this reason, the workerist conception of subjectivity also differed from traditional formulations of class consciousness. It was not the process whereby the workers came to realize their objective relation to the means of production (true consciousness) or were led astray from this realization (false consciousness). Nor could working-class subjectivity be imparted by the representatives of labor. With *operaismo*, class became an entirely political concept, one that was composed and decomposed through the workers' refusal of their own life condition.[62] As Marx had shown in his historical works, the workerists averred, proletarians became a class on the 1848 barricades.

The refusal of work

The industrial agitation that exploded with the Hot Autumn of 1969 confirmed *operaismo's* analysis. In September, negotiations over a labor contract sparked a wildcat strike by workers of the Fiat Mirafiori plant. Shortly after, similar strikes broke out at the Alfa Romeo and Pirelli factories, and within a month had spread throughout the industrial triangle. By the end of the year, some 5.5 million workers—more than 25 percent of the Italian labor force—had walked off the job, resulting in over 520 million worker hours lost. The strikes were initiated by the rank-and-file, violated no-strike contract clauses, and bypassed the union structures, which had, by December, lost all control. One worker from the Mirafiori body shop declared:

> Today we can make it with our own means. We don't need any union representation anymore, or nobody else's. This means that we now decide not only the form of the struggle, but also its goals, the style of its leadership, the way of organizing it and spreading it. This is what manufacturers and union bureaucrats alike are more afraid of.[63]

But what were the goals? Judging by their demands, workers were less concerned with pay and more with the hierarchical organization of labor within the workplace. Above all, workers demanded an end to practices that tied their wages to individual and collective productivity. This included an end to piecework, merit pay, production bonuses, and management control over promotions. The most popular slogan of the Hot Autumn, "Less work! More pay!" went to the heart of this radical demand, severing the nexus between remuneration and productivity—undermining a fundamental pillar of wage labor. They sought the elimination of established corporate practices that divided white- from blue-collar workers, lackeys from insubordinates, technicians from those on the assembly line.[64] Here, workers took aim at the stratified system of job classification, demanding the same work category for all employees. They demanded control over promotions, which they saw as a corporate mechanism reinforcing workers' submission to managerial authority, goals, and values. Or, in the words of the Autonomous Assembly of Alfa Romeo, an end to "selection based on . . . your willingness to lick ass."[65]

Initiated by unskilled laborers, this "rage against work" as one bourgeois commentator termed it, soon infected the white-collar and skilled laborers who benefited most from the existing system. Technical telecommunications workers in Milan called for "a human and anti-authoritarian way of working that enables the valorization of professional capacities." When unskilled workers at the Siemens plant went on strike, 90 percent of the white-collar force joined them, their autonomous committee declaring "their struggle is for the abolition of wage-labor and against the system of bosses."[66]

These worker statements and demands signified the collective desire for a different organization of work. Yet, to *operaismo*, the true revolutionary potential of 1969 lay in what the workers did, not what they asked for. It was through their direct actions, their refusal, their insubordination, that workers came to see themselves as a political class. Examples of this abound. On an individual level, workers would arrive late for their shifts and leave early. Or they simply refused to show up. Absenteeism was rampant throughout the factories of the industrial triangle, averaging 14 percent daily in the early '70s, with peaks of over 30 percent in certain months. Collectively, workers unilaterally declared paid rest periods, and held political meetings inside the factories, on the company's time. It was here, in these autonomous assemblies, that Italian workers developed new tactics of worker disruption. Some, such as the "hiccup" and "chessboard" strikes, were masterfully coordinated slowdowns of the assembly line, with successive sections of the plant, or workers with last names beginning with certain letters, downing tools at prearranged and staggered times. These "articulated strikes" caused enormous headaches for foremen, crippled production, easily bypassed union officials, and cost the rank-and-file workers nothing in terms of lost wages.[67] An article in *Rinascita* entitled "Pirelli: A Victory for Workers' Inventiveness" likened the new disruptive tactics to an autonomous symphony.

> The reduction of work speeds is a masterpiece of consciousness (*autocoscienza*) and technical ability. It is as if an orchestra had managed to play a difficult symphony, harmoniously, without the conductor, and at a tempo agreed upon and regulated by the players of the single instruments.[68]

Or as one worker stated more poetically, it was about "the workers learning to make the bosses dance to the rhythm of their own music." Other disruptive innovations, like the *corteo interno*—inside-the-factory marches that proceeded from shop to shop, harassing foremen, strike breakers, and management—had a more spontaneous, carnivalesque character, resurrecting medieval and early modern practices of charivari, or "rough music."[69]

Factory management and bourgeois commentators declared these new tactics "illegal" and their practitioners as "gangs of half-lunatics" and "self-improvised Zulus." The established unions were equally unimpressed. They saw in these worker disruptions "a political primitivism, stemming from a barely nascent trade-union consciousness," and, indeed, as "a cause for embarrassment."[70] Supporters saw in these coordinated disruptions workers' capacity for self-management and the fruits of workplace democracy.

For the workers, these disruptions were enjoyable in themselves. Slowing down production, moving freely around the factory floor, turning the tables on foremen, coming in late, and claiming paid breaks all gave workers a sense of control over their workplace while achieving what workers wanted: less work. Yes, the strikes impeded production and were adept displays of worker power. But more than their value in wresting concessions from management, these disruptions all had the immediate effect of reducing the tempo and length of work. They exemplified, as one radical student observed, the art of "practicing the objective."[71] A concept that would later come to be known as "prefigurative politics."

The struggle against labor

For Mario Tronti and other members of *operaismo*, the refusal of work had an even greater significance. These acts of refusal not only crippled production but, more fundamentally, were a challenge to the order of work itself, disrupting the role and function of the worker within the regime of movement. As Tronti argued in *Workers and Capital*:

> This refusal of work, this struggle against work, this relentless sabotage of its own identity as a commodity—labor power—that is sold in exchange for wages, cannot be reduced to a simple "resistance" on the part of a living, laboring humanity to its domination by capital. Its definition, if this word even applies, is articulated in its active

destruction or sabotage of its own objective existence as labor-power, its own identity as a category of capital.[72]

Just as Black Power disavowed "the Negro's" identity within the racial capitalism of the United States, the refusal of work was the workers' refusal to be categorized, ordered, dispensed, and defined by the regime of movement. This led to some startling arguments. For the Italian workerists, the creation of the proletariat required the nullification of their identity as laborers: the extraction of themselves from their assigned function within the regime of movement, a deactivation of their labor power. Quite radically, the workerists claimed that the labor struggle was not about recovering the wealth stolen from it. This is what socialism, in its aim to redistribute the gains, or even ownership, of productive activity had gotten wrong all along. The labor struggle was a struggle *against* labor. A workers' struggle against their own self-understanding as those who provided labor power.

Read in this light, the industrial agitation that crippled Italy's industrial triangle was the workers' attempt to render themselves, as workers, inoperable. The coordinated disruptions, the spontaneous factory marches, the organized passivity and absenteeism, the flouting of shift schedules and foremen directives, were all ways of practicing and showcasing their own debilitation.

"To struggle against labor requires proletarians to take themselves, their own condition as wage-laborers, as a limit to be overcome," Tronti wrote in "The Strategy of the Refusal." The working class must "reach the point of having as its enemy the whole of capital, including itself as part of capital."[73] Workerism wagered on the possibility that there was a force in workers that they could mobilize against themselves, not to extend but to destroy their own condition. It was therefore a workerism against work, refusing a naturalized subjectivity imposed by the capital relation.[74] In this sense, "the dignity of labor," the "pride of the producer," that the socialist movement had bestowed on the working class like some title of nobility, was nothing other than self-reification. Instead, true self-valorization began with sabotage. Worker sabotage, not of production but of themselves as a productive force. By becoming inoperable, Antonio Negri argued, "workers imagine their lives not as work but as the absence of it, their activity as free and creative exercise."[75]

Agnelli's Factory

Compared to the South, Turin is full of excitement. Windowed shops displaying blue jeans and radios, girls in miniskirts with purses walking into movies, and you want all of it. But everything in these northern cities costs money. The newspapers, the buses, the meat, the shirts all have a price. Not like back home, where you could still get by picking fruit off trees, fishing, wearing clothes your mother either made or found for you. And everything came down to that. To these prices. To live here, you needed money and the best money was at Fiat.

Fiat's Mirafiori is like a city unto itself. A massive complex with hundreds of buildings where 60,000 workers build thousands of cars a day. There are two main production streams that converge on the main assembly lines. The first starts in the Foundries, where the motor parts and aluminum heads are cast. Those are then taken to Mechanics, where the engines are put together. The second stream starts in the Presses, which stamp the car bodies out of sheet metal, then moves to Assembly, where these pieces are welded together. At this point, the two streams converge on the main lines for each model; the body shells are put together; moved along the line where the engine and mechanical parts are installed. The vehicles are then dressed, given tires, and deposited in the Yard.

But you don't know this, and you don't really need to, not yet anyway. Your job, like almost all the jobs at Fiat, is focused on one tiny fragment of this gigantic chain. You're quickly brought down a series of long perpendicular corridors to a large floor with hundreds of hollowed, almost-spectral cars moving horizontally, at different heights, above you. This, too, is exciting, but in a different way than the streets of Turin. You are introduced to your immediate boss, the foreman, and the leading hand, an older worker with leathery hands and weathered face who knows every process on that floor and will be teaching you one.

Overhead conveyors moving along Models 124 and
500 at the Fiat "Mirafiori" complex (1972).
©Alamy. Photographer: ZUMA Press

Your process is to attach two bolts, with washers, to predrilled holes
on two metal parts and then secure these from the back with nuts.
The metal parts are on the undercarriages of the Fiat 124, which
move toward your station at a pace of roughly one every twenty
seconds, depending on the speed of that day's line. It wasn't something you could learn how to do, or rather, your muscles learned
instead of you. It required precise movements at precise times; the
rhythmic motion of specific arm, hand, and finger joints, guided by
the careful calibration of ocular muscles, and it had to be repeated,
every twenty seconds, for nine hours a day, minus a half-hour break
for lunch. The line never stops. It keeps moving, and so must you.
You can't go to the bathroom, or have a smoke, or treat minor injuries, because someone would need to take over your station.

A few weeks in, and you start to get a hang of the place. Mirafiori
is organized through numbers. All Fiat workers have a gate
number, through which they enter and leave every day, a locker
room number, a locker number, a workshop number, a line

number, and of course their own identification number. There are numbers on corridors and staircases and numbers for the target of cars that will come out the line that shift. There are numbers you see and numbers you know are there that you cannot.

It makes sense, these numbers, for how else could all this happen? But they have a weird effect on the people working within them. The workers called it the *Neurosis*. The Neurosis was the way working at Fiat made you act after a while. Like the cafeteria, for example. Every day, the same men sat in the same exact place, talking to the same exact people. They didn't have to, nobody made them do it, but they did anyway. That was the Neurosis, the way the meticulous organization of dead matter shaped that of the living.

You get your first paycheck and, with it, a glimpse of those hidden numbers that organize work at Fiat. There is a category number, according to your process, that determines how much you get paid per hour. But this "base pay," it turns out, is close to nothing. The real part of your wage is in the variable components—productivity bonuses, piecework, bonuses for diligence, job allowances, merit increases, over-award payments, performance evaluations. These are absolutely essential if you want to live off your paycheck and so are the main way that the bosses make sure you're working your ass off.

Outside the gates one morning, a group of workers crowds around what look like university students. They're talking about having a discussion about the American worker, Dan, who came to Turin to talk about the working conditions in the factories of Detroit, the center of the American auto industry. From the little you overhear, things are even shittier over there. There, the bosses made sure that you only got paid for the minutes you were at your station. Washing up, rest breaks, job-preparation periods were all on your time. Temporary speedups of the line—something you have seen here— were regular and regularly became permanent. They even had mandatory overtime, including weekends, to squeeze the most out of each worker. You hear about how the Blacks have it worst. These guys, who had just come to Detroit from the South, get put into the foundry or the body shops: the dirtiest, noisiest, most back-breaking and dangerous spaces of the factory. They get harassed and insulted by white foremen who think it's still the slave days. You hear how the supervisors refuse to accept sick notes from Black doctors and use this or some other excuse to fire them before they worked long enough to come under union contract. It's pretty depressing stuff what this guy's saying. You're just about to walk away when you catch a smile slowly appear on his face. He pauses for a few seconds then reaches into his jacket pocket and pulls out a folded piece of paper. It's a letter that Dan gave him yesterday, he says. Written by a Black worker named General Baker to the Chrysler Corporation. He starts reading it, translating as he goes along. It's about a strike that the Black workers are planning. Near the end he pauses and in a louder voice reads out the General's last lines: "You have made the decision to do battle, and that is the only decision you will make. WE shall decide the arena and the time." There are shouts and applause. You move on, but what you heard sticks with you, and you'll remember it a few months later.

Where the Wildcats Roam

Workshop 54 got things going in the summer of 1969, with about thirty workers leaving their stations. They had whistles and cowbells and metal pipes, making all kinds of noise as they went section to section calling everybody out. By the time they got to us, the march was over 300 strong. You couldn't even see the back of it, but you could hear it, workers banging sheet metal, pushing car horns, and shouting down the corridors. The gathering sounds that reduced the bosses to piss.

It was an awesome sight. Groups would break off to hunt for terrified foremen, stuffing a red flag in their hands and a whistle in their mouths, screaming "Blow! Blow!" or "Hold it Higher!" as they pushed them into the march. The ones they could find, anyway. Most had ratted off to the supervisor's office. The bosses sent in a few reluctant guards, who were immediately surrounded. These shitheads that searched us when we left every day, keeping the company property safe. Now *they* got the pat-down, with the boys going rough in all the right places. The older Piedmontese workers, the ones who had looked down on us *Meridionali*, stunned at how quickly the bosses had lost control. We were turning Fiat upside down.

After a few hours, with the supervisors, their lackeys, and the scabs kicked out or in hiding, Mirafiori was ours. Groups of workers split off to their sections to hold meetings. It wasn't like the ones the unions had. Everybody got a chance to speak, to talk about how Fiat was breaking them and how we could break Fiat. Each worker explained their own process, how doing this or that would hold up the line or how to gum up their station if the scabs were sent in. We got a sense of the whole factory this way. We learned how it all fit together by teaching each other how to take it apart. It was our way of fighting the bosses, countering the assembly line with the autonomous assembly of workers. If the line made cars by atomizing workers, the assembly united the workers to break the line.

We began talking to other sections, using the same phones the supervisors used to coordinate work, this time to coordinate how to stop production: which section would go first and for how long, and who would take over to give them a break. That was the thing about Mirafiori—it worked when everybody did. All you had to do was stop one part of it, and eventually the whole thing would come crashing down. We called it the hiccup or chessboard or articulated strike, but the idea was the same. The bosses wouldn't know where or when they came from, and when they tried to put pressure on one section, another would take over.

A few weeks of this, and you could tell they were getting nervous. One time, during the height of the strikes, the managers even tried to restart the line, thinking some automated part of us would just assume our stations. The Neurosis. But that time had passed. We just laughed and watched until they shut it off again. Every so often, the bosses would send someone to ask us what we wanted or offer certain workers a jump in category. We would tell them we wanted an across-the-board increase of the base pay and an end to categories. Most of the time, we said nothing at all. I think that's what scared them the most. The union bureaucrats were scared, too. You could tell. They would try to take over our meetings, saying that they had reached some tentative agreement if we only returned to work, that now was not the best time to strike, that we didn't understand how this was undermining the larger struggle. But what's the point of striking in October, with the bosses knowing about it in advance and could stock up properly? The bosses didn't like talking to us, but they loved those union crats. They kept things predictable. And that meant policing us, making sure we didn't get out of line. Ha! In that, they were pretty much like the rest of the shitheads—the foremen, the parties, the cops, the fascists. At least with them, you knew what you were getting.

It's not as if the plant was down every day. We worked some shifts, but even then, the work was at our pace. We set the speed of the line, when it started and when it would end. We took breaks, when we decided, on company time. We called this "appropriation." Over the course of those months, we were slowly turning Mirafiori from a place of work into a base for political struggle. We started making leaflets, which we would hand out at the gates but also stuff into orders being shipped to other plants, a way to deliver news of what we were up to, urging them to join us. Soon we heard that the agitation had spread to Alfa Romeo and Pirelli. Students and other radical groups like *Potere Operaio* would meet us after shifts, holding meetings, passing out literature. It's from them that we heard about the wildcats in Detroit, how the Black workers at Ford and Chrysler had ditched their unions, who were even bigger shitheads than ours, and formed their own organizations. I mean, when the president of their union says he never went on or ordered a strike in his life, that he never even saw a picket line, and says it like that's a good thing, what do you expect? But the news from these other factories, from places as far as Detroit, was like music to our ears. We were beginning to see how what we were doing in the factory was connected to the workers' struggle in all of Italy, if not the whole world.

It's crazy to think about, but we kept this up for four whole years. Some days, we marched to claim the shop floor for ourselves; other days we held meetings, or just decided not to show up to work at all. It wasn't about contracts, which would come and go, but about the organization of work inside the factory. And the bosses knew this, too. The heads of the metal industry, the auto makers, led by our very own Agnelli, came to the bargaining table with their own demands: an end to the "permanent conflict," the regulation of absenteeism, full utilization of productive capacity, the restoration of workshop discipline. It was a fight over the space of the factory, what we did in that space and how we did it. And we were winning.

This was the real reason behind the occupations that blew up in 1973. The bosses threatening to lock us out or send in the police is what got the barricades up. It all started on an early Thursday morning near the end of March. A crowd of 10,000 picketers, shouting "Occupy Fiat—No Truce!" blocked all the entrances to Mirafiori. Inside, we set up permanent political assemblies, where Workers' Courts held mass trials of foremen and ruled that strike breakers would not be allowed to pick up their Friday wages. By the following evening, the occupations had spread throughout the city, and most of Turin's factories were in the hands of workers. We didn't occupy to take control of the "means of production" as the old party farts used to say. We occupied the factories so we could have power over that space. To turn it into a space where we could become something different, someone other than workers.

The Unmaking of the Italian Working Class

For the workerists, the disruptions at Mirafiori were not a reaction to working conditions imposed by capital, but rather the latest instance of a long history of worker revolt that had generated all capitalist development. Mario Tronti, in his 1966 opus, *Workers and Capital*, historicized this subjectivity of refusal to reinterpret the history of capital and class struggle. Rather than view the workers as a class created by capital (as almost all Marxist thought had done), Tronti began with the premise that the driving force of history was the workers themselves. From a workerist perspective, capital was a reactive force, adapting itself to the active and continual revolt of workers against their life condition. The technological and organizational innovations that had driven the development of capitalist society from its earliest days to the Fordist factory were nothing other than reactions to worker rebellion. "Where there are strikes," workerists argued, "machines will follow." As Marx himself had put it, "It would be possible to write a whole history of the inventions made since 1830 for the sole purpose of providing capital with weapons against working-class revolt."[76] This "Copernican Revolution," as it was soon dubbed, reversed the cause and effect of historical development as conceived by the Marxist tradition. Tronti explained:

> We too have worked with a concept that puts capitalist development first, and workers second. This is a mistake. And now we have to turn the problem on its head, reverse the polarity, and start again from the beginning: and the beginning is the struggle of the working class. At the level of socially developed capital, capitalist development becomes subordinated to working class struggles; it follows behind them, and they set the pace to which the political mechanisms of capital's own reproduction must be tuned.[77]

From the workerist perspective, capital was not the subject of history, it is not that which does and undoes, that which determines development or even the conditions for its own overcoming. Rather, history was nonteleological, and at its center was working-class struggle, its power of refusal and its autonomy.[78] Capital was forced to change, not because of its internal laws of motion but because of worker disruption. In a very odd twist, the workerists claimed that the constant movement and transformation of capital, its compulsion to flux and recomposition, that is, the engine that disruptive struggles had aimed to stop, was in fact produced by struggle itself.

As an autonomous political force, there were no guarantees about the direction and force of working-class disruption. Nonetheless, workerists theorized that worker refusal exerted certain "tendencies" on capitalist development. The direction of these tendencies, and the political response to them, would drive the various factions of workerism and its afterlives.

Some felt that worker disruption, by forcing capital to innovate new technologies to subdue or bypass it, were in fact a force strengthening the grip of capital. In this view, the struggles against capital made capital more formidable. These workerist strains argued that working-class liberation could only materialize when worker struggles became autonomous, that is, detached themselves from the composition of capital and its social forces (the worker included). As Adriano Sofri stated,

> The class struggle is the mainspring of development of every social system. The interest of the ruling class is to make this spring work for the extension and reinforcement of its own power. Workers' autonomy occurs when the class struggle stops working as the motor of capitalist development.[79]

Others drew the conclusion that the refusal of work forced capital to accelerate its productive forces, leading to a situation where labor would no longer be required. Thus, all worker refusal was positive, developing society to a point when human beings could "go beyond capitalism," the moment when liberation from exploitation became materially possible. A third strain advanced the line that the history of worker disruption effected fundamental changes to the organization and operation of the state. In this tendency, worker sabotage conditioned not just the technological development of capital (the machines and organization of work), but also its political history. To ensure worker subordination, the state, as the political arm of capital, grew ever more dictatorial, increasingly bent on command and domination for its own sake. In its later stages, the state became a pure empty form, detached from or "indifferent," as Negri states, to the laws of capital accumulation. At this phase, the worker struggle becomes a political (as opposed to industrial) one, aiming to free itself from the political domination of the state.

Despite these differing tendencies, workerists generally believed that capital was currently in transition to a new stage. As early as 1963, Tronti had argued that the disruptive struggles of the mass worker were effecting a contemporary shift in the composition of capital to a post-Fordist phase. Hampered by the industrial agitation of workers, capital accumulation had entered a crisis of immobility: a period when manufacturing profits fell below a certain threshold, triggering a precipitous drop in capital reinvestment. Its recomposition necessitated the appropriation of surplus value beyond capital's historical mode of industrial production: an expansion into, and value extraction from, the totality of social relations. The marketization of daily life, the rearrangement of urban spaces that channeled accumulation from leisure, health care, rents, and consumption, was, in this sense, the regime's attempt to reverse the petrification of capital. The phase where, as Tronti claimed, "the whole of society lives as a function of the factory and the factory extends its exclusive domination to the whole of society."[80]

Once again, the ideas of the *operaismo* proved prescient. Decreasing returns from European and North American manufacturing, precipitated by worker disruption and brought to a crisis point by the 1973 oil shock, forced a restructuring of the regime of movement that recomposed both capital and class. In this sense, and with an irony that the late great E. P. Thompson would have appreciated, North Atlantic workers were also present at their own unmaking.

Seeking new outlets, capital investment turned to circulation, logistics, and claims on future value, what Marx had termed "fictitious capital." Globally, this restructuring led to a massive finance-driven expansion of commerce. The emergence of intermodal shipping and containerization (a product of the Vietnam War) and its widespread adoption were one vector of the logistic revolution. Supply chain management and just-in-time manufacturing (first developed by the Japanese auto industry), was another. Together, they brought Taylorism into the realm of circulation, allowing for the global diffusion of manufacturing and the subordination of production to distribution as the main engine of capital accumulation.

Within the urban industrial centers of the North Atlantic, the restructuring of capital led to deindustrialization, corporate policies of relocation, and labor redundancy (greatly diminishing the power of worker militancy). It was no coincidence that the 1973 occupation of the Fiat Mirafiori plant proved to be the high point of radical and autonomous agitation in the factories. After this, the traditional unions reasserted control over the workers, using their diminishing strength not to arrest production but fighting alongside capital to continue it. That same year marked a similar turn in the manufacturing core of the United States, where for the first time in the history of the UAW, the union mobilized to keep a plant open.[81] This restructuring sounded the death knell for the radical subjectivity of the industrial worker. The moment when labor was forced to affirm capital in order to affirm its own existence— when it could no longer exist in antagonism to, or as the antithesis of, capital—marked the moment when disruption became all but symbolic on the factory floor.

For the Italian workers specifically, the final nail in the coffin was hammered in October 1980, during a protracted five-week strike against mass redundancy at the Fiat plant in Turin. News of the radical union Solidarity's actions in Poland had rekindled the labor militancy of the early 1970s, leading to the call, "Do as in Gdansk—Occupy!" Yet unlike earlier actions where the workers had unified into a homogeneous force opposing capital, the strike was actively opposed by a 20,000-strong demonstration of mid-level employees, foremen, and moderate workers. Their slogan, "Work is defended by working," was an explicit rebuttal of the radical subjectivity of the refusal of work and the affirmation of a worker identity as labor power ascribed to it by the regime of movement. Faced with this unprecedented show of support for the company, both union and party leaderships surrendered. The resulting agreement with FIAT accepted the redundancies and the prerogative of the company to fire whomever it chose.[82]

For the workerists, these developments signaled a shift in the site of autonomous conflict, away from the industrial plants to the entirety of the "social factory." The struggle for autonomy and self-determination, displaced from the shop floor, now migrated to the community: to struggles over housing and urban space; to grocery stores, utility bills, and childcare; to housework, health, and the human body. These new sites of conflict also involved production, not of goods but of the human beings who made them. And from this terrain of social reproduction, there emerged a new subject of human liberation.

Women's Liberation

Bitch is beautiful.
Bitches seek their identity strictly through themselves and what they do.
It is an act of affirmation by self and not negation by others.
The BITCH Manifesto

No longer daughters, no longer wives, we will destroy your families.
Witches of the March on Rome

Disrupting the Movement

In a speech for the citywide meeting of radical women's groups at the Free University in New York City on February 17, 1968, Anne Koedt remarked that, within New Left organizations, women's "roles centered on food-making, mimeographing, general assistance work, and as sexual supply for their male comrades after hours." "We never confronted men and demanded that unless they give up their domination over us," Koedt continued, "we would not fight for their revolution, work in their revolution."[83]

The accounts and memoirs of activists in the women's liberation struggle are filled with such realizations about the gender roles within the New Left. Sue Thrasher of the Southern Student Organizing Committee remembered, "The officers in the SSOC were all men except me. It became clear to me that I was doing all the shit work, holding the office together, keeping the mailing going on," while Elinor Langer, now editor of *The Nation*, recalled that within the New Left, "the women, come to think of it, were making drinks and setting the tables."[84] For Robin Morgan, a later WITCH member and author of the influential 1970 anthology *Sisterhood Is Powerful*, this led many women "to the depressing realization that we were doing the same work *in* the Movement as out of it; typing speeches men delivered, making coffee, but not policy."[85]

Despite the New Left's self-avowed questioning of hierarchy, activist women quickly found out that the Movement's antiauthoritarian bull-dozer stopped short of the gender wall. Rayna Rapp, who had joined the SDS in 1964, recalled how these "movement men . . . had empathy for the Vietnamese, and for Black Americans, but not for . . . the women in their lives; not the women they slept with, shared office space with . . . demonstrated with."[86]

Black women activists faced even greater hurdles. In addition to the challenges confronting white women, women in the Black Power struggle were haunted by a mythic "matriarchal" legacy of slavery, the untrue yet widely held assumption that Black women "were already liberated" as heads of Black families working outside the home. To this thinking, the reason for the impotence of Black men lay not in white supremacy but in Black women, whose authority and independence had shamed and usurped them. Kathleen Cleaver recalled how she had to "genuflect" to men of the Black Panther Party to be listened to, while Angela Davis was seen as "domineering" for never having done so. To become "real men," it was argued, Black men needed to undo the damage caused by slavery by bringing Black women back to their submissive role (an argument that had even greater resonance among Black Power activists in the Nation of Islam). As the SNCC leader Frances Beale pointed out, while the male Black militant was quick to renounce many white cultural values, "when it comes to women, he seems to take his guidelines from the pages of the *Ladies Home Journal*."[87]

In Europe, especially in Catholic countries, the situation was no better. Italian women made up a huge part of the student struggle, but were often relegated to secretarial roles within them, a situation later satirized by the quip, "From the angel of the hearth to the angel of the copying machine." Women within the German SDS found that even these lowly positions were tentative, subordinate to their primary function of child-rearing the moment they delivered "movement babies." Irrespective of race, on either side of the Atlantic, and despite their intense commitment to the cause, New Left women were silenced and ignored during important discussions, routinely assigned menial tasks, and forced to use their bodies as social currency, establishing sexual relationships with prominent movement men in order to earn concessions like the right to speak and be heard.

Drawn together by the Movement and the daily recognition of their subservience to men, women began to meet separately. Through these, at first informal, conversations, women came to perceive their subordination not as the product of individual faults or insecurities (either of themselves or of individual movement men), but as structural of the relations between sexes. When they attempted to state these grievances within the movement, they were met with resistance, derision, and violence. The leader of the Panthers, Huey Newton, refused to allow a Black women's caucus at the Revolutionary People's Constitutional Convention in 1969. Stokely Carmichael, when asked about the position of women in SNCC, charmingly replied, "prone." So fond of the joke, apparently, that he repeated it, with regularity, on his speaking tours. When Shulamith Firestone brought a women's resolution to the National Conference for New Politics in August 1967, Jo Freeman recalled how a man "patted Shulie on the head and said, 'Move along little girl: we have more important issues to talk about than women's liberation.' "[88]

In this regard, the new left was even worse than the old. In Italy, women's committees of the Italian Communist Party as well as the *Unione Donne in Italia* (Union of Italian Women), a semi-independent organization financed by the communists and active since 1945, provided a large platform to organize and advocate for issues faced by women. The student and extraparliamentary groups of the New Left had no comparable substructures. The CPUSA, though minuscule in size compared to the PCI, had also acknowledged the existence of "male chauvinism" and "the woman question." As Barbara Epstein noted,

> At least in the old left . . . one could bring up the issue, even if the communists regarded it as a "bourgeois matter" to be solved "after the revolution" . . . Inside SDS, you see, it was simply laughed at.[89]

Sarah Davidson, in a 1969 article in *Life Magazine*, recounted the story of a young woman attempting to speak at a political meeting during the turmoil at Columbia University.

> She was a pretty, soft-featured brunette who wore a loose gray sweater and no bra, and she was dead earnest. She said women are the most oppressed and underprivileged class in any society. The audience laughed and hooted. One man drew vulgar pictures on the black-board, SDS members yelled obscenities, and the girl walked out in tears.[90]

That same year, a speech by SDS veteran Marilyn Webb railing against the treatment of women as objects and property and contending that "women were mutilated as human beings so that we learn to function within the capitalist system" was interrupted by leftist men yelling, "Fuck her! Take her offstage! Rape her in a back alley!" while others jeered and shouted, "Take it off!"[91]

Worse scenes took place in Italy, where male "comrades" frequently interrupted women-only meetings. When women members of Lotta Continua (LC) in Rome demonstrated as a group against the ban on

abortion, they were violently attacked by male members of the organization's militia. For Vicky Franzinetti, a key member of LC Turin, it was
"the rupture of an alliance," a point of no return.[92]

Women's experiences in the Movement—the realization of their
subordinate status; the earnest airing of their grievances to the men they
fought with, respected, and loved; the anger provoked by the men's deri-
sive reaction—gave birth to the women's liberation struggle. In the
United States, activist women began forming autonomous women-only
groups within the structures of the New Left. By 1969, they were leaving
the Movement in droves. Italian women made the leap a year later.
Women-only groups emerged during the radically open political situation of 1969. Initially established in larger cities, they soon mushroomed
across Italy.

In this sense, the women's liberation struggle was both a product of,
and a response to, the politics and praxis of the New Left. The antiauthoritarian and anti-institutional impulses of the Movement, their questioning of the division of labor, their break from orthodox Marxism,
and the bringing together of human beings in new political groupings
were critical to the emergence of women's liberation. Equally so was the
male New Left's internal replication of gender roles, hierarchies, and
cultural assumptions of the very society they were so eagerly trying to
disrupt.

The Italian and American women's liberation struggle emerged
through the disruption of the Movement. Their self-extraction from
the New Left struggles and the simultaneous construction of an autonomous female politics led to a multifaceted questioning of the function and identification of women within society. Radical feminists
in both Italy and the United States rejected their ascription as sex
objects, as emotional crutches, as nurturing mothers, and daughters in
need of protection. They rejected long-standing conceptions of what a
women's body was, whose it was, and what it was for. They rejected
centuries-old binaries of sexual difference around male and female
endowments of reason, objectivity, agency, and completeness that had
legitimized their subordination. They rejected doing all the housework and not being paid for it. Perhaps most radically, they rejected
the past and present forms of disruptive politics, its theory, its practice, and its history as male—and therefore complicit in the world they
sought to dismantle. The shedding of old skins gave birth to many new

ones, as radical feminists in Italy and the United States created new definitions, new cosmologies, new practices and even new languages of womanhood.[93]

Getting together

In 1791, at the height of the French Revolution, Olympe de Gouges had asked, "Will women always be divided one from another? Will they never form a single body?" On the eve of women's liberation struggle, women across the Atlantic faced the same question. Though having attained franchise in most countries, in some respects, their situation had become worse. In the intervening 275 years, the regime of movement had etched stark lines between the "private" domestic realm and the "public" domain of politics and the economy. The demarcation had been entirely gendered, enacted through the forceful expulsion of women from the labor force and their subsequent confinement to the home. As the nuclear family gradually replaced larger kinship and community networks as the primary unit of society, this confinement became even more pronounced, tying women individually to men while segregating them from each other. The transfer of women from one male master to another—a transaction between father and husband sealed by the rebranding of a woman's name on her wedding day— remained the norm across the Atlantic.

This isolation from one another was singular to (particularly middle-class) women, an experience not shared by other social kinds. For most groups, the regime of movement's permeation throughout the Atlantic world had had the opposite effect. Industrial capitalism, uprooting a diffuse peasantry, concentrated workers in dense clusters within and around the factory. Racial segregation had led to a similar outcome for American Blacks. The need for skilled labor had conjured the student as a sociological unit and packed them into newly enlarged educational institutions. By contrast, the social function and spaces ascribed to women by the regime of movement had only furthered their atomization.

Social atomization made recognition of women's oppression particularly problematic. The forced concentration of workers by industrial capitalism had been pivotal to their consciousness. Working under the same roof, for the same boss, expressing and directing their frustrations at the point of their exploitation, had allowed workers to understand themselves as a collective class. The frustrations women felt, by contrast, went unshared, or were made illegible through an increasing array of twentieth-century psychiatric diagnoses targeting them. Betty Friedan's groundbreaking 1963 text, *The Feminine Mystique*, underscored the cold nature of this isolation, "suffering the nameless aching dissatisfaction . . . each one thinking she was alone."[94]

Finding one another became the first step. Women began with the political organizations they were already a part of, forming women-only collectives within SDS and the Black Panther Party in the United States and within the workers' unions of Italy. Some of these groups split off to create independent women's organizations that became the backbone of Italian and American radical feminism. In the United States, New York Radical Women (1967); WITCH, Women's International Terrorist Conspiracy from Hell (1968); The Feminists (1968); Cell 16 (1968); and Redstockings (1969) were established. In 1970, *Rivolta Femminile* (Feminine Revolt) opened its first chapters in Rome and Milan and *Lotta Feminista* (Female Struggle) groups formed in Rome and Padua.

While the performative actions of these organizations, the burning of "instruments of female torture" at the 1968 Miss America Pageant or the Witches' "Hex" on Wall Street, caught the media's attention, their real focus was on a turn inward, to an exploration of themselves and their life conditions. WITCH exhorted women to "form your own Coven of sister Witches" while *Rivolta Femminile* urged women to "Leave the piazzas!" and "Bring the street into the house!" Gathering in small groups of ten to thirty people, usually at someone's home, women began to share and analyze their individual experiences, frustrations, and feelings. This process, termed "consciousness raising" by the New York Radical Women in 1967, revealed to participants that the issues faced by individual women were, in fact, common, and that personal problems could have a social cause and a political solution. Daily experiences of inequality and unfreedom were taken as both narrative starting point and political compass into the workings of power.[95] Consciousness raising involved inquiry, not only of the structures that upheld male supremacy but also of women's internalization and performance of, and therefore complicity in, their own oppression. "Dismantling the feminine," as Carla Lonzi, the Italian pioneer of *autocoscienza*, put it, required erasing the effects of centuries of emotional and intellectual patriarchal domination, including the domination of their own sense of self. Joan Cassell, author of *A Group Called Women*, described consciousness raising as "the subjective identity-altering experience in the women's movement."[96] A process that "free[d] the group from the 'oppressor' ideology," creating what Lonzi called a "void," where an autonomous sense of being-woman could collectively emerge and exist. Topics varied by group and context, each opening up and politicizing areas of life that had previously drawn scant attention: female sexuality, childcare and housework, sexual violence, social functions and expectations, pornography, women's health, and the role of women within the Movement.

As a method, consciousness raising was not new. The poster nailed to the entrance of the Redstockings' "Bitch Sessions" in New York's Lower East Side put the process into context: "*Speak pains to recall pains.* – the Chinese Revolution. *Tell it like it is.* – the Black revolution. *Bitch, sisters, bitch!* – the final revolution." While feminists in the United States drew inspiration from Mao and the Black liberation struggle, the Italian variant, *autocoscienza* (self-awareness), was colored by its own context. *Operaismo*'s insistence on grounding analysis in the subjective experience of workers at the point of production as well as Catholic confessional practice, revived by young radical Catholics from the 1950s, inflected the translation of the practice from the United States to Italy.[97] In both cases, what made the feminist adoption of consciousness raising unique was not the method but the fact that it brought the oppression of women, previously experienced in isolation and shrouded by doubt, into a collective and relational space. The very act of coming together served to disrupt a patriarchal order whose smooth operation depended on keeping women apart.

In account after account of these sessions, women recalled the eye-opening effects of this defracturing. Edda Billi, active in the Roman feminist group *Movimento Femminista Romano* (MFR), described her experience of *autocoscienza*:

I finally viewed myself with my own eyes, no longer defined by others ... the capture of consciousness ... We had had enough of men's interpretations of who we were ... and desired to be another kind of woman, someone who was allowed to define herself for herself.[98]

Susi Kaplow, who organized four separate consciousness raising groups in New York City, felt the sessions allowed women "to restructure [themselves], putting new images, patterns, and expectations in place of the old, no longer viable ones."[99] For the Italian feminist writer Lea Melandri, consciousness raising created a new language. "It made it possible to 'say the unsayable': that for which in Italian culture no words existed, the realm of intimate sexual and emotional experiences based on one's sex."[100]

Not all radical feminists, much less all feminists, engaged in consciousness raising. Yet the centrality of the practice in the first days of women's liberation, the insights into women's oppression that emerged from them, ensured that consciousness raising had an outsized influence on the struggle as a whole. There were a number of significant effects of this influence for the theory and practice of disruptive politics.

Consciousness raising shifted the place of political struggle, away from the mass mobilization and heroic masculinity of the streets to the process of being-with and exploration inside the home.[101] These were not meetings held in private to plan "public" political (read public) events, but the practice of politics itself. Through this practicing, women politicized "private" sites that had remained outside the traditional realms of politics or had been studied neutrally, as sociological categories. Institutions such as hospitals, the family, and marriage, sites such as the bedroom, the kitchen, and the human body were thus scrutinized as terrains of political domination and reimagined in liberatory ways.

New York Wages for Housework Committee, "We
Can't Afford to Work for Love" (1974).

The Home

That was the flyer Alice gave me, and it's been hassling me all day.
I've been trying to figure out why exactly, 'cause—come on, it's a
little too much. My Jimmy works at the plant and I work here. So?

And a lot of the things it says I don't really mind doing. I mean, what else would I do all day? As my sister Lynette would say, this smells like white women's shit. Jimmy might bring home the bacon, but like my momma before me, it's my house and I set the rules. Still, it's hassling me, that and all her talk about us married women and the homes we make. Alice said she was going to their meeting Tuesday night and asked me to tag along. Why not? At least it would get me out of the house. So I tagged along.

The meeting was at the United Methodist Church on a quiet little street in Brooklyn, south of Prospect Park. It had already started by the time we got there, around thirty women, mostly white, nodding their heads as another women rapped about how our homes are really just a factory and that this factory produces the workers needed by capitalism. That means my Jimmy. Lady said I am the only worker in this factory and that my work is to keep Jimmy fed, clothed, satisfied, and rested so he can go to work each morning, all while raising my boy with the right toughness and discipline so he can grow up to be like Jimmy one day. She told us that there are millions of factories like this all over the world, each with one woman to work it. That we spend about 100 hours a week maintaining our homes, both physically and emotionally, and that it's a job. In fact, it's the most important job, since without the workers that we sisters produce, there would be no one to work all the other jobs. It's not love, it's not what we're good at, its grueling nonstop work and, she said, we should get paid for it.

Then an Italian woman got up and started rapping about how it hadn't always been this way. She said that up until a few hundred years ago, the home was a place that made stuff. Women, men, grannies, and kids, all did their part stitching, cutting, hammering, planting and harvesting round the home. But over time, where things got made shifted: to workshops and factories and offices, and the ones who worked in these places got a wage. The home became a space not for making things, but making and servicing the worker. That's when us women really got the shaft, she said. We got forced out of paid work, forced to have babies, and forced into the home, made dependent on our husbands, who became our bosses. When we protested, we were beaten and raped, or branded as witches and burned at the stake.

The factory part made sense to me. But the story about how we women got here wasn't my story. I told Alice as much on our walk back "to work." That the women I came from had been stolen from their homes and set to hard labor in the master's fields. That sex had always been part of our jobs, providing the master both relief and fresh cotton pickers. That even in our freedom, our story was more complicated; we still worked in white people's homes, were still mammies to their kids, but this time we got paid for it. We also worked in white people's prisons, making their shit for free. And while these women had gotten all riled up about how they turned our wombs into machines and why they don't want us getting abortions, they didn't say nothing about those same people sterilizing unmarried Black sisters on welfare. I had to say these things, well, because things are complicated. But after I did, I realized there was a lot in what was said that was also my story, our story.

I've been active in the campaign for four years now. Us Black sisters started up an associated group to organize in the community, based on our history, and our way of seeing the world. We got our own newsletter and meet every Sunday, but I still go by the main storefront to see Alice and help out when I can. We got all kinds of sisters in the campaign: married women, single women, old women, younger women, women who got second jobs on the outside—working days in offices or nights on the streets—and women who spend all day at home. The one thing we all got in common is housework.

Well, there's another thing, actually. It's how all this housework is done: by ourselves, in our homes. The thing about the home is that it's not just a factory, it's also a prison. Each of us locked up, watched over by our own families, guards of our own making. It's that doing it alone is what makes our job so much harder. The factory brought men together, gave 'em space where they could organize against it. They got solidarity, we got solitary. The box.

Ask anyone and they'll tell you, it's hard breaking out of prison. Shit, it's hard visiting people in prison. That's why we started going to the supermarkets, to the laundromats, the playgrounds where women do housework outside the home. Me and Alice hit up three laundromats last week. It's our version of the shop floor. No guards or bosses, where we can organize, educate, and agitate sisters to break out. It's busiest on Mondays, with women hauling, washing, sorting, and folding last weekend's clothes. We start rapping with whoever's there, asking if they like doing laundry, why they're the ones always doing it, why they don't get paid for it.

They always smirk at first, thinking we're either batshit crazy or just flew in from Mars. But we keep at it. They wave us away, saying they're busy, that they got *work* to do. But that's the goddamn point, we tell 'em. What we women do, day after day, year after year, here in the laundromat, at the grocers, in our homes, with no breaks, no sick days, no retirement, it's all work. We don't need to say it's a drag, how much it wears women down, wastes away our existence. You can read that story on their faces. All the neurosis, nerves, the acting out, the depression we sisters got? They're not women's but occupational diseases. Contracted from the factory that is our home. It's the work, we tell 'em, that's making us sick, and we're sick of doing it for free.

"So who's gonna pay us?" they ask. "My husband? His boss? The government? You want me to marry the state like some welfare bitch?"

"All of them!" and "Yes!" we say.

But demanding we get paid is just the first step. It gets us noticed. That's what most people don't get about the campaign. We actually don't want to do housework. We don't want to be homemakers at all. Not so we can get real jobs like some white women keep saying. Wearing overalls or pantyhose ain't no better than wearing an apron. For us, it's worse. 'Cause at the end of day, who you think is the one comin' home to start the cooking?

No, we're demanding wages 'cause it lets everyone know that what we do is work. Once we are seen as workers, that's when we can start holding back our labor. That's what the women who dropped off their kids with the men at the factory were doing. Same when nine out of ten sisters in Iceland went on a general strike, saying, "Fuck it, its Women's Day, we're not doing no housework." Whole country shut down.

But it's not just the stuff you read in the papers. We've been clogging up the homes, individually, every day—serving dinners late, not shopping or sticking to our schedules. When a sister refuses to lay with her man, he calls her frigid. We call it absenteeism. The moment we refuse to cook, smile, and fuck at command, we will have power over our men. At that moment, they're gonna realize that the home is not the glue holding the family together, but a space that divides us up, a place where we each discipline the other for the sake of capital. A sister Silvia said, in rejecting housework, we—their crutches, their slaves, their chains—will lead them by the hand into the struggle for our collective liberation.

I dig it, but I've been reading up for a while. Try explaining this to some of these sisters, though. It gets worse when we say, "But to do that, we gotta destroy the homes." Destroy the home as factory. That's why our real struggle is not with men—our immediate bosses—but with capital. Capital makes its money from our unpaid housework. It takes what we make—the workers we create and nurture and sustain—without paying us a dime. Anywhere else that's called stealing. To stop bankrolling it, we gotta shut down this space, break up the family and destroy the home. Then you get that smirk again. The thing is, they might not call it like I call it, but women are already doing it. Sisters all round the world are marry-ing later, having less kids, and divorcing more often. Or they're not getting hitched at all (here, Black sisters are leagues ahead of white women). The more we refuse to make the workers that capitalism needs, the more its gonna have to pay to make them itself. All them preschools, mental health clinics, and social workers you've been seeing in the community? They are the marks of our refusal. By upping the cost of making their workers, we take away the profits of capital.

Some lady asked me the other day why we want to destroy the home. Where is everyone supposed to live? That's like asking slaves why they wanted to burn their plantation. But still, it's not the dumbest question. We're not talking about burning down houses. The real question is why we do all this work where we do it. In this space everybody thinks is so natural for us to be in. As if doing this shit was our life's aspiration. Like we were hardwired for it. No, ma'am, we ain't gonna burn down your house. What we want to destroy is the space whose purpose is to create good workers for free. The space that imprisons sisters and exploits their labor. The space that isolates us from each other. We're not interested in the building, just what happens inside the building.

How we gonna shut down the home? What we gonna replace it with? Destroying the home means destroying the factory. Taking the work done there and moving it outside and into the community. Neighborhood clinics, childcare, communal kitchens, municipal laundromats, state-funded and community-run spaces, where men and women can work side by side, sharing the work. Public spaces where we can organize so this work is done on our own terms. We've already started setting up these spaces in Black neighborhoods. But in the end, it's going to require a whole shift in how this work is done, whose gonna do it, and who it's done for. Then people can live how they choose. You wanna stay with Jimmy? Shack up with a new group? There won't be anything holding you back. Not Jimmy, not money, not worrying about how you gonna feed the kids. So, come, sisters, let's get out of these homes and melt the city.

Whether discussing gender housework, gender roles, or sexuality, consciousness-raising groups rejected altogether the abstraction and objective analyses of society that had dominated male intellectual framings of disruption since the mid-nineteenth century. Much like the worker inquiries of *operaismo*, "The personal is political" of US radical feminists or the *partire da sé* (starting from oneself) method in Italy elevated a subjective narrative that began from how women experienced domination in their everyday lives. They were a dramatic departure from the Marxist vulgate of grand narratives and universalist claims that had pervaded Italian and American radical political discourse. As one member of the Roman MFR explained:

> *Partire da sé* was certainly a reaction against the languages of the leftwing groups many of us came from—you know, those typical long discussions that started with "the general framework," whereby "general" always, and inevitably, implied a male perspective. It was refreshing to know that we could be political by referring to our intimate relationships, by finding the political in our intimate desires, fears and hopes.[102]

In place of the theory-laden analyses of "objective conditions" or interpretations of the "present conjecture" that filled the pages of male leftist publications, feminist periodicals such as the Demau Collective's *Sottosopra* (Upside Down) printed diaries, narrative accounts, and autobiographical commentary by women describing their unmediated experiences of women's collectives.[103]

Taken together, the praxis and object of consciousness raising altered how many radical feminists conceptualized liberation; shifting the focus away from equality toward autonomy and self-determination. The equality sought by liberal organizations such as NOW, "to end sex discrimination in hiring, promotions and salaries, to establish a system of comprehensive child-care so women could join the wage-labor force, to place women in policy-making posts," failed to address the institutional and ideational entrapments that were brought up in consciousness-raising sessions.[104] Rather, consciousness raising revealed that the issues facing women—and their overcoming— could never be resolved through formal channels available in liberal democratic society. The personal was political, yes, but there was no mechanism within the existing framework of the regime of movement to address this politics. To underscore the point, in January 1969, New York Radical Women "gave back the vote" and burned their voter registration cards, a symbolic rejection of representative democracy and of women's franchise, which had been able to do so little to change women's situation within America.[105] Whether implicitly or explicitly, many radical feminists believed that "voting was a 'mockery of democracy' and equality in a fundamentally unequal society, an obscenity."[106]

Italian radical feminists saw the struggle for equality as not only counterproductive, but in fact a trap that led to the erasure of women (a position some radical feminists have stuck to despite the recent surge in trans activism). Feminine Revolt argued that formal or natural equality within categories created by patriarchal societies was a myth that veiled a fundamental contradiction. The category of the universal human being, though theoretically asexual, was in practice, male-sexed. The inclusion of women into the universal subject of the social contract implied that sexual difference could only be resolved by the obliteration of female characteristics. As one of the first Italian feminist collectives Demau (The Demystification of Authority) argued, the equal integration of women into male society was only possible through "the masculinization of women"[107] On the other hand, when sexual difference was affirmed, it was used to identify women with reproduction and thus to exclude them (as women) from the polis. As the New York Radical Feminists had earlier noted, woman's "sexual difference is rationalized to trap her within [social reproduction], while the male sexual difference is rationalized to imply access to all areas of human activity."[108] Equality, within this framework, implied that the polis was only open to women who agreed to neuter themselves.[109]

In both cases, becoming equal meant becoming like a man. Carla Lonzi took this perspective to its logical conclusion.

But do we, after thousands of years, really wish for inclusion, on these terms, in a world planned by others? Existing as a woman does not imply participation in male power, but calls into question the very concept of power. It is in order to avoid this attack that we are now granted inclusion in the form of equality.

For Lonzi, the framework of equality served to defang feminism of its disruptive power, a way to enervate the "unruly subject" of women through her assimilation into male society. Equality was a veil, a ruse, an "offer of legal rights to a colonized people . . . the mask with which their inferiority is disguised."[110]

Whether or not radical feminists subscribed to these ideas, consciousness raising cemented the belief that the cause of women's oppression lay in the structures of male society. Integration on equal terms within a system expressly designed to subordinate them was an absurdity akin to the integration of Blacks into Apartheid. For radical feminists, women's liberation could be achieved not through equality but rather by their refusal of the world of men.

The problem with men

In getting together and narrating their experiences, radical feminists realized that oppression came in multiple forms: Male domination over women was upheld by laws, acted through institutions, reinforced by language, and internalized by themselves. They termed this totalizing social system of domination the *patriarchy*. The range of approaches, theoretical frameworks, experiential worlds, ways of belonging and relating that feminists used to reject its mechanisms and articulate a new womanhood to the breadth of the radical social imaginary in a moment of self-institution. While many commentators have indicted radical feminism for its fractures and infighting, it is equally true to see these same features as their strength.

Radical feminists in Italy and the United States claimed that male domination over women was sanctioned and given legitimacy through a series of sexual differences that men had ascribed to each gender. Within this cosmology, men were seen as essentially rational, industrious, stable, outgoing, objective, active, strong, independent, guided by reason, and complete. Whereas women were projected as being irrational, lazy, unstable, shy, subjective, passive, submissive, dependent, guided by emotions, and incomplete. These sexual differences were confirmed and reproduced through a near-totalizing array of social institutions: from scientific discourse to family upbringing, marriage to child-rearing, historical narratives to the bodily comportments of men and women. Taken together, they enforced and naturalized male superiority throughout society. They were instrumental in striating the terrain of the regime of movement by gender, channeling women to low-level or auxiliary functions outside the home and to unpaid social reproduction within it.

Radical feminists' disruption consisted of a disavowal of this cosmology as a way of extracting themselves from their consigned roles within the regime of movement. Dana Densmore of the Boston women's collective Cell 16 saw in "the idea of a woman's nature: gentle, loving, unaggressive, tender, modest, giving, patient, naïve, simplistic, irrational, instinctual" a giant ruse to subordinate women and keep them in the home.[111] To Roxanne Dunbar (also of Cell 16), these were "the personality traits of slaves." "We have learned maternalism not from our closeness to reproduction," Dunbar averred, "but from our experience as Slaves to men and children, our closeness to shit."[112]

Other radical feminists believed this cosmology to be inscribed into the very definition of "women." Ti-Grace Atkinson, founder of the Feminists, argued that "women" was the outcome of a historical process that differentiated human beings into different social roles based on their sex. The oppression of one half of humanity by the other began with the political division of labor, the moment when "certain human beings *with* certain capacities are defined *by* that capacity." Atkinson claimed that "woman" was an artificial political category—the mutation of a biological classification into a sociological one, where the reproductive capacity of half of humankind became defined as its social function. The historical oppression of women, their "massacre," was thus inscribed into their definition. "Women" was nothing other than the name given to the one half of humanity through its oppression by the other half. In an argument similar to that of the Italian workerists, Atkinson argued that in order for "women" to regain their humanity, they needed to eradicate or annihilate themselves. Feminism was not the women's struggle but the struggle *against* women, against the way they had been defined and relegated by the patriarchy.

Still other feminists inversed the binary, reascribing to women traits that had historically been reserved for men. *The WITCH Manifesto*, published in 1968, argued that "Witches have always been women who dared to be: groovy, courageous, aggressive, intelligent, nonconformist, explorative, curious, independent, sexually liberated, revolutionary." There was a witch who "lives and laughs in every woman. She is the free part of each of us." Liberation for the members of WITCH lay in reclaiming and acting through these long-repressed traits. Valerie Solanas, the founder and sole member of the Society for Cutting Up Men (SCUM), provided perhaps the clearest if extreme example of this inversion. "The male is an incomplete female, a walking abortion, aborted at the gene stage," Solanas wrote in her *SCUM Manifesto*.

> The male spends his life attempting to complete himself, to become female. He attempts to do this by . . . claiming as his own all female characteristics—emotional strength and independence, forcefulness, dynamism, decisiveness, coolness, objectivity, assertiveness, courage, integrity, vitality, intensity, depth of character, grooviness, etc—and projecting onto women all male traits.[113]

Whether they believed sexual difference to be biological or socially produced, radical feminists across Italy and the United States agreed that the past and present of male civilization was not something to aspire to. The characteristics either possessed by men or revered by patriarchal society were repudiated for causing the untold suffering, violence, domination, and death that men had wrought on human-kind throughout its history. Carla Lonzi claimed that "male thought has sanctioned a mechanism which valorizes war, leadership, heroism, and struggle" and urged women to "abandon men to the depths of their solitude."[114] This "global devaluation of the male world," as Lonzi termed it in her infamous 1970 pamphlet, *Let's Spit on Hegel*, was a critical step for women in recognizing within themselves a radically different capacity, an "Unexpected Subject" that would "effect a complete transformation of life."[115]

For one of the earliest Italian feminist collectives, Demau, the value system of patriarchal society was authoritarian. They called upon women to demystify authority in all social relations and to "elaborat[e] values that will inform the new society."[116] This "new autonomy for women" entailed the search for and autonomous production of interpretive frameworks free from the models imposed by male patriarchy. In a different vein, *Revolta Femminile*'s Manifesto, hung up on the walls of Rome in 1970, took issue with the pervasive compulsion to productivity within male society. "We detest the mechanisms of competitiveness and the blackmail exercised in the world by the hegemony of efficiency," the Manifesto proclaimed, "Liberation for women does not mean accepting the life man leads, because this life is unlivable."[117]

Both SCUM and Cell 16 attributed the unliveability of contemporary society to the nature of man. Solanas claimed, "To be male is to be deficient, emotionally limited; maleness is a deficiency disease and males are emotional cripples." Rape, war, government, money, were all products of this male deficiency, caused by "man's attempts to disprove his error." The only solution, Solanas argued, was to abolish money and government and eradicate, through systematic murder, the male sex. Similarly, Lisa Leghorn of Cell 16 identified the features of the "male concept" as hierarchy, centralization, and aggression and stated that these patterns "were unknown in matriarchal cultures."[118] Building on this concept, Cell 16 member Betsy Warrior's article, "Man As an Obsolete Life-Form," claimed that the inner nature of men was dominated by "aggressive destructive drives" that made them "unfit for life today."[119]

Whatever the cause, radical feminists believed that the destructive tendencies of patriarchal civilization were reaching a critical stage, imperiling everything they touched, including themselves. "He is demolishing the world," the *Movimento Femminista Romano* stated succinctly, "self-destruction alone is the only goal offered, while we are dragged along, tied as we are to this great carriage of death." Rather than "participating in the defeat of man," many Italian and American radical feminists sought to extract themselves from their world. Only in separation, they argued, would women be free to create, "to find life in this cemetery that calls itself male society."[120]

The politics of separation

Almania Barbour, a Black militant woman from Philadelphia, made the sardonic yet incisive observation that "the women's movement is the first in history with a war on but no enemy."[121] If men, regardless of their individual beliefs, were the physical human beings who upheld and benefited from the structures of patriarchy, then most women were caught in the distinct situation of living alongside their adversaries. In this sense, women's liberation faced a particular difficult organizational problem. As The Furies, a lesbian-feminist collective based in Washington, DC, aptly summarized: "You can't build a strong movement if your sisters are out there fucking the oppressor."[122]

Though developed (and practiced) furthest by Italian and American radical feminists, separatism remained a loaded issue, particularly for the first women's groups formed from within the New Left. By 1970, many of these feminists were leading a double life. In the evenings, they went to their women's group. At night, they slept with movement men they had just criticized in front of other women. In the morning, they worked alongside those they had condemned the evening before.[123] The issue was especially vexing for Italian (particularly Roman) feminists, who were reluctant to abandon their connections to the broader left-wing struggle. This "double militancy" was seen as critical to engaging lower-class women who would not naturally come into contact with feminist politics, as well drawing on proletarian women's experiences as a way to diversify the largely educated middle-class composition of their founding members (escaping a siloization that often dogged their US counterparts).

Yet, as they discussed at length in their consciousness-raising sessions, these engagements hampered the women's liberation struggle. Just as integration had stunted Black subjectification, so too, radical feminists argued, had marriage. According to Judith Brown, cofounder of the first women's liberation organization in the American South, the political purpose of marriage lay in "the atomization of a sex so as to render it politically powerless."[124] Each day, their bodies and minds were being contaminated with male definitions, male gazes, male expectations, and male norms. If women were really at war, this clearly was not a very suitable battle position. What was needed was to withdraw and regroup as women on a more permanent basis, facing the enemy across clear lines of attack.

For some feminists, separatism was a temporary necessity. In 1970, the California Bay Area paper *It Ain't Me, Babe* carried an editorial arguing that while functioning among men within the patriarchy was extremely oppressive, the "creation of a woman's culture cannot simply be the carving off of an enclave to bear the status quo more easily—but a site to crystalize and strengthen our rebellion."[125] Separatism also did not necessarily rule out political alliances with men. Even militant feminist groups like *Revolta Feminnile* argued that "the woman who rejects the family and the young man who rejects military service are partners on the same path of refusing to participate in patriarchal structures."[126]

Others took a more hard-line stance. Cell 16 called for separation and celibacy, both personally and politically, as the only means to break out of the self-conditioning impressed upon women by patriarchal society.

They advocated forming and living in female-only communes and spoke only to female reporters, eschewing all interaction with men. The Feminists, led by Atkinson, institutionalized the principle of separation within their organization, stipulating that only one-third (and by 1971, none) of its membership could be composed of women living with men—in legal or informal partnerships.[127] For them, feminism, in both theory and practice, was synonymous with separatism. They described heterosexual love as a sort of Stockholm syndrome, "the response of the victim to her rapist," and married women as at best "hostages" and at worst "collaborators."

Sexually, separatism was intimately tied to feminist debates over the political significance of lesbianism. For lesbian-feminists in the United States, lesbianism was the logical outgrowth of feminism. The Radicalesbians claimed that lesbians, by virtue of their distance from contaminating maleness, were better positioned to "give each other a new sense of self" than heterosexual women, who were "bound in one-on-one relationships with their oppressors" and thus "dependent upon male culture for their self-definition."[128] The Furies took this approach to its limit, arguing against heterosexuality as itself a form of patriarchal oppression. To them, lesbianism was not a "bedroom issue" of sexual preference, but a political choice. "Lesbianism is a threat to the ideological, political, and economic basis of male supremacy," The Furies argued.

> It undermines the personal power that men exercise over women. Our rejection of heterosexual sex challenges male domination in its most individual and common form. We offer something better than submission to personal oppression. We offer the beginning of the end of collective male supremacy.[129]

While the issue of lesbianism created deep fissures within the US women's liberation struggle, it had a less divisive impact in Italy. For many Italian radical feminists, "political homosexuality" necessitated not so much a refusal of sexual relationships with men but, rather, the existence of separate spaces of theoretical production and political action. To a large degree, this was a product of the shifting object of *autocoscienza*, which by the mid-1970s had moved from an analysis of women's oppression to an analysis of the relationship between women, a move from the rejection of their definition within patriarchy to the articulation of a new female subjectivity. Through *autocoscienza*, the self was defined not as an individual woman but emerged relationally, created through the relationships formed in their coming together. If there was a subject of women, it was in the words, the language, that developed between women practicing *autocoscienza*. It was the symbolic and material universe of bonding, the collective discovery of each other, that defined women. Lesbianism was simply the name given by some radical feminists to this relational subject.

In just a few short years, radical feminists in Italy and the United States had achieved much. They had shifted the site of disruptive politics away from the factories and streets to the home, dissolving in the process the distinction between public and private realms.[130] They had introduced a totally new framing by which to analyze the regime of movement (the patriarchy) and explored the mechanisms, both overt and subtle, physical and psychological, through which it divided humanity by social kind. In doing so, they illuminated new or underexplored terrains of struggle, including reproductive and emotional labor, sex, and the family.

Despite these accomplishments, by the late 1970s, criticisms of the Italian and American radical feminist project began to mount. Leftists and liberal feminists indicted the insularity of consciousness raising and *autocoscienza*, arguing that the separatism it fostered had pigeonholed women into an irrelevance of their own making. Transgender, sexual lesbians, and women of color in both the global north and south charged them with ignoring their double or triple oppressions and universalizing to all women the subjectivities created by a small and privileged subset. Both accused them of a "cultural feminism" turned increasingly inward and away from the very real political struggles facing half of humanity. These indictments, however harsh, had legitimate basis. Yet, from the perspective of Italian and American radical feminists, they spoke from conceptions of politics and history that were themselves male, patriarchal, and unsuited for women's liberation. It was precisely in disrupting these conceptions that radical feminists had gone further than the contemporaneous struggles for Black Power and workerism.

In 1969, when the New York Radical Women burned their voter registration cards and "gave back the vote," they had rejected not only the liberal feminist struggle for gender equality, but also the suggestion that women's liberation was the completion of earlier feminist struggles. This sentiment, shared by many Italian and American radical feminists, had significant implications for the politics of disruption. On the most immediate level, it disrupted the notion of historical continuity and progress within the women's struggle—rejecting, at the moment of its birth, the metaphor of waves to describe the history of feminist politics.

More fundamentally, radical feminism denounced the very idea of progressive movement, prevalent since the mid-nineteenth century, as male. "The future of the world does not lie in moving continually forwards along a path mapped out by man's desire for overcoming difficulties," Carla Lonzi wrote. Rather than seek refuge in a struggle vouchsafed by the red star, men needed to instead "disrupt their historical role as protagonists."[131] An idea echoed by the American feminists Beverly Jones and Judith Brown, who urged the women's liberation struggle to "slow male-history making."[132] To a certain degree, the unruliness of the radical feminist subject lay precisely in her refusal of a progressive temporality that culminated in a redeemed future. Unlike almost every other struggle since the French Revolution, radical feminists refused to speak from what Derrida called "the grammar of the future anterior" (the emancipated position when liberation *will have* taken place). There was no arc of history, it did not bend toward justice, and it was certainly not propelled by historical subjects.

Black Power and workerism had sought to turn Blacks and workers from the objects to the subjects of this world they had defined self-determination (or self-valorization) as the autonomous deployment or entrance of the Black and worker into history. For radical feminists, by contrast, history itself was a patriarchal construct. As an anonymous woman of the *Movimento Femminista Romano* stated in 1979,

I don't want the word of history; rather I want to be subtracted from history; except that this subtraction must find a means of expression. Otherwise . . . having always been defined and used as my absence, [history] is filled by the greed of order.[133]

Almost a decade earlier, Lonzi had argued that "history was based on nonperishable traces." It was monumental, erected (and erectile), and male. Lonzi claimed that "women's difference [was] her millennial absence from history" and urged women to profit from this difference. If women had entered history at all, Lonzi maintained, it was in the brief episodes of a perishable and perished past, where woman had manifested herself as the "interruption, for the first time, of the monologue of patriarchal civilization." In such a temporality, "there are no goals." "We are the world's dark past, we are giving shape to the present," Lonzi declared. Freed from history, "the future of the world is open," shaped by "an entirely new word put forward by an entirely new subject. It ha[d] only to be uttered to be heard."[134]

Conclusion

From roughly the mid-1960s through the 1970s, the politics of disruption took on a different form. Its principal target was not the forced movement of the regime but the demarcation of the terrain of motion by social kind. The three disruptive struggles explored in this chapter all took issue with the ordering mechanism of this terrain, of how the regime of movement prescribed which subjects could and should do what and where. All three disavowed the subjectivity ascribed to them, be it as negro, woman, or worker. They defined themselves as an oppressed group and the values, culture, practices, and spaces of the regime of movement as exploitative, extractive, and appropriative. All three similarly questioned the normalized functioning of the spaces where their subjectivities took place. Significantly, all three struggles also rejected integration within the existing framework of the regime, specifically as they were offered by the PCI and Italian unions, the civil rights movement, and liberal feminism.[135]

Instead, the three struggles formed autonomous organizations that articulated new collective forms of subjectivity with their own practices, values, and spaces. These new subject positions demanded not only the eradication of their place and function within the hierarchy of social kinds, but, more profoundly, the destruction of the ordering system that made such divisions possible. As such, they were unassimilable by the regime of movement. Their disruptions were not distributive (seeking the social redistribution of power, wealth, and function), but were direct attacks on the regime's prerogative to define its subjects and what they could do in the spaces assigned to them.

For the regime of movement, the autonomous becoming-subject of Blacks, workers, and women registered as terror. And rightly so. There was simply no other way within the epistemic universe of capitalism, patriarchy, and white supremacy to understand "niggers with guns," the refusal of work, or witches chanting, "No longer daughters, no longer wives, we will destroy your families." Faced with these existential threats to its own continuation, the regime of movement struck back, responding with state violence, economic restructuring, co-option, and, later on, overt mechanisms of erasure and forgetting.

In America, Black Power organizations, particularly the Panthers, were singled out as the primary security threat to the United States, becoming the target of a relentless attack by federal and state governments entailing propaganda, blackmail, false flag operations, and targeted assassination. Where these failed, a much broader campaign of state terror under cover of the wars on crime and drugs brought an occupying and militarized police presence into Black communities, criminalizing Black existence and incarcerating (for profit) its surplus population. In Italy, the autonomous projects of workers and women became casualties of the ever-escalating violence between the Italian state and the armed terrorist resistance against it. This violence, actively encouraged by the state through a *strategia della tensione* (strategy of tension), had the intended consequence of pushing elements of the women's and workers' struggle toward armed confrontation and was used as an excuse for repressing the much larger autonomous struggles that refused to be drawn into the *Anni di Piombo* (Years of Lead).

At the same time, the regime of movement created and celebrated narrow pathways of social mobility previously denied to Black, working-class, and female subjects. For the price of accepting the regime's social order, the Italian PCI, lean-in feminists, and a nascent Black bourgeoisie were allowed access to the halls of corporate and governmental power. The scars of this Faustian bargain, where the entry of a privileged few were purchased at the expense of the many, are deep, numerous, and remain. They included a Communist Party actively backing neoliberal austerity in Italy, the 1985 aerial bombing of the Black environmental group MOVE by Philadelphia's first Black mayor Wilson Goode, and the inauguration of a postracial order by a Black president whose administration left unchanged rates of Black incarceration, Black poverty, and the murder of Blacks by police, while dramatically increasing deportations and drone warfare against other people of color.

Perhaps worst of all, this Faustian bargain relegitimized a politics of representation that the autonomous struggles of this chapter had viewed as an anathema, substituting their aim of autonomous self-determination with an identity-based politics seeking recognition and diversity. The most profound consequence of this shift has been the foreclosure of the project of liberation. The twenty-first-century mutations of these struggles have preserved the critiques of capitalism, white supremacy, and patriarchy, while abandoning the goal to remake the world anew. It has given rise to a pessimistic politics, at times verging on Nietzschean *ressentiment*, that mandates the recognition of past and present structural oppression but stops short of practicing ways to overcome it. The concept of privilege exemplifies this contradiction, continually demanding that society recognize its oppressive structure as its sole reality. The substitution of class warfare by the terms "classism," "class privilege," and "classist" over the past decade in US leftist discourse, becoming perhaps its most absurd and terrifying variant. Thankfully, these trends have been challenged by a global upsurge in disruptive politics, most recently by struggles that have developed a radical abolitionist agenda, autonomous zones practicing prefigurative politics, and new forms of multiracial organizing.

Historically, repression, selective integration, and the politics of representation were extremely effective mechanisms that foreclosed the promise of Black, worker, and women's liberation. Yet, these disruptive struggles should not be entirely absolved of blame, and bear partial responsibility for their demise. Their most persistent weakness—one present across all three struggles—was a tendency to replicate the forms of a system they struggled against. This mimicry was manifest in certain Black ethnonationalisms as well as the drift toward biological essentialism by some radical feminists. In both cases, the articulations of the Black or female subject simply inverted the content of the regime's ordering mechanism—substituting white and male with Black and female superiority—while preserving its form. The same could be said of the turn to armed resistance of groups like the Black Liberation Army or the Red Brigades that, as Christian Marazzi remarked, "are to be criticized not for being violent but not violent enough." They correlate the state's violence. "The Red Brigades, in their actions, *produce*

State-Power."[136] Of course, these struggles were far from alone in harboring such tendencies. From the tragic futures of the Zionist project to ethnic postcolonial violence in Africa and the subcontinent, duplication of violent forms remains just that.

By contrast, the most radical disruptive subjects were those who not only refused their subjugated role within the regime, but disavowed the ordering mechanism itself. It is such subjects who have formed the basis of this chapter. The incredible explosion of their deployments in such a short time span is a testament to the creative power of disruption.

Coda: The Southern Wind

They resist in order to persist. Because they can persist only by resisting the movement of a world that dissolves and negates their being.

Adolfo Gilly

On January 1, 1994, the day the North Atlantic Free Trade Agreement (NAFTA) went into effect, a large, armed, and masked Indigenous Mayan army emerged from the jungles and canyons of Southeast Mexico. They seized towns and ranches and occupied the old colonial capital of the Chiapas, San Cristóbal. In their first public announcement, the Zapatista Army of National Liberation (EZLN) declared their intention to march on Mexico City, defeat the federal army, and depose the government in order to allow Mexicans to exercise free and democratic control over their lives.

A relatively straightforward revolutionary agenda enacted successfully by dozens of militant groups since the days of Blanqui. Soon after, the Zapatistas called on the people of Mexico to join their uprising. They did not—seemingly dooming the EZLN to the dustbin of history.

If this had been all there was to the Zapatistas' disruptive script, there would be little to differentiate them from the thousands of other ill-timed and unsuccessful revolutionary struggles in history. However, though unwilling to take up arms against the federal government and army, large segments of Mexican society were ready to support the Zapatistas. As news of the Mexican government's brutal display of force against the lightly armed Indigenous poor spread, so did spontaneous and increasingly massive protests throughout Mexico and the world. After twelve days of mounting domestic and international pressure, the Salinas government was forced to back down. They issued a unilateral cease-fire and invited the EZLN to negotiations. The (inter)national solidarity, though falling short of expanding the Zapatista Army's "war against oblivion" into a global rebellion, did provide much-needed leverage against, and relative safety from, the Mexican state. Over the next three decades, the Zapatistas made use of this leverage to establish multiple spaces and subjectivities of autonomy.

Their story makes for a good transition from the twentieth- to a twenty-first-century form of disruptive politics. Begun in 1994 by a few thousand soldiers, the Zapatista struggle for "justice, dignity, and democracy" now involves more than 250,000 people, making it one of the longest lasting and largest disruptive struggles in history. Their success is even more remarkable if one considers the global context that they were up against.

The closing decades of the twentieth century were not a good time for disruption. The struggles of the 1970s detailed in the last chapter were over, their ideas and members co-opted, brutally suppressed, or reduced to the terrorist fringes of society. The fall of the USSR in 1990 made matters worse. The subsequent dawn of a unipolar world order and talk of the end of history severely constricted the world's ideological compass, cementing the cultural hegemony of the regime of movement and its economic colonization of the globe. By the close of the twentieth century, Thatcher's 1980 mantra, "There is no alternative," rang reassuringly or catastrophically true.[1]

Adding to the dismal conjecture was the regime's wholesale embrace and propagation of human rights. Coming into its own in the mid-1970s, human rights discourse posed a particular challenge for the politics of disruption, severely limiting the strategic options of the oppressed. The politics of this discourse acknowledged the oppressed, allowed them to presence, but only as victims whose fundamental humanity had been violated. It cornered the oppressed into a passive role, denying any agency save their appeals for recognition. Writing at the height of the anticolonial struggle, Fanon had argued that resistance was a cleansing force, endowing the oppressed with dignity and self-respect. On the new stage of human rights by contrast, human dignity was not realized through action but rather ontologized, manifest through the telling of, the bearing witness to, an unreciprocated suffering. In this, the global arena constructed by human rights was radically different from the one the New Left had operated within. Through the mid-1970s, the politics of liberation, of self-determination, was predicated on disrupting the regime of the oppressor. Its iconic symbols were images of strength and antagonism: the raised closed fist of a Black Panther or a Vietnamese woman holding an AK-47. A decade later, these images had all but disappeared. A new generation grew up among photographs of starving or sex-trafficked children, with the pop star–studded "We are the World" soundtrack as musical accompaniment.

To orchestrate this shift, the regime mobilized an entire army of charities and NGOs that drew attention to human suffering while simultaneously coding, in legal and moral terms, all resistance as terrorism. It was a strategically brilliant move, and one that proved disastrous for disruption. By forcing the oppressed to appeal to the conscience of their oppressor, human rights channeled discontent into a politics that legitimized the regime and criminalized those who destabilized its operations.

Some struggles adapted to the changed circumstances. Bishop Desmond Tutu and the South African UDC rebranded Mandela the armed militant into Mandela the political prisoner, and rather successfully at that. Greenpeace gradually phased out of its earlier direct actions and phased into shiny lobbying and fundraiser suits. Others stuck to their guns and went underground. Abandoned by their support networks, they were ruthlessly hunted down.

It was within this radically altered context that the Zapatistas began their armed uprising against the Mexican state and the global neoliberal order. The end of the Cold War and an international audience increasingly receptive to rights claims afforded them a certain measure of protection. It also severely limited the possible tactics for—and possible outcomes of—their struggle. To their credit, the Zapatistas masterfully navigated this new terrain, charting a politics of disruption that is still very much in use today.

Drawing Blood from Chiapas

The origin of the Zapatista uprising, Chiapas was and remains one of the poorest regions of Mexico, home to a large Indigenous population of Mayan decent (composed mainly of the Tzeltal, Tzotzil, Ch'ol, Zoque, Tojolabal, Lacandon and Mam peoples). In traditional markers of development, whether hospitals, schools, or access to electricity, roads, and running water, Chiapas ranks far below the average rates for the country. This underdevelopment is not due to a lack of resources. Chiapas generates 55 percent of all of Mexico's hydroelectricity and is the fourth largest producer of crude oil and natural gas. Add to this an export-oriented agricultural sector increasingly concentrated in the hands of absentee landlords, and it is little wonder that neither the products nor the profits from Chiapan labor remain within the state.

A few years before the Zapatista uprising, the unofficial spokesmen and poet of the EZLN, Subcomandante Marcos, offered a guided tour of the region, painting a vivid portrait of its extractive channels. "Chiapas is bled through thousands of veins: through oil ducts and gas ducts, over electric wires, by railroad cars, through bank accounts, by trucks and vans, by ships and planes, over clandestine paths, third-rate roads, and mountain-passes." These channels, Marcos argued, were the tributaries of neoliberalism.

Oil, electric energy, cattle, money, coffee, bananas, honey, corn, cocoa, tobacco, sugar, soy, melons, sorghum, mangoes, avocados, and Chiapan blood flow out through 1,001 fangs sunk into the neck of South-eastern Mexico . . . leaving behind the trademark of capitalism: ecological destruction, agricultural waste, hyper-inflation, alcoholism, prostitution, and poverty.[2]

Due to its difficult terrain and distance from the capital, Chiapas was a relatively late conquest for the regime of movement. Until the mid-nineteenth century, the mostly Indigenous population experienced Spanish rule much as they had the Aztec, working communal land and paying tribute to empire. The first fangs of the regime struck during the liberalization known as *La Reforma*, particularly with the implementation of the Lerdo Law that sought to "free" the Indigenous from their "traditional fetters" by privatizing their communal property. The reforms allowed for the confiscation of Indigenous land and its sale to a new, large, and largely absent landowning class.[3] For the Indigenous of Chiapas, the marketization of land, as elsewhere, resulted in expropriation and the creation of a labor force that was forced to work in order to survive. Indebted servitude, temporary migrant labor, and slavery became the hallmarks of the new labor regime, with landless Indigenous either tied by debt to large estates or forced to work as daily wage workers, sharecroppers, or renters.

Expropriation, as elsewhere, caused bitterness and unrest. In 1910, Emiliano Zapata organized this unrest into the Liberating Army from the South and, temporarily teaming up with northern elites, overthrew the forty-year Diaz dictatorship. Refusing to disarm or take state power, the Zapata army became an autonomous force, insisting on radical land reform, justice, and local control. As tensions with the newly elite–backed Madero government rose, the Zapatistas began to expropriate and redistribute land, institute village-based consensus democracy, and communalize production on their own initiative in areas they controlled. While ultimately defeated by the Federal Army, elements of the radical peasant struggle were incorporated into the Mexican constitution of 1917, particularly in its twenty-seventh article.

The cornerstone of land tenure law in Mexico, Article 27 outlined the agrarian reform demanded by the peasant armies of the Revolution. It declared all land, water, and mineral rights to be the property of the people of Mexico. It also gave the government a mandate and the requisite authority to expropriate land from large landholders and give it to eligible agrarian communities. Implementation was patchy and not without its own issues, but over the next sixty years, more than 3 million households were given access to land, living on some 28,000 rural communes, or *ejidos*.[4]

It was this partially restored system of communal land ownership that NAFTA intended to do away with. In preparation for the free trade agreement, Mexico amended Article 27 of its constitution, paving the way for the mass transfer of rural land from Indigenous communities to multinational food corporations.[5] The day the treaty went into effect was the moment the EZLN struck.

In the months and years that followed, the Zapatistas set loose their disruptive politics. These disruptions were both material and symbolic, directed inward and out, and operated upon local, national, and global terrains, creating new spaces and subjectivities of autonomy within each. Though treated individually below, for the Zapatistas, these terrains were all linked.

Becoming Indigenous—Autonomy

Like many other countries in the Americas, the Mexican state's approach to its Indigenous population has been Janus-faced. Under a civilizational logic of scientific modernization, it sought the assimilation and absorption of the Indigenous within Mexican society and the "citizenization" of Indians through public education and economic development. This process was formalized by the ending of Indigenous as a protected class. In the 1930s, the policies of erasure were matched by state-directed efforts to incorporate Indian history and culture into the official national ideology of Mexico. These contradictory approaches became the hallmark of the postrevolutionary Mexican state: one that valorized a glorious Indigenous past while consigning actually existing Indigenous peoples to oblivion in the present.[6]

The rallying cry, "Ya Basta!" of the Zapatistas when they emerged from the Lacandon Jungle in 1994 thus had a dual referent: a refusal of economic extraction by neoliberalism and the erasure of indigeneity by the Mexican state. The "war against oblivion" therefore required a twofold disruption, a withdrawal of their political *and* economic participation from the regime. This withdrawal was subnational. It was not a call to break up the Mexican state into fragments of Indigenous countries, nor was this withdrawal the birth announcement of the "Mayan Nation." Rather, the Zapatistas wanted recognition that Indigenous peoples have their own political, social, and economic forms of organization that differ from—and as such should be allowed to function independently of—the Mexican state. It was a call for self-determination and autonomy outside the registers of national sovereignty.

But if Indigenous people were to "be recognized as 'collective subjects' and not as individual subject-citizens of the Mexican state," as Marcos claimed, what was the basis of this collective subjectivity? What were the social, political, and economic forms of Indigenous organization? Were these rooted in an Indigenous past? Did they refer to current Indigenous practices? In answering these questions, the Zapatistas laid out a new Indigenous politics that disrupted both an essentialized indigeneity and its erasure/construction by the Mexican state.

The Zapatistas are a meeting of two worlds, two cultures, both of them exiled by the regime of movement. The first is the Indigenous Mayan people of Los Altos, who were compelled by land expropriation and population boom to move into the canyons and Lacandon Jungle of southeast Mexico. Young, landless, and deracinated, they formed new communities and experimented with new models of social organization—in particular, a consensus-based assembly model. The second culture was brought in by another migrant group, young mestizo urban guerrillas who, surveilled and repressed by the Mexican state, left the cities to organize the countryside.

These forced dislocations were crucial to the Zapatista project, conditioning practices and mentalities that disrupted inherited traditions, be they Indigenous customs or revolutionary agendas. In this, the Zapatistas followed a long line of disrupters traced throughout this book. The maritime radicalism of the eighteenth-century Atlantic, the proletarian consciousness of the nineteenth century, and the brazen refusals of southern Italian migrants in the 1970s were all products of a recent deracination by the regime of movement.

Zapatista women were a case in point. Indigenous women in Chiapas were traditionally secondary subjects within a patriarchal world. They were considered the property of men and were sold or traded by their fathers at a young age. They held no leadership positions, were subject to violence by male family members, overburdened with work, and unable to own land, collectively or individually. The introduction of the regime of movement into the Indigenous areas of the Chiapas had only worsened their position within the community. As wage labor gradually replaced subsistence economies, Indigenous women became further dependent on their husbands, resulting in a loss of autonomy, equality, and communal status.[7]

Yet, of the thousands of Mayan fighters who came out of the Lacondan Jungle on January 1, 1994, nearly one-third were women. And these women made it immediately clear that their revolt was as much against Indigenous society as it was against the Mexican state or capitalism.

They vehemently attacked assumptions about their lack of will and about the will of God in their subservience. They banned alcohol and distributed contraception. They formed working groups on "Indigenous Rights and Culture," asserting their cultural difference from the rest of Mexican society while, at the same time, asserting the need to change those same traditions that oppressed or excluded them. In doing so, the Zapatista women disrupted both an Indigenous essentialism advocating for the unquestioning defense of cultural traditions and their equally subservient position within neoliberalism.[8] For the women of the EZLN, tradition—as a marker of Indigenous difference—was central to their disruptive politics, but only in so far as this tradition was reinvented under new terms. It was a double-edged sword, cutting the sinews of capital and their own Indigenous upbringing. But it was catching on. By the early 2000s, women comprised over 45 percent of the Zapatista insurgents.[9]

Like the disruptive subjectivities of Blacks, women, and workers, becoming Indigenous required space. Yet, compared to the disruptive spaces established by these earlier groups (confined, by circumstance, to either small-scale or ephemeral undertakings), the spaces of autonomy carved out by the Zapatistas were vast and continue through to the present day.

In June 1994, after a two-month grassroots consulting process through their local assemblies, the Zapatistas rejected the Mexican government's proposed thirty-four-point peace plan as not adequately addressing questions of political democracy.

In the fall, following repeated incursions into Chiapas by the Mexican Army in violation of the cease-fire, the Zapatistas declared that they would no longer negotiate with the government, that they had mined their territory, and installed anti-aircraft units. On December 11, 1994, the EZLN announced the formation of nine new autonomous municipalities in the canyons of the Chiapas whose communities had voted to bar entry to state and federal officials, refused to pay taxes, utility bills, or debt on federal loans, and called for a National Liberation Movement across Mexico.

In response, the Mexican government sent 25,000 federal troops into the self-declared "Zapatista Territory in Rebellion," destroying homes, infrastructure, and personal belongings; poisoning corn and livestock; assaulting women; and driving entire communities into the mountains. Images of the military assault, even more than in the previous year, catapulted the Zapatistas to national and international fame, forcing the government to retreat and restart negotiations. These negotiations would, in turn, lead to the San Andrés Accords that granted autonomy, recognition, and rights to the Indigenous population of Mexico. They were never ratified by the Mexican Congress and subsequently undermined by the federal government, prompting the Zapatistas to press forward unilaterally with their project of autonomy.

Autonomy, to not be cosmetic, meant autonomy over land, of how it was used and what it was for, as well as who decided the answers to these questions. The EZLN handed the nine newly created Rebel Municipalities over to their inhabitants, instituting various forms of radical democratic self-governance. These newly formed territories, renamed by their residents as the Municipality of General Emiliano Zapata, of the Freedom of the Mayan Peoples, of Ernesto Che Guevara, Lucio Cabañas, Magdalena de la Paz and so on became the central organs of autonomous government. The municipalities were in turn beholden to, and took orders from, the hundreds of local assemblies contained within each. In 2003, the Rebel Municipalities were replaced by a new organizational unit, the *Caracoles* (snails), whose shell (blending metaphor and reality) offered inhabitants protection from the regime of movement, reflected the slower pace of democratic processes and Mayan ancestry, and served as chambers of dialogue with the outside world.

The Caracoles are termed to be "in resistance." They are disruptive spaces that not only refuse to pay the tribute exacted by the regime of movement (such as taxes and debt payments), but also reject all external development aid that aims to incorporate Chiapas into the global economy. When the regime has sought to force entry, the Zapatistas have stood ground, most notably during their successful sixteen-month blockade of a highway project designed for the extraction of timber, uranium, and oil.

Within these disrupted spaces, the Zapatistas have built structures to serve their own needs. All of the Caracoles have clinics. In some places, these are high-level hospitals with ambulances, dormitories, dentists, doctors, and laboratories. They have set up over 300 autonomous Zapatista schools, where 1,000 teachers each oversee a curriculum collectively decided upon by children and their elders. The schools operate based on the principle, "Nobody educates anybody else; nobody is educated alone." There are no grades.

Much of the economy is organized communally, divided into democratically run cooperatives. Some maintain connections with the larger regime of movement, exporting coffee or importing consumer goods, but on their own terms. Others, such as the bread-baking cooperatives, the cattle cooperatives, or the collective cornfields worked on lands recovered from wealthy estate owners, produce for local consumption.

Despite near-constant harassment by government and paramilitary forces, the "Zapatista Centers of Autonomous Resistance and Rebellion" have persisted and even expanded. In August 2019, the Zapatistas established eleven new Caracoles that now encompass the more than 2,000 villages housing nearly 250,000 Indigenous people in the canyons and jungles of southeast Mexico.[10]

Becoming Mexican—Dialogue

As the Zapatistas were establishing their autonomy in Chiapas, they simultaneously engaged in a national dialogue with Mexican society and state. Within weeks of the rebellion, condemnation of the armed forces slaughtering Indigenous rebels forced the government into a cease-fire and began a long and punctured process of negotiations for a resolution to the conflict.

Perhaps more telling than the negotiations were the drawn-out discussions on where to hold them. The EZLN proposed several sites in Mexico City, all of which the government refused, insisting that the meetings be held in Chiapas. Just as the French state had sought to isolate students from workers during those critical months of 1968— cordoning their respective rebellions to "education" and "wage" concerns—the Mexican government, by conceding to negotiate only in Chiapas, tried to sequester the Zapatista uprising to "Indigenous issues." The Zapatistas first refused, then finally relented to the government's chosen location. But the back-and-forth over the site of negotiations was just the opening salvo of a much larger battle between the Mexican government, which constantly sought to regionalize, "ethnify," and reduce the terrain of the conflict, and the Zapatistas, who constantly disrupted this consignment in an effort to expand the material and symbolic scope of their rebellion.

The same tension was present in the themes and protocol of the negotiations themselves. While the government sought to limit discussion to Indigenous rights and culture, the Zapatistas insisted on a broader dialogue over justice and democracy in Mexico, inviting over 100 advisers, including Mexican historians, anthropologists, and Indigenous leaders, to weigh in on what they saw as national concerns.

Throughout the negotiation process, in comments made to the press, the government's position was clear. We will engage in a politics of recognition. We will reluctantly recognize your existence and negotiate over your claims, but in turn, you must recognize us as the legitimate arbiter of Mexico. In short, we will let you into the order as long as we retain material and symbolic control over the ordering mechanism. It was an attempt to diffuse the threat posed by the Zapatistas by turning them into an Indigenous social movement: an interest group (alongside women, landowners, or unions) that could be identified, defined, and acknowledged as an actor on the Mexican stage.

Time and time again, and to their credit, the Zapatistas refused to be pigeonholed. In fact, the refusal of any definition, of any identity, was an active and continuous effort on the part of the Zapatistas. As John Holloway noted, "The state is pure *is*-ness, pure definition, pure identity, and this is what it demands from its enemies. To be defined, to be imprisoned within an identity." The Mexican state's main strategy against the Zapatistas was to identify, to classify, to limit. On the other hand, the Zapatista struggle has been the opposite, to disrupt the closure and refuse definition because the "revolt of dignity is the revolt against definition."[11]

For the Zapatistas, this meant a refusal to acknowledge the ordering power of the Mexican state: a power that was naturalized by a laying claim to the past. To counter the state's power, it was necessary to disrupt this claim, "to open," as Subcomandante Marcos stated, "a crack in History."[12] The Zapatistas argued that the current Mexican government was just the latest in a long list of traitors of the Mexican people.

The same ones that had opposed Hidalgo and Morelos, the same ones that sold half our country to a foreign invader, that imported a European prince, that installed a "scientific" Porfirista dictatorship, that massacred workers in 1958 and students in 1968.[13]

The PRI government had "usurped" the legacy of the Mexican Revolution, and the Zapatistas were here to take it back. They declared "the Mexican flag, the justice system of the Nation, the Mexican Hymn, and the National Emblem" to be under the safekeeping of the "resistance forces" until "legality, legitimacy, and sovereignty are restored to all of the national territory."[14]

Through these disruptions, the Zapatistas channeled the arguments of all modern democratic revolutions in challenging the legitimacy of the Mexican state. The rebellion was not about recognition. It was the people's assertion of their native, original, inherent, and unlimited sovereignty against the historically contingent, delegated, and derived sovereignty of instituted government. As their Fourth Declaration made clear, "We do not need permission to be free. The role of the government is the prerogative of society and it is its right to exert that function."[15]

If the Zapatistas were not a social movement of the Indigenous seeking recognition and rights, they were likewise far from being a typical revolutionary force. January 1, 1994, marked the Zapatistas' first and only offensive. By the fall of 1994, with parallel uprisings failing to materialize, the Zapatistas, though remaining armed, swerved away from the legacies of Lenin, Mao, and Castro. Like much of the New Left as well as their namesake Emiliano Zapata, the Zapatistas had a strong distrust of power and its ability to reproduce, repeat, or resemble that which it overthrew. The EZLN maintained, "Our army is very different from others because its proposal is to cease being an army . . . The worst thing that can happen to [the EZLN] would be to come to power and install itself there as a revolutionary force."[16]

They rejected the armed struggle for state power. They refused to be a social movement demanding rights and recognition by the Mexican state. Or rather, they played one role off the other to resist both. It was a hard tightrope act, particularly as it was in everyone's inherited framework and interest to peg them as one or the other. But, in walking this tightrope, the Zapatistas disrupted the two established methods by which the oppressed could enter the "national space." In doing so, they opened up the possibility of writing a new script, one that would introduce a new kind of political space, fundamentally reconfiguring the meaning of Mexico and being Mexican.

The new space the Zapatistas proposed was to be the staging ground for a new political force, one which neither worked within established channels of power nor sought to forcibly impress a new one. The Zapatistas described this political space as "the antechamber looking onto the new world" and called upon "National society, those without a party, the citizen and the social movement, all Mexicans" to its construction.[17]

Eight months into their rebellion, the Zapatistas instituted the first of these antechambers, physical "spaces of encounter" that sought to bring together the different elements of Mexican society. In August 1994, they convened a National Democratic Convention in the town of Guadalupe Tepeyac, the site where the various revolutionary forces had convened in 1914. The Zapatistas worked for nearly a month setting up the space for the encounter, one that would last five days and bring together over 7,000 people. They included Mexicans from all walks of life, some attending as individuals (artists, homosexuals, farmers, intellectuals), others as representatives of leftist groups, workers, women, and the Indigenous. The encounter was a space to listen to others' experiences, to ask questions, and to learn from one another. Only through this kind of dialogue, the Zapatistas believed, could a new framework of struggle for a new world emerge, a common framework that would unify without encapsulating, one that would simultaneously bring together and maintain the differences in experience, expression, and history of its constituent parts.

Marcos, in his very first interview after the EZLN's liberation of San Cristóbal de las Casas, claimed that the Indigenous of Mexico had given everyone a lesson in dignity. "We cannot let ourselves be treated like this," he stated, and urged other groups to hear the call of dignity and do the same "within your ideology, within your means, within your beliefs, and make your human condition count."[18] Through these spaces of encounter, the Zapatistas hoped the Mexican people would find new ways of relating to one another, replacing the centralized hierarchical institutions of the Mexican nation-state with a network of autonomous communities that shared and learned from each other.

Becoming Us—The Mask

While its main and immediate adversary was the Mexican government and federal army, the Zapatistas were keenly aware that modern nation-states were nothing other than the agents and instruments of a thoroughly globalized neoliberal economy. The real threat was global capital and the oblivion of humanity it was presiding over. The Zapatistas believed that the globe was engaged in a Fourth World War (the third having ended with the fall of the Soviet Union) that pitted a neoliberal "New World Order" with its agents—military, sociopolitical, and economic—against the vast majority of humanity. A global machine "that fed on blood and defecated dollars" into the bank accounts of the superelite. Within this New World Order, the rest of humanity were given two options: to enter into the world as servants or to "remain outside of this world, outside of life."[19]

The lumpen and the laborers. Rather than privileging one over the other, the Zapatistas claimed these distinctions played into the hands of the regime. Capitalism had not homogenized the toilers into a single class, but had cut and sliced a majority into a thousand different minorities, differentiating humanity into social kinds in order to better exploit it. Marginalization, the Zapatistas argued, was its preferred method of exploitation. Marcos wrote,

> In the complex equation that turns death into money, there is a group of humans who fetch a very low price in the global slaughterhouse. We are the indigenous, the young, the women, the elderly, the homosexuals, the migrants, all those who are different. That is to say, the immense majority of humanity.[20]

There were two major implications to such a worldview. First, that while the vast majority of humanity was oppressed by neoliberal capital, their oppressions were experienced differentially. Not only did this not guarantee a single class consciousness, as Marx had predicted, but, quite the reverse, it created multiple experiences of injustice and multiple dreams of liberation. Second, reducing this multiplicity of nightmares and dreams to a singular analysis guiding a singular praxis was bound to reproduce the very hierarchies that the Zapatistas sought to subvert. To avoid the historical mistakes of past liberation movements, the Zapatistas needed to scale up the national spaces of encounter, to construct a global political space where these nightmares and dreams could be expressed and heard by others.

The Intercontinental Gatherings for Humanity and Against Neo-Liberalism, the first of which convened in the spring and summer of 1996, were the Zapatistas' attempt to configure such a global political space. An heterogeneous antechamber to "a world," as the Zapatistas were fond of saying, "where many worlds fit."[21] In preparation, the Zapatistas gave notice, inviting "all human beings without a home, without land, without work, without food . . . without peace, without democracy, without tomorrow" to join "the struggle of the world people" against the New World Order.[22] Preceded by continental planning meetings across five continents, the first *Encuentro* brought 5,000 people from forty-five countries into rebel territory to learn about and connect to one another's struggles. Within this global antechamber, the Zapatistas argued, would emerge a universal subject: a marginalized humanity, threatened with oblivion, determined to disrupt the regime of movement.

Compared to the media blitz surrounding the initial phases of the war or even the negotiations with the government, the encounters garnered much less attention. Yet, in these spaces erected upon a collective "Ya Basta!" in order to bring to birth something new, we can see the traces of much of twenty-first-century thought and struggle. The reconceptualizations of constituent and destituent power, of the multitude, of solidarity and allyship; the political praxis of disruption that resonated from Seattle (1999), Prague, Melbourne, (2000), Buenos Aires, Genoa (2001), Greece (2008), and through the 2011 uprisings to the present owes much to the disruptive politics of the Zapatistas.

There is a Zapatista poem written for this first global encounter. A poem read aloud by the General Command of the EZLN at the 1996 opening ceremony, held in the ubiquitous mud and blazing tropical July sun of the village of La Realidad (reality) in the Lacandon Jungle. It's too beautiful not to cite at length.

This is what we are. The Zapatista National Liberation Army.
The voice that arms itself to be heard.

The face that hides itself to be seen.
The name that hides itself to be named.
The red star that calls out to humanity and the world to be heard, to
	be seen, to be named.
The tomorrow that is harvested in the past.

Behind our black mask. Behind our armed voice.
Behind our unnamable name. Behind what you see of us.
Behind this, we are you.

Behind this, we are the same
simple and ordinary men and women that are
repeated in all races,
painted in all colors,
speak in all languages
and live in all places.

The same forgotten men and women. The same excluded.
The same untolerated. The same persecuted.
The same as you. Behind this, we are you.

Behind our masks is the face of all excluded women. Of all the forgotten native people. Of all the persecuted homosexuals. Of all the despised youth. Of all the beaten migrants. Of all those imprisoned for their words and thoughts. Of all the humiliated workers. Of all those dead from neglect. Of all the simple and ordinary men and women

who don't count,
who aren't seen,
who are nameless,
who have no tomorrow.

The poem is full of the contradictions that framed the Zapatistas' struggle. In arming themselves, they underscored the denial of agency by the regime of human rights. In masking, they refused a particular identity for a universal one. In giving multiple names to this universal, they rejected its homogenizing tendencies. As Major Ana Maria stated in her

closing address to the Intercontinental Gathering, "There are thousands
of different paths present . . . each of you are a guiding red star."[23]

The universal subject that emerged from these antechambers was
both the mirror image of, and a retort to, the newly emerging global
subject of capital—one that celebrated human diversity by commodify-
ing its differences. The following are but a few examples. In 1982, Walt
Disney opened Epcot Center, a sprawling theme park in Florida showcasing the array of human cultures, cuisines, architectures, and traditions: a permanent World's Fair of clichéd pavilions erected around an
artificial lake. In the late 1980s, the Italian multinational Benetton Group
coined the slogan "*tutti i colori del mondo*," changed its logo to the *United
Colors of Benetton*, and began using smiling mixed-race models for its
photo shoots. In the late 1990s, the European Union, needing an adage
to accompany the rollout of its new single currency, organized a competition where "Unity in Diversity" beat out "Peace, Liberty, Solidarity" to
become the EU's official motto. Around the same time, HSBC launched
its "The World's Local Bank" campaign, blanketing airport jetways with
adverts of how a global financial giant was attuned to cultural
difference.

Neoliberalism forged its global markets by flattening difference
through the commodified celebration of the world's cultures. The
Zapatistas responded by underscoring how the peoples of this world,
though experiencing a differentiated oppression based on their race,
class, gender, and geography, were oppressed by a single enemy: global
capital. The invitation to the Intercontinental Encounter had drawn
these lines clearly:

> Disregarding borders, the power of money humiliates dignities,
> insults honesties, and assassinates hopes. Re-named as "Neoliberalism,"
> the historic crime in the concentration of privileges, wealth, and
> impunities, democratizes misery and hopelessness . . . Each country,
> each city, each rural area, each house, each person, everything is a
> large or small battleground. On the one side is neoliberalism with all
> its repressive power and all its machinery of death; on the other side
> is the human being.

But, for this subject to come into being, anonymity was critical. The
universal subject was a masked subject, and this, the Zapatistas believed,

made it impervious to sequestration by the regime. Not that the regime did not try. From the very start, the Mexican government was hell-bent on "unmasking" Marcos, to strip him of his mystique by pegging him as a specific individual and assigning him discrete labels. Facing fascism in 1930s Vienna, the German-speaking Bulgarian author Elias Canetti had remarked on the regime's need for definition. "A ruler wages continuous warfare against spontaneous and uncontrolled transformation," Canetti wrote. "The weapon he uses in this fight is the process of unmasking, the exact opposite of transformation . . . If it is practiced often, the whole world shrinks."[24] In February 1995, the Mexican government finally succeeded in pinning down Marcos and staged a public unmasking. The subcomandante's real identity was revealed as a philosophy professor named Rafael Sebastián Guillén, but the attempt at definition failed. Within hours, thousands of Zapatistas and their supporters took to the streets shouting, "We are all Marcos!" Marcos himself responded with a passage that has probably become his most famous.

> Who is Marcos? Yes, Marcos is gay. Marcos is gay in San Francisco, Black in South Africa, an Asian in Europe, a Chicano in San Ysidro, an anarchist in Spain, a Palestinian in Israel, a Mayan Indian in the streets of San Cristóbal, a Jew in Germany, a Gypsy in Poland, a Mohawk in Quebec, a pacifist in Bosnia, a single woman on the Metro at 10 pm, a peasant without land, a gang member in the slums, an unemployed worker, an unhappy student and, of course, a Zapatista in the mountains. Marcos is all the exploited, marginalized, oppressed minorities resisting and saying "Enough."[25]

He was everyone and no one. Or more specifically, he was a man named Rafael. He became everyone and no one in resistance. More so, he claimed that anyone could become everyone by simply putting on a mask. The passage seems a little out of place from our current political conjecture, a well-intentioned if ill-delivered statement of universalism that smacks of reductionism and privilege. From the standpoint of the Zapatistas, such criticism replicates the discourse of the regime— its representational framework, its need for definition—and is therefore itself suspect. Against the polarization of the left—caught between a class reductionism that effaced the oppression of all but white, male industrial workers and an equally reductionist identity politics that recreates and polices hierarchical divisions among the oppressed—the Zapatistas offered a middle ground. Through their encounters, behind their masks, in "the face that hides itself to be seen," the Zapatistas presented a universal subject of resistance based upon difference. Revisiting their disruptive praxis is a great starting point in our search for a way out of the present impasse.

Conclusion:
Disrupt or Be Disrupted

In March 2017, tickets went on sale for the sixth annual Disrupt Berlin, a three-day "disruptothon" expected to bring in 10,000 attendees. The Innovator Pass ($1,600) gets you access to all the main events plus the *VIP Disrupt* experience, giving you exclusive access to *CrunchMatch*, where tech disruptors pitch their disruptive ideas to venture capitalists. Closely watching the festivities are reporters from the tech and mainstream media, who compile yearly lists of Top Disruptors—companies whose products disrupt existing markets and accustomed ways of consuming and being.[1] The climax of the event is the Startup Battlefield, where one lucky winner walks away with the *Disrupt Cup* and an equity-free check for $100,000.

A few months earlier, several thousand people flooded to Washington, DC for Disrupt J20, a coordinated series of direct actions intending to shut down the inauguration of US president Donald Trump. Its website claimed that Disrupt J20 would be the "start of the resistance" and urged participants to "take to the streets and protest, blockade, disrupt, intervene, sit in, walk out, rise up, and make more noise and good trouble than the establishment can bear. The parade must be stopped." That day, Disrupt J20 activists formed human chains blocking several security checkpoints, smashed dozens of corporate storefronts, and set luxury cars and limousines on fire. Two-hundred and thirty-four lucky people, among them journalists, medics, and legal observers, were arrested and subsequently charged with felony inciting to riot, rioting, conspiracy to riot, and destruction of property, carrying combined sentences of at least fifty years in prison.[2]

This book has traced the long history of the groups, tactics, and mentalities that inform Disrupt J20. It has had less, if anything, to say about Disrupt Berlin. Like most things that have challenged capitalism, disruption too has faced capture and co-option. There are now disruption consultants, disruption conferences, and disruption workshops. In 2013, the University of Southern California opened a new program funded by Andre Young (a.k.a. Dr. Dre). You can now get a "degree in disruption."

Disruption has also entered the political arena, having recently been used to (self-)describe right-wing populists in their attempts to shake up the established consensus. In the United States, Florida governor Jeb Bush sought to revive his faltering presidential bid by calling himself "the disruptor." Trump regularly played up his self-styled maverick persona, enough at least to convince Slavoj Žižek to endorse him as a figure who fundamentally disturbed the political status quo. Trump's victory, Žižek predicted, "will be a kind of big awakening. New political processes will be set in motion, will be triggered," opening up a space of possibility and reorientation.[3] When Trump became president, Rudy Giuliani, the former mayor of New York and Trump's personal lawyer, seemed to embrace this new role, humbly stating his mission to "disrupt the world."[4] Disruption has even worked itself into the "stay calm and carry on" of British politics. In a 2022 speech defending her proposed neoliberal tax and spending cuts, the short-lived prime minister Liz Truss stated, "In Britain we need to do things differently. Whenever there is change, there is disruption. Not everyone will be in favour. But everyone will benefit from the result."[5] A dubious statement only made true by her resignation two weeks later.

The recent co-option of disruption by both neoliberal capital and right-wing populist politics is neither total nor, at the moment, hegemonic. Born from the tech sector, capital's eager embrace of disruptive discourse exists within, and is made possible by, its opposite: long-term capital accumulation in blue chip stocks and safe-haven investments such as gold, bonds, and global currency. Politically, the new purveyors of disruption stand in an uneasy tension with more traditional upholders of the neoliberal order. A tension perfectly drawn out by Angela Merkel's portraiture of Franco–German relations. "I understand your desire for disruptive politics," then-chancellor Merkel said to President Macron. "But I'm tired of picking up the pieces. Over and over, I have to glue together the cups you have broken so that we can then sit down together and have a cup of tea."[6]

Is the neoliberal co-option of disruptive methods and mentalities a passing fad? A long-term trend of cultural capitalism? The conscious and explicit self-projection of what it has been all along? It is hard to tell. But, for the near future, at least, the politics of liberatory disruption described in this book now operates within a contested and more ambiguous field. Embraced by capital and its discontents, disruptive practices and imaginaries are increasingly animating both the regime of movement and those who struggle against it. It makes sense to know the enemy. How has capital historically made use of disruption? What is its contemporary cultural and political currency? Answering these questions is, I believe, crucial to staking out a path for a politics of disruptive liberation today.

Capital and Disruption

In one sense, capitalism has always been disruptive. Its entrance into any terrain (natural, social, psychic) has, in short time and then continuously, reordered and recoded the possible ways of being, reproducing, and desiring according to newly striated lines of motion. From the violent expropriations and kidnappings that accompanied its birth to the precarity, gentrification, biospheric alterations, and normalized warfare that mark its present, capitalism has uprooted, upended, and destabilized the lives of billions of human beings and animals on our planet. On a much less violent level, it has also ceaselessly rendered obsolete existing habits, practices, and norms, altered how we interact with family, strangers, and friends, ways we experience distance and time, and so on. Yet this perspective on capitalism as itself a disruptive force—one informing a long strand of reactionary and conservative politics—is mired in a traditionalism that *The History of Disruption* has been at pains to avoid.

Instead, it has positioned capital as a coercive regime of movement that invades and reterritorializes terrain according to capitalism's internal laws of motion: the *imperatives* of competition and profit maximization, a *compulsion* to reinvest surpluses, and the systematic *need* to improve labor productivity. It is the disruptions of *these* laws, of its own internal logic, and not the dislocations or crises produced by them that I want to trace here.

As an economic practice, capital's use of disruption against its own perpetual motion first appeared in the late nineteenth century. In this moment, the capitalist laws of motion that drove the relentless expansion of the regime of movement were counteracted by the profits to be made by retarding it. Two historical developments were crucial to creating this counterforce: first, the concentration of industry and the consequent ability of large firms to influence price by adjusting production; second, the emergence of financial corporate managers making decisions over industrial output. The combination of these developments, referred to as "monopoly" and "managerial" capitalism, respectively, allowed for profit generation through reducing output below capacity or through the purposeful reduction of productive capacity itself.[7]

The Norwegian-American economist Thorstein Veblen called this *sabotage*. In a 1919 article, he used sabotage as an umbrella term referring to any "peaceable or surreptitious restriction, delay, withdrawal, or obstruction within the economic system." Copying verbatim the IWW's definition, "sabotage," Veblen claimed, "was a conscious withdrawal of efficiency," utilized not only by labor but equally by corporate managers through the routine underemployment of workers and plant capacity in order to maximize profit.[8] Timothy Mitchell, in his book *Carbon Democracy*, expanded on Veblen's conception of sabotage, arguing that both capital and labor derived their economic and political power from their ability to disrupt the production and flow of goods to market.[9]

Writing nearly a century apart, both Veblen and Mitchell trace a shift in the kinetic logic of the economy of movement: the transition from unrelenting motion to one that found profit in its tempered hindrance. Their texts describe the means of this tactical sabotage, detailing lockouts, manufactured unemployment, divestment, and the underdevelopment of infrastructure used for both economic and political advantage—the latter to undermine organized labor's ability to disrupt capital on its own terms.[10]

By the 1970s, these disruptions to the laws of motion became systematized through the active manufacture of disruptive crises. As Mitchell and Naomi Klein have argued, these crises, beginning with the "oil shock" of 1973, continuing through the "war on terror," to the financial destabilizations of the twenty-first century all restructured the terrain of struggle, forcing policies of deflation, privatization, and austerity, while effectively removing significant aspects of collective life beyond the reach of democratic contestation.[11]

Yet throughout the twentieth century, these disruptive practices of capital were concealed, purposefully so, behind a widely accepted narrative of expansion, linking capitalism to national, imperial, and later, global growth (what is good for General Motors is good for America). Capitalism's own cosmology helped cement this view. From its birth, on a cultural and ideological level, capital has systematically presented itself as a liberating force against barriers to human advancement, establishing a link between movement, freedom, and progress that has informed a vast number of political and theoretical projects. This link allowed capitalism, despite its constant dislocations, to furnish the social scripts of modernity (progress, civilization, development, integration, modernization, and growth) that were subsequently forced on, or voluntarily adopted by, the states and peoples of the world. Through these scripts, the coerced motion of goods and bodies became compatible with, if not the engine of, the progressive movement of society through time. However paradoxical, these ideas have remained a constant and central feature of capital's cultural imaginary as it oversaw the kinetic reterritorialization of the globe. This perception is equally shared by many Marxist critics of capitalism, who credit the bourgeoisie for its historic role in advancing human production *and* absolve them of agency for the periodic breakdowns of capitalist accumulation, now reified as "objective crises of overproduction."

Absent from, or masked by, such narratives was the intentional politics of a capitalist class to disrupt this very movement. Veblen had already noted as much in 1919:

Men of a liberal and commercial mind not only credit the business-like captains of industry with having created this productive capacity, but also overlook all what the same captains of industry have been doing in the ordinary course of business to hold productive industry in check.[12]

Mitchell has similarly argued that behind the heroic narrative of intrepid oil company explorers provisioning the world, there lay the hidden reality of a parasitic entity hell-bent on delaying, restricting, and limiting the production and flow of Middle Eastern oil.[13] Mitchell and Veblen are of course not alone in pointing out the incommensurability between capitalism's self-projection of progressive movement and its actual economic practices. Nevertheless, the association of capitalism with growth, progress, and development has proved quite enduring.

This conceit has vanished in the twenty-first century. Over the past two decades, capital discarded the robes of progressive movement (whether liberal, civilizational, national, or global) it had worn since its inception.[14] In its place, capital has increasingly come to understand its incessant kinetic reordering of the world's social terrain through the category of disruption. This is a significant shift in conceptual framing, with large consequences.

The reasons for this shift are overdetermined. The end of communism and capitalism's consolidation as the planet's only economic system. The transition from industrial production to finance as the main site of capital accumulation. Capital's decreased reliance on the modernist state (and its attendant ideologies) as a quasi-independent entity. Neoliberal policies that have reduced the health, income, security, and prospects for the majority of the world's population. An increasing understanding that the solution of the climate crisis was fundamentally at odds with capitalism's own logic. Whatever the driving causes, the combination of these developments has both removed capital's need for progressive narratives and made such associations harder to sustain.

By the turn of the millennium, a new cultural logic of disruption began to establish itself. There are innumerable sites to trace its polyvalent propagation: film and television's fascination with dystopian and postapocalyptic themes, the emergence of a disruptive right-wing populism, the gaslighting of precarity as personal freedom, to name a few. But the most prevalent entrenchment of the new cultural logic is to be found within the habitus of capital itself: in the rise of what has now become the preeminent business theory of the twenty-first century—*disruptive innovation.*

In his 1997 book, *The Innovator's Dilemma,* Harvard Business School professor Clayton Christensen presented a "new" management theory, arguing that substantial changes to our ways of being and interacting are brought about through disruptive innovation.[15] According to the theory, a disruptive innovation is a product or practice that fundamentally interrupts an existing market, reordering the rules, customs, institutions, behaviors, and principles by which we do things. Examples would include the travel and dating apps on smartphones (not to mention the phone itself) or the introduction of the Model T Ford and the personal computer. Since the publication of the book, Christensen has gone on to coauthor others, urging disruptive innovation in higher education (*The Innovative University*), public schools (*Disrupting Class*), and health care (*The Innovator's Prescription*).

As a concept, *disruptive innovation* is change without the need to justify improvement. As Jill Lepore writes, it "is the idea of progress stripped of the aspirations of the Enlightenment . . . and relieved of its critics." Unlike progress, innovation has no long-term goals. It doesn't care about advancing humanity or the project of human freedom or even growth. What disruptive innovation does, according to Lepore, is provide sparkle for the "nihilism of contemporary neoliberalism." Ironically, the sparkle comes through mimicry of many of the disruptive struggles detailed in this book. Disruptive innovation parodies the contours of an asymmetrical war between empire and colony, between corporations and labor, where large entities are confronted by rebels, insurgents, and freedom fighters. Except in this scenario, capital gets to play Che Guevara.

> Disruption casts capital in the role of guerrilla cadre—improvisatory, unencumbered, rhizomatic. The enemy in this scenario is always the entrenched fortification of all non-capitalized aspects of social reproduction: infrastructure and public works (increasingly managed by private equity), public education (undermined by charter schools and for-profit colleges), or the attack on unions and collective bargaining (in favor of a "gig economy" of contingent workers).[16]

Unhinged from all telos and social narrative, disruptive innovation nakedly trumpets itself as the kinetic restructuring of social and economic terrain. It is concerned with pure encumbrance and its removal, with making social relations more fluid, more mobile, more flexible, more accessible for their commodification by capital.[17]

Over the past two decades, the concept of disruptive innovation has spread virally throughout capital's institutional landscape. Steve Jobs was "deeply influenced" by the theory, and it is required reading for all of Jeff Bezos's chief executives at Amazon. Nearly every major multinational company has hired a "Chief Innovation Officer," and countless US school districts have adopted "Innovation Agendas," not to improve their products or education, but out of fear of being left behind.

"Disrupt or be disrupted," the venture capitalist Josh Linkner warns in a new book, *The Road to Reinvention: How to Drive Disruption and Accelerate Transformation*, claiming that "fickle consumer trends, friction-free markets, and political unrest," along with "dizzying speed, exponential complexity, and mind-numbing technology advances," mean that the time has come to panic as you've never panicked before.[18] Larry Downes and Paul Nunes, who blog for *Forbes*, insist that we have entered a new and even scarier stage: "big bang disruption." "This isn't disruptive innovation," they warn. "It's devastating innovation."[19] In these and countless other writings, disruption becomes, according to Lepore, "the heedless churn of innovative subversion, in which the catastrophic waste of capitalism is simply ontologized as the fact of incessant transformation."[20] For the members of the Invisible Committee, "this is the logic of a world straining to maintain itself while giving itself an air of historical rupture."[21]

The political equivalent to this business model is crisis capitalism: the active promotion of incessant disruptions that then require, or prevent us from seeing, the continued kinetic reterritorialization of our life-worlds. Manufactured wars, sovereign debt and banking crises, drug epidemics, defunded public services, bursting speculative bubbles, and terror are recycled at regular intervals that "shake up" accumulated capital, creating new pathways for the regime of movement while maintaining its subjects in states of perpetual anxiety. A continually (re)generated *stasis*, "in which," Balibar claims, "the whole mode of production moves with an immobile movement."[22]

Within this worldview of disruptive capital, movement becomes its own virtue. In "this image of a frozen reality that is nevertheless caught up in an unremitting, ghostly movement" that Lukács foretold a century ago, time is flattened out.[23] With no future direction and a past understood only as outmoded innovations (be they political, social, economic in nature), humanity under capital becomes marked by temporal self-closure. We are living in a perpetually convulsing, precarious present without meaning or aim, jumping from one crisis to the next, each one registering as the ones before. A present that has become the nightmarish inversion of Benjamin's redemptive temporality, "where time stands still and has come to a stop."

The most catastrophic implication of this self-closure concerns the regime's ability to listen. The narrative of human advancement, for two centuries shared by it and social movements, is no longer an operational feature of capital. This common narrative had partially allowed social movements to challenge the regime's imagined past and future, contesting its purpose, scope, and the social kinds embraced or excluded by it. In fact, the history of social movements teaches us the maxim that the regime of movement can be made responsive to our needs. It is this maxim that now needs revisiting. Locked in an eternal present of incessant innovation, the regime of movement has become increasingly heedless to the value, direction, and pace of its motion. To expect to persuade an unthinking, unhearing machine (to quote Fanon), one that operates outside of historical time, adept only at mobilizing all dead and living matter, is delusional. You cannot negotiate the terms of a future within a system that no longer believes humanity can determine its own. The only thing you can do is stop it.

In the nineteenth century, the politics of disruption intertwined itself with movement. For the past two centuries, the struggle between capital and those who fought against it was waged over the category of movement—who would appropriate the term and, with it, the future of modernity. As late as 1923, Lukács argued that proletarian consciousness of its historical role would put into motion the frozen image of reified capital. Perhaps the last instance of such certainty. For the better half of the twentieth century, we have been contending with the reality that the forces of liberation either lack a coherent working-class subject or have sought this subject elsewhere (in women, in youth, in the colonized, the precarious, the multitude, and so on). At the turn of the twenty-first century, theorists such as Fredric Jameson had returned to the pessimism of the early Frankfurt School, remarking, "Stasis today, all over the world . . . certainly seems to have outstripped any place for human agency, and to have rendered the latter obsolete."[24]

One reason I wrote this book is because I believe many of us are looking in the wrong place. As long as we continue to search for a movement to counter that of capital, we shall continue to draw blanks. Rather, as this conclusion argues, we are entering a moment when social struggle will take place not over movement, but rather the category of disruption. Between a disruptive capital and those seeking to free themselves from it. The battlelines of this new terrain are emergent and not yet solidified. In these last few pages, I will try to outline their contours, limits, and possibilities as I see them.

Disrupt Everything! Except Capital

Capitalism was born through the struggle to gain control over movement. In its early days, it fought both ideological and material battles against a previous socioeconomic system over who, how, and what could move. With its eventual takeover of the state, it secured a monopoly over the power of movement. A similar struggle is now taking place over disruption. Now that capital has embraced disruption, are we all free to disrupt? Of course not. While the regime of movement welcomes, thrives on, and promotes a certain nihilistic disruptive chaos, it is at the same time drawing rigid boundaries to contain disruptions that threaten its validity or operation. Examining what kinds of disruption the regime of movement permits, is neutral toward, or actively suppresses thus provides a good metric for thinking through the possible deployments of disruption for liberatory ends.

What was true at its emergence remains true today: material disruptions that directly affect its profits pose the most immediate and therefore serious threat to the regime of movement. But disruptions of what? To what? How can capital be disrupted now? The monumental shift of Atlantic capital from production to circulation over the last half century has significantly altered the answers to these questions.

Faced with diminishing returns from further labor productivity increases, capital's response to the 1970s crisis of industrial production was to transition investment toward circulation: speeding up and reducing the cost of both commodity flows (through containerization, modal transport, the reconfiguration of wholesale and retail industries) and money capital (banking and financial instruments). Aiding this process were "innovations" that calibrated supply much more closely to demand. Demand flow technology, just-in-time production, demand-driven manufacturing, logistics automation, and mixed-model production all reduced forecasting risk and gradually eliminated inventory overhead. The result was a large-scale shift in capital investment away from production locations to the ordering and management of financial and material infrastructure. Or, put more simply, a shift from institutions to flows. Jürgen Habermas, in a different context, captured the essence of this transition. "The new relevance of 'flow volumes' also signals how the locus of control has shifted from space to time: as *'masters of speed'* come to replace the *'rulers of territory.'* "[25] As a consequence, capital became less and less dependent on specific sites of production and thus less vulnerable to their disruption. On the other hand, the increased significance of circulation has opened up new possibilities.

Not surprisingly, capital's active suppression of social disruption has likewise shifted (particularly in the postindustrial Atlantic). In the first three quarters of the twentieth century, the regime of movement was concerned with controlling and limiting industrial action. Until World War II, capital's preferred tactic was outright violence. In the postwar period, it turned to a strategy of containment. This it sought to accomplish in two ways. The first was working through union bureaucracy to mitigate a strike's disruptive impacts. The second was through legally delineating the boundaries of an acceptable strike: one that was predictable, organized by leadership, and presented no path to a generalized revolt or the coordination of worker control. Within Europe, capital opted to work with and deradicalize unions. In North America, its preferred strategy was criminalization. The United States outlawed wildcat strikes in 1935, sit-ins in 1939, and solidarity and general strikes in 1947. Canada was, and remains, one of the worst abusers of mandatory back-to-work legislation in the world.

It has been decades since the United States last deployed the military to break a strike. Yet, in 2019, it charged two women with crimes carrying 110-year prison sentences for damaging a pipeline valve.[26] The Earth Liberation Front, which carries out nonviolent acts of ecotage against environmentally harmful industries, was labeled as the number one domestic terrorist threat by the FBI. Simply protesting the fossil fuel industry has become a felony in numerous US states and is investigated as a national security threat in both the United States and Canada. Sentences for the sabotage of circulatory infrastructure, of pipelines, railways, ports, and information and electricity grids have risen dramatically over the past two decades across the Atlantic world.[27] Taken together, the draconian criminalization of such nonviolent acts are the clearest indication of the regime's new emphasis on preventing the disruption of flows and infrastructure.

Aside from material disruptions to its operation, the regime of movement has also targeted disruptions that either challenge its validity or offer models of human existence outside of its prescribed lines. Over the past decade, the regime's intolerance to such threats has reached totalitarian heights as liberticidal laws against public protest have been passed or ramped up across the Atlantic. Spain's Citizens' Security Law, which allows police to issue fines of up to €650,000 for protesting near transit hubs or government buildings, tops the list. Quebec, in response to massive student unrest, began slapping $5,000 fines on each individual participating in an unapproved protest containing fifty or more people, while in the United States, House Resolution 347 made protesting near government buildings, political conventions, or global summits—except in heavily policed and encaged "free speech zones"—a federal crime. Following the mass disruptions of Extinction Rebellion, the UK government drafted a bill criminalizing protests that "are not primarily violent or seriously disorderly," but had an avowed intent to "intentionally" or "recklessly" cause a "public nuisance" or "bring the city to a halt."[28] Faced with the choice of alleviating the roots of neoliberal discontent or criminalizing its expression, the proliferation of such laws are a clear indication of the regime's future direction.

Parallel to these liberticidal laws has been the regime's ongoing commodification of all social relations. This capillary colonization has, like all intrusions of capital, been accompanied by force: the political policing of practices that exist outside—and offer alternatives to—the movements permitted by corporatized market exchange. The evictions of squatter communities and social centers, the privatization of once-public space, and the militarized surveillance of minority subcultures across the Atlantic have been among the most widely used vectors of attack. A marked increase in microregulations—the enforcement of the minute rules governing which people can do what and where—has been pivotal to these attacks. The trading permit is a great example. Lack of one has led, in different contexts, to the shutting down of lemonade stands in white suburbia, Eric Garner's murder by the New York police, and the confiscation of a Tunisian fruit seller's produce cart, his subsequent self-immolation, and the spark for the Arab Spring.[29] We live in a world where, on the pretext of hygiene codes, people are routinely arrested for distributing food to the poor. It is only against the backdrop of this regulatory policing of our life-worlds that the communal and free kitchens, medical clinics, and day care centers that organically sprouted within the 2011 occupations take on their true significance.

On the other hand, there are types of disruption that do not threaten the legitimacy or profits of the regime of movement and toward which it is indifferent. Representative identity politics, as the transference of discontent against the regime into discourses for recognition of its past and present discriminatory practices, is one such example. Rather than suppress its expression, the regime of movement has been quite adept at incorporating them to bolster its own legitimacy. The capture, co-option, and rebranding of identity discourses via diversity initiatives, corporate pinkwashing, or woke imperialism speaks to capital's present indifference vis-à-vis the racial and gendered makeup of its target markets and labor force. This is not to say that individual capitalists, not to mention the law enforcement officers who protect their interests, cannot be racist, sexist, or homophobic. In fact, they often are. Nor does it discount the significant status property—the material benefits and privileges—that whiteness, maleness, and sexual normalcy have conferred upon socially reproduced identities.[30] It is simply to observe that just as capital historically fostered hierarchies and enmities of race, gender, geography, and sexual preference to redirect anger away from itself, it can as easily operate within, and profit from, frameworks of inclusion.

Disruption Now

Looking at what forms of disruption the regime of movement permits, heavily polices, or is indifferent to has historically been a good way to figure out where it is most vulnerable and, conversely, which pathways of resistance it can tolerate or even profit from. Historians have a bad track record in prognostication, but the trends related previously, if true, do offer some insight into what forms of disruptive politics might be effective in the near future.[31]

Disrupting circulation

"Power is logistic. It's through flows that this world is maintained. Block everything!" writes the Invisible Committee, reorienting disruption away from the fixed sites to the streams of capital.[32] Have we come full circle? Back to the initial strategy deployed by peasants, pirates, slaves, and sailors to forestall the regime of movement in the eighteenth-century Atlantic world. As Joshua Clover convincingly argues in *Riot. Strike. Riot*, the riot's resurgence coincided with the restructuring of capitalist accumulation from production to circulation that began fifty years ago.[33]

Eighteenth-century disruptors resisted the immediate vehicles (the slavers, press gangs, the grain carts, and barges) that forced their bodies and goods into motion. Yet, what are the targets of today? Where is such intervention viable, given the rhizomatic nature of global capital? If the unintentional grounding of the super container *Ever Given* that shut the Suez Canal and disrupted global shipping is any indication, one should look for the nodal points and bottlenecks of capital circulation. Charmaine Chua argues that logistic processes create crucial sites of political intervention in core capitalist countries, where new accumulation strategies emphasize movement over location.[34] Specifically, this means looking into the physical and cyber infrastructure by which goods and information move: ports, warehouses, railroads, pipelines, data centers, fossil fuel depots, interstate highways, and electricity and fiber optic grids. Disruptions to these nodal points can be enacted through work stoppages of transit and infrastructural employees in related industries, from longshoremen, truck drivers, and warehouse workers to utility and information technicians.[35] Ninety percent of all commodities are shipped across the world's oceans by container vessels. A 2014 report by *Interindustry Forecasting Project* predicted that "the [US] economy could lose as much as $2.5 billion a day and disrupt thousands of jobs if labor . . . forced a shutdown of West Coast seaports."[36]

The people behind Empire Logistics have put together interactive maps of supply-chain infrastructure, allowing anyone to examine how many goods move through each transit hub, railway line, and shipping lane across the globe. The daily volume of raw materials, particularly coal, that passes through one unguarded rail intersection in the United States is, simply put, staggering.[37] It is the strategic targeting of such choke points, argues Degenerate Communism, that will be key to disrupting capital. Just as the early twentieth-century general strike was articulated as "widespread time of non-production," the generalized disruptions in circulation they propose would manifest as a "widespread time of non-circulation."[38]

These maps are revealing for another reason. They show that disruptions to the circulation of capital, unlike production, need not be carried out by workers. Anyone can close a road, liberate a marketplace, shut down a port or a pipeline. As evidenced by the actions of Occupy Oakland, Black Lives Matter, or the Yellow Vests, disruptors "are unified not by their possession of jobs but by their more general dispossession."[39]

Such a unification of the dispossessed is perhaps strongest in the territories known as Canada. Over the past decade, the choke-point protests of settler organizers in cities and distribution centers have converged with the much longer history of First Nations blockading territory and disrupting settler infrastructure on stolen land. As Tiny House Warrior Kanahus Manuel made clear, "Canada is not going to listen to any of us until we start disrupting their economy." In connecting Indigenous land defenders to urban resistance, these disruptions draft new possibilities for settler anticapitalist, environmentalist, and working-class solidarity with anticolonial struggle. This form of solidarity could collate geographically distant struggles and paradoxically empower regional interventions within global markets by traversing the very infrastructure it would obstruct.[40]

We are living in a moment in which accustomed forms of solidarity and allyship are being contested. While these are certainly welcome developments, they have also made a global resistance to the regime of movement more complicated. Directing attention to the logistic arteries of this regime offers one path to practicing global solidarity anew.

Extraction

A technology professor writes about the questions asked by five hedge fund managers who paid to hear his wisdom: Which region will be less impacted by the coming climate crisis: New Zealand or Alaska? How do I maintain authority over my security force after the *event*? For these men preparing to insulate themselves from the dangers posed by climate change, mass migrations, global pandemics, nativist panic, and resource depletion, the future, "is really about just one thing: escape."[41] The one properly monied person I know has bought a walled farming compound on Turkey's Aegean coast and is educating his six-year-old son in aquaponics. He too thinks about the loyalty of his guards.

These fantasies of self-extraction aren't being mapped out in secret cabals of the ultrarich. They are everywhere, playing out in high definition, often with us as cheering spectators. Silicon Valley billionaires are filling up the Nectome waiting list to upload the contents of their brains onto a computer that will preserve their consciousness beyond their mortal bodies. Richard Branson, Jeff Bezos, and Elon Musk are actively pursuing plans for privatized space flight and colonization. Like the Once-ler's extended family in Dr. Seuss's *The Lorax*, one gets the sinking feeling they are packing up and moving out, leaving the rest of us to a slow death on the earth they have destroyed.

The tragicomic plot of Pixar's *Wall-E* aside, this is not what *our* extraction will look like. Much like the targeting of circulation, extraction as a disruptive impulse is coeval with the establishment of the regime of movement. It was put into practice by maroon societies of the Caribbean in the eighteenth century and formed the backbone of every decolonization struggle. Hippies, radical feminists, Black Power advocates, and Italian workerists all equated liberation with its praxis. But what pathways will today's extraction take? Who will initiate it? What forms can it create? Can these forms resonate? How will this extraction relate to disruption? These are old questions, given new life by the wave of global uprisings that began in 2011. They are also all-too-often abstracted questions, debated and dissected at a remove from the radical contingency, needs, and possibilities of a concrete situation. It's preferable to start with something we can all relate to.

"Natural disasters bring out the best in people." A cliché peddled by the inescapable personal interest stories covering the breakdown of the regime's ability to provision its subjects. The cobbler who traveled 500 kilometers to mend shoes on devastated streets following the 2023 Turkish earthquake. The informal networks of food and first aid set up after every major hurricane. Families taking in strangers whose houses have flooded or burned down. In these moments when a natural disaster temporarily disrupts the regime of movement, renders its regular motions inoperable, we celebrate the rapid and spontaneous organization of provisions, informalized labor, and collectivity that human beings are capable of.[42] Just underneath the numbing religious or patriotic rhetoric deployed to frame such actions, there is a palpable sense of freshness when the regime's breakdown is filled by new ways of being-with, of distribution and exchange, shared agency, recently claimed competencies, aid, and care. We get excited at the chance to display and observe our humanity.

The disruptions to the regime of movement created by natural disasters are not the result of intentional human action (not counting the intentional negligence of the regime to prevent or protect us from them). Nor can we speak of extraction in anything but a passive sense. Humans do not extract themselves from the regime during a natural disaster; they are involuntarily extracted from it, that is, left to fend for themselves. Nevertheless, these disruptions create space, openings, for people to practice ways of relating to one another that differ substantially from the ones sanctioned by the regime. This space, when produced intentionally, becomes the staging ground for a politics of extraction.

Political extraction begins with a negative gesture, a refusal to be governed by the regime of movement. The content of this gesture, be it the rejection of authoritarian government, austerity, police brutality, climate change, or the influence of corporations on democratic institutions, is less important than its consequences: the creation of new forms of life.

The occupations of urban public space since 2011 are one form of this disruption. On January 25, 2011, hundreds of thousands of people from all over Egypt descended on Cairo's Tahrir Square. Over the following weeks, they organized and orchestrated their own security, dealt with human and regular waste, and opened a kindergarten so that mothers with small children could come to participate. They converted a Hardee's restaurant into a free kitchen and a Kentucky Fried Chicken into a free clinic, organized networks for digital and print information, set up a pharmacy, handled hired agitators, and protected each other's religious practices. Similar structures and social relations mushroomed throughout the global occupations, each building upon previous iterations and instituting new forms fitting their particular situation. In Greece's Syntagma Square, the occupation paid particular attention to the how of participation, detailing bans on union and party insignia, the drawing of lots, and the arranging of transportation. Occupy Wall Street added a

People's Library and a gray water filtration system; Istanbul's Taksim Square built barricades and LGBTQ and gender visibility tents.

The occupations, by withdrawing their consent to the regime, allowed for the democratic and explicit institution of social forms. The People's Assembly of Syntagma Square resolution underscored the power of this extraction: "For a long time, decisions have been made for us, without us. We are here . . . to take life into our own hands."[43] In the space created by the occupations, not everything was organized, but everything organized itself. The difference was meaningful. One requires management, the other attentiveness—dispositions that are incompatible in every respect.[44]

As the urban rebellions of the twenty-first century have consistently proved, extraction need not be organized. By refusing the rules of law, property, police, and commodity, the riot likewise clears space for new forms of social life. As a young looter in Birmingham during the 2011 UK uprising expressed with much joy:

> It's not like any other day today is it . . . not just some normal, routine shit day, same-old same-old. I mean it's mental innit, its just crazy, you can come out, get what you can, it's just like a party today, you got to join in![45]

Taken together, the blockades, riots, and occupations of the twenty-first century underscore the intimate connection between the interruption of circulation and the creation of new forms of life. It was no surprise that Occupy Oakland's first foray outside of its base in Oscar Grant Plaza was the 100,000-person-strong shutdown of the Port of Oakland (the fifth largest container terminal in the United States). As the Invisible Committee noted, "Tahrir and Taksim squares are central hubs of circulation in Cairo and Istanbul. To block those flows was to open up the situation."[46] In 2016, Indigenous water protectors formed an encampment to disrupt the construction of the Dakota Access Pipeline. Within weeks, tens of thousands of settlers from all walks of life and struggle had joined them. Much like those occupying the squares in 2011, they set up tents, distributed food, organized resistance, and, perhaps most importantly, learned from each other's experiences and practices.

In this sense, the interruption of the regime's circulatory system and the extraction of humans from it are two faces of the same coin. If the former focuses on the material effects of disruption—what is to be interrupted or broken—the latter is concerned with creating forms of life not permitted by the regime of movement.

It's at these moments that disruption releases those involved (or witnessing) from the coercive pull of the regime's imposed meanings and imperatives. The pauses and rifts opened by disruption have the power to decode our fundamental social relations. These include the potential decoding of work as labor power by the strike; space as property by the occupation; entities as commodities by the riot; language as male by the consciousness-raising group; or a person's subjectification through the law by a nighttime act of ecotage. Through these disruptions, human beings are freed to reformulate their own understanding of—and relationship to—work, space, entities, language, and subjecthood. In these reformulations, undertaken with others, on uncarved terrain, lie the possible paths for a new human flourishing.

Notes

Introduction

1 See Miha Hribernik and Tim Campbell, "Emerging Markets Face Acute Instability as Pandemic Fuels Unrest," July 16, 2020, maplecroft.com; Rupert Steiner and Steve Goldstein, "Millennials to Redistribute Wealth From Older Generations to the Young in New 'Age of Disorder,' Warns Deutsche Strategist," September 12, 2020, marketwatch.com.

2 Christian Stirling Haig, Katherine Schmidt, and Samuel Brannen, "The Age of Mass Protests: Understanding an Escalating Global Trend," March 2, 2020, csis.org.

3 James Baldwin, "The Creative Dilemma," *Saturday Review*, February 8, 1964.

4 Giorgio Agamben, "Movement," transcribed and translated by Arianna Bové, 2005, generationonline.org. Yet its first analysis as a political category does not appear until midcentury. See Karl Marx, *The Communist Manifesto* (2013); Lorenz von Stein, *The History of the Social Movement in France: 1789–1848* (1964).

5 Ralph Waldo Emerson, "Historic Notes of Life and Letters in New England," *Atlantic Monthly* (October 1883): 1. Also Emerson, *Collected Works Volume 10* (2010): 572.

6 Agamben, "Movement." At this time, the term *movement* was picked up by radical/revolutionary wings of European socialist parties and unions. For use of the term within the reformist/radical debates of the German SPD, see Eduard Bernstein, *The Preconditions of Socialism and the Tasks of Social Democracy* (1993) and Rosa Luxemburg's response, Rosa Luxemburg, "Sozialreform oder Revolution," in Rosa Luxemburg, *Gesammelte Werke, 1893–1919*, 6 (1990): ii, 369–71. For its use by Lenin, see V. I. Lenin, "What Is to Be Done?" in Joseph Gusfield (ed.), *Protest, Reform, Revolt: A Reader in Social Movements* (1970): 458–72.

7 The new role of movement was most famously articulated by Nazi jurist Carl Schmitt in his 1933 essay "State, Movement, People," in which he equated movement with National Socialism and differentiated its dynamic quality from both the

state (the static apparatus of civil servants and officers) and the People (the unpo-
litical and undifferentiated element to be fashioned by the party). Carl Schmitt,
State, Movement, People: The Triadic Structure of the Political Unity (2001).

8 Since 1933, the term *movement* has been included in the names of radical right
parties in Chile, Denmark, Finland, France, Italy, the Netherlands, Portugal,
Romania, Sweden, Switzerland, Turkey, the UK, and the United States.

9 Around the same time, the term *movement* also gained currency throughout the
Third World. Though the Non-Aligned Movement had its origins in the 1950s, the
term itself did not appear until the Fifth Conference of Heads of State or
Government of Non-Aligned Countries in 1976, where participating countries
were for the first time denoted as members of "the Movement." See "Fifth
Conference of Heads of State or Government of Non-Aligned Nations," James
Martin Center for Nonproliferation Studies, cns.miis.edu.

10 Steven M. Buechler, *Understanding Social Movements: Theories from the Classical
Era to the Present* (2011): 75–7; Rudolf Heberle, *Social Movements: An Introduction
to Political Sociology* (1951). The French *Le Mouvement Social*, founded in 1960 by
Jean Maitron, was one of the first journals in the field. The diffusion of the category
of movement within academic analysis has also impacted our historical understanding of social struggle. As part of the "historic turn in the human sciences,"
historical sociologists led by Sidney Tarrow, Doug McAdam, and Charles Tilly
have, since the 1980s, engaged in theoretical and empirical work on the history of
"social movements." In 1994, Sidney Tarrow called for social movement theory to
be embedded "into the concrete record of history," while Doug McAdam argued in
1996 that the future for social movement studies lay "in getting in closer to the
lived experience of the social movements themselves." See Craig Calhoun, "The
Rise and Domestication of Historical Sociology," in Terrence McDonald (ed.), *The
Historic Turn in the Human Sciences* (1996): 305–38; Sidney Tarrow, *Power in
Movement: Social Movements and Contentious Politics* (2011); Doug McAdam,
John D. McCarthy, Mayer N. Zald (eds.), *Comparative Perspectives on Social
Movements: Political Opportunities, Mobilizing Structures, and Cultural Framings*
(2011); and Charles Tilly, *Social Movements: 1768–2004* (2004).

11 Beginning in the late 1990s, a newer trend in social movement studies coalescing
around the concept of *contentious politics* has sought to address this ingrained
assumption. See Charles Tilly and Sidney Tarrow, *Contentious Politics* (2007);
David A. Snow, Daniel Cress, Liam Downey, and Andrew Jones, "Disrupting the
'Quotidian': Reconceptualizing the Relationship between Breakdown and the
Emergence of Collective Action," *Mobilization: An International Journal* 3, no. 1
(1998): 1–22; Doug McAdam, Sidney Tarrow, Charles Tilly, "To Map Contentious
Politics," *Mobilization* 1, no. 1 (1996): 17–34; Ron Aminzade et al. (eds.), *Silence
and Voice in the Study of Contentious Politics* (2001); Sidney Tarrow, *Power in
Movement: Social Movements and Contentious Politics* (1998).

12 Hannah Arendt, *Men in Dark Times* (1968): 9.

13 Arendt, *Origins of Totalitarianism* (1951): 297.

14 The relations between movement and political community were first systematically
taken up by Plato. In *The Republic*, Plato crafted a triangular connection between
liberty, danger, and movement that was central to his conception of democracy. As
Hagar Kotef points out, for Plato, democracy is the mode of governance of those who
are bound to move. "While we have become accustomed to thinking of the demos as

the body of citizens or 'the people,' its original meaning was 'country' (or land), and later the concept came to refer to the people of the countryside, and thus the poor. The demos, therefore, was composed of those who did not live in the city but had to walk to participate in acts of legislation and governance. When the demos entered the city, their movement violated the stability which was the privilege of the citizens-as-the-few, and subjected the city to its rule of excessive freedom." Or as Plato put it in his satirical version of Athenian democracy, "where animals roam freely and proudly along the streets, bumping into anyone who doesn't get out of their way." For Plato, democracy's excessive movement constantly failed to produce and sustain order. In this formulation, movement becomes, both literally and figuratively, the interruption of established political order. The ambivalence of movement within Platonic thought, especially the tension between (an excess of) freedom and order, would later be worked out by the paradigmatic ideology of movement: liberalism. Hagar Kotef, *Movement and the Ordering of Freedom: On Liberal Governances of Mobility* (2015): 4; Plato, *The Republic* (2000), especially Book VIII.

15 Hannah Arendt, *On Revolution* (1963): 32.

16 Kotef, *Movement,* 5, 63, 59, 74.

17 L. T. Hobhouse, *Liberalism and Other Writings* (1994): 8.

18 Hagar Kotef argues that, while modern theorists of liberalism such as Kant and Mill increasingly equated liberty with human will and an abstracted reason, the connection between movement and freedom remained a latent strain surfacing throughout the entire history of the liberal project. Kotef, *Movement,* 80.

19 William Blackstone, *Commentaries on the Laws of England: In Four Books* (2010): 130.

20 Kotef, *Movement,* 85.

21 Frantz Fanon, *The Wretched of the Earth* (2004): 15.

22 See Mikhail Bakhtin, *Rebelais and His World* (1984); Michel de Certeau, *The Practice of Everyday Life* (1984); Edward Said, *Culture and Imperialism* (1994); Gilles Deleuze and Felix Guattari, *Nomadology: The War Machine* (1986).

23 Michael Hardt and Antonio Negri, *Multitude: War and Democracy in the Age of Empire* (2004): 137.

24 Michel Foucault, *Discipline and Punish* (1977): 218; James C. Scott, *Seeing like a State: How Certain Schemes to Improve the Human Condition Have Failed* (1998): 1.

25 Marx, *Manifesto,* 223.

26 Marx, *Manifesto,* 225.

27 Marshall Berman, *All That Is Solid Melts into Air: The Experience of Modernity* (1982): 92.

28 P. S. Atiyah, *The Rise and Fall of Freedom of Contract* (1985).

29 Peter Linebaugh and Marcus Rediker, *The Many Headed Hydra: Sailors, Slaves, Commoners, and the Hidden History of the Revolutionary Atlantic* (2000); Greg Grandin, *The Empire of Necessity: Slavery, Freedom, and Deception in the New World* (2014); Ian Baucom, *Specters of the Atlantic: Finance Capital, Slavery, and the Philosophy of History* (2005).

30 Ann Laura Stoler, "Colony," *Political Concepts: A Critical Lexicon* 1 (2012), politicalconcepts.org.

31 An obvious statement for those who, like Marx himself, saw primitive accumulation not as an initial or precursory step to the organization and operation of capital,

but as an ongoing and constant process of expropriation central to its functioning.

32 Midnight Notes Collective, "Introduction to the New Enclosures," *Midnight Notes*, no. 10 (1990): 4.

33 Sandro Mezzadra, "The Gaze of Autonomy: Capitalism, Migration, and Social Struggles," in Vicki Squire (ed.), *The Contested Politics of Mobility: Borderzones and Irregularity* (2010).

34 See Gil Anidjar, "Blood," *Political Concepts* 1 (2012); Gil Anidjar, *Blood: A Critique of Christianity* (2014); and Timothy Cresswell, *On the Move: Mobility in the Modern Western World* (2006): 14.

35 Karl Polanyi, *The Great Transformation, The Political and Economic Origins of Our Time* (2001): 155.

36 See Linebaugh and Rediker, *Many Headed Hydra*, 40–61; A. L. Beier, *Masterless Men: The Vagrancy Problem in England 1560–1640* (1985).

37 Paul Virilio, *Speed and Politics: An Essay on Dromology* (2006): 53.

38 John Torpey, *The Invention of the Passport: Surveillance, Citizenship, and the State* (2000). One must also add to this official monopoly the state's active interventions into society to certify the smooth operation of the economy of movement. From a kinetic standpoint, seemingly disparate state initiatives as Keynesianism, the deployment of the military and police as strike breakers (and replacement workers), Soviet collectivization, or the development of information and transportation infrastructure can be understood as part of a broader effort to ensure the efficient movement of the economy.

39 Louis Althusser described how individuals are interpellated as subjects by the state. To illustrate his point, he gave the now-famous example of a police officer shouting out, "Hey, you there!" in a public square. For Althusser, as the individual stops and turns to look at the officer—"by this mere one-hundred-and-eighty-degree physical conversion"—he becomes a subject. In the act of acknowledging that it is indeed s/he who is addressed (arrested), the individual, for Althusser, recognizes his/her subjecthood. In this formulation, the state apparatus (and the correlative subjectivity produced by it) is predicated on the mechanism of arrest. See Louis Althusser, "Ideology, and Ideological State Apparatuses," *Lenin and Philosophy and Other Essays* (1971).

40 Jacques Rancière, *On the Shores of Politics* (1995): 177.

41 *Mustafa Abdullah v. County of Saint Louis, Missouri et al.*

42 Bryce Covert, "'You're Breaking the Law as Soon as You Stop Walking': How Colorado Cities Criminalize Homelessness," *The Appeal*, April 2, 2018.

43 Lee Grimsditch, "Police Officer 'Assaulted' and 27 Arrests Made During City Centre Lockdown Protest," November 14, 2020, *The Liverpool Echo*.

44 Virilio, *Speed and Politics*, 56.

45 Brad Evans, "The Violence of the Algorithm," May 6, 2019, *Los Angeles Review of Books*.

46 Gilles Deleuze and Felix Guattari, *A Thousand Plateaus: Capitalism and Schizophrenia* (1987): 386.

47 Barry Boubacar, *Senegambia and the Atlantic Slave Trade* (1998): 121.

48 Joe Hill, "Workers of the World, Awaken!" in *The Industrial Worker "Little Red Songbook"* (1916).

49 Ti-Grace Atkinson, "Radical Feminism," in Barbara Crow (ed.), *Radical Feminism: A Documentary Reader* (2000): 82.

50 Rita Mae Brown, "The Shape of Things to Come," in Nancy Myron and Charlotte Bunch (eds.), *Lesbianism and the Women's Movement* (1975): 74.

51 The Feminists, "A Political Organization to Eliminate Sex Roles," in *Notes from the Second Year* (1970): 117.

52 Fredric Jameson, "Dresden's Clocks," *New Left Review*, no. 71 (2001): 150.

53 Benjamin Noys, "Emergency Brake," leniency.blogspot.com.

54 Tilly, *Social Movements*, 3.

55 Ibid., 4.

56 Here the anarchist millenarianism of nineteenth-century Spain serves as the quintessential boundary line. For an argument against this thesis, see Temma Kaplan, *Anarchists of Andalusia, 1868–1903* (1977): 206–12.

57 See Frederic Jameson, *A Singular Modernity* (2002): 29 and Joshua Clover's response to Alberto Toscana: Joshua Clover, Final Remarks, in "The Crisis and the Rift: A Symposium on Joshua Clover's *Riot. Strike. Riot,*" *Viewpoint Magazine*, September 29, 2016.

58 There are notable exceptions. Within social movement studies, the term *contentious politics*, first deployed in the mid-1990s by Sidney Tarrow, Charles Tilly, and Doug McAdam and since sprouting a cottage industry of its own, has sought to bridge this divide. Historians, for their part, have studied "revolutionary movements" (though often the term is used to describe radical struggles that never came to fruition) or have implicitly traversed the gulf between revolution and social movement by radically expanding their periodizations of revolutionary history.

59 As an example, in the over 200 pages of Tilly's foundational textbook, *Social Movements*, there is not a single mention of the concept of revolution.

60 An agenda most famously set forth in the opening lines of the Manifesto, "The history of all hitherto existing society is the history of class struggles." Marx, *Manifesto*, 14.

61 Marx, *Capital*, 167.

62 For a counterinterpretation of the origin of Marx's laws, see Burkett, "Marx's Concept of an Economic Law of Motion," *History of Political Economy* 32, no. 2 (2000): 380–94.

63 Marx, *Capital*, 10.

64 Ellen Meiksins Wood, *The Origin of Capitalism* (1999): 103. From these come other laws of capitalism; fall in rate of profit, concentration, and centralization of capital; technological revolution; inevitability of economic crisis; social polarization and so on.

65 Marx, quoted at length here: "The bourgeoisie has stripped of its halo every occupation hitherto honored and looked up to with reverent awe. It has converted the physician, the lawyer, the priest, the poet, the man of science, into its paid wage laborers. The bourgeoisie has torn away from the family its sentimental veil, and has reduced the family relation to a mere money relation. It has pitilessly torn asunder the motley feudal ties that bound man to his 'natural superiors,' and has left remaining no other nexus between man and man than naked self-interest, than callous 'cash payment.' It has drowned the most heavenly ecstasies of religious fervour, of chivalrous enthusiasm, of philistine sentimentalism, in the icy water of egotistical calculation. It has resolved personal worth into exchange value, and in place of the numberless indefeasible chartered freedoms, has set up that single, unconscionable freedom—Free Trade." Marx, *Manifesto*, 16.

66 See Deleuze and Guattari, *Capitalism and Schizophrenia*. Especially plateau 12, "1227: Treatise on Nomadology—The War Machine," and plateau 14, "1440: The Smooth and the Striated."

67 This is not to say that it eradicates these older conflicts. In fact, keeping and often accentuating them is necessary to sublimate conflict away from the source of the real violence—the regime of movement itself. Capital has continually fostered conflict between men and women and white and non-white people as a way to divert coordinated struggle against its order.

68 To be sure, social disruption has a much older history, itself coeval with the institution of human coercion. More to the point, specific disruptive practices detailed in the book, such as the barricade or food riot, have their origins deep in the early modern, if not late medieval, periods. The first strikes are as old as ancient Egypt. Yet, as I hope will become clear, the kinetic reordering of terrain that accompanied the regime of movement fundamentally shifted the stakes and signification of these disruptions.

69 Jock Young, "Cannibalism and Bulimia: Patterns of Social Control in Late Modernity," *Theoretical Criminology* 4, no. 3 (2007): 387–407.

70 This view has been reinforced not least by the "two sixties" of the New Left, segregating it into an earlier reformist and integrationist period and its later degeneration into chaos and violence. See Todd Gitlin, *The Sixties: Years of Hope, Days of Rage* (1987); David Chalmers, *And the Crooked Places Made Straight* (1996): 68, 77–8, 86; Dan Berger, *Outlaws of America: The Weather Underground and the Politics of Solidarity* (2006): 7–8. A similar bifurcation exists in German and Italian popular narratives that marks a shift from the positively remembered late-1960s student movements to the much more infamous descent into armed conflict of the late 1970s. See Karrin Hanshew, *Terror and Democracy in West Germany* (2012); Timothy S. Brown, *West Germany and the Global Sixties* (2013). For the Italian version, see George Katsiaficas, *The Subversion of Politics* (1997): 8–59.

71 From Paul Gilroy, "Never Again: Refusing Race and Salvaging the Human," *New Frame*, June 20, 2019.

72 Ross, *May '68 and Its Afterlives*, 6.

73 An argument that applies equally well to the role of the "environmental movement" as the necessary transformation of capitalism from an extractive to an ecological enterprise.

1. Movement

1 World-system theorists have long contended that these developments marked the slow transition of human societies from a multitude of mostly self-sufficient regional empires to a single integrated modern world system. Other historians have seen in these developments the early conditions for the emergence of industrial capitalism. Specifically, these historians note the transformation of agriculture from subsistence to commercial farming and pasturage, the institutionalization of regional, national, and international markets for goods and credit, and the expansion of wage labor as precursors to the Industrial Revolution.

 2 David Armitage, "Three Concepts of Atlantic History," in David Armitage and Michael J. Braddick (eds.), *The British Atlantic World 1500–1800* (2002): 12.
 3 E. P. Thompson, "The Moral Economy of the English Crowd in the Eighteenth Century," *Past and Present*, no. 50 (1971): 76–136; Cynthia A. Bouton, *The Flour War: Gender, Class, and Community in late Ancien Régime French Society* (1993): xviii.
 4 Thompson, "Moral Economy," 83.
 5 Ibid., 83.
 6 Bouton, *The Flour War*, 10.
 7 Thompson, "Moral Economy," 86–8.
 8 Bouton, *The Flour War*, 5.
 9 Charles Sellers, *The Market Revolution: Jacksonian America, 1815–1846* (1994): 5.
10 See Christopher Clark, "Economics and Culture: Opening Up the Rural History of the Early American Northeast," *American Quarterly* 43, no. 2 (1991): 279–301; Allan Kulikoff, "The Transition to Capitalism in Rural America," *The William and Mary Quarterly* 46, no. 1 (1989): 120–44. Earlier articles that developed the debate include Michael Merrill, "Cash Is Good to Eat: Self-Sufficiency and Exchange in the Rural Economy of the United States," *Radical History Review*, no. 14 (1977): 42–71; James A. Henretta, "Families and Farms: Mentalité in Pre-Industrial America," *The William and Mary Quarterly* 35 (1978): 3–32; Christopher Clark, "The Household Economy, Market Exchange and the Rise of Capitalism in the Connecticut Valley, 1800–1860," *The Journal of Social History*, no. 13 (1979): 172–5. For an important work detailing the intersection of rural social and cultural change, see Christopher Clark, *The Roots of Rural Capitalism: Western Massachusetts, 1780–1860* (1990).
11 Bruce Mann, *Neighbors and Strangers: Law and Community in Early Connecticut* (1986).
12 Merrill, "Cash Is Good to Eat," 42–71.
13 The binary drawn by Sellers and others was, in reality, more complicated. The relative prosperity, if not the existence of, many backcountry farming communities was deeply intertwined and made possible by the culture of the market. It was the profits to be made from transatlantic commerce that cleansed the Native Americans from these lands, opening them up to colonial farming. Many of the new backcountry towns were commercial ventures financed by coastal merchants, whose interests lay not in the meager rents to be collected from propertyless craftsmen, but as collection and distribution points for integrating the rural interior within the transatlantic economy. "Philadelphia and Baltimore merchants were essential to the process of getting the flour, flaxseed, and iron of the backcountry to consumers in the Atlantic world and in bringing . . . European and East India goods [and Irish immigrants] to backcountry farmers." As the interior became more commercially integrated into the transatlantic economy, transatlantic capital began to penetrate into these communities. The local networks of credit became more and more tied to international credit as British merchants supplied long lines to East Coast merchants, who advanced lines of credit to local shopkeepers, who in turn did the same to local craftsmen and farmers in their regions. In the South, the mortgaging of human property, itself predicated on the transatlantic economy of movement, became an essential means of supplying credit to rural communities, serving as an engine for the slave economy. For the creation of rural towns in colonial America, see Richard K. MacMaster, "Philadelphia Merchants, Backcountry Shopkeepers,

and Town-Making Fever," *Pennsylvania History: A Journal of Mid-Atlantic Studies* 81, no. 3 (2014): 351–4; for slavery's role in capital accumulation, see Bonnie Martin, "Slavery's Invisible Engine: Mortgaging Human Property," *The Journal of Southern History* 76, no. 4 (2010): 817–66.

14 Thompson, "Moral Economy," 93.

15 Ibid., 101.

16 Charles Smith, *Three Tracts on the Corn-Trade and Corn-Laws* (1766); Adam Smith, *The Wealth of Nations, Vol. 2* (1982): 32.

17 Smith, *The Wealth of Nations*, 32.

18 Ibid., 42.

19 Bouton, *The Flour War*, 8, 13.

20 The French physiocrats, particularly Vincent de Gournay, had a great impact on Turgot, Louis XVI's Controller-General of Finances, who abolished police regulations and established free trade in grain throughout France on September 13, 1774. In England, by 1772, many of the local practices and the regulations governing them had become obsolete.

21 Cynthia Bouton, "Provisioning, Power and Popular Protest from the Seventeenth Century to the French Revolution and Beyond," in *Crowd Actions in Britain and France from the Middle Ages to the Modern World* (2015): 81.

22 Restrictions to transatlantic trade were most notable during the French Revolutionary wars. The shift in power balance to landed interests in England allowed for the passage of the notorious Corn Laws (1815–1846) over the objections of both the poor and new manufacturing interests that would have benefited from lower grain prices. In France, the General Maximum of the Jacobin era (1793–1794) was partially resurrected during the Napoleonic era, but, by and large, restoration and July Monarchy governments remained committed to liberalization.

23 Joshua Clover, *Riot. Strike. Riot. The New Era of Uprisings* (2016): 29.

24 Thompson, "Moral Economy," 120.

25 See John Bohstedt, "Food Riots and the Politics of Provision in Early-Modern England and France, The Irish Famine and WWI," in *Crowd Actions in Britain and France from the Middle Ages to the Modern World*, (2015): 119; Bouton, "Provisioning, Power and Popular Protest," 89.

26 Eric Hobsbawm, "The General Crisis of the European Economy," 40.

27 Silvia Federici, *Caliban and the Witch: Women, the Body and Primitive Accumulation* (2004): 89.

28 Marcus Rediker, *Villains of All Nations: Atlantic Piracy in the Golden Age* (2004): 23.

29 Alison Games, "Migration," in David Armitage and Michael Braddick (eds.), *The British Atlantic World 1500–1800* (2002): 41.

30 Alan Everitt, *The Agrarian History of England and Wales: Vol. 4* (1967): 405.

31 Ellen Meiksins Wood, *The Origin of Capitalism* (1999): 103.

32 "The Goose and the Common," unionsongs.com.

33 A. L. Beier, *Masterless Men: The Vagrancy Problem in England 1560–1640* (1985): 21.

34 Enclosed lands normally could demand higher rents than unenclosed, and thus landlords had an economic stake in enclosure, even if they did not intend to farm the land directly. Leigh Shaw-Taylor, "Parliamentary Enclosure and the Emergence of an English Agricultural Proletariat," *Journal of Economic History* 61, no. 3 (2001).

35 Beier, *Masterless Men*, 21.

36 Games, "Migration," 34.

37 Ibid., 35.

38 Karl Marx, "Grundrisse," in *Karl Marx, Frederick Engels: Collected Works* (1975): 501.

39 For a wonderful synopsis of the major vectors of the primitive accumulation debate over the past 150 years, see Robert Nichols, "Disaggregating Primitive Accumulation," in *Radical Philosophy* vol. 194 (2015).

40 Beier, *Masterless Men*, xxii.

41 Marcus Rediker and Peter Linebaugh, *The Many Headed Hydra: Sailors, Slaves, Commoners, and the Hidden History of the Revolutionary Atlantic* (2002): 18.

42 Jesse Lemisch, "Jack Tar in the Streets: Merchant Seamen in the Politics of Revolutionary America," *William and Mary Quarterly*, no. 25 (1968): 375.

43 Karl Marx, *Capital* (1977): 899.

44 Games, "Migration," 37–8. See also Spencer Dimmock, *The Origin of Capitalism in England, 1400–1600* (2014).

45 See Eric Williams, *Capitalism & Slavery* (1944).

46 Games, "Migration," 36–8.

47 Edmund Morgan, "Slavery and Freedom: The American Paradox," *Journal of American History* 59, no. 1 (1972): 15. David Galenson confirms this view, stating that most indentured servants were farmers, either yeomen, husbandmen, or agricultural day laborers who, for reason of the changing economy, could no longer find adequate subsistence through such work. David Galenson, *White Servitude in Colonial America* (1981): 190–1.

48 For shorter articles and book-length studies on white indentured servitude in the New World, see Theodore Allen, *The Invention of the White Race* (1994); P. C. Emmer (ed.), *Colonialism and Migration: Indentured Labour Before and After Slavery* (1986); David Galenson, *White Servitude in Colonial America: An Economic Analysis* (1981); Don Jordan and Michael Walsh, *White Cargo: The Forgotten History of Britain's White Slaves in America* (2008); Russell Menard, *Migrants, Servants, and Slaves: Unfree Labor in Colonial British America* (2001); Kenneth Morgan, *Slavery and Servitude in Colonial North America: A Short History* (2001); Sharon Salinger, "Labor, Markets, and Opportunity: Indentured Servitude in Early America," *Labor History*, no. 38 (1997): 311–338; Abbot Emerson Smith, *Colonists in Bondage: White Servitude and Convict Labor in America, 1607–1776* (1971).

49 Rediker and Linebaugh, *The Many Headed Hydra*, 110.

50 Jordan and Walsh, *White Cargo*, 119.

51 Ibid., 13.

52 Morgan, *Slavery and Servitude in Colonial North America*, 54. See also Rodger Ekirch, *Bound for America: The Transportation of British Convicts to the Colonies, 1718–1775* (1990).

53 Ibid., 58.

54 Marcus Rediker, *Outlaws of the Atlantic: Sailors, Pirates, and Motley Crews in the Age of Sail* (2014): 50.

55 Morgan, *Slavery and Servitude in Colonial North America*, 44–5.

56 Ibid., 56.

57 Ibid., 9.

58 Christopher Magra, "Anti-Impressment Riots and the Age of Revolution," in Anderson, Frykman, Voss, Rediker (eds.), *Mutiny and Maritime Radicalism in the Age of Revolution: A Global Survey* (2014): 134.

59 For further reading on impressment, see Denver Bausman, "Men of War: British Sailors and the Impressment Paradox," *Journal of Early Modern History*, no. 14 (2010): 9–44; Nicholas Rodgers, *The Press Gang* (2007); John Hutchinson, *The Press Gang Afloat and Offshore* (1913).

60 Games, "Migration," 49.

61 In the North American colonies, the transition from servitude to slavery occurred in the four decades between 1680 and 1720.

62 The end of the legal transatlantic slave trade did not end forced movement, but led to new patterns of coerced migration with a large internal trade that developed to transfer slaves to regions where labor was in highest demand. Games, "Migration," 49.

63 Rediker, *Outlaws of the Atlantic*, 7.

64 Marcus Rediker, *The Slave Ship: A Human History*, (2007): 347.

65 Erin McKenna, Scott L. Pratt, *American Philosophy: From Wounded Knee to the Present* (2015): 375.

66 Rediker, *Villains of the Atlantic*, 17.

67 Ibid., 17.

68 E. S. Ferguson, "The Measurement of the 'Man-Day,'" *Scientific American* (October 1971): 99–100.

69 Charles Babbage, *The Exposition of 1851: Or, Views of the Industry, the Science, and the Government, of England* (1851): 1–5.

70 Caitlin Rosenthal, *Accounting for Slavery: Masters and Management* (2018).

71 Alan L. Olmstead and Paul W. Rhode, "Productivity Growth and the Regional Dynamics of Antebellum Southern Development," NBER Working Paper 16494, www.nber.org.

72 E. P. Thompson, "Time, Work-Discipline, and Industrial Capitalism," *Past and Present*, no. 38 (1967): 81.

73 Ibid., 83.

74 Ibid., 90.

75 Ibid., 88.

76 Michel Foucault, *Discipline and Punish: The Birth of the Prison* (1995): 135–6.

77 Ibid., 136, 138.

78 Thompson, "Time, Work-Discipline, and Industrial Capitalism," 85.

79 William J. Ashworth, "England and the Machinery of Reason: 1780 to 1830," in Iwan Rhys Morus (ed.), *Bodies/Machines* (2002): 40.

80 David H. Shayt, "Stairway to Redemption: America's Encounter with the British Prison Treadmill," *Technology and Culture* 30, no. 4 (1989): 908–38.

81 *Gloucester Journal*, January 16, 1823. As cited in Jill Evans, "On the Treadmill: Hard Labour at Gloucester Prison," gloscrimehistory.wordpress.com.

82 Ashworth, "England and the Machinery of Reason," 51.

83 Ibid., 39.

84 Rediker, Outlaws of the Atlantic, 23.

2. Obstruction

1 Anonymous. This African-American spiritual, first sung by slaves, has a fascinating transatlantic afterlife. It was picked up by American workers in the 1930s, when it was sung by workers in various industries, including the West Virginia coal mines, Southern textile mills, and General Motors plants in Detroit. In the 1950s and '60s, civil rights activists added new verses and sang it as they united for racial justice. The song crossed the Atlantic Ocean and was sung as "*No nos moverán*" in protests against Spanish dictator Francisco Franco. It journeyed back to the Americas and was the last song played on Chilean radio immediately before the military over-threw the democratically elected government in a bloody coup d'état in 1973. See Matthew Sabatella, "We Shall Not Be Moved," balladofamerica.org.

2 Cynthia Bouton, "Provisioning, Power and Popular Protest from the Seventeenth Century to the French Revolution and Beyond," in M. T. Davis (ed.), *Crowd Actions in Britain and France from the Middle Ages to the Modern World* (2015): 85; John Bohstedt, *The Politics of Provisions: Food Riots, Moral Economy, and Market Transition in England, c. 1500–1850* (2010).

3 David Halle and Kevin Rafter, "Riots in New York and Los Angeles: 1935-2002," in David Halle (ed.), *New York and Los Angeles: Politics, Society and Culture—A Comparative View* (2003): 347; Paul Gilje, *Rioting in America* (1999): 4; Joshua Clover, *Riot. Strike. Riot. The New Era of Uprisings* (2016): 37.

4 Clover, *Riot. Strike. Riot,* 83.

5 Ibid., 4.

6 E. P. Thompson, "The Moral Economy of the English Crowd in the Eighteenth Century," *Past and Present*, no. 50 (1971): 76.

7 "John Bohstedt, "Food Riots and the Politics of Provisions in Early Modern England and France: The Irish Famine, and World War I," in Michel T. Davis (ed.), *Crowd Actions in Britain and France from the Middle Ages to the Modern World* (2015): 107.

8 Charles Tilly, "Speaking Your Mind Without Elections, Surveys, or Social Movements," *Public Opinion Quarterly* 47, no. 4 (Winter, 1983): 470.

9 Clover, *Riot. Strike. Riot,* 54.

10 Thompson, "Moral Economy," 99.

11 Ibid., 78.

12 Adam Smith, *The Wealth of Nations, Vol. 2* (1982): 34.

13 Cynthia A. Bouton, *The Flour War: Gender, Class, and Community in late Ancien Regime French Society* (1993): 84–6.

14 Thompson, "Moral Economy," 100.

15 Andrew Charlesworth (ed.), *An Atlas of Rural Protest in Britain 1548–1900* (1983): 81; E. P. Thompson, *The Making of the English Working Class* (1963): 70-3.

16 Bouton, "Provisioning Power and Popular Protest," 88.

17 Clover, *Riot. Strike. Riot,* 44; Thompson, "Moral Economy," 120, 134.

18 Thompson, "Moral Economy," 110.

19 Ibid., 111.

20 Barbara Clark Smith, "Food Rioters and the American Revolution," *The William and Mary Quarterly* 51, no. 1 (1994): 7.

21 Bouton, *The Flour War,* 83, 96.

22 Tilly, "Speaking Your Mind," 470.

23 Smith, "Food Rioters and the American Revolution," 14.

24 Ibid., 24.

25 Ibid., 25.

26 Ibid., 23.

27 Terry Bouton, *Taming Democracy: "The People," The Founders, and the Troubled Ending of the American Revolution* (2009).

28 Terry Bouton, "A Road Closed: Rural Insurgency in Post-Independence Pennsylvania," *Journal of American History* 87, no. 3 (2000): 855–87.

29 Bouton, "Provisioning Power and Popular Protest," 93.

30 The debate among economic and social historians has revolved around two poles. One set by Karl Marx, who saw these riots as the birth pangs of social revolution, the other by Karl Polanyi, who claimed that rioters sought little more than a return to bucolic self-sufficiency. More recent historians have shied away from these categories, asserting that food riots were motivated more by the deep conviction that the rich were bound to help in times of need. See Bohstedt, *The Politics of Provisions*.

31 Peter Linebaugh and Marcus Rediker, *The Many-Headed Hydra: Sailors, Slaves, Commoners, and the Hidden History of Revolutionary Atlantic* (2000): 13.

32 Ibid., 13.

33 Anita Rupprect, "All We Have Done, We Have Done for Freedom: The *Creole* Slave-Ship Revolt (1841) and the Revolutionary Atlantic," in Clare Anderson et al. (eds.), *Mutiny and Maritime Radicalism in the Age of Revolution: A Global Survey* (2013): 269.

34 Ibid., 275.

35 The New England Historical Society, "The Boston Impressment Riot of 1747," newenglandhistoricalsociety.com. See also Jack Tager, *Boston Riots: Three Centuries of Social Violence* (2001).

36 Christopher Magra, "Anti-Impressment Riots and the Age of Revolution," in *Mutiny and Maritime Radicalism in the Age of Revolution*, 132.

37 Linebaugh and Rediker, *The Many Headed Hydra*, 214.

38 Nicolas Rodgers, *The Press Gang: Naval Impressment and Its Opponents in Georgian Britain* (2007): 5, 40.

39 Don. M. Wolfe (ed.), *Leveller Manifestoes of the Puritan Revolution* (1944): 95.

40 Magra, "Anti-Impressment Riots and the Age of Revolution," 148.

41 Ibid., 146.

42 Linebaugh and Rediker, *The Many Headed Hydra*, 215.

43 Magra, "Anti-Impressment Riots and the Age of Revolution," 149.

44 Ibid., 141.

45 Linebaugh and Rediker, *The Many Headed Hydra*, 215.

46 Walther Hawthorne, "Strategies of the Decentralized: Defending Communities from Slave Raiders in Coastal Guinea-Bissau, 1450–1815," in Sylviane Diouf (ed.), *Fighting the Slave Trade: West African Strategies* (2003): 158.

47 Thierno Mouctar Bah, "Slave-Raiding and Defensive Systems South of Lake Chad from the Sixteenth to the Nineteenth Century," in *Fighting the Slave Trade*, 25.

48 Adama Gueye, "The Impact of the Slave Trade on Cayor and Baol," in *Fighting the Slave Trade*, 56.

49 Barry Boubacar, *Senegambia and the Atlantic Slave Trade* (1998): 121.

50 Robert Norris, "Log of 'Unity' for a Slaving Voyage," Merseyside Maritime Museum, Maritime Digital Archives, www.liverpoolmuseums.org.uk.

51 Marcus Rediker, *The Slave Ship, A Human History* (2007): 32.

52 Eric Robert Taylor, *If We Must Die: Shipboard Insurrections in the Era of the Atlantic Slave Trade* (2006): 3. For as complete a list as is available of recorded resistance, see The Transatlantic Slave Trade Database: slavevoyages.org.

53 David Richardson, "Shipboard Revolts, African Authority, and the Atlantic Slave Trade," *The William and Mary Quarterly*, no. 58 (2001): 69–92; S. Behrendt, D. Etlis, and D. Richardson, "The Costs of Coercion: African Agency in the Pre-modern Atlantic World," *Economic History Review*, no. 54 (2001): 454–76; Johannes Postma, *The Dutch in the Atlantic Slave Trade: 1600–1815* (1990).

54 Taylor, *If We Must Die*, 122.

55 C. B. Wadstrom, *An Essay on Colonization Particularly Applied to the Western Coast of Africa with Some Free Thoughts on Cultivation and Commerce. 1794* (reprint 1968): 79.

56 Ibid., 87.

57 Rediker, *The Slave Ship*, 285.

58 Ibid., 287.

59 Terri Snyder, "Suicide, Slavery, and Memory in North America," *Journal of American History*, no. 97, 1 (2010): 39.

60 Ibid., 288.

61 Ismail Rashid, "A Devotion to Liberty at any Price: Rebellion and Anti-slavery in the Upper Guinea Coast in the Eighteenth and Nineteenth Centuries," in *Fighting the Slave Trade*, 137.

62 Rediker, *The Slave Ship*, 291. Taking one's life as a means of property damage was a harrowing practice that carried over from the ships to the plantation system. Observing such suicides, the Dominican Jean-Baptiste Labat, on a mission to Saint-Domingue, wrote in 1701, "They destroy themselves, they off-handedly slit their throats for trivial reasons, but most often, they do this to cause damage to their masters." This view was seconded by M. de Gallifet, one of the wealthiest slaveholders in Saint-Domingue: "Last night a slave chocked himself to death with his tongue. This happens quite often, as there are slaves desperate enough to kill themselves in order to inflict loss upon their masters." See: Carolyn Fick, *The Making of Haiti: Saint Domingue Revolution from Below* (1990): 48.

63 Rediker, *The Slave Ship*, 291.

64 Issac Dookhan, *A History of the Virgin Islands of the United States* (1974); Col. C.L.G. Harris, "The True Traditions of my Ancestors," in Kofi Agorsah (ed.), *Maroon Heritage: Archaeological Ethnographies and Historical Perspectives* (1994): 47.

65 Louis Perez, *To Die in Cuba: Suicide and Society* (2005): 34–53.

66 Alvin O. Thompson, *Flight to Freedom: African Runaways and the Maroons in the Americas* (2006): 93.

67 Thomas Clarkson, *An Essay on the Slavery and Commerce of Human Beings 1786* (reprint 1969): 143–4.

68 Kevin Mulroy, *Freedom on the Border: The Seminole Maroons in Florida, the Indian Territory, Coahuila, and Texas* (1993): 1.

69 Thompson, *Flight to Freedom*, 129.

70 Richard Price, *Maroon Societies: Rebel Slave Communities in the Americas* (1996): 6–7.

71 Thomas Flory, "Fugitive Slaves and Free Society," *Journal of Negro History*, no. 64, issue 2 (1979): 124; Mavis Campbell, *The Maroons of Jamaica 1655-1796: A History of Resistance, Collaboration, and Betrayal* (1990): 21; Price, *Maroon Societies*, 11.

72 William Freehling, "Why the US Fugitive Slave Phenomenon was Crucial," Paper presented at Gilder Center for the Study of Slavery Resistance and Abolition, Yale University, 6–7 December 2002.

73 Behrendt, Etlis, and Richardson, "The Costs of Coercion," 475.

74 Thomas Clarkson, *Newburyport Herald*, December 4, 1801, as cited in Rediker, *The Slave Ship*, 301.

75 Marcus Rediker, *Villains of All Nations: Atlantic Pirates in the Golden Age* (2004): 4.

76 Colin Woodard, *The Republic of Pirates* (2007): 3.

77 Rediker, *Outlaws of the Atlantic*, 64.

78 Rediker, *Villains of All Nations*, 67.

79 Ibid., 34.

80 Ibid., 9.

81 Ibid., 15.

82 Ibid., 33.

83 Woodard, *The Republic of Pirates*, 131, 139, 159.

84 Having said all this, one must be careful not to draw too rosy a picture of New Providence. Racial and gendered hierarchies, though more fluid, were still very much present on the island. This reality was even more pronounced on the ships, where female pirates often had to hide their gender and distinctions between pirate vessels that welcomed the enslaved and those that had few qualms about profiting off their sale were not always easily drawn. Nevertheless, given the alternatives offered by the regime of movement, it was a welcome home for tens of thousands.

85 Marcus Rediker, "Hydrarchy and Libertalia: The Utopian Dimensions of Atlantic Piracy in the Early Eighteenth Century," in David Starkey (ed.), *Pirates And Privateers: New Perspectives on the War on Trade in the Eighteenth and Nineteenth Centuries* (1997): 37–8.

86 See Julius Scott, *The Common Wind: Afro-american Currents in the Age of the Haitian Revolution* (2018); Marcus Rediker, "The African Origins of the Amistad Rebellion, 1839," *International Review of Social History*, no. 58 (2013): 15–34.

87 Lenin, *What Is to Be Done?*, 27, marxists.org.

Excursus I: Disruption and Revolution

1 William Sewell, "Historical Events as Transformations of Structures: Inventing Revolution at the Bastille," *Theory and Society* 25 (1996): 857.

2 Ibid., 852.

3 Thomas Jefferson, *Declaration of Independence* (1997).

4 Keith Baker, *Inventing the French Revolution: Essays on French Political Culture in the Eighteenth Century* (1990): 206–7.

5 Pierre Retat, *Les Journaux de 1789* (1988); Claude Labrosse and Pierre Retat, *Naissance du Journal Révolutionnaire 1789* (1990).

6 Baker, *Inventing the French Revolution*, 207.

7 Baker, *Inventing the French Revolution*, 219.

8 C. L. R. James, *Black Jacobins* (1989); Robin Blackburn, *The Overthrow of Colonial Slavery, 1776–1848* (1988); Carolyn E. Fick, *The Making of Haiti: The Saint Domingue Revolution from Below* (1990); Eugene Genovese, *From Rebellion to Revolution: Afro-American Slave Revolts in the Making of the Modern World* (1992); Laurent Dubois, *A Colony of Citizens Revolution and Slave Emancipation in the French Caribbean, 1787–1800* (2004); Laurent Dubois, *Avengers of the New World: The Story of the Haitian Revolution* (2004); Lynn Hunt, *Inventing Human Rights: A History* (2008); John Thornton, "I Am the Subject of the King of Congo: African Political Ideology and the Haitian Revolution," *Journal of World History* 4, no 2 (1993): 181–214.

9 Most scholars of Saint-Domingue have recognized the significance of marronage to the Haitian Revolution. The historian Jean Reynold Jean-Pierre has gone so far as to claim that the Haitian Revolution was a grander form of the practice "that established a marronage on an entire island." See Alvin Thompson, *Flight to Freedom: African Runaways and Maroons in the Americas* (2006): 15; Jean Reynold Jean-Pierre, *Sur la Route de l'Esclave: Saint-Domingue, Une Terre d'Enfer, 1503–1791* (2000). For Geggus's counterargument, see David Geggus, "The Colony of Saint-Domingue on the Eve of Revolution," in David Geggus and Norman Fiering (eds.), *The World of the Haitian Revolution* (2009).

10 Part of the difficulty in establishing long-term maroon communities on Saint-Domingue was the saturation of mountainous zones by coffee plantations. Indeed, the limits on marronage may have propelled plantation slaves to direct insurrection as the only path open to overcoming their condition.

11 Carolyn Fick, *The Making of Haiti: Saint Domingue Revolution from Below* (1990): 67.

12 Ibid., 66.

13 Leslie Manigat, "The Relationship Between Marronage and Slave Revolts and Revolution in St. Domingue-Haiti," in *Annals of the New York Academy of Sciences*, no. 292 (1977): 433–4.

14 Ibid., 428.

15 Ibid., 422.

16 Fick, *The Making of Haiti*, 86.

17 Fick, *The Making of Haiti*, 100.

18 James, *Black Jacobins*, 88.

19 Fick, *The Making of Haiti*, 51.

20 Ibid., 150.

21 Laurent Dubois, *Avengers of the New World: The Story of the Haitian Revolution* (2005): 141.

22 Ibid., 141.

23 For a wonderful recent study of these impacts, see David Geggus (ed.), *The Impact of the Haitian Revolution in the Atlantic World* (2020).

3. Control

1 Eduard Bernstein, *The Preconditions of Socialism* (1993): 190.
2 Benjamin, "Thesis on the Philosophy of History," 393.
3 Ibid., 393.
4 In addition to labor, the mid-nineteenth and early twentieth centuries saw an explosion of social struggle across the Atlantic world, from the emancipation of women and slaves to struggles for democracy and national self-determination. I have focused on workers because labor struggles were present across the entire Atlantic world, were the most theorized (and thus self-reflexive) of struggles during this period, and employed the widest range of tactics. It was the sphere where disruption, as mentality and practice, were most forcefully developed. The workers' struggle also became *the* point of reference, departure, and rejection for social struggles that came after it, forming the backdrop for the emergence and development of the New Left and its successors. As such, it serves as a bridge between eighteenth-century Atlantic disruption and its more recent history.
5 Agamben, "Movement."
6 Maximilien Robespierre, "Speech to the National Convention, 5 November 1792," as cited in Slavoj Žižek, *In Defense of Lost Causes* (2008): 163.
7 Susan Buck-Morss, *Hegel, Haiti, and Universal History* (2009).
8 Susan Buck-Morss, "Hegel and Haiti," *Critical Inquiry* 26, no. 4 (2000): 848–9.
9 Ibid., 849.
10 Karl Marx, *The Communist Manifesto* (1996).
11 Daniel Guerin, *No Gods No Masters: An Anthology of Anarchism, Book I* (1998): 41.
12 Pierre-Joseph Proudhon, *The Evolution of Capitalism: The Philosophy of Misery* (2016): 20.
13 Mikhail Bakunin, "The Paris Commune and the Idea of the State," in Sam Dolgoff (ed.), *Bakunin on Anarchy: Selected Works of the Activist-Founder of World Anarchism* (1973): 272.
14 Ibid., 57.
15 Peter Marshall, *Demanding the Impossible: A History of Anarchism* (2010): 270.
16 E. H. Carr, *Michael Bakunin* (1961): 379. The second text, *Catechism of a Revolutionary*, was cowritten with Sergei Nechaev, though recent scholarship has disputed the extent of Bakunin's contribution. See Mark Leier, *Bakunin: The Creative Passion* (2006): 232.
17 Mikhail Bakunin, "Letter to a Frenchman on the Present Crisis," in *Bakunin on Anarchy*.
18 Guerin, *No Gods No Masters*, 141.
19 Ibid., 152.
20 Ibid., 208.
21 Ibid., 208.
22 P. A. Kropotkin, *Selected Writings on Anarchism and Revolution* (1970): 305.
23 Guerin, *No Gods No Masters*, 265.
24 Ibid., 266.
25 For a recent historiographical summary of the main arguments, see Robert Graham, *We Do Not Fear Anarchy—We Invoke It: The First International and the Origins of the Anarchist Movement* (2015).

26 Revolutionary millenarianism dates back, according to Eric Hobsbawm, to Joachim of Flora (1145–1202), the inventor of the doctrine of the three Ages of the World: the Age of the Father (Law), the Age of the Son (Faith), and the future age, that of the Holy Ghost. See Eric Hobsbawm, *Primitive Rebels. Studies in Archaic Forms of Social Movement in the 19th and 20th Centuries* (1959): 25; Michael Löwy, "Eric Hobsbawm, Sociologist of Peasant Millenarianism," *Estudos Avançados* 24, no. 69 (2010).

27 Norman Cohn, *The Pursuit of the Millennium: Revolutionary Millenarians and Mystical Anarchists of the Middle Ages* (1970); Rochard Landes, *Heaven on Earth: The Varieties of Millennial Experiences* (2011); Hillel Schwartz, *The French Prophets: The History of a Millenarian Group in Eighteenth-Century England* (1980); Temma Kaplan, *Anarchists of Andalusia, 1868–1903* (1977): 206–12.

28 Löwy, "Eric Hobsbawm, Sociologist of Peasant Millenarianism," 105–18.

29 Karl Marx, *Thesis on Feuerbach*, marxists.org.

30 Marx, *The Communist Manifesto*.

31 James Billington, *Fire in the Minds of Men: Origins of the Revolutionary Faith* (1999): 243.

32 Gareth Stedman Jones, *Karl Marx: Greatness and Illusion* (2016): 462.

33 Marshall, *Demanding the Impossible*, 271.

34 Ibid., 277.

35 Ibid., 346.

36 Rosa Luxemburg, *Reform and Revolution* (*Chapter 8: The Conquest of Political Power*), marxists.org.

37 Eduard Bernstein, *The Preconditions of Socialism* (1993): 190.

38 Luxemburg, *Reform and Revolution*.

39 Vladimir Lenin, *What Is to Be Done?* marxists.org.

40 Vladimir Lenin, *The State and Revolution, Chapter 5: The Economic Basis of the Withering Away of the State*, marxists.org.

41 H. L. E. Howarth, *The Syndicalist*, November 1912.

42 IWW, *Proceedings of the First Annual Convention of the Industrial Workers of the World* (1905): 1.

43 Tom Mann, *The Industrial Syndicalist*, July 1910.

44 Ralph Darlington, *Radical Unionism, The Rise and Fall of Revolutionary Syndicalism* (2008): 57–69.

45 Roger Magraw, *A History of the French Working Class*, vol. 2 (1992).

46 F. F. Ridley, *Revolutionary Syndicalism in France* (1970): 176.

47 Ibid., 176.

48 A. Bar, "The CNT: The Glory and Tragedy of Spanish Anarcho-Syndicalism," in Marcel Van der Linden and Wayne Thorpe (eds.), *Revolutionary Syndicalism: An International Perspective* (1990): 123, 125–6.

49 Melvyn Dubofsky, "The Rise and Fall of American Syndicalism," in Marcel Van der Linden and Wayne Thorpe, *Revolutionary Syndicalism: An International Perspective* (1990): 214; Melvyn Dubofsky, *Industrialism and the American Worker* (1975): 36.

50 Darlington, *Radical Unionism*, 28–9.

51 Sasha Lilley, *Capital and Its Discontents: Conversations with Radical Thinkers in a Time of Tumult* (2011): 22.

52 Darlington, *Radical Unionism*, 80.

53 Emmet O'Conner, *Syndicalism in Ireland* (1988): 29–53.

54 Rosa Luxemburg, "What Does the Spartacus League Want?" in Gabriel Kuhn (ed.), *All Power to the Councils! A Documentary History of the German Revolution, 1918–9* (2012): 99.

55 The tensions between industrial versus political forms of disruption and the later historiographical divide between syndicalist versus communist histories of worker struggle have obscured the shared radicalization of workers in the immediate postwar years.

56 John T. Murphy, *Preparing for Power* (1972): 172.

57 Mark Traugott, "Barricades as Repertoire: Continuities and Discontinuities in the History of French Contention," *Social Science History* 17, no. 2 (1993): 309–23.

58 Carl Douglas, "Barricades and Boulevards: Material Transformations of Paris, 1795–1871," *Interstices* 8 (2006): 32.

59 Mark Traugott, *The Insurgent Barricade* (2010): 70–1.

60 Traugott, "Barricades as Repertoire," 315.

61 Douglas, "Barricades and Boulevards," 31.

62 Traugott, *The Insurgent Barricade*, 72.

63 Douglas, "Barricades and Boulevards," 37.

64 Fredrich Engels, Introduction to *Karl Marx, The Class Struggles in France, 1848–1850* (1934): 14.

65 Leon Trotsky, *1905* (2016): 332.

66 Douglas, "Barricades and Boulevards," 39.

67 Victor Hugo, *Les Misérables* (1982): 989–90.

68 Roger Price, *Documents on the French Revolution of 1848* (1986): 90.

69 Douglas, "Barricades and Boulevards," 38.

70 Mikhail Bakunin, "Confession to Tzar Nicholas I—1851," in Sam Dolgoff (ed.), *Bakunin on Anarchy: Selected Works of the Activist-Founder of World Anarchism* (1973): 69–70.

71 Traugott, *The Insurgent Barricade*, 212.

72 Ibid., 197.

73 Ibid., 205.

74 Ibid., 189.

75 Ibid., 189.

76 Avrahm Yarmolinsky, *Road to Revolution: A Century of Russian Radicalism* (1956): 114.

77 Ibid., 114.

78 Billington, *Fire in the Minds of Men*, 388.

79 Richard Jensen, "Daggers, Rifles and Dynamite: Anarchist Terrorism in Nineteenth Century Europe," *Terrorism and Political Violence* 16, no.1 (2004): 116.

80 Yarmolinsky, *Road to Revolution*, 117.

81 See Derek Offord, *The Russian Revolutionary Movement in the 1880s* (1986); Philip Pomper, *The Russian Revolutionary Intelligentsia* (1970).

82 Jensen, "Daggers, Rifles and Dynamite," 124.

83 Wendy McElroy, "The Schism Between Individualist and Communist Anarchism in the Nineteenth Century," *The Journal of Libertarian Studies* 15, no. 1 (2000).

84 Paul Avrich, *Anarchist Voices: An Oral History of Anarchism in America* (1996): 132.

85 Beverly Gage, *The Day Wall Street Exploded: A Story of America in its First Age of Terror* (2009): 44–5.

86 Stephen Naft, *The Social General Strike* (1905): 5. Ralph Chaplin, editor of the IWW publication, *Solidarity*, makes a similar distinction. See Ralph Chaplin, *The General Strike* (1933).

87 For more detailed histories of the general strike as both theory and practice, see: Phil H. Goodstein, *The Theory of the General Strike from the French Revolution to Poland* (1984); Robert Brécy, *La Grève Générale en France* (1969); A. G. Phillips, *The General Strike: The Politics of Industrial Conflict* (1976); Wilfred H. Crook, *Communism and the General Strike* (1960); Wilfred H. Crook, *The General Strike: A Study of Labor's Tragic Weapon in Theory and Practice* (1931); Jeremy Brecher, *Strike!* (2014). For histories of specific general strikes, see: Philip Sheldon Foner, *The Great Labor Uprising of 1877* (1977); David Burbank, *The Reign of the Rabble: The St. Louis General Strike of 1877* (1966); Gerald Dennis Surh, *1905 in St. Petersburg: Labor, Society, and Revolution* (1989); Vincent Knapp, "Popular Participation in European General Strikes before 1914," *Studies in History and Society*, no. 5 (1973): 16–33; Jeffrey Skelley, *The General Strike, 1926* (1976); Christopher Farman, *The General Strike, May 1926* (1972); Victoria Johnson, *How Many Machine Guns Does It Take to Cook One Meal?: The Seattle and San Francisco General Strikes* (2008); Irving Abella, *On Strike: Six Key Labour Struggles in Canada, 1919–1949* (1974).

88 Goodstein, *The Theory of the General Strike*, 13.

89 Jean Jaurès, *Studies in Socialism* (1906): 127.

90 There were, of course, notable exceptions. The Grand National Holiday, proposed by William Benbow and nearly implemented by the Chartist Convention in 1839, was almost realized by the 1842 general work stoppage in England. See Niles Carpenter, "William Benbow and the Origin of the General Strike," *Quarterly Journal of Economics*, no. 35 (1921): 491–99. W.E.B. Du Bois would later famously argue that the Southern slave's gradual work stoppage during the American Civil War constituted a general strike. W.E.B. Du Bois, *Black Reconstruction in America* (1997): 55–84.

91 The Bakuninist wing had advocated the idea of general strike at the Geneva Congress of the Alliance in 1873 and had flirted with its practice in Andalusia the same year. Engels's critique of it as a strategy for worker emancipation was to provide the basis for subsequent Marxist critiques over the next half century. Predictably, it asserted the primacy of political over industrial struggle. "Although it was universally admitted that [the mass strike] required a well-formed organization of the working class and plentiful funds. And there's the rub. On the one hand the governments, especially if encouraged by political abstention, will never allow the organization or the funds of the workers to reach such a level; on the other hand, political events and oppressive acts by the ruling classes will lead to the liberation of the workers long before the proletariat is able to set up such an ideal organization and this colossal reserve fund. But if it had them, there would be no need to use the roundabout way of a general strike to achieve its goal." Karl Marx and Fredrich Engels, "The Bakuninists at Work," in *Revolution in Spain* (1939).

92 Georges Sorel, *Reflections on Violence* (1999): 128, 132.

93 Ibid., 133.

94 William E. Trautmann, *One Big Union: An Outline of a Possible Industrial Organization of the Working Class, With Chart* (1911).

95 Victor Griffuelhes and Louis Neil, *Les Objectifs de Nos Luttes de Classe* (1908).

96 Ridely, *Revolutionary Syndicalism in France*: 146.

97 Naft, *The Social General Strike*, 7.

98 Justus Ebert, *The Trial of a New Society* (1913): 61.

99 Darlington, *Radical Unionism*, 41.

100 Ridely, *Revolutionary Syndicalism in France*, 150.

101 Georges Yvetot, *L'ABC Syndicaliste* (2015): 52.

102 Marshall, *Demanding the Impossible*, 271.

103 Naft, *The Social General Strike*, 9.

104 R. A. Leeson, *Strike: A Live History 1887/1971* (1973): 89.

105 William Lyon Mackenzie King, Industry and humanity a study in the principles underlying industrial reconstruction (1973), 494–5.

106 Eric Partridge, *Origins: A Short Etymological Dictionary of Modern English* (1977): 2843.

107 Elizabeth Gurley Flynn, *Sabotage: The Conscious Withdrawal of the Workers' Industrial Efficiency* (1915).

108 The quote is from Arturo Giovannitti, an Italian-American leader of the 1912 Lawrence Strike, in the introduction to the 1913 English translation of Pouget's *Sabotage*. Emile Pouget, *Sabotage* (1913): 6.

109 Ridely, *Revolutionary Syndicalism in France*, 121–3; Walker C. Smith, *Sabotage: Its History, Philosophy, and Function* (1913); Bill Watson, *Counter Planning on the Shop Floor* (1971): 17.

110 Smith, *Sabotage*.

111 Ridely, *Revolutionary Syndicalism in France*, 114.

112 Pouget, *Sabotage*, 16.

113 Arturo Giovannitti, in Pouget, *Sabotage, 6*.

114 Amédée Bousquet, "Il Faut Saboter!" *La Voix du Peuple*, May 21, 1905.

115 Watson, *Counter Planning on the Shop Floor*, 17.

116 Naft, *The Social General Strike*, 10.

117 Pouget, *Sabotage*, 34.

118 Charles M. Carlson, *The Clog in the Machine or Sabotage: A Harmful and Obsolete Weapon for the Workers* (1913): 18.

119 Rudolph Rocker, "The Methods of Anarcho-Syndicalism," in *Anarcho-Syndicalism* (1987): 69.

120 Darlington, *Radical Unionism*, 37.

121 This is essentially the main thesis of Timothy Mitchell's *Carbon Democracy*, which argues that the ability of workers to disrupt the global economy of coal was undermined by the transition to the oil economy. Timothy Mitchell, *Carbon Democracy: Political Power in the Age of Oil* (2011).

122 This consciousness was radically different from, though often operating in concert with, the worker-subject that emerged through collective bargaining, manifestations, or parliamentary politics.

Excursus II: The New Left

1 Mario Savio, "Sit-In Address on the Steps of Sproul Hall, 2 December 1964, The University of California at Berkeley," in A. Bloom and W. Breines (eds.), *Takin' It to the Streets: A Sixties Reader* (2011): 94.

2 Gerd-Rainer Horn, *The Spirit of '68: Rebellion in Western Europe and North America, 1956–1976* (2007): 85.

3 George N. Katsiaficas, *The Imagination of the New Left: A Global Analysis of 1968* (1987): 52.

4 United States President's Commission on Campus Unrest, *The Report of the President's Commission on Campus Unrest* (1970): 17.

5 Todd Gitlin, *The Sixties: Years of Hope, Days of Rage* (1989): 410.

6 Katsiaficas, *The Imagination of the New Left*, 123.

7 L. A. Kauffman, *Direct Action: Protest and the Reinvention of American Radicalism* (2017): 1–4.

8 Michael A. Schmidtke, "Cultural Revolution or Cultural Shock? Student Radicalism and 1968 in Germany," *South Central Review* 16, no. 4 (1999): 87.

9 Of note is the largely spontaneous nature of many of these tactics of social arrest. The building of the barricades in the Latin Quarter, the occupations of the Pentagon steps and the French factories were initiated on the spot without any prior planning and, in the case of the workers, against the orders of union and party leadership. See Ronald Fraser, *1968: A Student Generation in Revolt* (1988): 211; Breines, *Community and Organization in the New Left*, 33.

10 First utilized on a large scale in 1906 by 3,000 workers of the General Electric plant in Schenectady, New York, the original intent of "sit-in strike" was to deter scabs from resuming work. See Joel Seidman, *Sit-Down* (1937). Thirty years later, in 1936, over 150,000 French *métallos*, or metal workers, hunkered down in their factories, followed six months later by workers at the great General Motors auto plants in Flint and Cleveland. See Michael Torigian, "The Occupation of the Factories: Paris 1936, Flint 1937," *Comparative Studies in Society and History* 41, no. 2 (1999): 324–47. The resounding success of these sit-in strikes, leading to closed-shop agreements across America's mass production sector and the world's most progressive system of industrial relations in France, brought them international renown. Factory occupations had also been part of a more disruptive revolutionary history, particularly in Italy, where, in 1920, over half a million metal workers occupied their workplaces, formed factory councils and armed Red Guard units, barricaded the factories, and attempted to resume production under worker control.

11 In Nashville, police demanded that Blacks leave the store, then arrested eighty-one students for the kinetic offense of loitering. Within a few years, sit-ins spread to sixty-eight other cities of the segregated South, challenging the accepted practice of where Black bodies could be situated. See James Talley, "75 Students Arrested Here," *Tennessean*, February 28, 1960. All told, more than 50,000 individuals participated in one or more sit-ins in the American South, with more than 3,600 spending some time in jail. See Howard Zinn, *SNCC: The New Abolitionists* (2002): 16.

12 Kristin Ross, *May '68 and Its Afterlives* (2002): 66.

13 Alain Touraine, *The May Movement: Revolt and Reform* (1971): 268.

14 Jean-Paul Sartre, *Situations VIII, autour de 68* (1972): 194.

15 David Caute, *The Year of the Barricades: A Journey Through 1968* (1988): 151.

16 Ross, *May '68 and its Afterlives*, 74.

17 Luisa Passerini, *Autobiography of a Generation: Italy 1968* (1996): 111.

18 Robin Blackburn, "A Brief Guide to Bourgeois Ideology," in Alexander Cockburn and Robin Blackburn (eds.), *Student Power: Problems, Diagnosis, Action* (1969): 163–213.

19 Carl Schmitt, *Roman Catholicism and Political Form* (1996): 13.

20 See Horn, *The Spirit of '68*, 131–6; Martin Klimke, "1968 in Europe," in M. Klimke and J. Scharloth (eds.), *1968 in Europe: A History of Protest and Activism, 1956–1977* (2008): 1–9.

21 Theodor Adorno and Max Horkheimer, *Dialectic of Enlightenment* (1997): 1.

22 Tom Hayden, "Two, Three, Many Columbias," in Alexander Bloom, Wini Breines (ed.), *"Takin' It to the Streets": A Sixties Reader* (1995), 345.

23 Eldridge Cleaver, "Introduction," in Jerry Rubin, *Do It! Scenarios of a Revolution* (1970): 8.

24 Herbert Marcuse, *One-Dimensional Man: Studies in the Ideology of Advanced Industrial Society* (1964).

25 Douglas Kellner, "Marcuse and the Quest for Radical Subjectivity," in *Dogma: Revue de Philosophie et de Sciences Humaines* (2000).

26 Richard Petersen and John Bilorusky, *May 1970: The Campus Aftermath of Cambodia and Kent State* (1971): 141.

27 Angelo Quattrocchi and Tom Nairn, *The Beginning of the End: France, May 1968* (1998): 45.

28 Rubin, *Do It! Scenarios of a Revolution* (1970): 105.

29 Stokely Carmichael, *Ready for Revolution: The Life and Struggles of Stokely Carmichael* (2003).

30 Tom Fawthrop, "Education or Examination?" in Alexander Cockburn and Robin Blackburn (eds.), *Student Power: Problems, Diagnosis, Action* (1969): 102.

31 Blackburn, "A Brief Guide to Bourgeois Ideology," 164.

32 Touraine, *The May Movement*, 259.

33 Horn, *The Spirit of '68*, 199. Early efforts for Free Universities in the United States drew inspiration from the Freedom Schools opened as part of the Civil Rights Struggle in the American South. As part of the Freedom Summer of 1964, forty-one Freedom Schools, enrolling 2,500 students, engaged in free-flowing discussion on the Citizenship Curriculum, based around the following question for the Black community: What does the majority culture have that we want? What does the majority culture have that we don't want? What do we have that we want to keep? See Daniel Perlstein, "Teaching Freedom: SNCC and the Creation of Mississippi Freedom Schools," *History of Education Quarterly* (1990): 297–324.

34 Jan Kurz and Marisa Tolomelli, "Italy," in M. Klimke and J. Scharloth (eds.), *1968 in Europe: A History of Protest and Activism, 1956–1977* (2008): 83–96.

35 Julien Besançon, *Les Murs ont la Parole* (1968).

36 Black Panther Party, *Ten-Point Program of the Black Panther Party*, marxists.org.

37 Gruppe Spur, "January Manifesto," in Jürgen Miermeister and Jochen Staadt (eds.), *Provocations: The Student and Youth Revolts in their Leaflets 1965–1971* (1980): 13.

38 Cleaver, "Introduction," 9.

39 Herbert Marcuse, *An Essay on Liberation* (1969): 11.

40 Besançon, *Les Murs ont la Parole*, 43.

41 Raoul Vaneigem, *The Revolution of Everyday Life* (2003): 26.

42 Richard Kempton, *The Provos: Amsterdam's Anarchist Revolt* (2007). See also Katsiaficas, *The Imagination of the New Left*, 123.

43 Urban Research Corporation, *On Strike, Shut It Down: A Report on the First National Student Strike in US History* (1970): 37.

44 *The Village Voice* XIII, no. 24 (March 18, 1968).

45 Schmidtke, "Cultural Revolution or Cultural Shock?", 83. See also Marcuse, *One Dimensional Man*, 15. For guerrilla theatre as a tactic of social arrest, see John Weisman, *Guerrilla Theater: Scenarios for Revolution* (1973).

46 Guy Debord, "All the King's Men," *Internationale Situationniste*, no. 8 (1963): l.

47 Faces of Recuperation, *Situationist International*, no. 1 (June 1969).

48 Marcuse, *An Essay in Liberation*, 8.

49 Stokely Carmichael, *Black Power: The Politics of Liberation* (1992): 38.

50 Michel de Certeau, *The Capture of Speech and Other Political Writings* (1997): 11.

51 Marcuse, *An Essay on Liberation*, 24.

52 See Maurice Isserman, *If I Had a Hammer: The Death of the Old Left and the Birth of the New Left* (1987), 77–125, 171–221; Gregor Kritidis, *Linkssozialistische Opposition in der Ära Adenauer* (2008).

53 Rubin, *Do It! Scenarios of a Revolution*, 56.

4. Extraction

1 Kristin Ross, *May '68 and Its Afterlives* (2002): 69.

2 Alain Touraine, *The May Movement: Revolt and Reform* (1971): 60.

3 Johan Kugelberg et al. (eds.), *Beauty is in the Street: A Visual Record of the May '68 Paris Uprising* (2011).

4 During this period, Black Power activists drew attention to the politics of naming, explicitly associating the term *black* with autonomy and *negro* with heteronomy. As in other instances throughout the book, and in an effort to bring out their voices, I have retained the terminology used by the historical subjects themselves. My use of the terms *woman* and *women* in the third section follows this same logic.

5 Akinyele Umoja et al., *Black Power Encyclopedia: From Black Is Beautiful to Urban Uprisings* (2018): 113.

6 The ideas underlying Black Power had been floated by Malcolm X and others a few years prior. The concept of the "second ghetto" as a "power base" for African American organizing is seen by some as a precursor to Black Power. Additionally, the National Negro Labor Council and the Organization for Afro-American Unity articulated such ideas, though without the guns, rhetoric, and internationalism of the 1970s Black Power movements. Robert Self, "Negro Leadership and Negro Money," in Jeanne Theoharis and Komozi Woodard (eds.), *Freedom North: Black Freedom Struggles Outside the South, 1940–1980* (2003): 115.

7 The history of Black radicalism in the CPUSA offers a quite different story. See Michael C. Dawson, *Blacks In and Out of the Left* (2013).

8 Joshua Bloom and Waldo Martin, *Black against Empire: The History and Politics of the Black Panther Party* (2013): 85.

9 See Angela Davis, *Are Prisons Obsolete?* (2003); Alex Lichtenstein, *Twice the Work of Free Labor: The Political Economy of Convict Labor in the New South* (1996); Mary Ellen Curtin, *Black Prisoners and Their World, Alabama, 1865–1900* (2000).

10 Singh, *Black Is a Country*.

11 Ira Katznelson, *When Affirmative Action Was White: An Untold History of Racial Inequality in Twentieth-Century America* (2005).

12 Interestingly, white America was, despite the civil rights movement, blissfully igno-
   rant of this reality. The 1968 Kerner Commission reported that 75 percent of whites
   felt that Negroes were at least partially to blame for their second-class status. In
   many cases, they believed the opposite. A 1969 Gallup Poll reported how a plurality
   of whites felt that Blacks had a greater chance of receiving a better education, better
   jobs, better housing, and preferential government assistance than whites. Alan
   Altshuler, *Community Control: The Black Demand for Participation in Large
   American Cities* (1970): 17–18.

13 Carmichael and Hamilton, *Black Power*, 47.

14 Manning Marable, *Race, Reform, and Rebellion: The Second Reconstruction in Black
   America, 1945–1990* (1991): 107.

15 W. E. B. Du Bois, *The Souls of Black Folk* (1969): 45.

16 Singh, *Black Is a Country*, 185.

17 Carmichael and Hamilton, *Black Power*, 34–5.

18 Harold Cruse, "Revolutionary Nationalism and the Afro-American," in *Studies on
   the Left* 2, no. 3 (1962): 13.

19 S. E. Anderson, "Revolutionary Black Nationalism and the Pan-African Idea." in
   Floyd Barbour (ed.), *The Black Seventies* (1970): 113. An activist within the Student
   Nonviolent Committee (SNCC), S. E. Anderson was one of the founding members
   of the Black Panther Party.

20 Stokely Carmichael and Michael Thelwell, *Ready for Revolution: The Life and
   Struggles of Stokely Carmichael* (2005): 527.

21 Robert S. Browne, "The Case for Black Separatism," *Cross Currents* 18, no. 4 (1968):
   471–82.

22 James Boggs, "The Revolutionary Struggle for Black Power," in Barbour, *The Black
   Seventies*, 43.

23 To be sure, Black historiography has a long history that predates the Black Power
   struggles of the '60s and '70s. It's important to add, though, that the revisiting and
   contributions to this historiography at a moment of radical self-definition lent
   these histories an almost existential quality.

24 Robin Kelley, "Stormy Weather: Reconstructing Black (Inter)Nationalism in the
   Cold War Era," in Robin Kelley and Eddie Glaude (eds.), *Is It Nation Time?:
   Contemporary Essays on Black Power and Black Nationalism* (2002): 78–80.

25 C.L.R. James and Scott McLemee, *C. L. R. James on the "Negro Question"* (1997):
   63–89.

26 Boggs, "The Revolutionary Struggle for Black Power," 39.

27 Orlando Patterson, "Rethinking Black History," in *Harvard Educational Review*,
   no. 4 (1971): 297–8.

28 A name he once again changed to El-Hajj Malik El-Shabazz following his pilgrim-
   age to Mecca.

29 Stokely Carmichael, "Black Power," speech given at the University of California,
   Berkeley, October 29, 1966, audio recording available at americanradioworks.
   publicradio.org.

30 James Wilson, *Negro Politics: The Search for Leadership* (1965): 133.

31 Marable, *Race, Reform and Rebellion*, 111.

32 Cruse, "Revolutionary Nationalism and the Afro-American," 16.

33 Albert B. Cleage, *The Black Messiah* (1968).

34 Browne, "The Case for Black Separatism," 472.

35 Carmichael and Hamilton, *Black Power*, xi, 41.

36 Singh, *Black Is a Country,* 44.

37 Carmichael and Hamilton, *Black Power,* vii.

38 Kelley, "Stormy Weather," 67–90.

39 Alys Eve Weinbaum, "Reproducing Racial Globality: W.E.B. Du Bois and the Sexual Politics of Black Internationalism," *Social Text* 19, no. 2 (2001): 19.

40 Ula Taylor, "Elijah Muhammad's Nation of Islam: Separatism, Regendering, and a Secular Approach to Black Power after Malcolm X (1965–1975)" in *Freedom North*, 179. As Robert Reid-Pharr has argued, "the Nation of Islam produced a historical self-definition of black-Americans that was 'imagined as larger than blackness,' even though 'very few others were allowed to share this identity.'" (Including, at times, Black Africans themselves.) Robert Reid-Pharr, "Speaking Through Antisemitism," *Social Text* 14, no. 2 (1996): 140.

41 John Oliver Killens, *Black Man's Burden* (1965): 176.

42 Antony Hamilton, "Malcolm X: The Road to Revolution," *Socialist Review*, no: 299 (2015).

43 RAM, *Black America* (1965).

44 Ibid., 19.

45 Robin Kelley and Betsy Esch, "Black Like Mao: Red China and Black Revolution," in Fred Ho, Bill V. Mullen (eds.), *Afro Asia: Revolutionary Political and Cultural Connections Between African Americans and Asian Americans* (2002): 97–154.

46 Maxwell Stanford, "The Revolutionary Action Movement: A Case Study of an Urban Revolutionary Movement in Western Capitalist Society," master's thesis, Atlanta University (1986): 79.

47 Stanford estimates that the Black Guards in the various branches of RAM numbered as follows: 350–500 in Philadelphia, 800–1,000 in Cleveland, 200 in Chicago, 200 in Detroit, and 100 in New York City. At its height, total RAM membership was estimated at 3,000, with 2,000 supporters. Stanford, "The Revolutionary Action Movement," 130.

48 RAM was by no means alone in advocating and organizing Black liberation along these models. However, RAM, as an early Black Power organization, influenced many subsequent branches of the Black Power struggle, having put forward all three models of Black autonomous organization in embryonic form.

49 The Republic of New Africa was proclaimed on March 31, 1968, at a Black Government Conference held in Detroit, Michigan. The attendees produced a Declaration of Independence (signed by 100 conferees out of approximately 500), a constitution, and the framework for a provisional government.

50 Fanon, *The Wretched of the Earth*, 130.

51 David Hilliard and Lewis Cole, *This Side of Glory: The Autobiography of David Hilliard and the Story of the Black Panther Party* (1993): 122.

52 Bristol Radical History Group, *Interview with General Baker*, December 2011, brh. org.uk.

53 Behind their seeming spontaneity was a surgical calculation to disrupt the choke points of automobile production in the United States. ELRUM (Eldon Avenue Revolutionary Union Movement) was a case in point. As Dan Georgakas, author of *Detroit, I Do Mind Dying,* explained: "Why Eldon? Because that was the factory that made all the axles for all the cars. So if you could win control at Eldon Avenue Gear and Axle, you would have Chrysler hostage." *Working Class History*, Interview

with Dan Georgakas, Episode 12: The League of Revolutionary Black Workers, 2018. Workingclasshistory.com.

54 Boggs, "The Revolutionary Struggle for Black Power," in Barbour, *The Black Seventies*, 41.

55 Marable, *Race, Reform and Rebellion*, 110. For earlier RAM analysis of the white working class, see RAM, *World Black Revolution* (1966): 5, Viewpointmag.com.

56 George Katsiaficas, *The Subversion of Politics: European Autonomous Social Movements and the Decolonization of Everyday Life* (2006): 25.

57 Potere Operaio, "Italy, 1973: Workers' Struggles in the Capitalist Crisis," *Radical America* 7, no. 2 (1973).

58 Ibid., 15–32.

59 The Johnson–Forest Tendency was founded by C.L.R. James and Raya Dunayevskaya, and later joined by Grace Lee Boggs. They studied working-class life and struggles within the Detroit auto industry, publishing pamphlets such as "The American Worker" (1947), "Punching Out" (1952), and "Union Committeemen and Wildcat Strikes" (1955). Through their publishing arms, *Correspondence* and *News and Letters*, the Tendency advocated both for workers' autonomy and self-organization, theorized on the critical role of the Black worker in the socialist revolution. They were among the first to popularize the 1956 Hungarian workers' struggles in the United States. See Martin Glaberman (ed.), *Marxism for our Times: C.L.R. James on Revolutionary Organization* (1999). In 1949 in Paris, two former Trotskyites, Cornelius Castoriadis and Claude Lefort, founded *Socialisme ou Barbarie*, the name both of a group and of a journal that argued for the importance of the workers' struggle at the point of production, unhindered by official unions or party organizations. For an analysis of the group, see Stephen Hastings-King, *Looking for the Proletariat: Socialisme ou Barbarie and the Problem of Worker Writing* (2014); Philippe Gottraux, *Socialisme ou Barbarie, Un Engagement Politique et Intellectuel dans la France de l'Après Guerre* (1997).

60 Between 1951 and 1970, the number of people working the land fell from 7,200,000 to 3,800,000.

61 Asad Haider and Salar Mohandesi, "Workers' Inquiry: A Genealogy," *Viewpoint Magazine*, issue 3 (2013).

62 Gigi Roggero and Davide Gallo Lassere, " 'A Science of Destruction': An Interview with Gigi Roggero on the Actuality of Operaismo," *Viewpoint Magazine*, April 30, 2020.

63 Nicola Pizzolato, "Workers and Revolutionaries at the Twilight of Fordism: The Breakdown of Industrial Relations in the Automobile Plants of Detroit and Turin, 1967–1973," *Labor History* 45, no. 4 (2004): 419–43.

64 Potere Operaio, "Italy 1969–70: A Wave of Struggles," *Potere Operaio*, no. 27 (1970).

65 Autonomous Assembly of Alfa Romeo, "Against the Boss," translated by Bruno and Judy Ramirez, *Radical America* 7, no. 2 (1973).

66 Katsiaficas, *The Subversion of Politics*, 19.

67 For an early English account of factory disruption, see S. G. Tarrow, *Democracy and Disorder: Protest and Politics in Italy, 1965–1975* (1989).

68 Robert Lumley, *States of Emergency: Cultures of Revolt in Italy from 1968 to 1978* (1990): 303.

69 Ilaria Favretto, "Rough Music and Factory Protest in Post-1945 Italy," *Past and Present* 228, no. 1 (2015): 207–47.

70 Ibid., 210.

71 Lumley, *States of Emergency*, 305.

72 Tronti, *Workers and Capital* (2019), as cited in Jason E. Smith, "Form-of-Life: From Politics to Aesthetics (and Back)," *Nordic Journal of Aesthetics*, no. 44–5 (2012–2013): 50–67.

73 "The Strategy of the Refusal" was written in 1965 as #12 of the "Initial Theses," in *Workers and Capital*. See Tronti, *Workers and Capital*, 234–52.

74 Roggero and Lassere, "A Science of Destruction."

75 Antonio Negri, "The Workers Party Against Work," in Antonio Negri and Arianna Bove, *Books for Burning: Between Civil War and Democracy in 1970s Italy* (2005).

76 Karl Marx, *Capital: A Critique of Political Economy,* chapter 15, section 5 (1977): 290.

77 Mario Tronti, "Lenin in England," *Classe Operaia*, no.1, January 1964.

78 Roggero and Lassere, "A Science of Destruction."

79 Adriano Sofri, "Organizing for Workers' Power," *Radical America* 7, no. 2 (1973).

80 Tronti, *Workers and Capital*, 26.

81 Dan Georgakas, Marvin Surkin, and Manning Marable, *Detroit, I Do Mind Dying: A Study in Urban Revolution* (2012): 189.

82 Marco Revelli, "Defeat at Fiat," *Capital & Class* 6, no: 1 (1982): 95–109.

83 Anne Koedt, "Women and the Radical Movement," in Barbara A. Crow (ed.), *Radical Feminism: A Documentary Reader* (2000): 26.

84 Ruth Rosen, *The World Split Open: How the Modern Women's Movement Changed America* (2000): 109.

85 Robin Morgan (ed.), *Sisterhood Is Powerful: An Anthology of Writings from the Women's Liberation Movement* (1970).

86 Rosen, *The World Split Open*, 118.

87 Alice Echols, *Daring to Be Bad: Radical Feminism in America, 1967–1975* (1989): 107.

88 Rosen, *The World Split Open,* 117.

89 Barbara Epstein, *Free Speech Movement Oral History Project*, interviews conducted by Lisa Rubens (1999): 10.

90 Sara Davidson, "An 'Oppressed Majority' Demands Its Rights," *Life Magazine*, December 12, 1969, 66.

91 Rosen, *The World Split Open,* 102.

92 Maud Anne Bracke, *Women and the Reinvention of the Political: Feminism in Italy, 1968–1983* (2014): 79.

93 Emerging in the United States in the late 1960s, the struggle for women's liberation became, by the early 1970s, a transnational phenomenon involving the translation and circulation of texts, international conferences, and collaborative networks across the Atlantic. My focus on Italy and the United States stems from the desire to bypass the dominant historiographical binary between empirical Anglo-American and theoretical French feminisms and to underscore how the becoming-subject of women was informed by national context, specifically the influence of Black Power and Italian workerism that this chapter has already explored. These traditions lent a particular separatist and autonomous force to Italian and American radical feminist struggle, informing practices aimed not at gender equality but towards the formation of "unexpected subjects"—political beings that could not be

counted or assimilated by the existing order. A short note on terminology. The terms *equality* and *separation* were hotly debated and often confusing concepts within Italian and American radical feminist struggles. I will be using these terms in a general way, with *equality* referring to feminist projects that aimed at the integration of women into the existing public sphere on equal terms (i.e., the eradication of male privilege and access) and to *separation* as a strategy for autonomous organizing in women-only groups. This general usage is different than the context-specific feminist debates over the natural or essential *equality/difference* between men and women as well as debates over *separatism* within the feminist struggle.

94 Betty Friedan, *The Feminine Mystique* (1963): 33. To be sure, the middle-class white American woman Friedan referred to, one trapped inside her nuclear home with fewer and fewer encounters outside of it, was a specific if extreme case of this atomization.

95 Bracke, *Women and the Reinvention of the Political*, 20.

96 Joan Cassell, *A Group Called Women: Sisterhood and Symbolism in the Feminist Movement* (1977): 79, 161.

97 Bracke, *Women and the Reinvention of the Political*, 20.

98 Ibid., 67.

99 Susi Kaplow, "Getting Angry," in Anne Koedt, Ellen Levine, and Anita Rapone (eds.), *Radical Feminism* (1973): 40.

100 Bracke, *Women and the Reinvention of the Political*, 67.

101 Ibid., 67.

102 Bracke, *Women and the Reinvention of the Political*, 102.

103 Eva Rus, "From New York Radical Feminists to Rivolta Femminile: Italian Feminists Rethink the Practice of Consciousness Raising, 1970–1974," *Irish Feminist Review* 1 (2005): 190.

104 Davidson, "An 'Oppressed Majority' Demands Its Rights," 71.

105 Voichita Nachescu, "Radical Feminism and the Nation: History and Space in the Political Imagination of Second-Wave Feminism," *Journal for the Study of Radicalism*, no. 3 (2009): 35.

106 Marilyn Webb, "We Are Victims," *Voice of the Women's Liberation Movement* (February 1969): 6.

107 Demau Collective, "Manifesto Demau," in Bono and Kemp (eds.), *Italian Feminist Thought: A Reader* (1991): 35.

108 New York Radical Feminists, "Politics of the Ego," *Notes from the Second Year* (1970): 126.

109 Paola Bono and Sandra Kemp, "Introduction: Coming from the South," in *Italian Feminist Thought*, 15.

110 Carla Lonzi, "Let's Spit on Hegel," in Bono and Kemp (eds.), *Italian Feminist Thought: A Reader* (1991): 41.

111 Dana Densmore, "On Female Enslavement . . . and Men's Stake in it," *No More Fun and Games, a Journal of Female Liberation*, no. 1 (1969).

112 Roxanne Dunbar, "What Is to Be Done?" in *No More Fun and Games*. Though Dunbar would a few months later change course and promote these same slavish traits as "the female principle" that needed to replace the competitive aggressive "male principle."

113 Valerie Solanas, *The SCUM Manifesto* (2013).

114 Lonzi, "Let's Spit on Hegel," 54.

115 Ibid., 41.

116 Demau Collective, 35.

117 Revolta Femminile, "Manifesto of Revolta Femminile," in Bono and Kemp (eds.), *Italian Feminist Thought: A Reader* (1991): 37.

118 Lisa Leghorn, "Feminism Undermines," *No More Fun and Games, a Journal of Female Liberation,* no. 4 (1970): 61.

119 Betsy Warrior, "Man As an Obsolete Life-Form," *No More Fun and Games: A Journal of Female Liberation,* no. 2 (1969).

120 Movimento Femminista Romano, "Towards a Project," in Bono and Kemp (eds.), *Italian Feminist Thought: A Reader* (1991): 74.

121 Ti-Grace Atkinson, "Radical Feminism," in Barbara Crow (ed.), *Radical Feminism: A Documentary Reader* (2000): 82.

122 Rita Mae Brown, "The Shape of Things to Come," in Nancy Myron and Charlotte Bunch (eds.), *Lesbianism and the Women's Movement* (1975): 74.

123 Rosen, *The World Split Open,* 120.

124 Beverly Jones and Judith Brown, "Toward a Female Liberation Movement," in Barbara A. Crow (ed.), *Radical Feminism: A Documentary Reader* (2000): 45.

125 Berkeley Women's Liberation Group, "Towards a New Culture," *It Ain't Me Babe* 1, issue 5 (1970): 2.

126 Katsiaficas, *The Subversion of Politics,* 35.

127 The Feminists, "A Political Organization to Eliminate Sex Roles," in New York Radical Women (eds.), *Notes from the Second Year* (1970): 117.

128 Radicalesbians, "The Woman-Identified Woman," Duke Library Digital Collections.

129 Charlotte Bunch, "Lesbians in Revolt," in Barbara A. Crow (ed.), *Radical Feminism: A Documentary Reader* (2000): 332–6.

130 The radical feminists of the 1970s were not first to challenge these boundaries. As Dolores Hayden remarked, between 1880 and the Great Depression, US feminists "challenged two characteristics of industrial capitalism: the physical separation of the household space from public space, and the separation of the domestic economy from the political economy." Dolores Hayden, *The Grand Domestic Revolution: A History of Feminist Designs for American Homes, Neighborhoods, and Cities* (1985): 3.

131 Lonzi, "Let's Spit on Hegel," 57.

132 Jones and Brown, "Toward a Female Liberation Movement," in Barbara A. Crow (ed.), *Radical Feminism: A Documentary Reader* (2000): 43.

133 Movimento Femminista Romano, "Towards a Project," 72.

134 Lonzi, "Let's Spit on Hegel," 41, 58–9.

135 The disruptive subjects traced in this chapter were neither the first and certainly not the only political subjects to manifest through this dual gesture of extraction and self-definition. The most prominent antecedent was that of European Jewry, who since the late eighteenth century had been torn between the two paths of assimilation and separatism. In fact, there were striking parallels between them and the Black struggle of the 1950s and '60s in the United States: a diasporic culture debating the merits of integration into an existing order, a universalist and revolutionary socialism, and an ethnonational Zionism that mimicked the settler colonial tendencies of their oppressors. The charged environment of these debates, the existential stakes they evoked and involved, led to some of the most provocative and

beautiful experiments in human thought, art, and politics before they were dramatically cut short by the most murderous regime in human history. The workerist,
Black Power, and women's liberation struggles were in turn followed by other
disruptive subjects, including gay liberation, Indigenous struggle, and the radical
environmentalism of groups such as Earth First!, the Animal and Earth Liberation
Fronts, and Water Protectors, whose actions, on behalf of the wild, posit the nonhuman as a political subject—disrupting both the ascription of nature as natural
resource and our conception of society as human.

136 Christian Marazzi, "The Return of Politics," in Hedi El Kholti et al. (eds.),
  Autonomia: Post-Political Politics (2007): 18.

Coda: The Southern Wind

1 The same year as the Zapatista uprising, its German variant, *Es Gibt Keine Alternative,* served as the slogan for the Christian Democratic Union.
2 Subcomandante Marcos and the EZLN, *Shadows of Tender Fury* (1995): 32–3.
3 Richard Sinkin, *The Mexican Reform, 1855–1876: A Study in Liberal Nation-Building* (1979).
4 The downside was the creation of a patron–client relationship with the PRI-controlled state, making the granting of *ejidos* dependent on state favor and clientelism, one that benefited a Chiapan oligarchy with connections to federal government. See James J. Kelly, "Article 27 and Mexican Land Reform: The Legacy of Zapata's Dream," *Columbia Human Rights Law Review 25*, no. 2 (1994): 541.
5 Ibid., 541.
6 Gilly, *The Mexican Revolution*, 278.
7 Rosalva Castillo, "Between Hope and Adversity: The Struggle of Organized Women in Chiapas Since the Zapatista Uprising," *Journal of Latin American Anthropology* 3 (1997): 104.
8 Ibid., 102–20.
9 As soldiers within the EZLN, women receive not only military training, but also education in Spanish, international law, and the politics and history of social struggle. They are offered opportunities not available to many civilian women in the Chiapas, including access to contraception, choice of sexual partners, and freedom from domestic violence. Yet, as Lynn Stephen points out, this movement toward gender equality has been more easily accomplished among the Zapatista activists themselves than among the communities in which they operate. "While significant experimentation in gender roles may be taking place among groups of men and women who live completely separated from their communities while training as full-time insurgents in special camps, women in Zapatista base communities often continue to struggle for recognition and participation in decision-making." Lynn Stephen, *Zapata Lives! Histories and Cultural Politics in Southern Mexico* (2002).
10 For a good journalistic account of the Zapatista struggle, see Gloria Ramirez, *The Fire and the Word: A History of the Zapatista Movement* (2008).
11 John Holloway, "Dignity in Revolt," in John Halloway (ed.), *Zapatista: Reinventing Revolution in Mexico* (1998): 168.

12 Subcomandante Marcos, "To Open a Crack in History," in Juana Ponce de Leon (ed.), *Our Word Is Our Weapon* (2001): 212.

13 EZLN, *Shadows of Tender Fury*, 52.

14 EZLN, *Third Declaration of the Lacandon Jungle* (1994), schoolforchiapas.org.

15 EZLN, *Fourth Declaration of the Lacandon Jungle* (1995), schoolforchiapas.org.

16 Interview with Marcos in Tom Mertes, Walden Bello (eds.), *A Movement of Movements: Is Another World Really Possible?* (2004): 4.

17 EZLN, *Fourth Declaration of the Lacandon Jungle.*

18 "Testimonies of the First Day," in Tom Hayden (ed.), *The Zapatista Reader* (2002): 212.

19 Subcomandante Marcos, "The Slaves of Money—and Our Rebellion," *The Guardian,* September 11, 2003.

20 Ibid.

21 EZLN, *Second Declaration of the Lacandon Jungle* (1994), schoolforchiapas.org.

22 EZLN, *First Declaration of La Realidad for Humanity and against Neoliberalism* (1996), schoolforchiapas.org.

23 Peter Brown, *Zapatistas Launch International of Hope* (1996), nadir.org.

24 Elias Canetti, *Crowds and Power* (1984): 378.

25 Subcomandante Marcos, Professionals of Hope: The Selected Writings of Subcomandante Marcos (2017).

Conclusion: Disrupt or Be Disrupted

1 CNBC has been compiling a Top-50 Disruptors list since 2012.

2 After failing to convict a single person of any crime, federal prosecutors dropped all charges on the remaining J20 accused. Sam Adler-Bell, "With Last Charges Against J20 Protesters Dropped, Defendants Seek Accountability for Prosecutors," *The Intercept,* July 13, 2018.

3 Slavoj Žižek, Interview, Channel 4 News (UK), November 3, 2016.

4 Daniel Chaitin, "Rudy Giuliani Says His Mission Is 'To Disrupt the World,'" *Washington Examiner,* October 5, 2019.

5 Rowena Mason, "Liz Truss Promises 'Growth, Growth and Growth' in Protest-Hit Speech," *Guardian*, October 5, 2022.

6 Steven Erlanger, "Merkel and Macron Publicly Clash Over NATO," *New York Times*, November 23, 2019.

7 While Marx had noted the rise of financial speculation and its effects on the economy in volume III of *Capital*, he still expressed an optimistic faith that financial capital would become subordinate to industrial capital and that the rationality of the system would overcome these growing pains. By the early twentieth century, critics were taking a markedly different view. The socialist Rudolf Hilferding coined the term "finance capitalism" in 1910, and Veblen himself commented on the distortions of pecuniary relations on the economy. See Michael Hudson, *Financial Capitalism v. Industrial Capitalism*, 1998.

8 Veblen has a very good summary of the history of capitalism from the economy of movement to a fixation on restricting productive capacity by late nineteenth century. Thorstein Veblen, *The Engineers and the Price System* (2001): 21–33.

9 Timothy Mitchell, *Carbon Democracy* (2011): 8, 154. Mitchell ascribes the transition from coal to oil, as well as the transportation and logistics revolutions of the 1970s as part of capital's efforts to remove global bottlenecks that could be leveraged by labor through disruptive strike action (specifically the historical power held by western coal miners and longshoreman). Moreover, it allowed the long-term outsourcing of industrial production to countries with less unionized workforces.

10 For a brilliant analysis of Veblen, see Jeff Shantz, "Reflections on Sabotage, Theirs and Ours," libcom.org.

11 Mitchell, *Carbon Democracy*; Naomi Klein, *The Shock Doctrine: The Rise of Disaster Capitalism* (2007).

12 Veblen, *The Engineers and the Price System*, 21.

13 See Mitchell, *Carbon Democracy*, chapter 2.

14 Not only does it have no need for these myths, capital is openly disavowing them in order to flex its disruptive muscle. Kevin Young, Michael Schwartz, Tarun Banerjee, "When Capitalists Go on Strike," *Jacobin Magazine,* March 2, 1917.

15 As with almost all other business theories I have come across, disruptive innovation is not based on original analysis but rather copied, without much adaptation, from its critics. The term basically describes a variant of Joseph Schumpeter's concept of *creative destruction* first developed in his 1942 work, *Capitalism, Socialism and Democracy*. Schumpeter, through a close reading of Marx, defined creative destruction as "the process of industrial mutation that continuously revolutionizes the economic structure from within, incessantly destroying the old one, incessantly creating a new one." Joseph A. Schumpeter, *Capitalism, Socialism and Democracy* (1942): 82–3.

16 Jill Lepore, "The Disruption Machine: What the Gospel of Innovation Gets Wrong," *New Yorker*, June 16, 2014.

17 This too is not a new logic of capital, but the intensification of a centuries-long process. As Marx noted in the Manifesto, "[The Bourgeoisie] has pitilessly torn asunder the motley feudal ties that bound man to his 'natural superiors,' and has left remaining no other nexus between man and man than naked self-interest, than callous 'cash payment.' It has drowned the most heavenly ecstasies of religious fervor, of chivalrous enthusiasm, of philistine sentimentalism, in the icy water of egotistical calculation. It has resolved personal worth into exchange value . . . stripped of its halo every occupation hitherto honored and looked up to with reverent awe." Marx, *The Communist Manifesto* (1996): 16.

18 Josh Linkler, *The Road to Reinvention: How to Drive Disruption and Accelerate Transformation* (2014)

19 Larry Downes and Paul Nunes, "Big Bang Disruption," *Harvard Business Review*, March 2013, 44–56.

20 Lepore, "The Disruption Machine."

21 The Invisible Committee, *The Coming Insurrection* (2009), 17.

22 Étienne Balibar, "The Basic Concepts of Historical Materialism," in Louis Althusser and Étienne Balibar (eds.), *Reading Capital*, trans. Ben Brewster (1970): 291.

23 Georg Lukács, *History and Class Consciousness* (1971): 181.

24 Frederic Jameson, *Brecht and Method* (1998): 4.

25 Jürgen Habermas, "The Post National Constellation and the Future of Democracy," in *The Postnational Constellation: Political Essays* (2001): 67.

26 Julia Shipley, "You Strike a Match," *Rolling Stone*, May 26, 2021.

27 See "Alleen Brown, Ohio and Iowa are The Latest of Eight States to Consider Anti-Protest Bills Aimed at Pipeline Opponents," *The Intercept*, February 2, 2018; Alleen Brown, "Dakota Access Pipeline Activists Face 110 Years in Prison," *The Intercept*, October 4, 2019.

28 Luke McGee, "With UK Police Under Fire, Boris Johnson Pushes New Bill That Could End Peaceful Protests," *CNN.com*, March 16, 2021.

29 Shaun Boyd, "Child's Lemonade Stand Shut Down for Lack Of Permit," *CBS Local Denver*, May 29, 2018.

30 See Christopher Chitty, *Sexual Hegemony: Statecraft, Sodomy, and Capital in the Rise of the World System* (2020); Cheryl Harris, "Whiteness as Property," *Harvard Law Review* 106, no. 8 (1993): 1707–91.

31 Though, if this book has shown anything, it is the profound creativity of disruption, its ability to adapt and mutate to new terrains and circumstances.

32 The Invisible Committee, *Letter to Our Friends* (2015): 32.

33 Joshua Clover, *Riot. Strike. Riot: The New Era of Uprisings* (2016).

34 Charmaine Chua, *Logistics, Capitalist Circulation, Chokepoints*, September 9, 2014, thedisorderofthings.com.

35 For a global survey of logistics workers disrupting such nodes, see the excellent edited volume: Jake Alimahomed-Wilson and Immanuel Ness (eds.), *Choke Points: Logistics Workers Disrupting the Global Supply Chain* (2018).

36 Degenerate Communism, "Choke Points: Mapping an Anti-Capitalist Counter-Logistics in California," *Libcom.org*, July 21, 2014.

37 Empire Logistics, *Supply Chain Infrastructure*, www.empirelogistics.org.

38 Degenerate Communism, "Choke Points."

39 Clover, *Riot. Strike. Riot*, 151.

40 Cam Scott, "Below the Barricades: On Infrastructure, Self-Determination, and Defense," *Viewpoint Magazine*, October 11, 2021.

41 Douglas Rushkoff, "Survival of the Richest: The Wealthy Are Plotting to Leave Us Behind," *CNBC*, July 11, 2018.

42 There are, of course, exceptions, and ugly ones at that. The Crescent City Connection Bridge, where mostly white officers fired shots to prevent Black residents from evacuating to safety during Hurricane Katrina, comes to mind.

43 "Vote of The People's Assembly of Syntagma Square," June 1, 2011, blog.p2pfoundation.net.

44 The Invisible Committee, *To Our Friends*, 35–43.

45 Matt Clement, *A People's History of Riots, Protest, and the Law* (2016): 186.

46 The Invisible Committee, *To Our Friends*, 31.